OCEANS ODYSSEY 3

OCEANS ODYSSEY 3

The Deep-Sea Tortugas Shipwreck, Straits of Florida: A Merchant Vessel from Spain's 1622 Tierra Firme Fleet

Edited by
Greg Stemm & Sean Kingsley

Odyssey Marine Exploration
Reports 3

Oxbow Books
Oxford and Oakville

Published by
Oxbow Books, Oxford, UK

© Oxbow Books and Odyssey Marine Exploration, 2013

ISBN 978-1-78297-148-1

This book is available direct from:

Oxbow Books, Oxford, UK
(Phone: 01865-241249; Fax: 01865-794449)

and

The David Brown Book Company
PO Box 511, Oakville, CT 06779, USA
(Phone: 860-945-9329; Fax: 860-945-9468)

or from our website

www.oxbowbooks.com

A CIP record for this book is available from the British library

Library of Congress Cataloging-in-Publication Data

Oceans Odyssey 3 : the deep-sea Tortugas shipwreck, Straits of Florida : a merchant
vessel from Spain's 1622 Tierra Firme fleet / edited by Greg Stemm & Sean Kingsley.
    pages cm. -- (Odyssey marine exploration reports ; 3)
    Includes bibliographical references.
    ISBN 978-1-78297-148-1
    1. Buen Jesús y Nuestra Señora del Rosario (Ship : Carrack) 2. Shipwrecks--Florida--
Dry Tortugas Region. 3. Underwater archaeology--Florida--Dry Tortugas Region.
4. Excavations (Archaeology)--Florida--Dry Tortugas Region. 5. Florida--Antiquities. I.
Stemm, Greg. II. Kingsley, Sean A. III. Odyssey Marine Exploration (Firm)
    VK1273.F6O35 2013
    910.9163'64--dc23
                    2013003214

*Printed and bound in
Wales by Gomer Press*

Contents

Preface by *Greg Stemm*.. vii

Introduction by *Sean Kingsley* xix

1. The Deep-Sea Tortugas Shipwreck, Florida: Technology
   John Astley & Greg Stemm... 1

2. The Deep-Sea Tortugas Shipwreck, Florida:
   A Spanish-Operated Navio of the 1622 Tierra Firme Fleet.
   Part 1, the Site
   Greg Stemm, Ellen Gerth, Jenette Flow,
   Claudio Lozano Guerra-Librero & Sean Kingsley....................... 17

3. The Deep-Sea Tortugas Shipwreck, Florida:
   A Spanish-Operated Navio of the 1622 Tierra Firme Fleet.
   Part 2: the Artifacts
   Greg Stemm, Ellen Gerth, Jenette Flow,
   Claudio Lozano Guerra-Librero & Sean Kingsley....................... 55

4. The Identity and Maritime History of the
   Deep-Sea Tortugas Shipwreck
   Sean Kingsley... 123

5. The Deep-Sea Tortugas Shipwreck, Florida: the Animal Bones
   Philip L. Armitage 151

6. The Deep-Sea Tortugas Shipwreck, Florida: the Silver Coins
   Carol Tedesco 171

Preface

"I know of no other field where funds have been set aside to bribe scholars to publish their projects, nor any discipline that has field reports a half-century old still waiting to be written. Most scholarly fields complain about the lack of adequate publishing outlets. In archaeology, it is the reverse. There are plenty of outlets but not enough finished works."

Mitch Allen, 'Field Guide to Archaeological Publishing',
SAA Archaeological Record 3.1 (2003), 5.

*

During the last decade a tsunami of new data, research and issues have surfaced that have changed the face of underwater archaeology. High profile shipwreck discoveries, a disappearance of funding for underwater cultural heritage management and the UNESCO Convention on the Protection of the Underwater Cultural Heritage have all caused much soul-searching, particularly concerning the umbilical cord linking project design, fieldwork, funding and public outreach. The cooperative and conflicting interests of all the various stakeholders in shipwrecks are in the spotlight now more than ever.

As much as everyone with a passion for underwater archaeology loves the thrill of the dig, for the scientist and society at large the publication of an archaeological project and dissemination of the data generated from the site should be the ultimate end goal. Archaeological excavation is destructive, no matter who undertakes it – and publication should ideally enable a site to be reconstructed and reinterpreted any time in the future based on the written record (supported by graphics). Odyssey Marine Exploration has strived to honor these commitments to science in

our work. Our philosophy is to share our results in scientific form swiftly, accurately and in a palatable way that will hopefully delight as well as inform.

The anxiety of whether to publish and be damned – a psychological condition highly familiar to Odyssey's scientists – has exposed myriad skeletons in the discipline's cupboard. But has it resulted in a new wave of improved standards?

In the United Kingdom, *From The Ground Up. The Publication of Archaeological Projects* (Jones *et al.*, 2001), commissioned from the Council for British Archaeology by English Heritage, Cadw, Dúchas, Historic Scotland and the Northern Ireland Environment & Heritage Service, revealed widespread dissatisfaction with the state of archaeological publishing practices, primarily:

- With the structure of reports, and diversity of opinion about the purposes of writing them;
- Burgeoning grey literature, inadequate synthesis, delay in the appearance of summaries of new work, and imbalances in reporting, are all held to be militating against the current use of much of what is being produced;

Fig. 1. Interpretive graphic panel at the Museum of the History of Science, Oxford, for the 2010 display of the world's earliest wooden folding rule found on a shipwreck. Discovered by Odyssey Marine Exploration in the Western Approaches to the English Channel on site 35F, an English merchant vessel of c. 1672-85 involved in trade with West Africa.

- Inadequacies in provision for editorial support and training, standards of preparation, consistency in procedures, and capacity for prompt production;
- The absence of any single template for archaeological publication, which might be suited to all branches of the discipline in all parts of the United Kingdom and Ireland.

Grey literature, in particular, was singled out as a genre that was neither being read by those who might find some of it useful, nor appreciated by those who produced or used it. While fieldwork publications in monographs and journals were consulted frequently by around one-third of the professional archaeologists surveyed, only 22% regularly consulted grey literature fieldwork publications and 17% never consulted them. Only 15.6% stated positively that they utilized grey literature in their own research.

When English Heritage assumed the role of managing UK underwater cultural heritage in 2002, the situation was arguably even worse within maritime archaeology. *Taking to the Water: English Heritage's Initial Policy for the Management of Maritime Archaeology in England* determined that "Over the last twenty-five years many licenses have been issued for survey and excavation work within areas designated under the Protection of Wrecks Act. Few of the

Fig. 2. A display of the photomosaic of the wreck of the side-wheel steamer the Republic (sunk 1865, 150km off south-east USA) in Odyssey's traveling exhibition, SHIPWRECK! Pirates & Treasure. This interactive, multimedia exhibit featuring over 500 artifacts recovered from Odyssey's worldwide deep-sea shipwreck expeditions has traveled across the USA since 2005.

licenses issued required the academic reporting of fieldwork results and, as the vast majority of this work took place on a voluntary basis, lacking adequate financial support for subsequent analysis and dissemination of the results, very little of this work has been formally published" (Roberts and Trow, 2002: 25).

Few robust preliminary articles and fewer final reports have reported on UK Protected Wrecks (the rare exceptions being the *Mary Rose* and the *Invincible*, both of which had unusually strong private-sector support: Jones, 2003; Marsden, 2003; Bingeman, 2010). Before such work can appear, understandably often disparate old archives need to be synthesized, understood and interpreted. As was obligatory for the current Tortugas shipwreck project, which we undertook two decades ago, most UK Protected Wrecks need to be subjected to 're-excavation of the excavation' (whether just a survey or a full excavation took place) to make sense of the primary data, and drag the whole body of recorded information into the modern digital age, before publication can be considered.

As the Institute of Field Archaeologists' *Slipping Through the Net. Maritime Archaeological Archives in Policy and Practice* (2007: 5) has pointed out, the current situation in the UK is "a culture of ad hoc solutions... Archives are frequently split prior to interpretation and publication; ownership of material assemblages often remains in private hands. There is little common or accepted knowledge about policy, Best Practice or maritime archival standards. There is simply no coherent long-term strategy. Consequently, thus far, the vast majority of maritime archives have fallen through this policy gap – and are curated, split or sold very much on the basis of luck or the tenacity of individuals involved with the site or project."

Although a phase of house-cleaning of underwater archaeology archives is essential for many countries prior to their ability to roll out publications, any initiative would be purely hypothetical without funds being sourced for writing, production, printing or publication. Ideally, and increasingly compulsorily, this means allocation at the start of a project, not a doomed scramble for funding when the fieldwork has finished and the research team has been largely disbanded. UNESCO's Rule 17 on the Protection of the Underwater Cultural Heritage requires that "Except in cases of emergency to protect underwater cultural heritage, an adequate funding base shall be assured in advance of any activity, sufficient to complete all stages of the project design, including conservation, documentation and curation of recovered artefacts, and report preparation and dissemination." UNESCO also requires projects to prove the availability of funds before commencement and through to completion, such as by securing a bond (Rule 18).

Fig. 3. A display of artifacts, accompanied by interpretative graphics, highlighting the wreck of the steamer the Republic *in Odyssey's traveling exhibition,* SHIPWRECK! Pirates & Treasure. *The showcases are presented beneath a reconstructed side-wheel.*

Fig. 4. A selection of the 8,429 glass and stoneware bottles recovered from the wreck of the steamer the Republic *on display in Odyssey's traveling exhibition,* SHIPWRECK! Pirates & Treasure.

Anywhere on Earth, from the academic community to government circles, this is nothing short of a pipedream, not least because it is simply impossible to predict the absolute character and complexity of a site at the start of a project. Only under optimum legal regimes (and ironically through the for-profit sector) is funding security achievable, such as the 2007 mitigation management in the Gulf of Mexico, which resulted in the swift publication of the 1,220m-deep, early 19th-century Mardi Gras wreck found on the development path of the Okeanos Gas Gathering Company pipeline (albeit with just two and a half weeks being allocated to fieldwork: Ford *et al.*, 2008; 2010). It is questionable whether this achievement would have been accomplished without the early 19th-century Mica wreck's disastrous bisection in the same waters in 2001 by an ExxonMobil Corporation pipeline (Jones, 2004).

A tough approach to guarantee standards is Israel's Antiquities Law (1978), whereby the issuing of licenses for excavation on land and underwater demands preliminary reports to be submitted to government authorities in less than one year; future licensing is dependent on the appearance of "an appropriate scientific publication" within five

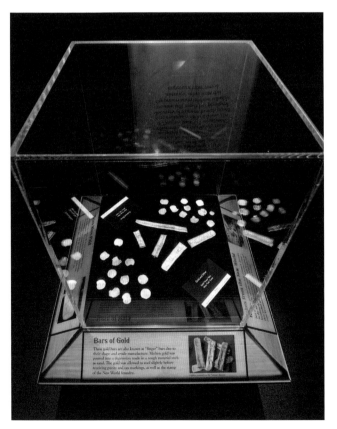

Fig. 5. A selection of gold bars and silver coins from the Tortugas shipwreck, a merchant vessel from the Tierra Firme fleet lost off the Florida Keys in 1622. On display in Odyssey's traveling exhibition, SHIPWRECK! Pirates & Treasure.

years. A rule of thumb is that 20% of projects' funding in Israel be allocated to post-excavation publication preparation. Project direction by qualified archaeologists with an academic background, and a proven track record in writing up projects, has promoted a strong publication record. No comparable legal protocols exist for the majority of countries. In the absence of national legislation models laying out compulsory demands for funding, archive curation and publication, projects are typically left to the passion, management skills and funding streams of inspired individuals.

In reality, very little difference exists in the published record of colonial Spanish shipwrecks between sites sought and studied by commercial groups, universities and government groups. Positive and negative trends are evident within all structures, and it is misleading to argue otherwise. Affiliation with no single group guarantees a final report as the end product. Commercial groups are often criticized for a perceived incompatibility between the idea of the select sale of artifacts and doing good science that leads to respectful treatment of cultural remains and, ultimately, the scientific publication of results. While such criticism is undoubtedly reasonable for various parts of the world (cf. Castro, 2011), certainly Latin America and the Caribbean, my experience in the USA is that commercial influences can be positive.

While final reports are pending for Mel Fisher's work on the *Atocha* and *Margarita*, the celebrated treasure galleons from the same 1622 Tierra Firme fleet in which the Tortugas ship sailed, numerous significant notes have been made available about bale seals, pewter wares, a swivel gun, ammunition, an astrolabe, copper ingots, porcelain, emeralds and lead hull sheathing (Malcom, 1990; 1996b; 1997; 1998a; 1998b; 1998c; 2000; 2001; Tedesco, 2002). Mathewson's popular treatment of the discoveries and excavation, *Treasure of the Atocha* (1986), credibly introduces the sites and finds. The organic remains and coins have been examined in great detail, the animal bones studied in a comprehensive MA thesis at the University of Arizona (Chapin, 1990; Malcom, 1993; Tedesco, 2010), and Marken's analysis (1994) of the two ships' ceramics is the most important contribution to the study of early 17th century Spanish pottery from any archaeological context. Data related to work on the 1715 Spanish treasure fleet by private companies has resulted in both popular and more scientific catalogued treatments (Clausen, 1965; Burgess and Clausen, 1982). All of these sources were invaluable for the parallel study of the Tortugas shipwreck.

The *Nuevo Constante*, a merchant vessel from the New Spain fleet sailing from Veracruz, Mexico, to Spain, and wrecked off the coast of Louisiana in 1766, came to light when shrimp fishermen's nets recovered numerous artifacts over 20 years preceding 1979. The fisherman and his associates founded Free Enterprise Salvage, Inc., which was permitted to excavate the wreck by the State of Louisiana under the guidance and direction of professional archaeologists. The salvors were to be compensated for their work by receiving 75% of the value of precious metals recovered (ultimately receiving silver, copper and gold ingots in lieu of payments), and the results were well published by the University of Louisiana. The site's basic distribution maps, and substantial assemblages of iron cannon, anchors, Hawksbill turtle shells, complete logwoods for dyeing, indigo, fragments of annatto dye, animal figurines, ceramics and glass wares, brocaded cloth and concretion conglomerates containing gun flint, animal bone, ceramics glass, iron bolts, shot and wood, provide illuminating insights into mercantile commerce with the Americas soon after the mid-18th century (Pearson and Hoffman, 1995: 5-6, 98, 133, 153, 157-8, 179, 185, 196, 201-203).

Although the activities of a for-profit shipwreck company on one of the three small Spanish ships wrecked off Padre Island in the Texas Gulf Coast in 1554 led to litigation with the State of Texas, this episode brought the sites to the attention of the authorities and resulted in an excellent scientific publication following fieldwork sponsored by the Texas Antiquities Committee. This study of the *Santa María de Yciar* and the *San Esteban*, which were carrying considerable silver to Spain from the newly opened mint in Mexico City, led to detailed analyses of nearly 12 tons of iron concretions containing rich assemblages of iron spikes, chains, iron cannon breech chambers, ballast stones, 358 silver coins, silver bullion, gold bars, pewter plates, barrel hoops, an iron pick adze, lead sheathing, wood, an iron gudgeon, planking, bones, obsidian blades, potsherds and other artifacts recovered between 1972 and 1975.

One wonders whether greater loss of data from the site was caused by the treasure hunters or by the man-made Mansfield Cut, constructed in the late 1950s, "totally obliterating" one of the 30 x 50m wreck sites. The mysterious disappearance from the agency files of field notes and site plans plotting the locations of artifacts covering the 1972 and 1973 seasons is an example of problematic management and accountability inflicted by government agencies, not commercial forces (Arnold and Weddle, 1978: 188, 190-1, 195, 326-7).

Fig. 6. Visitors get close up and personal to examine a model of the 8-ton ROV Zeus used by Odyssey to conduct its worldwide deep-sea archaeological operations. On display in 2012 in Odyssey's traveling exhibition, SHIPWRECK! Pirates & Treasure.

Preface

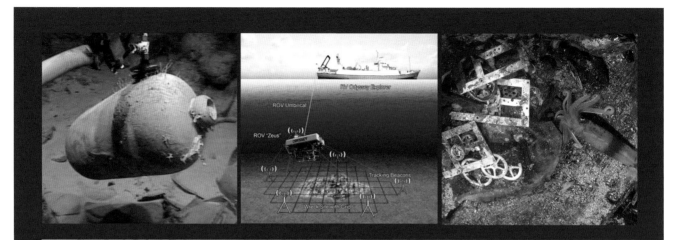

Exploring The Deep

ARCHAEOLOGY in the deep ocean requires the same rigorous standards as those used on land and shallow water sites. ⇨

The ROV ZEUS works at the SS Republic wreck site.

No Need to Get Wet
With two agile manipulator arms and high-resolution cameras, the ROV ZEUS becomes the hands and eyes of the archaeologist.

Recording What You've Found
The archaeological excavation begins with a pre-disturbance survey:
- Includes a site photomosaic documenting the site
- Permits the team to develop excavation strategies

Creating a Virtual Grid
- Acoustic transponders are placed around the perimeter of the site and on the ROV
- Electronic virtual grid of one-meter squares is generated
- Permits recording of each artifact location with an accuracy up to 5 cm

Artifact Recovery
- Artifacts are carefully picked up by ZEUS and placed in numbered plastic containers
- The plastic containers are set in a sub-divided metal lifting basket (called a fourplex) prior to recovery to the surface vessel

Documentation
- Data loggers and video record the date, dive time and precise location of each artifact on the wreck site
- The entire archaeological operation is recorded 24 hours a day, seven days a week

Fig. 7. An interpretative graphic panel explaining how Odyssey scientifically explores the deep, created to showcase Odyssey's exhibit program.

Fig. 8. A showcase panel explaining the presence of English ceramics on the Jacksonville 'Blue China' shipwreck (lost 1854, 70 nautical miles off Florida), created for Odyssey's traveling exhibition, SHIPWRECK! Pirates & Treasure.

Further afield, Martin's study of the pottery assemblages and other research from the Spanish Armada ships of Ireland lost in 1588 (Martin, 1979) relied on excavations conducted by a commercial group headed by Robert Sténuit focused on the *Girona*, lost off the Antrim coast (Sténuit, 1972). Key artifacts from the site, including the renowned gold salamander inset with rubies, remain in the collection of Ulster Museum.

Contrary to the views of armchair archaeologists, it is not easy to find such sites, for which substantial funds and energy need to be expended. Commercial models and motivation have proven highly successful in uncovering lost colonial Spanish shipwrecks. Their subsequent management should become a question of national legislation and its enforcement, including oversight and involvement of commercial firms, which in many ways are best suited to fund these operations. Failure to include legitimate for-profit firms will surely result in unauthorized destruction of the sites in most cases – which will result in a total loss of the archaeological record.

The best example of a state-led study of a Spanish shipwreck in Florida is the Emanuel Point I site discovered in 1992 during a submerged cultural resource survey of Pensacola Bay. This ship from the *flota* of Tristán de Luna was lost in a hurricane in 1559 during the first European attempt to colonize Florida. Recognizing its importance as the earliest colonial vessel found in Florida, in 1993 a five-year plan was agreed for the investigation, conservation and display of its recovered remains in a public exhibit, plus the development of a university program in marine archaeology. The site's discovery represented an opportunity for Florida to attempt a new strategy for the development and management of a shipwreck for research and public benefit in a cooperative partnership between public and private sectors. The University of West Florida became an academic partner, partly due to the university's record of public-oriented archaeology in the Pensacola community. Two extensive multi-disciplinary scientific publications have been published (Smith *et al.*, 1995; Smith *et al.*, 1998). The plant remains have been studied in a University of West Florida MA thesis (Lawrence, 2010).

Another favored line of argument pursued by heritage critics is that commercial groups only conduct research into sites that generate profits. In reality, an important side-effect of the search for high-value targets is the discovery of internationally important wrecks, for which funds are made available for excavation, study and publication. A case in point is the St. John's Bahamas Shipwreck Project, a non-profit study by the Mel Fisher Maritime Heritage Society of an armed vessel lost on the Little Bahama Bank between *c.* 1554 and 1575 (Malcom, 1996a).

Of great historical importance is also the *Henrietta Marie*, a 24m-long, 120-ton English slaver wrecked on New Ground Reef, Florida, in 1700. Found by Mel Fisher's divers in 1972 during the search for the *Atocha*, the *Henrietta Marie* is the world's largest source of tangible objects related to the early years of the slave trade. Excavated finds included over 80 sets of shackles, two cast-iron cannon, Venetian glass trade beads, iron trade bars, elephant's teeth and a large collection of English pewter tankards, basins, spoons and bottles (Moore, 1997; Moore and Malcom, 2008).

The collection was not sold, but is being used for educational purposes through the Mel Fisher Maritime Heritage Society's *A Slave Ship Speaks: The Wreck of the Henrietta Marie*, the first major museum exhibition in America devoted to the transatlantic slave trade. This critically acclaimed exhibition was prepared with the assistance of America's leading scholars in African-American history, and used as a focal point to examine the slave trade and its enduring effect on society. Overall, it is no accident that two of the slaver wrecks found to date (*Henrietta Marie* and *Adelaïde*) were discovered by private companies investigating Caribbean routes plied by Spanish treasure fleets, while two ex-slavers (*Whydah Galley* and Beaufort Inlet shipwreck) were found by shipwreck hunters in search of pirate gold. Until recently, academic archaeologists took little interest in slave shipping (Webster, 2008: 9, 10).

The discovery of internationally significant wreck sites during Odyssey's survey projects is the rule, not the exception, in all seas. Archaeology has surely been the winner of the Atlas Shipwreck Survey Project in the Western Approaches and western English Channel. Contrary to what one might believe based on the hysterical cries of some members of the archaeological community, to date not one artifact has been sold from any of the scores of shipwrecks discovered. Rather the published results of extensive surveys and small-scale excavations of a possible Royal Africa Company English merchant vessel of *c.* 1672-85 (Site 35F: elephant tusks, copper manilla bracelets, iron cannon saleable ballast, world's earliest wooden folding rule; Fig. 1), the mid-18th century French privateer the *Marquise de Tourny*, and several German U-boats, amongst other discoveries, have enriched our understanding of the maritime record of the Narrow Seas (Cunningham Dobson, 2011; Cunningham Dobson, 2013; Cunningham Dobson and Kingsley, 2011; Johnston, 2011; Kingsley, 2011; Niestlé, 2011).

The study of pristine Punic and Roman shipwrecks found in deep seas in the Western Mediterranean during the search for the English warship the *Sussex* (Kingsley, 2012), itself the subject of a former Odyssey publication (Cunningham Dobson *et al.*, 2010), shows that the image of commercial groups as profit-obsessed archaeological mercenaries is an inaccurate stereotype or – for some politically-motivated heritage bodies – wishful thinking. Very heavily impacted by shrimp trawlers for 35-40 years, Odyssey's rescue excavation of the mid-19th century Jacksonville 'Blue China' shipwreck resulted in five scientific papers (Tolson, 2010; Gerth, 2011; Gerth *et al.*, 2011; Gerth and Lindsey, 2011; Sudbury and Gerth, 2011). Retained in our permanent collection in Tampa, some of the wreck's finds have been enjoyed by nearly two million people in traveling exhibitions (Figs. 1-8).

Compared to the extensive multi-sourced data on colonial Spanish shipwrecks published from America by commercial firms, Spain's own publication record is sadly almost non-existent. Government authorities propose that between 1,500 and 1,800 "treasure-laden" shipwrecks alone lie in the country's territorial waters, while over 400 shipwrecks dated between 1473-1868 have been catalogued for the Bay of Cadiz (Lakey, 1987). The absence of even preliminary reports from Spain for their major sites is at odds with its well-publicized and heavy-handed overseas crusade to 'protect' its heritage. The limited coverage in an exhibition catalogue of the wreck of the *Nuestra Señora de la Concepción*, lost off Hispaniola in 1641 (Borrell, 1983), offers more insights into the site than exists for Spain's colonial wrecks. Compared to the treasure oriented work on the *Atocha* and *Margarita* in the Florida Keys, subjected to numerous popular books (Lyon, 1989; Smith, 2003), even Spain's hugely publicized granting of salvage permits to foreign groups in the 18th to mid-20th centuries to recover the treasures of Vigo Bay failed to result in any scientific publications (Iberti, 1908; Potter, 1958). One wonders where the numerous finds and archives from these operations, 20-50% of which were typically returned to Madrid, can be found today?

The self-proclaimed reason for Spain's poor publication record is an educational system failure. Spain's *Green Paper. A National Plan for the Protection of Underwater Cultural Heritage* (2009: 62-3) admits that "over the last 25 years a large group of new underwater archaeologists has received very competent training and are able to compete from a methodological and technical perspective with their counterparts in economically and culturally comparable countries. But they have not reached, barring a few noteworthy exceptions, the same level in terms of scientific knowledge or research capacity. Clear evidence of this is the lack of scientific production in Spain in this field over the last several years judging from the number of publications." One of the five clearly differentiated components of all maritime archaeology projects in Spain is now scientific study, dissemination and publication (*Green Paper*, 2009: 71).

The same absence of publications pervades Latin America and, indeed, is a global problem: very few studies about Iberian ships have been conducted, and even less published, despite the discovery of more than 70 suspected Iberian shipwrecks worldwide built and sailed between 1500 and 1700 (Castro, 2008: 9). The near future will show how seriously Spain manages this dilemma and whether 'citizenship' of the UNESCO brotherhood will excuse it from such duties while it focuses on a policy of preserving sites *in situ*, ignoring the danger to the sites from man and nature.

This first of two anticipated volumes on the archaeology of the Tortugas shipwreck seeks to present the artifacts in a reconstructed historical context that both respects the site and Odyssey's commitment to share results with society. When we are all long gone, and the overweight fuss generated over the ethics of commercial archaeology is a distant memory, it is this written and graphic record that we hope will keep the world interested in this testimony to long-distance trade between Seville and the Americas during the Golden Age of Spain. Meanwhile, over 8,000 artifacts from the Tortugas shipwreck are held in Odyssey's permanent collection in Tampa, Florida, where they are stored for ongoing research, loans to exhibitions and museums, and are available to fellow scholars for study.

Greg Stemm
Co-Founder & CEO
Odyssey Marine Exploration
Tampa, January 2013

Bibliography

Arnold, J.B. and Weddle, R., *The Nautical Archaeology of Padre Island. The Spanish Shipwrecks of 1554* (New York, 1978).

Bingeman, J., *The First HMS Invincible (1747-58). Her Excavations (1980-1991)* (Oxford, 2010).

Borrell, P.J., *Historia y Rescate del Galeon Nuestra Señora de la Concepcion* (Museo de las Casas Reales, Santo Domingo, 1983).

Burgess, R.F. and Clausen, C.J., *Florida's Golden Galleons. The Search for the 1715 Spanish Treasure Fleet* (Port Salerno, Florida, 1982).

Castro, F. Vieira de, 'A Group for the Study of Iberian Seafaring'. In F. Vieira de Castro and K. Custer (eds.), *Edge of Empire* (Casal de Cambra, Portugal, 2008), 7-22.

Castro, F., 'Archaeologists, Treasure Hunters, & the UNESCO Convention on the Protection of the Underwater Cultural Heritage: a Personal Viewpoint'. In G. Stemm and S. Kingsley (eds.), *Ocean Odyssey 2. Underwater Heritage Management & Deep-Sea Shipwrecks in the English Channel & Atlantic Ocean* (Oxford, 2011), 7-9.

Chapin, R.L., *A Faunal Analysis of the 17th Century Galleon Nuestra Señora De Atocha* (MA Thesis, the University of Arizona, 1990).

Clausen, C.J., *A 1715 Spanish Treasure Ship* (University of Florida, Gainesville, 1965).

Cunningham Dobson, N., '*La Marquise de Tourny* (Site 33c): A Mid-18th Century Armed Privateer of Bordeaux'. In G. Stemm and S. Kingsley (eds.), *Ocean Odyssey 2. Underwater Heritage Management & Deep-Sea Shipwrecks in the English Channel & Atlantic Ocean* (Oxford, 2011), 69-108.

Cunningham Dobson, N., *German U-Boats of the English Channel and Western Approaches: History, Site Formation and Impacts* (OME Papers, Tampa, Forthcoming 2013).

Cunningham Dobson, N. and Kingsley, S.A., *A Late 17th-Century Armed Merchant Vessel in the Western Approaches (Site 35F)* (OME Papers 23, Tampa, 2011).

Cunningham Dobson, N., Tolson, H., Martin, A., Lavery, B., Bates, R., Tempera, F. and Pearce, J., 'The HMS *Sussex* Shipwreck Project (Site E-82): Preliminary Report.' In G. Stemm and S. Kingsley (eds.), *Oceans Odyssey. Deep-Sea Shipwrecks in the English Channel, the Straits of Gibraltar and the Atlantic Ocean* (Oxford, 2010), 159-90.

Ford, B., Borgens, A., Bryant, W., Marshall, D., Hitchcock, P., Arias, C. and Hamilton, D., *Archaeological Excavation of the Mardi Gras Shipwreck (16GM01), Gulf of Mexico Continental Slope* (US Department of the Interior, Minerals Management Service, Gulf of Mexico OCS Region, New Orleans, LA. OCS Report MMS, 2008).

Ford, B., Borgens, A. and Hitchcock, P., 'The 'Mardi Gras' Shipwreck: Results of a Deep-Water Excavation, Gulf of Mexico, USA', *International Journal of Nautical Archaeology* 39.1 (2010), 76-98.

Gerth, E., 'The Jacksonville 'Blue China' Shipwreck (Site BA02): the Ceramic Assemblage.' In G. Stemm and S. Kingsley (eds.), *Ocean Odyssey 2. Underwater Heritage Management & Deep-Sea Shipwrecks in the English Channel & Atlantic Ocean* (Oxford, 2011), 221-62.

Gerth, E., Cunningham Dobson, N. and Kingsley, S., 'The Jacksonville 'Blue China' Shipwreck (Site BA02): A Mid-19th Century American Coastal Schooner off Florida'. In G. Stemm and S. Kingsley (eds.), *Ocean Odyssey 2. Underwater Heritage Management & Deep-Sea Shipwrecks in the English Channel & Atlantic Ocean* (Oxford, 2011), 143-220.

Gerth, E. and Lindsey, B., 'The Jacksonville 'Blue China' Shipwreck (Site BA02): the Glass Assemblage'. In G. Stemm and S. Kingsley (eds.), *Ocean Odyssey 2. Underwater Heritage Management & Deep-Sea Shipwrecks in*

the English Channel & Atlantic Ocean* (Oxford, 2011), 287-332.

Iberti, C.L., *The Treasure Hunt in Vigo Bay* (London, 1908).

Johnston, S., 'A Note on the Wooden Carpenter's Rule from Odyssey Shipwreck Site 35F'. In G. Stemm and S. Kingsley (eds.), *Ocean Odyssey 2. Underwater Heritage Management & Deep-Sea Shipwrecks in the English Channel & Atlantic Ocean* (Oxford, 2011), 39-50.

Jones, M. (ed.), *For Future Generations. Conservation of a Tudor Maritime Collection* (Portsmouth, 2003).

Jones, S., MacSween, A., Jeffrey, S., Morris, R. and Heyworth, M., *From The Ground Up. The Publication of Archaeological Projects. A User Needs Survey* (Council for British Archaeology, 2001).

Jones, T.N., *The Mica Shipwreck: Deepwater Nautical Archaeology in the Gulf of Mexico* (MA Thesis, Texas A&M University, 2004).

Kingsley, S.A., 'The Art & Archaeology of Privateering: British Fortunes & Failures in 1744'. In G. Stemm and S. Kingsley (eds.), *Ocean Odyssey 2. Underwater Heritage Management & Deep-Sea Shipwrecks in the English Channel & Atlantic Ocean* (Oxford, 2011), 109-42.

Kingsley, S., 'Commerce, Controversy, Science and Sustainability in Deep-Sea Shipwrecks'. In H. Tan (ed.), *Marine Archaeology in Southeast Asia. Innovation and Adaptation* (Asian Civilisations Museum, Singapore, 2012), 132-49.

Lakey, D., *Shipwrecks in the Gulf of Cadiz: A Catalog of Historically Documented Wrecks from the Fifteenth Through the Nineteenth Centuries* (MA Thesis, Texas A&M University, 1987).

Lawrence, C.L.R., *An Analysis of Plant Remains from the Emanuel Point Shipwrecks* (MA Thesis, Department of Anthropology College of Arts and Sciences, University of West Florida, 2010).

Lyon, E., *The Search for the Atocha* (New York, 1989).

Malcom, C., 'Glass from *Nuestra Señora de Atocha*', *Astrolabe: Journal of the Mel Fisher Maritime Heritage Society* 6.1 (1990).

Malcom, C., 'The Flotation of Waterlogged Organics: the *Atocha* Example', *Astrolabe: Journal of the Mel Fisher Maritime Heritage Society* 8.1 (1993), 2-7.

Malcom, C., *St. John's Bahamas Shipwreck Project. Interim Report I: the Excavation and Artifacts 1991-1995* (Key West, 1996a).

Malcom, C., 'Remarkable *Atocha* Ammunition Emerges from Laboratory', *The Navigator: Newsletter of the Mel Fisher Maritime Heritage Society* 10.11/12 (1996b).

Malcom, C., 'The 1622 Swivel Gun', *The Navigator: Newsletter of the Mel Fisher Maritime Heritage Society* 11.4 (1997).

Malcom, C., 'Pewter from the *Nuestra Señora de Atocha*', *The Navigator: Newsletter of the Mel Fisher Maritime Heritage Society* 13.11-12 (1998a).

Malcom, C., 'The Mariner's Astrolabe', *The Navigator: Newsletter of the Mel Fisher Maritime Heritage Society* 13.5 (1998b).

Malcom, C., 'Copper on the *Nuestra Señora de Atocha*', *The Navigator: Newsletter of the Mel Fisher Maritime Heritage Society* 13.3 (1998c).

Malcom, C., '*Atocha* Emeralds Help to Shed New Light on History of Gem Trade', *The Navigator: Newsletter of the Mel Fisher Maritime Heritage Society* 15.3 (2000).

Malcom, C., 'Lead Hull-Sheathing of the *Santa Margarita*', *The Navigator: Newsletter of the Mel Fisher Maritime Heritage Society* 16.1 (2000/2001).

Marken, M.W., *Pottery from Spanish Shipwrecks 1500-1800* (University Press of Florida, 1994).

Marsden, P., *Sealed By Time. The Loss and Recovery of the Mary Rose* (Portsmouth, 2003).

Martin, C.J.M., 'Spanish Armada Pottery', *International Journal of Nautical Archaeology* 8.4 (1979), 279-302.

Mathewson, D., *Treasure of the Atocha* (Houston, 1986).

Moore, D., *Site Report. Historical and Archaeological Investigations of the Shipwreck Henrietta Marie* (Key West, 1997).

Moore, D.D and Malcom, C., 'Seventeenth-Century Vehicle of the Middle Passage: Archaeological and Historical Investigations on the *Henrietta Marie* Shipwreck Site', *International Journal of Historical Archaeology* 12.1 (2008), 20-38.

Niestlé, A., 'The 'Atlas' Survey Zone: Deep-sea Archaeology & U-boat Loss Reassessments'. In G. Stemm and S. Kingsley (eds.), *Ocean Odyssey 2. Underwater Heritage Management & Deep-Sea Shipwrecks in the English Channel & Atlantic Ocean* (Oxford, 2011), 333-54.

Pearson, C.E. and Hoffman, P.E., *El Nuevo Constante. The Wreck and Recovery of an Eighteenth-Century Spanish Ship off the Louisiana Coast* (Louisiana State University Press, 1995).

Potter, J.S., *Treasure Divers of Vigo Bay* (New York, 1958).

Smith, J., *Fatal Treasure* (Hoboken, New Jersey, 2003).

Smith, R.C., Bratten, J.R., Cozzi, J. and Plaskett, K., *The Emanuel Point Ship Archaeological Investigations 1997-1998* (Report of Investigations No. 68 Archaeology Institute University of West Florida, 1998).

Smith, R.C., Spirek, J., Bratten, J. and Scott-Ireton, D., *The Emanuel Point Ship: Archaeological Investigations, 1992-1995, Preliminary Report* (Bureau of Archaeological Research, Division of Historical Resources, Florida Department of State, 1995).

Sudbury, J.B. and Gerth, E., 'The Jacksonville 'Blue China' Shipwreck (Site BA02): Clay Tobacco Pipes'. In G. Stemm and S. Kingsley (eds.), *Ocean Odyssey 2. Underwater Heritage Management & Deep-Sea Shipwrecks in the English Channel & Atlantic Ocean* (Oxford, 2011), 263-86.

Tedesco, C., '*Santa Margarita* Lead Bale Seal: Artifact 49987', *The Navigator: Newsletter of the Mel Fisher Maritime Heritage Society* 18.6 (2002).

Tedesco, C., *Treasure Coins of the Nuestra Señora de Atocha & the Santa Margarita* (Key West, 2010).

Tolson, H., 'The Jacksonville 'Blue China' Shipwreck and the Myth of Deep-Sea Preservation'. In G. Stemm and S. Kingsley (eds.), *Oceans Odyssey. Deep-Sea Shipwrecks in the English Channel, the Straits of Gibraltar and the Atlantic Ocean* (Oxford, 2010), 145-58.

Webster, J., 'Slave Ships and Maritime Archaeology: An Overview', *International Journal of Historical Archaeology* 12 (2008), 6-19.

Introduction

Oceans Odyssey 3 presents the archaeological results of a particularly enthralling and consequential marine archaeological site – the Tortugas shipwreck, the subject of the world's first comprehensive deep-sea excavation conducted exclusively using a Remotely-Operated Vehicle. Seahawk Deep Ocean Technology of Tampa, Florida, discovered the wreck in 1989 at a depth of 400m in the Straits of Florida and 20km south of the Dry Tortugas, the southernmost islands of the Florida Keys. From the outset the decision was made not to pursue salvage, as had been unsuccessfully attempted at this site by other groups on several previous occasions, but to record the deposits archaeologically. The vision called for the documentation of all artifacts *in situ*, site mapping by photomosaic, the retention and sieving of deposits and the safe recovery of delicate finds. Between June 1990 and October 1991, 16,903 artifacts were recorded and recovered after a total dive time of 1,489 hours.

The post-excavation history of the Tortugas wreck has taken many twists and turns. Today the surviving archive and collection is stored and curated by Odyssey Marine Exploration. The current publication appears courtesy of the company's investment and commitment to scientific publication.

Chapter 1 of the first of two volumes dedicated to the Tortugas shipwreck examines the technological package designed around the 3-ton ROV Merlin. The fieldwork permitted extensive trials and tests, and the thousands of hours of video documenting every dive demonstrate how systematic daily operations became. These ground-breaking operations in the Straits of Florida witnessed the birth of a new discipline, deep-sea archaeology, for which the core tools of the trade were fine-tuned to enable: accurate surveying using a Sonardyne acoustic long baseline positioning system; stratigraphic excavation using a customized suction dredge with integrated sediment removal and filtration (SeRF) system prototyped from a beer keg; heavy duty lifting with two advanced Schilling manipulators; and delicate artifact recovery based on several successive stages of limpet suction device innovations. All underwater activities were fully documented by video camera and three still photography cameras.

Chapter 2 sets the site within its environmental, biological and archaeological context and defines the character of its formation. As with many important shipwrecks off Florida and Louisiana (see below), the background to the Tortugas shipwreck's study signifies the role of fishing impacts on site discovery and, indeed, deterioration. The wreck extends over a surface distance of 19.2m on a northwest/southeast axis and was excavated to depths of 0.30-1.0m. The recording of all finds demonstrated

that technically they were not preserved *in situ*, but had been substantially disturbed: 25.2% overlay the main ballast and hull nucleus, while 74.8% were scattered closely around its perimeter. Artifacts were identified both on the site's surface and within this uppermost 30cm-deep stratum. The hull was subjected to small-scale exposure, which revealed a coherent and continuous entity whose well-preserved remains included the sternpost and stempost, the collapsed rudder, a pump well retaining shaft and stanchions.

Chapter 3 introduces the Tortugas ship's finds, which are without doubt the most important archaeological contribution of this wreck. The 16,903 artifacts include significant assemblages of pearls, ceramics, glassware, lead musket shot, silver coins, gold bars, trade beads, animal bones, and seeds that enable the vivid maritime history of the ship to be reconstructed. The combination of artifact types and date leave no doubt that the ship was a small merchant vessel from the Tierra Firme fleet that was returning to Seville in 1622 when part of the *flota* sank off the Florida Keys during a hurricane on 5-6 September.

Volume encapsulates just one dimension of the wreck's narrative. The gold bars and silver coins testify to well-documented colonial Spanish exploitation of the Americas. The trade in pearls harvested off Cumana adds a lesser-known layer of brutality to the reality of early 17th-century treasure shipments that led to both the demographic eradication of tribal groups and history's first recorded case of species collapse for the oyster, *Pinctada imbricate*. The 64 pieces of intriguing tortoise shell identified across the Tortugas wreck, cut from the hawksbill turtle, *Eretmochelys imbricate,* may reflect the presence of an industrious crew member onboard, who idled away the hours cutting lice combs and cases.

The scientific value of individual finds fully justified the site's painstaking study. A well-appointed shipboard merchant probably owned the onyx inkwell and stylish octagonal ivory sundial manufactured in Nuremberg, useless for telling the time in either Seville or the Americas. Most curious of all are two wooden drop spindles typically used by women for spinning fibers, two tiny ceramic objects of apparent South American or circum-Caribbean origin, two greenstone whetstones and a single greenstone labret (tribal lip ornament), unique finds that raise speculation that an Indian woman accompanied the ill-fated Tortugas ship, whether as slave or dependent is uncertain.

The artifact assemblage's characterization as originating from the 1622 Tierra Firme fleet, combined with an analysis of the ship's magnitude (lower sternpost to lower stempost, 17.4m: 30 *codos* keel length and a 10 *codos* beam), results in a suggested identification of the Tortugas ship as the *Buen Jesús y Nuestra Señora del Rosario* (Chapter 4). This 117-ton Portuguese-built and Spanish-operated ship owned by Juan de la Torre Ayala and with Manuel Diaz as Master rejoined the Tierra Firme fleet at Havana after striking out for Nueva Cordoba (Cumana) on the Costa de las Perlas in modern Venezuela.

The ship's daredevil itinerary into waters teeming with Dutch and English privateers is examined in relation to early 17th-century Spanish mercantile economics and foreign policy. 1622 was a time of crisis, when the Crown was instigating desperate measures to retain its monopoly over pearls, tobacco and salt along north-east Venezuela, a battle that Spain was fast losing and would usher in the end of its Golden Age. As a small merchant vessel operating at the opposite spectrum to the great Tierra Firme treasure ships *Atocha* and *Margarita* celebrated off the Florida Keys, the Tortugas shipwreck emerges ultimately as a rare window into everyday maritime entrepreneurship of colonial Spain's trade with the Americas.

The 165 animal bones from the Tortugas wreck (Chapter 5) are largely a typical assemblage for the period, in which pig bones predominated over cattle and sheep/goat. The crew also ate chicken and possible turkey. Other faunal remains introduce further color into our image of daily life at sea. Rats were a significant presence and nuisance on the ship, running wild beneath the feet of the ship's cat and a caged blue-headed parrot. The latter is the first archaeological evidence from any shipwreck worldwide of the historically attested shipment of high-status rare birds to Spain from central and northern South America.

The final chapter of *Oceans Odyssey 3* quantifies and discusses the 1,184 silver coins excavated from the wreck (Chapter 6). These seem to have been shipped in bags as opposed to wooden crates and may be interpreted, alongside the gold bars, as revenue obtained from the sale of the outward-bound consignments. The majority are poorly preserved, having decomposed extensively within an exposed water-worn environment. The greater majority are 8 *reales* denominations, followed by 4 *reales*, and originated mainly in Mexico, followed by Potosi, with a small number of Bogotá/Cartagena or Old World issues. Chapter 6 examines the coins' assayers and the value of silver coins *c.* 1622. One example dated to '1621' serves as a crucial index of the wreck's date.

Stepping back from the wealth of data excavated from the Tortugas shipwreck, three trends dominate the characterization of this site. The first is the often neglected complexity of finding deep-sea wrecks, the second the Tortugas project's key position in the history of marine exploration, and thirdly the vulnerable condition of much of the world's underwater cultural heritage.

Fig. 1. The shrimp fleet at dock in Key West, Florida, in 1960. Photo: © State Archives of Florida.

These points interconnect to create a balanced equation: protecting many shipwrecks at high risk is only achievable by challenging ourselves to find innovative means to obtain the funding and skills to excavate sites before they are eradicated. Of course, it is impossible to predict what the condition of the Tortugas wreck would have been if it had been left to the ravages of time in these very heavily fished waters, but there is good reason for pessimism.

Other sites found within America's economically crucial 'Pink Gold' shrimp fishery waters, which overlie the former West Indies and American trade route of colonial Spain (Fig. 1), include a deep-water wreck probably associated with Spain's 1715 fleet, again identified by Seahawk Deep Ocean Technology based on reports of a shrimp boat landing 450kg of cannonballs, metal wares and ballast in 1954. In the late 1970s a different fishing vessel snagged an iron cannon off the Marquesas shrimp grounds, 80km off Key West; a few years later the *Casey Jones* netted further cannonballs, olive jars, ship's timbers and a 10cm-high wooden figurine from the same site that was subsequently identified as originating from a late 18th or early 19th-century vessel (Vorus, 1997: 21).

Continuing southwards, some 80km off Louisiana a shrimp trawler landed hundreds of silver coins in 1993, which led to the infamous discovery of the *Cazador*, a Spanish warship lost in 1784 en route from Veracruz, Mexico, to New Orleans. A salvage operation recovered the ship's bell, cannon and over 12,000 silver coins in ten days. The site has not been published in any form. The 24m-long *Lady Barbara* shrimper was stopped in its tracks in 1979 off Constance Bayou, southwest Louisiana, when its nets snagged on the *Nuevo Constante*, a Spanish galleon lost in a hurricane in 1766. Its nets hauled up three copper ingots, each 50cm wide and weighing 32-36kg, part of a collection of iron canon, hull structure and other artifacts ripped up over a 20-year period preceding 1979 (Pearson and Hoffman, 1995: xv, 3). Off Texas a huge anchor from the 1554 fleet snagged by a shrimper, whose concretion conglomerate included chain rigging and rope fragments, was later donated to the Raymondville Chamber of Commerce (Arnold and Weddle, 1978: 322).

All these wrecks were excavated by various commercial and state groups. Whether they would have survived for future study without such intervention is highly debatable. The fate of the Jacksonville 'Blue China' shipwreck, a mid-19th century New York schooner discovered and excavated by Odyssey Marine Exploration at a depth of 370m off Florida, calls into serious question the robustness of such sites in fishing impacted seas. Local fishermen confirmed that shrimp trawlers had extensively impacted the wreck for 35-40 years prior to its discovery. Furrows cut into the site's surface and the disappearance of over three-quarters of the ship's cargo illustrates the immense vulnerability of important historic wrecks (Gerth *et al.*, 2011; Fig. 2).

The lottery of fishing impacts versus wreck preservation off eastern America is confirmed by an important case study of 52 mid-Atlantic sites in depths of 20-76m (Atlantic City to Virginia), which yielded a 64% presence of nets and 17% presence of scallop dredges. Recently snagged wreckage included a 3m timber wedged inside a

Fig. 2. Photomosaic of the Jacksonville 'Blue China' shipwreck, a New York schooner lost in 1854 some 70 nautical miles off Florida. Discovered by Odyssey in 2003 at a depth of 370m. The cargo of English Staffordshire ceramics and American glass bottles have been heavily impacted by bottom trawling. Only one 4.1 x 1.9m section of cargo remains in situ *in the bows. The rest of the cargo has been dragged out.*

clam dredge, a 4.9m-long rudder and a 4.6m-long anchor. Formal fishermen's hang lists were found to be of limited reliability: 50% of 'recorded' hangs did not exist, 30% were not big enough to change fishing behavior, and just 20-25% were true hangs. Comparisons between a second-generation offshore netter's database of 19,000 hangs with a confirmed shipwreck database revealed that the fishermen's records had missed 16 large shipwrecks within 50 miles of their homeport (Steinmetz, 2010: 3, 16, 19, 81, 88, 119, 120, 129).

Even in protected marine zones, typified to the north of America's East Coast by Stellwagen Bank National Marine Sanctuary, an 842 square-mile protected marine zone at the mouth of Massachusetts Bay managed by the National Oceanic and Atmospheric Administration (NOAA), impact prevention has proven all but impossible. Fishing gear was found to have impacted nearly all historic shipwrecks. Underwater surveys initiated in 2008 revealed the "severe impact" that fishing has caused on an annual basis because "virtually every square kilometer of the sanctuary is physically disturbed by fishing activities, including bottom trawling and dredging. Some wrecks are covered in nets while others have been stripped of all upper structure and metal hardware" (Marx, 2010: 8).

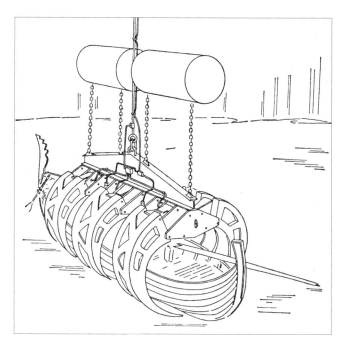

Fig. 3. Willard Bascom's early 1970s scientific impression of what a deep-sea shipwreck recovery system might look like. By modern standards his 'super tongs', as he called the tool, resemble a destructive elongated grab bucket. From: W. Bascom, Deep Water, Ancient Ships *(1976: 192).*

Fig. 4. Modern deep-sea shipwreck archaeology requires a sophisticated Remotely-Operated Vehicle system, like Odyssey's ROV Zeus, to serve as the hands and eyes of the archaeologist conducting high-level recording and artifacts recovery.

The East Coast to Gulf of Mexico pattern of fishing impacts on shipwrecks, typically resulting in the publication of minimal archaeological information, is a global trend that ranges geographically from the Wadden Sea to the North Sea and English Channel, the Mediterranean, Black Sea (Brennan *et al.*, 2012), Atlantic and all across South-East Asia (Kingsley, 2012). The huge scale of the issue leaves little alternative but to consider preservation *in situ* to be politically inappropriate for such sites for which research-oriented excavation, as on the Tortugas wreck, or rescue archaeology is both warranted and obligatory. As Bass has argued (2011: 10), in order to avoid misinterpretation full excavation is not to be feared or shunned:

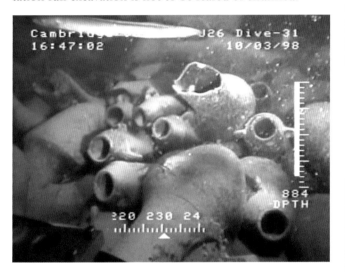

Fig. 5. A large cargo of 5th-century BC Mañá-Pascual A4 Punic amphoras from a shipwreck discovered by Odyssey in the Western Mediterranean. At a depth of 900m, this wreck remains untouched beyond the reach of trawling fleets.

Fig. 6. A vast cargo of Baetican Dressel 7 and 12 Roman fish-sauce amphoras of c. 30 BC to AD 20 from a shipwreck discovered by Odyssey in the Western Mediterranean. At a depth of 750m, this wreck is untouched.

"A shipwreck, being a coherent whole, is more like just one burial. It is hard to imagine an archaeologist excavating only part of a skeleton and leaving the rest… Sampling wrecks can lead only to historical inaccuracies. The debate should be closed."

Society considers this trail of man-made destruction to be an inevitable and acceptable casualty of feeding the planet. The footprint of the industry on underwater cultural heritage is not mitigated. The days of romantically envisioning the deep blue sea to be a virgin wonderworld populated by rare fish species and intact wooden wrecks is a dreamland.

In the first issue of the *International Journal of Nautical Archaeology,* Willard Bascom, the hugely experienced pioneering marine scientist, considered the chances of preservation between the shallows and oceans depths to be promising (Bascom, 1972):

"The important difference is that there is a big increase in the chances of survival of the hulls and artefacts in deep water (which I will define for the present as depths of 200m and greater) compared with those wrecked against a shore. Below the zone of light and waves the bottom is cold and quiet;

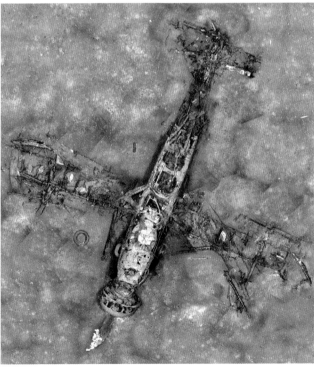

Fig. 7. Photomosaic of a well-preserved World War II 'Fairy Swordfish' class biplane. Discovered by Odyssey at a depth of 850m in the Western Mediterranean. By comparison, the remains of no airplanes were recorded in Odyssey's extensive Atlas survey of the Western Approaches and western English Channel, where the relatively shallow sea bottoms under 150m are easily accessible to fishing boats.

chemical reactions proceed slowly. Without wave action to smash and abrade, one can visualize a ship settling quietly on the bottom to rest unaltered on the mud indefinitely. There are no plants and far fewer animals than in shallow water; there are no divers and no trawls… Thus, deep sea conditions greatly favour the survival of complete ships."

In the space of a few decades this perceived reality has faded into fiction. Of the hundreds of wrecks discovered by Odyssey Marine Exploration worldwide, using ROV technology that is far removed in terms of sophistication to Bascom's scientific perception (Figs. 3-4), the dreamland lives on in rare pockets of seabed. Below 750m in the Western Mediterranean, vast cargos of Punic, Roman and post-medieval shipwrecks lying untouched beyond the ravages of mankind offer hope for future studies (Figs. 5-7).

In recent years it has become clear that when some heritage groups deliberately use disproportionate propaganda and sensationalism in an attempt to stop commercial groups operating beyond territorial waters, they demonstrate little understanding or concern about the real pressures exerted on global underwater cultural heritage. Blaming commercial groups for all the ills of the deep is myopic, when heavy damage is perpetuated daily by fishing boats and their bottom gear. Signing up to the UNESCO Conventional on the Protection of the Underwater Cultural Heritage will only generate positive change if national governments back up their signatures with legislation and funds. Otherwise, we are just cynically window dressing the deep. The governmental failure to protect both shallow and deep-sea shipwrecks from the most quantitatively menacing threats – fishing, oil and gas pipelines, recreational divers trophy hunting and wind farms – leaves no alternative but to redefine the term international waters as 'unprotected waters'.

The relative innocence of the silent seas of course has always been an illusion. Jacques Cousteau was both a highly experienced pioneer of marine exploration and a pragmatist, who fully grasped the wide scope of the sea as a form of education, entertainment, finance and, ultimately, as a resource. Cousteau had no hesitation in appreciating that even in his day the sea was open for business once and for all, writing 60 years ago in *The Silent World* (1953: 147-8) how:

> "There is no choice in the matter. The human population is increasing so rapidly and land resources are being depleted at such a rate, that we must take sustenance from the great cornucopia. The flesh and vegetables of the sea are vital. The necessity of obtaining mineral and chemical resources from the sea is already widely recognized, as is plainly indicated by the intense political and economic interest being shown… in tidal oilfields."

In an ideal world, submerged resources would rest untouched. Idealism is a luxury that science can ill afford. Attempting to impose a blanket ban on commercial archaeology, which occupies such a small slice of the underwater cultural heritage pie, and tie the administration of marine archaeology in a straightjacket, will not save sites long-term or contribute to the procurement and dissemination of knowledge.

The Tortugas shipwreck represents an exciting moment in the history of marine exploration. I hope that the publication of this volume will demonstrate through the presentation of excavated data and its interpretation that the potential of deep-sea studies is a matter to be celebrated.

On a personal note, in the editing of this volume I am conscious that I stand on very tall and broad shoulders. In addition to the acknowledgements presented on Pages 113-115 of this book, special thanks are extended to John Astley, the Offshore Project Manager of Seahawk and one of the great innovators of deep-sea shipwreck archaeology, for providing data, confirming facts and sharing his memories of the project. This publication would have been impossible without the on-site diligence and passion of David Moore, the project archaeologist, and the post-excavation dedication of Jenette Flow.

Numerous unsung heroes at Odyssey's offices in Tampa shared in this production, to all of whom I extend great appreciation: John Oppermann as chief conductor of the orchestra, Ellen Gerth for working closely and relentlessly on artifact identifications and interpretation, Gerri Graca for the tedious yet central task of converting thousands of hours of underwater video to DVD, Alan Bosel for artifact photography, Eric Tate for the careful sorting of coin types, Chad Morris for assisting with cataloguing and preparing scientific samples for analyses, Mark Sullivan for facilitating the translation of Spanish historical sources, and Mark Mussett for map making and fish species identification. Melissa Dolce designed the chapters of this book and attended to my endless stream of pedantic requests for editorial changes with her usual charm and professionalism. Quite simply it has been an experience of a lifetime to have had the opportunity to help bring such an incredible and important shipwreck back to life.

Finally, many thanks to Clare Litt and Val Lamb at Oxbow Books for guidance in publishing the *Oceans Odyssey* series and for accommodating our work.

Sean A. Kingsley
Director
Wreck Watch Int.
London, January 2013

Bibliography

Arnold, J.B. and Weddle, R., *The Nautical Archaeology of Padre Island. The Spanish Shipwrecks of 1554* (New York, 1978).

Bascom, W., 'A Tool for Deep-Water Archaeology', *International Journal of Nautical Archaeology* 1 (1972), 180-4.

Bascom, W., *Deep Water, Ancient Ships. The Treasure Vault of the Mediterranean* (London, 1976).

Bass, G., 'The Development of Maritime Archaeology'. In A. Catsambis, B. Ford and D.L. Hamilton (eds.), *The Oxford Handbook of Maritime Archaeology* (Oxford University Press, 2011), 3-24.

Brennan, M.L., Ballard, R.D., Roman, C., Bell, K.L.C., Buxton, B., Colemana, D.F., Inglisc, G., Köyagasioglu, O. and Turanlıe, T., 'Evaluation of the Modern Submarine Landscape off Southwestern Turkey through the Documentation of Ancient Shipwreck Sites', *Continental Shelf Research* 43 (2012), 55-70.

Gerth, E., Cunningham Dobson, N. and Kingsley, S., 'The Jacksonville 'Blue China' Shipwreck (Site BA02): A Mid-19th Century American Coastal Schooner off Florida'. In G. Stemm and S. Kingsley (eds.), *Ocean Odyssey 2. Underwater Heritage Management & Deep-Sea Shipwrecks in the English Channel & Atlantic Ocean* (Oxford, 2011), 143-220.

Kingsley, S.A., *Out of Sight, Out of Mind? Fishing and Shipwrecked Heritage* (London, 2012).

Marx, D., 'NOAA's Stellwagen Bank National Marine Sanctuary', *INA Quarterly* 36.4 (2010), 8.

Pearson, C.E. and Hoffman, P.E., *El Nuevo Constante. The Wreck and Recovery of an Eighteenth-Century Spanish Ship off the Louisiana Coast* (Louisiana State University Press, 1995).

Steinmetz, J.H., *Examining Mid-Atlantic Ocean Shipwrecks and Commercial Fish Trawling and Dredging* (MA Thesis, East Carolina University, 2010).

Vorus, S., 'Trawling for Treasure,' *National Fisherman* (June 1997), 19-29.

The Deep-Sea Tortugas Shipwreck, Florida: Technology

John Astley
Tortugas Shipwreck Project Offshore Manager, Seahawk Deep Ocean Technology

Greg Stemm
Odyssey Marine Exploration, Tampa, USA

Between 1989 and 1991 Seahawk Deep Ocean Technology of Tampa, Florida, conducted the world's first robotic excavation of a deep-sea shipwreck, in this case lost in 405m off the Tortugas Islands in the Florida Keys, USA. The study of this merchant vessel from the 1622 Spanish Tierra Firme fleet required the development of cutting-edge technological solutions ranging from an appropriate research ship to a sophisticated Remotely-Operated Vehicle. The latter was custom-tooled with a specialized pump and suction system, which included a limpet device to lift delicate artifacts and a Sediment Removal and Filtration (SeRF) filtering unit to save small finds recovered during the extraction of sediment spoil. The Tortugas shipwreck's technology package successfully enabled 16,903 artifacts to be recorded and safely recovered.

1. Introduction

In July 1989 when the location of the Tortugas shipwreck was first identified using a Deep Ocean Engineering Phantom ROV (Remotely-Operated Vehicle), underwater technology was developing at a rapid rate due to vast budgets being made available for complex projects across the world. Between 1978 and 1988 the offshore oilfield industry had made significant advances in their capabilities for deep-sea work ranging from pipeline surveys to offshore oil rig support and inspection.

The navigational precision of the data demanded for rig support and the laying of oil pipelines needed to be to centimetric accuracy in critical areas near structures and lesser (1m) in open water. These systems were highly automated: data recorders only needed to press one or two keys to record all positional data and references to video, still photographs and anomaly identity. Seahawk chose to adapt recognized and well-developed offshore oil and gas technology to the recording and recovery of artifacts from the Tortugas shipwreck as the most realistic and efficient methodology for a scientific deep-sea excavation.

While some cursory exploration and salvage work had been accomplished on other deep shipwreck sites, the excavation of the early 17th-century Tortugas shipwreck represented the world's first comprehensive archaeological excavation of a deep-sea shipwreck entirely remotely using robotic technology. The project called for appropriately respectful technology suited to the removal of sedimentary overburden, accurate positioning and recording systems, as well as sensitive artifact recovery tools. The project resulted in the recovery of 16,903 artifacts, ranging from gold bars to ballast stones and extensive ceramics, animal bones, pearls and tiny seeds, and the procurement of an enormous quantity of scientific data in the form of video, still photographs and records. The Tortugas shipwreck excavation's pioneering technology package served as the backbone to the archaeological reconstruction of this shipwreck.

Fig. 1. The 86ft-long research vessel RV Seahawk.

Fig. 2. The Seahawk Retriever *in port. Photo: John Astley.*

Fig. 3. The Seahawk Retriever *anchored over the Tortugas shipwreck site on a four-point mooring. Photo: John Astley.*

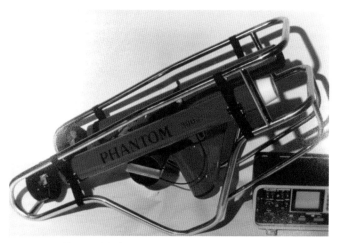

Fig. 4. A DOE Phantom 300 ROV used for visual reconnaissance from the RV Seahawk.

2. Survey Equipment

The operation's platform used during the Tortugas shipwreck survey was the 26.2m-long research vessel *Seahawk* (Fig. 1), equipped with side-scan sonar, sector-scanning sonar, magnetometer, a multi-target acquisition/tracking system, an integrated navigation system, Remotely-Operated Vehicles, HF, VHF radios and a very long range cellular telephone. The integrated navigation system was capable of generating search grids and graphically displaying the real time position of the research ship. The side-scanning sonar (consisting of a Klein 590 paper recorder, a 100/500 khz towfish, a Sintrex high-resolution magnetometer and an EG & G magnetometer), a Mesotec 971 and UDI sector-scanning sonar, a Loran C Integrated Seatrac Navigation System, and a Track Point II Dynamic Relative Positioning System facilitated the initial survey.

The side-scan sonar featured transducers on a tow fish that emitted and received acoustic pulses, which were transmitted to the research vessel. The data from the Klein side-scan sonar tow fish (100/500 khz) were transmitted to a model 595 recorder for processing. The system was able to record a swathe of up to 300m to each side, depending on the frequency. Conditioned by density and material, features and objects rendered a dark silhouette created by acoustic shadows on thermal paper, which fed out of the recorder at a speed proportional to the tow fish's movements along the survey lines. The resulting image provided a detailed representation of the ocean floor features and characteristics: an accurate picture of a wide area, which could be interpreted to construct a three dimensional image of the seafloor's contours.

Aboard the RV *Seahawk* were three ROV's equipped with video and still cameras to provide visual access and documentation in deep water, and a manipulator device

Figs. 5-6. The initial visual wreck survey was accomplished using a Phantom DHD2 ROV (top) being launched by Scott Stemm, Dr. James Cooke, David Six and Steve Dabagian.

that enabled the mechanical retrieval of artifacts. The largest and most versatile of the ROV's was a Phantom DHD2, custom built for this project by Graham Hawkes of Deep Ocean Engineering. The DHD2 had a depth rating of 610m, a low-light color video camera and relatively simple articulated arm (Figs. 5-6). A Phantom 500, with a depth rating of 150m and a color video camera, was

Fig. 7. The 3-ton ROV Merlin built for the Tortugas shipwreck excavation;
with its SeRF system hose and nozzle at front right, two manipulator arms and limpet suction
device at center. Along the badge bar are two 35mm cameras and two 70mm still cameras.

a mid range ROV. Finally, a Phantom 300, with a depth rating of 90m and color video, functioned in shallow water (Fig. 4). The RV *Seahawk* was capable of holding station under its own power without anchoring by 'liveboating' the vessel during ROV operations.

Initial visual survey of the wreck site was accomplished using the Phantom DHD2 ROV (Figs. 5-6), which was equipped with a Mesotech 971 sector scanning sonar and was utilized to define the location and perimeter of the site. The ROV was linked to *Seahawk* via 610m of shielded 42 separate conductor umbilical cable (no single wire multiplex control system was available in 1990-91) and was fitted with two 250-watt halogen lights and two Panasonic CCD low light video color cameras to illuminate the site. The Phantom DHD2 had a single function manipulator arm to provide dexterity for the retrieval of artifacts and was equipped with an ORE multi-beacon, which emitted an analog signal received by a Trac Point II tracking system. DHD2, with dimensions of 0.6 x 0.9 x 1.2m,

including its protector bars, weighed approximately 68kg and was propelled by six thrusters. The pilots flew the ROV using a 'joy stick' control and observation via a small TV monitor mounted in the control console. A 'co-pilot' managed the camera adjustments, recorders and manipulated the retrieval arm.

The launch system onboard the RV *Seahawk* consisted of a winch, an A frame, armored tether and depressor weight that allowed ROV operations to be conducted in depths of up to 600m of water. The ROV was free-swimming, relying on the depressor weight connected to the armored umbilical, with a 50m neutrally buoyant excursion tether from the depressor that provided a 100m footprint for the ROV.

The video survey of the Tortugas deep-water wreck initially revealed a shipwreck site measuring approximately 15m long and 10m wide characterized by wooden hull remains, piles of ballast stone and numerous 17th-century olive jars. All videotapes recorded throughout the excavation were, and continue to be, held for permanent reference.

3. Excavation Equipment

In order to commence excavations with suitable technology, a second vessel, the 64m-long *Seahawk Retriever*, was dispatched to the site in May 1990 (Figs. 2-3). Originally called the *Tera Tide*, this vessel was built in 1974 by Burton Shipyard, Texas, as a twin screw supply vessel for transporting and pump drilling mud in the oilfields of the Gulf of Mexico. Of welded steel construction, and with a flush deck aft and raised deck forward, a model bow, square stern and steel deckhouse, the ship was retro fitted for the Tortugas shipwreck excavation with low pressure Bratvaag winches for managing a four point mooring system (Fig. 3), cranes for hoisting equipment and artifacts, a billeting module for housing additional personnel, a complete suite of communications and security technology and a control module for the ROV. The *Seahawk Retriever* was equipped with living facilities for a 30-person crew (Appendix 2).

While manned submersibles capable of operating at the depth of the Tortugas wreck were available to the project, the relatively short duration capability of manned subs, the low power available in their DC systems and difficulty of working in heavy currents made such an approach to the site impractical. Seahawk considered robotic excavation to be the best solution to the unique problems of excavation at 400m depth. After lengthy consultation with archaeologists and subsea engineers, a large work ROV, nicknamed Merlin, was designed and constructed to the specifications laid out by Seahawk's technology team specifically for archaeological excavation in deep water. The system was manufactured by AOSC, formerly AMETEK Offshore Scotland, Ltd., of Aberdeen, Scotland (Appendix 1).

Merlin was fitted with advanced Schilling manipulators, a customized suction dredge, an acoustic long baseline

Fig. 9. The SeRF (Sediment Removal and Filtration System) tool for sieving small finds custom-designed for the Tortugas shipwreck excavation and installed onto the rear of the ROV Merlin. Photo: John Astley.

positioning system and weighed approximately 3 tons out of water (Figs. 7-12). Buoyancy blocks of syntactic foam (to resists the crushing effects of pressure at 400m) made Merlin 272kg positively buoyant. The ROV had six hydraulic-powered positioning thrusters; vertically oriented thrusters allowed it to work above the seafloor without stirring up sand or silt. In other words, Merlin floated and used thrusters to push itself down, which enabled the system to hover safely over the site. Thrusters also held the ROV steady when artifacts were lifted. Either manipulator arm could lift up to 113kg without affecting Merlin's position in the water. One of the manipulators used a master/slave system controlled by a master replica of the manipulator at the surface desk; the jaw pressure could be dialed up to 500lbs or reduced to a few ounces. Positioning was determined and recorded by a system of long baseline transponders installed on the site, which communicated with transponders on Merlin and the ship.

A crew of three technicians operated the ROV from the control room onboard the *Seahawk Retriever* (Figs. 13-14) under the supervision of the project archaeologist. Video was relayed to the control room via fiber optic cable, where three 30in video screens provided a 180-degree view of the underwater excavation site. One Photosea 35mm camera and two 70mm cameras (oriented so that stereoscopic still photos of artifacts *in situ* were possible) provided still photography. Merlin's Schilling manipulators were made of titanium and included a five-function and a seven-function unit. Pilots watched events on the seafloor live in real time on monitors and commanded the manipulator arms using joysticks at the control console aboard the *Retriever*.

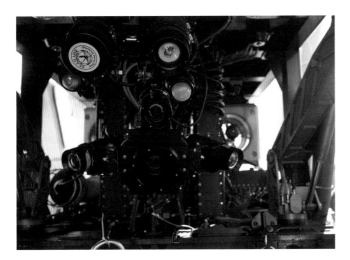

Fig. 8. Cameras and strobe lights at the front of the ROV Merlin. Photo: John Astley.

Fig. 12. The ROV Merlin docked onto the deck
of the Seahawk Retriever. Photo: John Astley.

Fig. 13. The archaeological recording and datalogger
room on the Seahawk Retriever from where excavations
were observed and documented. Photo: John Astley.

Figs. 10-11. The custom-designed receiver and venturi
pump from the SeRF (Sediment Removal and
Filtration System) unit installed onto the rear of
the ROV Merlin (with an early prototype at top).
Photo (Fig. 11): John Astley.

Fig. 14. Monitoring archaeological operations on the
Tortugas shipwreck from the Seahawk Retriever.
The top screens displayed sonar and navigation.
The three middle colour screens revealed a very wide
view of the site under investigation. The lower row
of screens depicted compass, vehicle instrumentation
and stern camera data, plus other cameras monitoring
the ROV parts. In the foreground the datalogger runs four
SVHS recorders and the logging system. Photo: John Astley.

Fig. 15. A Sonardyne transponder, with the transducer at left and the hook release at right, all encased in a buoyancy jacket to facilitate recovery. Photo: John Astley.

Fig. 16. Alan Crampton rigging a Sonardyne transponder for deployment. Photo: John Astley.

4. Operations

The approximate location of the Tortugas shipwreck in 405m of water was determined by a Loran C navigational fix obtained when the site was first discovered. To position the ship for the excavation, four Sonardyne Compatt transponders were placed approximately 200m away from the wreck perimeter, their positions at this stage not being critical (Figs. 15-16). Four large anchors were situated 1,600m apart in a box group around this position. These were connected by 30m of chain to a steel wire leading straight up to the surface, where they were attached to 3m-diameter mooring buoys. The ship connected its mooring winches to these buoys and wound itself into the middle of the array. It was imperative to use mooring buoys in this operation because if the research ship attempted to connect directly to the anchors in this depth of water it would have jeopardized the integrity of the wreck as the connecting wires could have swept across the site. The buoy system also allowed the vessel to hook into and release itself from the system without recovering the anchors.

The Sonardyne long baseline system used for positioning included a set of transponders that were placed in a seabed array and interrogated by the ROV, or the ship, to obtain positional information. Calibrating arrays of this type and gauging the precise distance between transponders on the seabed had always been an inherent problem. Traditionally this had been executed using transponders that 'ping' (transmit a single tone but no telemetry) and by steaming the ship around the site and interrogating the transponders to compare positions with surface radio navigation systems, thereby obtaining a calibration. This method produced a reasonable result in shallow water, where the temperature and salinity of the local water column was known and in an area where surface navigation facilities were good (bearing in mind that in 1989 GPS was not yet available).

The Sonardyne Pans system used on the Tortugas shipwreck project removed errors caused by distortion of the speed of sound in water due to the vertical water column. All of the transponders are 'intelligent': they passed information between themselves through water as sound, rather like the RS232 system used in computer telemetry. They possessed a vast repertoire of commands and abilities, which could all be controlled from the surface or by the ROV. The procedure designed for this system involved placing an array of four transponders in the optimum positions. The calibration procedure functioned as follows:

Figs. 17-18. Removing overburden on the
Tortugas shipwreck using the SeRF system.

1. The transponders measured the temperature and salinity of the water at the seabed. This information was passed to the surface as data, and used to derive the speed of sound in water at the seabed level.
2. The transponders were then instructed from the surface to interrogate each other about 20 times each in all directions and between all paths between each transponder.
3. Each transponder that was interrogated replied to its interrogator. The total out and return time across the local seabed was sent to the surface as data.
4. At the surface a histogram was constructed of each interrogation path. From this the actual distance between any two transponders could be established to a high degree of accuracy. Any small error was then eliminated by iterating a 'best fit scenario' for the complete array. The result was a calibration that determined the relative positions of the transponders to better than 5cm

spatial accuracy. No data relying on sound velocity was ever determined through the vertical water column, only horizontally through the water at the local work site.
5. When the system was calibrated, the array could be interrogated by the ROV on the seabed. The return times were collected by the vehicle's ROVNAV system and sent up the vehicle umbilical as data via a modem.

During the course of the excavation, using this system a repeatable recording accuracy of approximately 10cm for the ROV's position was obtained. The array could also be interrogated vertically through the water column from the ship via a transducer to place the ship within 5m for the launching of the ROV or retrieval of anchors.

A Navigation Camera was situated on the front of the ROV that looked down vertically to navigate movements safely. A video overlay system generated a white cross-site in the center of this picture (Fig. 23). The ROVNAV transducer carried by the ROV was fitted just above this camera so its crosshairs were centered directly below the transducer, which provided the known location on the site. This camera served as the vehicle's datum.

Transponders can be moved due to local tide or current variations. Thus, at the beginning of each dive the ROV followed an exercise that recalibrated them. At the start of operations two metal plates, each 30cm square with a cross-painted on them, had been placed on the sea bottom to create south and north datum points. One was located 60m south of the site and the other 60m to the north. When the ROV arrived on the seabed at the beginning of each dive the local temperature and salinity were established from the sensors on the array.

After the water density, and therefore the speed that sound would travel through the water, was established the ROV would position its navigation camera directly over the target on the south datum. If the x,y,z co-ordinates of this position did not agree within a few centimeters with the data observed after calibration, then the array would be 'virtually shifted' in the x,y plane by software to fit again. The ROV would then transit to the north datum, 120m away, and set up again over this target. Any error now observed with scale or skew could thus be corrected by rotating or rescaling the calibration to fit. If these two datums were kept consistent, then recording locations on the wreck site between them maintained a high degree of accuracy.

During operations, the 98 Series Hewlett Packard Navigation computer ran two displays. The first was located at the surveyor's station and displayed time returns, standard deviation of fixes and a graphic display of the 'cocked hat' triangle formed by the array returns. The second monitor at the pilot's station displayed a graphical representation of the site, with a moving icon representing the ROV and any other features on the site that had been logged into the system. The representation of the site was updated from time to time from the logging database as the excavation progressed. The navigation computer accepted and processed information on gyro, pitch, roll and depth from the ROV's computer. The raw data was then corrected for pitch, roll and the orientation of the ROV. The positional data was stored at the navigation computer and passed on to the logging computer.

The logging computer accepted positional data and kept track of any other operational event related to artifacts, camera stills taken and videotapes running. All data was placed in a FoxBase database using in-house software utilized with minimum keystroke activity by the operator to avoid typo errors. Although the facility to enter individual comments was available, most events could be registered using a single function key. At the end of a dive session the database was backed up to a WORM drive (Write Once Read Many), an early form of CD.

During the excavation, events recorded included, but were not be limited to (Fig. 33):

- Artifact Observed: all positional data and videotape numbers recorded across line of the database.
- Artifact Identified: eg. jar, sherd, pottery, porcelain, coin, gold bar, wood, ballast, utensil, etc.
- Artifact Removed: all the above date plus an ID Inventory Number and ID Basket Number.
- Artifact Basket Placed: As above information, plus data on the partition number of the 4Plex container in which the basket was secured. Also the excursion number of the 4Plex.
- Positional and recording data were taken for the following events: dredging started, dredging stopped, video started, video paused, still taken 35mm, still taken 70mm, frame grab.

Two Schilling Titan manipulators were fitted to the ROV Merlin. One was a seven-function position feedback unit used for all delicate operations. The other was a Schilling Titan five-function unit utilized mainly for holding the sediment removal nozzles and for lifting artifacts already contained in baskets (Fig. 17). The seven-function unit was controllable by the operator in jaw grip pressure ranging from a few ounces to 45kg. The main arm could lift object weighing up to 226kg.

Perhaps the most resourceful modification custom-made by the Tortugas team was the attachment to the ROV of a small, 5cm-diameter bellows type suction cup (Figs. 19-21, 36-37). The suction delivered to this device

Fig. 19. An early limpet suction device developed for the Tortugas project being used to recover an olive jar.

Figs. 20-21. An evolved small limpet suction bellows device used to recover artifacts from the Tortugas shipwreck inspired from paper printing industry technology.

Fig. 22. Observation of Merlin excavating, using the ROV's vertical black and white still camera.

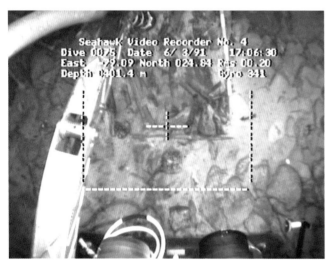

Fig. 23. Observation of Merlin excavating using the ROV's vertical black and white still camera, with its electronic grid position and geospatial data superimposed over the image. Similar data could be observed on all live and recorded video data.

was controllable by the operator. The cup could pick up the most delicate porcelain and olive jars without causing damage, yet could still remove large angular ballast stones. The invention and adoption of this limpet system on the Tortugas shipwreck went through several phases of on-site development and was the first application of this tool on a deep-sea archaeological excavation. The system is now a standard tool utilized by Odyssey Marine Exploration and other archaeological operatives.

Artifacts were initially secured in circular fishing baskets, which were numbered for input into the database and for recording onto videotape. They were fitted with 'jug' handles on the sides and 'bucket' handles on top to facili-

tate carrying by the ROV manipulator arms. The baskets were placed in sectioned off partitions in the large steel basket designed for retrieving artifacts from the sea bottom, nicknamed the 4Plex, which had a lifting capability of 3 tons (Fig. 24).

When the 4Plex was ready for recovery, a wire was lowered from the research vessel's recovery winch. Near the hook on this wire was a transponder that enabled the ship to reposition itself using its winches to guide the hook to within 50m of the 4Plex. When the hook arrived near the sea bottom the ROV approached it, grasped it with a manipulator and conveyed it to the 4Plex, where it could be hooked on and lifted to the ship (Figs. 25-30).

After recovery, an empty 4Plex would be sent down again with a transponder on the wire. The transponder relayed depth, thus permitting its descent to be halted just above the seabed. The ROV then pushed the 4Plex to the appropriate position before it was lowered completely onto the seabed. Merlin finally unhooked the wire from the 4Plex to allow the empty wire to be winched back to the surface. Due to the careful navigation of the ROV using the positioning system, at no time during the excavation were any entanglement problems encountered between the ROV umbilical and the 4Plex lift wire during deployment or recovery operations.

The sediment removal and filtration (SeRF) system used on the Tortugas excavation was a 25hp hydraulically-driven three-stage water pump (Figs. 17-18). This venturi pulled water and unobserved small finds through the main system (Fig. 36). No artifacts passed through any mechanical portion of the pump, so there was no damage to cultural remains that might have traversed the system. In addition to working sensitively around archaeological remains, this system could extract solid clay at full power. It could also be reversed to back flush the system or blow away silt and sand.

Many methods were tried and tested to filter sediment that might contain small finds unnoticed during excavation. Any form of screen or filter inserted into the venturi soon blocked up and curtailed the dive. A successful method was subsequently evolved based on the principle of a fuel filter using a container on which liquid is dropped from the top onto a domed plate. Solid objects fall to the bottom of the vessel beneath the domed plate. Excess water and fine silt was then discharged at the top, where it was ejected through a 2m-high stack.

A ram-operated, three-way select gate valve was utilized to select between usage of the main dredge nozzle and the suction limpet used for lifting artifacts. The venturi used was a 'Banjo' type, which ejected water through a ring. The aperture in the center, 9.0cm diameter, passed the

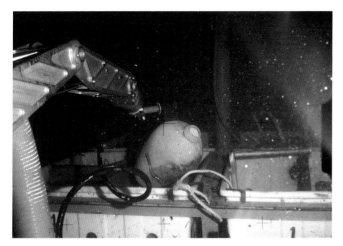

Fig. 24. An olive jar being secured into a 4Plex unit by the ROV Merlin using its limpet suction device.

induced flow through the dredge nozzle. The main water pump relied on was a three-stage turbine, which required about 80 liter/min at 200 bar. The dredge nozzle and lifting suction limpet were stowed on hooks positioned near the Schilling Titan manipulator. The SeRF system nozzle measured 10.2cm in diameter and was attached by a flexible tube. The lifting limpet was adapted to a self-coiling airline hose.

The dredge receiver into which spoil was filtered was constructed from two 18 US gallon stainless steel pressure beer barrels built onto the rear of the ROV Merlin (Figs. 9-11). Its content size was suitable for dredging a cubic meter of clay (about one ton). When full the receiver typically held about 25% clay and 25% hard objects (stones, shell and small finds including pearls, seeds, coins, beads, glass, and human and animal teeth: Figs. 31-32). Simultaneously, nearly a ton of clay had exited via the three exhaust stacks in the form of fine debris that drifted away from site and created no visibility issues.

The size of the domed plate proved to be critical and was determined by trial and error. If the dome was too small it allowed too much turbulence in the bottom of the receiver. It was discovered that the best results were obtained by cutting the domed plate a little on the large side so that some clay was retained alongside any artifacts collected. The clearance between the edge of the dome and the receiver rim was 2.5cm. This served to protect and cushion the small artifacts, but demanded more intensive sorting after ROV recovery.

The SeRF system was attached to the stern of the ROV Merlin and could only be removed at the surface. In practice a bottom working time of about three to four hours proved feasible before the SeRF unit was full and had to be recovered.

Figs. 25-26. Artifacts secured in a 4Plex unit being winched onto the deck of the Seahawk Retriever. Photos: John Astley.

Figs. 27-28. Numbered 4Plex units were recovered with a closed lid protecting the artifacts. Photos: John Astley.

*Figs. 29-30. Archaeology team members examining the finds freshly
recovered from the Tortugas shipwreck. Photos: John Astley.*

*Figs. 31-32. Archaeologist David Moore examines sieved spoil recovered from within the ROV Merlin's SeRF
(Sediment Removal and Filtration System) unit. Photo (Fig. 31): John Astley.*

```
PAGE NO.    7
06/17/91
                              REPORT OF ROV DIVING
                  .Seahawk Deep Ocean Technology,Inc. Dive Number: 84
                  .Ship: Seahawk Retriever         Dive Date: Jun 16, 1991.
                  .ROV: Merlin                      Data File: D84-v1.dbf  .
```

TIME hr:mm:ss	EVENTNAME		COMMENT	EAST	NORTH	DEPTH (m)	RMS	GYRO
18:23:45	Artifact Removed #	1822	sherd	210.56	-95.31	403.26	34.27	48
18:23:56	Artifact Placed #	1822	basket 12	210.38	-95.32	403.26	34.26	48
18:24:50	Artifact Removed #	1823	sherd	210.47	-95.31	403.26	34.23	46
18:25: 1	Artifact Placed #	1823	basket 12	-80.53	16.89	403.00	0.08	45
18:29:46	Dredging End			-80.37	16.97	403.26	0.06	46
18:32:27	Stop VCR 1		Pause	-80.56	16.86	403.26	0.03	50
18:32:29	Stop VCR 2		Pause	-80.43	17.01	403.26	0.07	50
18:32:32	Stop VCR 3		Pause	-80.60	16.90	403.26	0.05	50
18:34:16	Start VCR 1		Continue	-80.52	17.19	403.00	0.04	50
18:34:18	Start VCR 2		Continue	-80.52	17.19	403.00	0.04	50
18:34:20	Start VCR 3		Continue	-80.43	17.03	403.26	0.13	51
18:34:25	Dredging Start			-80.43	17.03	403.26	0.13	50
18:39: 3	35mm Taken # 4		e.o.	-80.54	16.95	403.26	0.09	44
18:39:31	35mm Taken # 5		e.o.	-80.59	17.00	403.26	0.07	45
18:47:22	Dredging End			-80.50	16.94	403.26	0.16	45
18:48:45	Stop VCR 1		Pause	-80.59	16.98	403.26	0.07	48
18:48:50	Stop VCR 2		Pause	-80.62	17.01	403.26	0.14	50
18:48:56	Stop VCR 3		Pause	-80.55	17.02	403.26	0.10	49
18:49: 5	Dredging End			-80.55	17.08	403.26	0.07	49
18:49:21	Artifact Removed #	1824	sherd	-80.58	16.99	403.26	0.07	48
18:49:34	Artifact Placed #	1824	basket 12	-80.59	17.10	403.00	0.11	49
18:53:59	Start VCR 1		Continue	-80.64	17.05	403.26	0.05	49
18:54: 2	Start VCR 2		Continue	40.83	265.72	403.26	23.10	50
18:54: 5	Start VCR 3		Continue	40.83	265.72	403.26	23.10	51
18:54:12	Nav. Fix		close up video of large E.O.	-80.56	17.15	403.26	0.00	50
18:57:44	Stop VCR 1		Pause	-80.44	16.90	403.26	0.04	50
18:57:47	Stop VCR 2		Pause	-80.52	16.90	403.26	0.09	50
18:57:49	Stop VCR 3		Pause	-80.52	16.90	403.26	0.09	49
19: 9: 4	Start VCR 1		Continue	-81.39	15.86	403.26	0.09	54
19: 9: 9	Start VCR 2		Continue	-81.49	15.61	403.00	0.16	55
19: 9:10	Start VCR 3		Continue	-81.49	15.61	403.00	0.16	55
19: 9:24	Dredging Start		Continue	-81.29	15.64	403.26	0.12	55
19:15:23	Artifact Removed #	1825	sherd	-81.32	15.56	403.26	0.04	51
19:15:38	Artifact Placed #	1825	basket 12	-81.32	15.56	403.26	0.17	50
19:23:12	Dredging End		port	-81.30	15.67	403.26	0.15	54
19:24:32	Stop VCR 1		Pause	-81.58	16.12	403.26	0.08	39
19:24:35	Stop VCR 2		Pause	-81.66	16.25	403.26	0.09	38
19:24:39	Stop VCR 3		Pause	-81.66	16.25	403.26	0.09	39
19:28: 8	Dredging Start		port into aft reciever	-80.74	17.18	403.26	0.10	336
19:28:37	Start VCR 1		Continue	-80.85	16.99	403.26	0.09	335
19:28:41	Start VCR 2		Continue	-80.66	17.10	403.26	0.14	334
19:28:44	Start VCR 3		Continue	-80.74	16.99	403.26	0.17	334
19:37:57	Nav. Fix		backflush to basket 12	-80.73	17.08	403.26	0.12	334
19:41:17	Artifact Removed #	1826	wood frag	-80.68	17.20	403.26	0.09	336
19:41:31	Artifact Placed #	1826	basket 12	-80.70	17.01	403.00	0.23	336
19:44:36	Artifact Removed #	1827	sherd	-80.66	17.21	403.26	0.08	336
19:44:52	Artifact Placed #	1827	basket 12	-80.59	17.24	403.26	0.14	335

*Fig. 33. Typical dive sheet maintained
during the 1991 Tortugas shipwreck excavation.*

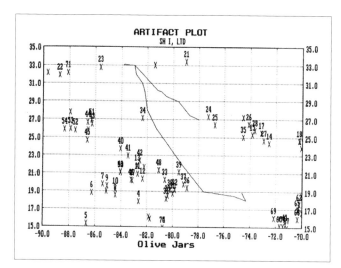

Fig. 34. An example of an original computer generated artifact plot from the Tortugas shipwreck excavation, in this case showing the positions of olive jars.

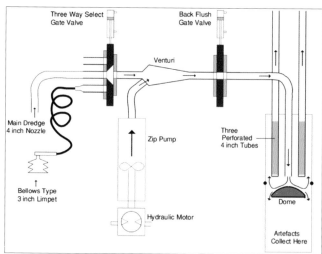

Fig. 36. A schematic diagram of the construction and operation of the venturi SeRF system developed for ROV Merlin for the Tortugas shipwreck excavation. Drawing: John Astley.

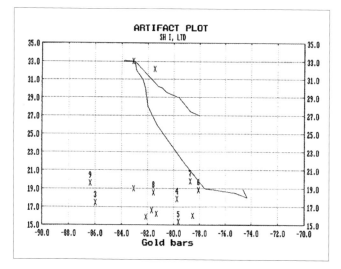

Fig. 35. An example of an original computer generated artifact plot from the Tortugas shipwreck excavation, in this case showing the positions of gold bars.

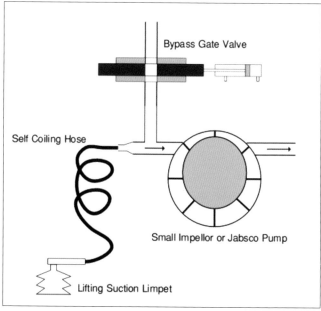

Fig. 37. A schematic plan of the limpet suction device developed for the Tortugas shipwreck excavation. Drawing: John Astley.

5. Excavation

Using the Long baseline navigational system already decribed, the position of Merlin was recorded every five seconds. Along with various vehicle orientation information received from Merlin's computers, this data was passed to a computer system developed by Todd Robinson of Seahawk Deep Ocean Technology to manage artifact provenience. Called the 'On Line Data Storage and Logging System', this system was run by the third member of the pilot crew, designated the 'datalogger'.

The system first took the received information, processed it and sent it to the display system that overlaid the data onto the video recorders. As activities unfolded on site, the datalogger entered appropriate comments and assigned artifact numbers to items as they were first seen, photographed and prepared for storage and recovery. That information was recorded immediately onto a paper log transcript and to an electronic database for further review by the team archaeologist. The paper log included a heading with Dive Number and Date and a continuous log of Time in hours, minutes, and seconds, followed by the Event Type, Comment, then the Position Coordinates.

The electronic database, stored on computer disc, could be accessed through a variety of methods. For example, a category of artifacts (ie. olive jars) could be imposed on an outline of the site so that the distribution could be studied. Any combination of categories could be plotted together showing their distribution over the site and contextual relationships. The computer could also be commanded to generate a plot (either on screen or paper) showing the distribution of the gold bars, glazed ceramic bowls or astrolabes, for example (Figs. 34-35). These plots proved invaluable in determining relationships between artifacts and site contexts during the course of the excavation – and then to recreate the site through post-processing after the project was completed.

During the excavation of the site the project archaeologist directed all activities undertaken by the ROV technicians. One of the key benefits of this remote system, as opposed to archaeological excavations by divers, was the ability of the entire team to view, discuss and contemplate the excavation strategy. This unique ability to share ideas during the course of the excavation was exceptionally useful when nearly every activity on the site required the development of new techniques and tools. The fact that every second of the excavation was recorded on video allowed thorough review and documentation of the project two decades after the excavation took place.

After ten months of excavation, thorough documentation of the site and recovery of just under 17,000 artifacts, the Seahawk team proved that it was possible to undertake a detailed archaeological excavation remotely using robotics, something never before accomplished. More than just allowing a primitive excavation, as one would expect from the inaugural attempt at such a complex task, the systems designed and utilized on this project provided a level of repeatable accuracy, artifact recovery and efficiency of recording that would serve to provide a model for the evolution of robotic excavation in the deep ocean for future generations.

Appendix 1:
Scorpio 2000 ROV, 'Merlin'

Specification
- L. 2.4m.
- W. 1.85m.
- H. 2.5m.
- Weight (in air): 3,300kg.
- Payload: 150kg.

- Depth rating: 1,000 msw.
- Through frame lift: 3,000kg.

Hydraulic Power Unit
- HPU voltage: 3000 volts.
- Maximum current: 23 amps.
- HPU shaft power: 75 kW.
- Maximum flow: 190 1/min (50 US gpm).
- Supply pressure: 204 bar (3000 psi).
- Over ambient compensation pressure: 1.0 bar (14.7 psi).

Axial Thrusters
- Number: 2.
- Manufacturer: Innerspace.
- Type: 1002.
- Motor Type: RHL A70.

Vertical Thrusters
- Number: 4.
- Manufacturer: Innerspace.
- Type: 1002.
- Motor Type: RHL A70.

Bollard Pull
- Forward: 408 kgf (900 lbsf).
- Aft: 340 kgf (750 lbsf).
- Lateral: 408 kgf (900 lbsf).
- Vertical: 649 kgf (1430 lbsf).

Valve Packs
- One 12-station solenoid valve pack.
- One eight-station proportional valve pack.

Optics & Lighting
- Provision for five cameras with separate focus or zoom and on/off controls.
- Provision for one two-channel fiber-optic video multiplexer.
- Six 115-volt ac lighting power supply circuits at 250W each.

Sensors/Indicators
- Depth Digiquartz sensor.
- Heading gyro compass updated by fluxgate sensor.
- Pitch and roll sensor.
- Hydraulic pressure.
- Hydraulic temperature.
- HPU temperature.
- Water ingress.
- Pod temperature.
- Tether turns.

- ROV multiplexor status.
- Status of each analogue and digital signal.
- Analogue and digital signals to offset and span set from control console.

ROV Control
- Manual horizontal and vertical joystick control.
- Trim pot control.
- Full/half auto heading with trim pot offset.
- Manual pitch control.
- Manual roll control.
- Full/half auto altitude with trim pot control.

Additional Equipment
- Schilling 'Titan' seven-function manipulator with position feedback.
- Schilling five-function manipulator.
- Simrad Sonar system with 600khz.
- One Photosea TV1200 3 chip CCD TV Camera with 10:1 zoom.
- Two CCD colour fixed TV cameras.
- One OE1323 SIT TV camera.
- One OE1356 B+W TV camera.
- One Photosea 1000 35mm still camera.
- One Photosea 1500 strobe.
- Two Photosea 2000 70mm still cameras.

Umbilical
- Triple wire armored main lift umbilical.
- L. 1,000m.
- Two twisted screened quad.
- Two optical fibers.
- 12 3,000v rated conductors.
- Three 120v rated conductors.
- Four coaxial RG59 conductors.
- One safety shield/screen.
- Weight in air: 2,240 kg/km.
- Theoretical breaking strain: 15,260kg.
- Minimum bend radius: 75cm.

Appendix 2: Ship-Based & Navigational Specification

Control Shack
- External L. 6.1m.
- External W. 2.44m.
- External H. 2.72m.
- Air conditioned.
- Control Console.
- Three 30in Barcho monitors.

- Five 14in TV for video monitoring.
- One 14in vehicle position monitor.
- One 17in sonar monitor.
- One 17in site navigation monitor.
- Four Sony SVHS video recorders.
- One video switching matrix.
- One video overlay system.
- One data recorder computer and monitor.
- One navigation computer and PANS control unit.

Deck Equipment
- A Frame launch over the side from midship position.
- Umbilical winch: line pull 4,620kg.
- Generator: 440 volts (150 kva).
- Crane 1: 5-ton mounted near launch to assist if required.
- Crane 2: 5-ton mounted near stern to deploy moorings.
- Winch: 8-ton pull 800m cable to recover 4Plex.
- Two 4Plex recovery containers.
- Four 5-ton Bruce anchors.
- Four 3m-diameter mooring buoys.
- 122m of 8.9cm studlink chain to connect anchors.
- Four mooring winches, each 25-ton pull, loaded with 2km of 6.3cm wire.
- One two-drum waterfall winch, each 50-ton pull.

Research Ship
- Originally named the Tera Tide, a supply boat with all accommodation forward leaving a long low deck area, renamed the Seahawk Retriever.
- L. 64m.
- Beam 9.8m.
- Engines: 2 x V18 Alcho railroad engines. (These could provide the considerable power to deploy the anchors and drag out the suspended wire cables, but used 14 tons of fuel per day. Once anchored the engines were shut down for the season.)
- Propellers: 2 x 305cm variable pitch.
- Accommodation: modified for 15 people.

Navigation
- Four Sonardyne compact transponders, with depth, temperature and salinity sensors.
- One Sonardyne compact transponder with ability to interrogate, receive and relay data from bottom array to the ship.
- One Sonardyne ROVNAV system.
- One Sonardyne PANS system.
- Interrogation rate 1,500ms.
- All transponders set to operate between 28 and 32 khz.

2

The Deep-Sea Tortugas Shipwreck, Florida: A Spanish-Operated *Navio* of the 1622 Tierra Firme Fleet. Part 1, the Site

Greg Stemm, Ellen Gerth
Odyssey Marine Exploration, Tampa, Florida, USA

Jenette Flow
Pasco-Hernando Community College, New Port Richey, Florida, USA

Claudio Lozano Guerra-Librero
Stratigraphy Area, Faculty of Experimental Sciences, University of Huelva, Spain

Sean Kingsley
Wreck Watch Int., London, UK

In 1990 and 1991 Seahawk Deep Ocean Technology of Tampa, Florida, conducted the world's first archaeological excavation of a deep-sea shipwreck off the Tortugas Islands in the Florida Keys, USA, exclusively using robotic technology. Located at a depth of 405m, 16,903 artifacts from a small merchant vessel identifiable as a Spanish *navio* from the 1622 Tierra Firme fleet were recorded and recovered using a Remotely-Operated Vehicle.

Archival and archaeological research suggests that the most plausible identification of the Tortugas ship is the Portuguese-built and Spanish-operated 117-ton *Buen Jesús y Nuestra Señora del Rosario* owned by Juan de la Torre and captained by Manuel Diaz that sailed for Nueva Cordoba (Cumana) on the Pearl Coast in modern Venezuela before attempting to return to Spain in September 1622.

The shipwreck's significance lies in its relative coherent preservation compared to the scattered character of the *Atocha* and *Margarita* from the same 1622 fleet. This condition enabled the distribution of the original cargo and domestic wares to be examined in context. As a small *navio* the Tortugas vessel operated at the opposite commercial spectrum to these large royal 'treasure' ships and thus reflects the more common everyday world of early 17th-century long-distance Spanish commerce and seafaring.

1. Introduction

In 1989 Seahawk Deep Ocean Technology of Tampa, Florida, identified the site of a colonial-era shipwreck in deep waters off the Dry Tortugas islands in the westernmost Florida Keys (Fig. 1). The following year a pioneering archaeological project was initiated. Throughout 1990 and 1991 the site's cargo and domestic assemblage were extensively recorded and recovered exclusively using pioneering remote technology developed around a Remotely-Operated Vehicle (ROV).

The Tortugas shipwreck excavation was unique in many respects. No humans ever physically visited the site. Instead, the operation was completed entirely using a ROV governed by computers and remote technology aboard a recovery vessel at the ocean surface. Remote archaeological excavation was untried at the time and innovation was required for every phase of the operation. Methods for capturing and recording contextual data were complex and environmental conditions at the site, such as extreme pressure, currents and total darkness, complicated all procedures. Mariners, offshore technicians, pilots and ship's officers and crew, as well as experts in robotics, mechanical engineering, computer technology, marine biology and electronics were instrumental in the project's technical success.

Historically this was the world's first comprehensive deep-sea wreck excavation conducted using a ROV. Although a commercial venture with one of the objectives aimed at identifying valuable cargo, the project was also planned scientifically in parallel to examine the site's

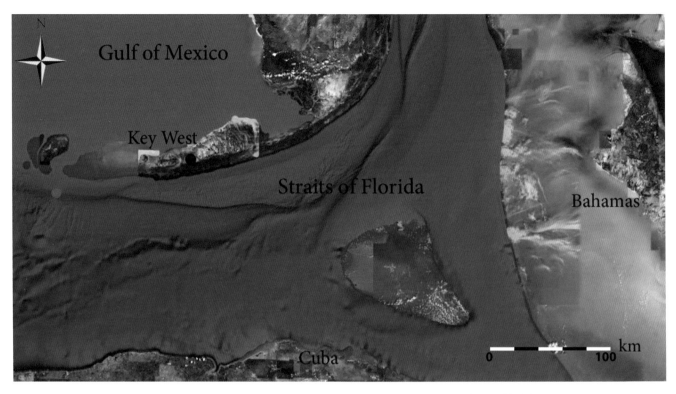

Fig. 1. Location map of the Tortugas shipwreck off the Dry Tortugas islands, Florida Keys.

Fig. 2. The 64m-long Seahawk Retriever used as the research platform during the Tortugas shipwreck excavation.

archaeological character in detail. The positions of all finds were spatially plotted using a recording system developed by John Astley, Gordon Richardson, Greg Stemm and John Morris. The reliance on a limpet suction device to lift delicate artifacts was successfully evolved and sediments were collected for sieving and the detection of small finds through a pioneering SeRF (Sediment Retrieval and Filtration) system built onto the back of the ROV, from which an important set of artifacts and environmental data were obtained for analysis (cf. Astley and Stemm, 2013).

The Tortugas wreck's material culture – from olive jars to the domestic pottery, silver coins, gold bars and astrolabes (Figs. 3-6) – so closely matches the assemblages associated with the *Nuestra Señora de Atocha* and *Santa Margarita* discovered by Mel Fisher in the Florida Keys that there is no doubt that this wreck comprised part of the ill-fated homeward-bound Tierra Firme fleet of 1622. A combination of historical research examined in conjunction with archaeological data suggests that the most plausible candidate for the Tortugas shipwreck is the 117-ton Portuguese-built and Spanish-operated *Buen Jesús y Nuestra Señora del Rosario* owned by Juan de la Torre and captained by shipmaster Manuel Diaz that sailed for Nueva Cordoba (Cumana) on the Pearl Coast in modern Venezuela (Kingsley, 2013). Unlike the more celebrated *Atocha* and *Margarita*, whose sites are largely disarticulated and scattered across enormous sections of the Florida Keys beneath dense and dynamic sediments, the Tortugas wreck is fundamentally coherent and continuous.

Although elements of the upper stratum of the well-preserved Tortugas hull were documented, notably the stern, bows and a square feature identified as a pump well, it is the extensive artifact assemblages that are of greatest evidential value to historical archaeology. In volume and variety these are unparalleled in published scholarly literature from other 16th and 17th-century Spanish shipwrecks worldwide.

Following its dramatic sinking, pioneering recovery and post-excavation fate, on the twentieth anniversary of the completion of the site's excavation Odyssey Marine Exploration – the owner and curator of the surviving collection today – is publishing a series of specialist papers, in addition to two introductory main reports summarizing the site and artifact assemblages, on the Tortugas wreck's assemblages, focusing on:

• Underwater technology
• Artifacts summary
• Ceramic kitchenwares and tablewares
• Olive jars (*botijas*)
• Inductively-coupled Plasma Spectrometry (ICPS) ceramic analysis

Fig. 3. Seahawk co-director Greg Stemm (right) and Dan Bagley (left) with a variety of artifacts from the Tortugas wreck.

• Tobacco pipes
• Glass wares
• Gold bars, bits and belts
• Silver coins
• Venezuelan pearls
• Tortoiseshell craftsmanship
• Trade beads
• Animal bones
• Leather shoes
• Sundial
• South American greenstone artifacts
• Archaeology of 16th and 17th-century Spanish fleets

This introductory paper presents the background to the excavation and summarizes the technology used. The marine environment is defined and the anatomy of the site characterized.[1]

2. Background to the Excavation

Consciousness of the presence of a shipwreck in deep waters off the Dry Tortugas, a group of islands located at the westernmost point of the Florida Keys, first arose in 1965, when the shrimp trawler *Trade Winds* snagged its nets and came to a shuddering halt. When the badly

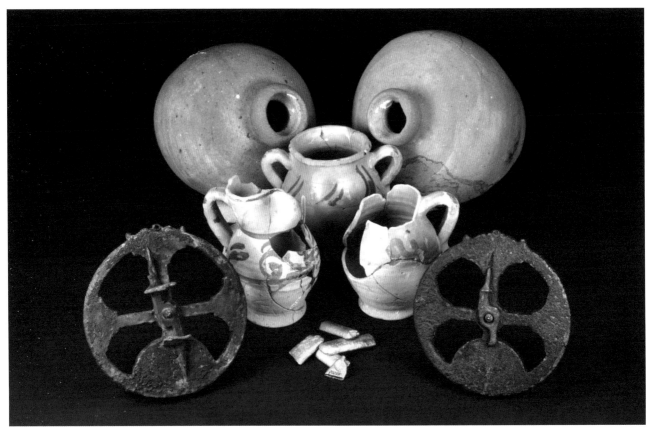

Fig. 4. Bronze astrolabes, gold bars, olive jars and linear-decorated Blue Morisco wares from the Tortugas shipwreck.

Fig. 5. Lead musket shot, tortoise shell lice comb and case, pearls, a sounding lead and wooden spindle weaving battens from the Tortugas shipwreck.

Fig. 6. A sample of ceramic olive jars and tablewares from the Tortugas shipwreck.

ripped nets were pulled in the crew discovered three intact Spanish olive jars, various metal artifacts, pieces of ship's rigging and a considerable amount of wood, including a well preserved section of ornately carved railing. In the absence of technology appropriate for working at such depths, Bob Marx collaborated without success in 1972 with a team of oceanographers from California on the research vessel *Alcoa Seaprobe* to conduct recovery operations. A steel cable was dragged between two shrimp boats several months later and a large anchor snagged and recovered (Marx, 2009: 57).

The character of the fishing hang was finally identified on 20 April 1989 by Seahawk Deep Ocean Technology at a depth of 405m using a Deep Ocean Engineering Phantom ROV operated by Graham Hawkes and Scott Stemm. Later that year on 21 June 1989 a bronze bell was the first artifact recovered from the site. A request for admiralty and maritime jurisdiction was filed in the United States District Court, Southern District of Florida, Miami Division. The motion was granted and title to the wreck was awarded to Seahawk on 29 November 1989.

Due to its depth an archaeological excavation of the Tortugas shipwreck could only be conducted remotely through robotic technology. The 64m-long *Seahawk Retriever* was developed for appropriate use as an archaeological research platform (Fig. 2), and the on-site surveying, excavation and recovery was conducted exclusively using a 3.3-ton Scorpio ROV nicknamed 'Merlin', designed and constructed by AOSC of Aberdeen, Scotland, and tooled for archaeological excavation in deep water (Figs. 7-9).

Merlin was fitted with two manipulators capable of lifting up to 113kg each, a suction dredge and positioning systems. A Sonardyne long baseline acoustic navigation system enabled the location of the ROV underwater to be plotted to an accuracy of 10cm (intra-site was of greater precision). The precise positions of all artifacts recovered during the excavation were mapped *in situ* in custom-designed data logging software. Technical and archaeological ROV activities were recorded using live video and both vertical and horizontal color and black and white photography (both 35mm and 70mm). A typical activity would log: the time, event type (eg. artifact removed, dredging stopped, 35mm photo taken, etc.), the artifact number, event action (eg. sherd recovered to basket), east and north co-ordinates, RMS and gyro. Artifacts were initially placed in large 4Plex lifting containers situated on the seabed prior to recovery (Astley and Stemm, 2013).

Under the direction of offshore Project Manager John Astley and marine archaeologist David Moore, the excavation of the Tortugas shipwreck was conducted over the course of 138 dives in 1990 and 1991, when the contexts of 16,903 shipboard objects were recorded prior to recovery (including 6,639 pearls, around 3,935 ceramic wares and sherds, 1,658 ballast stones 1,590 organic items, 1,184 silver coins and 176 intrusive items). The first of 65 dives commenced on 9 June 1990 and operations finished on 25 November 1990; 659 hours of ROV diving were conducted during the season. The fieldwork recommenced on 19 May 1991, when 73 dives were continued until 3 October 1991; around 830 hours of diving were completed in the second season. The total dive duration for 1990 and 1991 was approximately 1,489 hours.

The entire perimeter around the ballast mound was excavated to a depth of 0.30-0.75m, and 0.75-1.0m around the sternpost and stem, for a total north/south distance covering 24.6m and east/west across an area of 17.0m. A pre-disturbance photomosaic was produced prior to operations (Figs. 12-14), which facilitated the production of the site plan (Fig. 10). Whereas all artifacts were excavated and recovered, the central hull was largely left untouched, with the exception of the removal of extensive ballast stones at the stern, minimally in the bows and along the starboard edge to expose the planking perimeter. Tightly packed, it is unlikely that anything other than the smallest artifacts would have slipped through small cracks between the stones to now underlie the ballast. A comprehensive pulse induction metal detector survey was conducted across the site during different periods between July and October 1991 that identified ferrous materials down to depths of 35cm and non-ferrous objects to 20cm below the sea bottom. A total of 131 targets were investigated as result of this survey (Fig. 11).

Conservation and analysis of the collection continued until July 1998 under the management of Odyssey Marine Exploration, supervised by archaeologist Jenette Flow. An additional phase of conservation, recording and research in preparation for the production of the final reports was undertaken by Odyssey between 2010 and early 2012 under the direction of Sean Kingsley (Wreck Watch Int., London) and Ellen Gerth (Odyssey Curator, Tampa), including conversion of all video to DVD for purposes of long-term archive curation and research, scanning underwater slides to digital form, full re-photography of the artifact collection, select artifact illustrations, animal bone, seed, ceramics, tobacco pipes, tortoise shell and ballast analysis, artifact cataloguing and research, and conversion of the localized artifact positional geospatial data into modern software to generate distribution maps of assemblages.

Fig. 7. *The ROV Merlin being winched onto the deck of the* Seahawk Retriever. *Photo: John Astley.*

3. The Marine Environment

The 'Tortugas Deep-sea A' shipwreck (henceforth abbreviated to the Tortugas shipwreck in this report) lies at a depth of 394-406m, approximately 20km south of the Dry Tortugas, a group of islands situated near the southwest corner of the Florida Platform.[2] The Tortugas Islands are located around 113km west of Key West and 60km west of the Marquesas Keys. The Gulf of Mexico borders the area to the north and the Straits of Florida lie directly to the east and south. The region displays a low tidal range, which achieves 0.52m in spring. Current measurements taken to the west of the Dry Tortugas indicate a dominant north/northeast flow at a maximum rate of <0.10m/s; cyclic reversals to the south/southwest at times exceed 0.10m/s. Surface measurements indicated maximum current rates of 3 knots during the fieldwork seasons, the result of the meandering Gulf Stream current that sometimes flowed over the site.

Fig. 8. The ROV Merlin docked on the deck of the Seahawk Retriever. *Photo: John Astley.*

Fig. 9. The ROV Merlin being launched from the Seahawk Retriever. *Bottom photo: John Astley.*

Fig. 10. Pre-disturbance site plan of the Tortugas shipwreck.

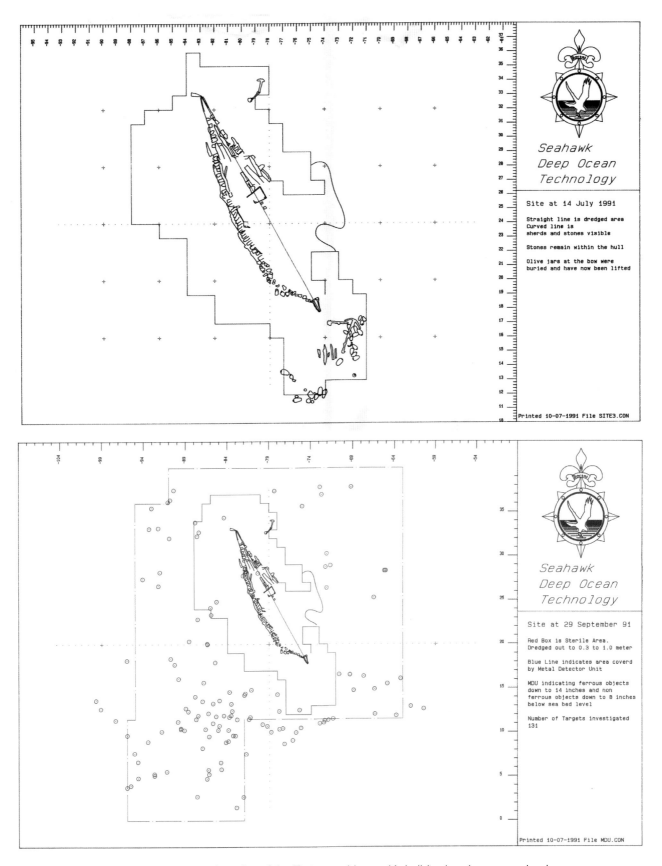

Fig. 11. Post-excavation plan of the Tortugas shipwreck's hull (top) and area examined during the metal detector survey (bottom) (scans of hard copy archival printouts).

Fig. 12. The master site photomosaic being manually assembled.

The study region is blanketed by Holocene sediments varying in thickness from less than 1m in the northeast to greater than 3m in the northwest and averaging about 2m. The sediments consist of soft, carbonate muds and sandy muds (Induced Polarization impedances of 2.01-2.44 ip), soft carbonate muddy sands (impedances of 2.45-2.97 ip) and coarse sands. Core samples reveal compositions comprising 32-34% sand, 43-47% silt, 18-21% clay and 5.3-5.9% Phi. The sediment column is dominated by the calcareous green algae Halimeda in varying states of dia-genesis. A minimal amount of small shell is present in the upper fine section (< 5 phi) of the sediment column 0.9-1.4m below the seafloor. Beneath this stratum the sediment structure and content change to a desiccated lag layer up to 0.4m thick dominated by coarse molluscan shells consist-ing of partial and broken gastropods and pelecypods and coral debris. At depths beyond a maximum of 1.8m below the surface, sediments studied from the deepest cores con-sist of a bioturbated layer of fine-grained (< 6.5 phi) gray sandy mud (Walter *et al.*, 2002: 162, 168-9, 171), which corresponds to visual observations made on the Tortugas shipwreck site, where shell content was low.

Measurements taken in less than 25m water depth around the Dry Tortugas islands suggest that sediments accumulate steadily at rates of 0.3-0.4cm/yr (Ingalls *et al.*, 2004: 4364). Since this zone is relatively shallow com-pared to the Tortugas shipwreck site, and is dominated by fine-grained carbonate sediments compared to the stiff muds within the wreck environment, the latter's sediment accumulation rate is likely to be significantly lower (Walter *et al.*, 2002: 162). Visual observations from the Tortugas wreck reveal a dominance of stiff and heavily bonded clay mud, sufficiently dense to enable vertical sections to be cut by the ROV dredge into the sediments without collapsing (Fig. 22). Numerous olive jars were exposed under mud accumulations covering at least three-quarters of their widths (Figs. 34-35), which indicated a maximum un-dulating sediment drift of 30cm since 1622 on the lower slopes below the elevated ballast pile, which was discov-ered entirely exposed, as was the upper surface of the hull towards the stern. All artifacts were identified either on the site's surface or within this uppermost 30cm-deep stratum. The impact of hurricane activity on sediment transport remains undetermined for these depths.

The Tortugas wreck lies within one of America's most famous fishing grounds, where 'Pink Gold' was struck in 1949 with its epicenter 112km off Key West. The vast, formerly untouched, shrimp fisheries indigenous to these waters were identified by the Federal Fish and Wildlife Service as perhaps the most productive ever located in America. When news of the discovery broke in 1949,

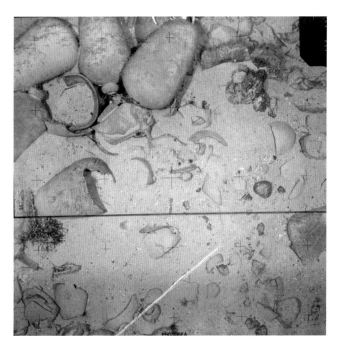

Fig. 13. Detail of the master site photomosaic.

no shrimp boats operated out of Key West. Within three weeks, however, trawlers from North Carolina, northern Florida, Georgia, Mississippi, Louisiana and Texas occu-pied every space in the town's dock. One month later five new packing-houses were built and local wharfage expand-ed to the maximum.

The shrimp beds covered around 160 square kilometers and were believed to extend for another 224km north-wards to Fort Myers in western Florida. Within a very short period of time 200 diesel-powered shrimp trawlers of 18m length were based in Key West. Crewed by three to four men per boat, full capacity catches weighed 1.6-1.8 tons, which were loaded into refrigerated trucks as soon as they were landed for transport north (Van Dresser, 1950: 124, 126).

The new pink gold grounds were considered so important to the US economy that Government fisheries scientists worked hand in hand with fishermen to develop optimum catch efficiencies. In the 1950s National Marine Fisheries Service engineers experimented with electric tick-ler chains that shocked the shrimp out of the mud and into nets (Rudloe and Rudloe, 2010: 36).

Gulf fisheries are some of the most productive in the world. According to the National Marine Fisheries Service, in 2008 the commercial fish and shellfish harvest from the five US Gulf states was estimated to be 1.3 billion pounds valued at $661 million. The Gulf also contains four of the top seven fishing ports in the nation by weight and is home to eight of America's top 20 fishing ports by dollar value.

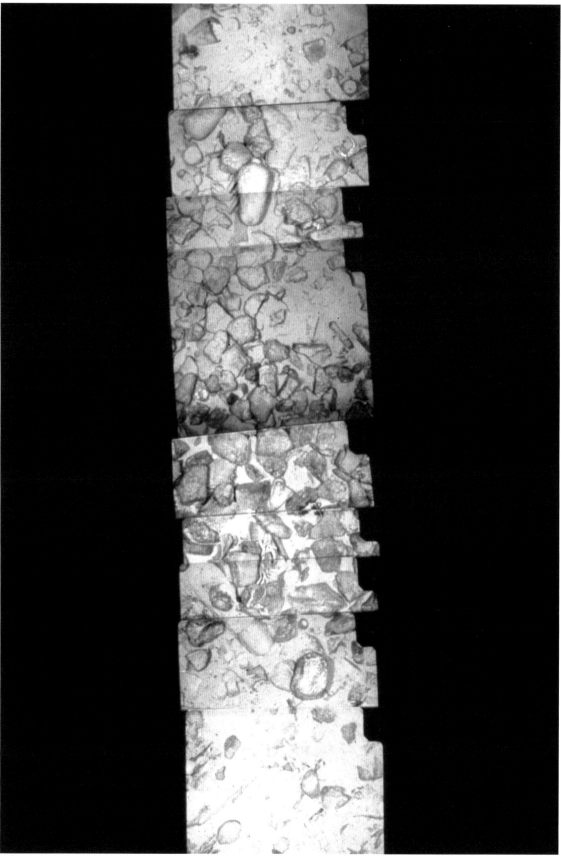

Fig. 14. Detail of the master site photomosaic.

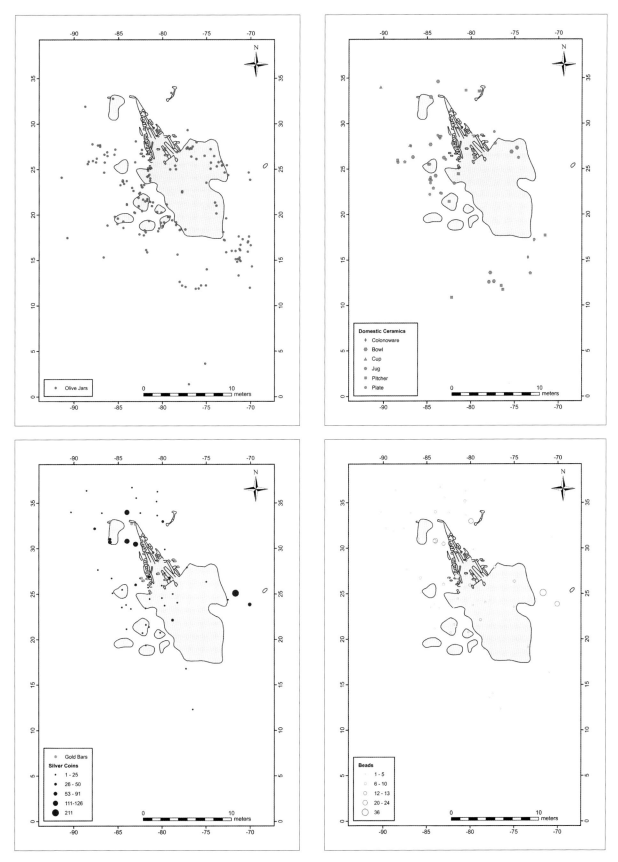

Figs. 15-18. Distribution plans of botijas *(olive jars); kitchen and tablewares; gold bars and silver coins; and beads on the Tortugas shipwreck (top left to bottom right).*

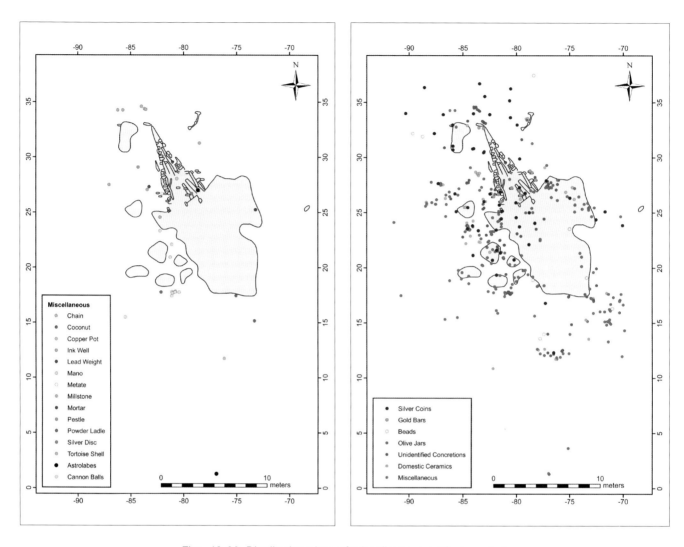

*Figs. 19-20. Distribution plans of miscellaneous artifacts and all
artifact groups combined on the Tortugas shipwreck (left to right).*

Gulf landings of shrimp led the nation in 2008 with 188.8 million pounds at $367 million dockside value, accounting for about 73% of the US total. The Gulf also led the production of oysters in 2008 with 20.6 million pounds of meat valued at $60.2 million and representing 59% of the national total.[3]

In 1997-98 the Tortugas fishery caught 873,620lbs lobster, 665,500lb shrimp, 522,402lb reef fish and 88,695lb king mackerel.[4] The three species of penaeid shrimp (white, pink and brown) comprise more than 99% of landings in the Gulf of Mexico shrimp fishery. Nearly 85% of the pink shrimp harvested in the United States comes from the west coast of Florida, with a commercial value in 2010 of over $17.5 million. Since 2002 catches have declined sharply due to economic conditions in the fishery and hurricane damage, particularly in 2005 when landings dropped from

150 million pounds to approximately 92 million pounds. A total of about 8.4 million pounds of pink shrimp were landed in US fisheries in 2008, mostly off western Florida.[5] Peak concentrations of shrimp are usually found at depths of 250-475m (Stiles *et al.*, 2007: 6), which coincides with the Tortugas wreck's location. As an artificial reef, the wreck site is densely inhabited primarily by crabs and catsharks, but also with lesser amounts of lobster, squirrelfish, shrimp and squid (Figs. 23-28).

The site formation displays conspicuous impacts caused by bottom fishing, primarily in the form of the displacement of artifacts off the main ballast mound onto the lower lying surrounding levels (see Section 4 below). Despite the relative coherent nature of the shipwreck, the original stowage points of the cargo and domestic assemblage are not preserved.

Fig. 21. Ballast stones from the Tortugas shipwreck (top left to bottom right): chert nodule (TOR-90-00342-BL), granite (TOR-90-00341-BL & TOR-90-01098-BL), basalt (TOR-90-00339-BL), the site dominant sandstone ballast (TOR-90-01103A-BL & TOR-90-01103B-BL), quartz sandstone (TOR-90-00340-BL & TOR-90-01104-BL) & oolitic limestone (TOR-90-01100-BL).

Fig. 22. Excavation of the site in horizontal stratigraphic strips.

Fig. 23. A slipper or shovel-nose lobster (Scyllarus americanus).

Fig. 24. Rock crabs (Cancer irroratus) were particularly common on the wreck.

Fig. 25. Catshark (Scyliorhinus), common across the site, and present above the ballast mound and broken olive jars.

Fig. 26. Squirrelfish (Holocentrus) on the wreck site.

Fig. 27. A white-striped cleaner shrimp or a peppermint shrimp (Lysmata).

Fig. 28. *Either long-finned squid* (Loligo pealei), *brief squid* (Lolliguncula brevis) *or arrow squid* (Loligo plei).

Fig. 29. *A typical deposit of intact and broken olive jars on the outer edge of the ballast mound.*

Fig. 30. *An olive jar being prepared for recovery using the ROV's limpet suction device.*

Fig. 31. *Olive jars and a Seville White ware dish in situ on the wreck edge.*

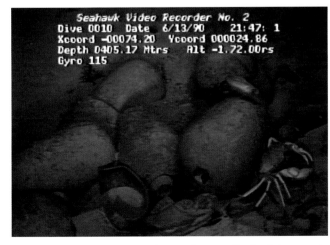

Fig. 32. *Intact olive jars in situ on the east flank of the wreck.*

Fig. 33. *A Type 3 olive jar in situ surrounded by catsharks.*

Fig. 34. Ceramics were located both on the surface
and immediately beneath sediments in a stratum
typically 30cm deep (and 50cm maximum).

Fig. 35. Broken olive jars immediately
beneath surface sediments.

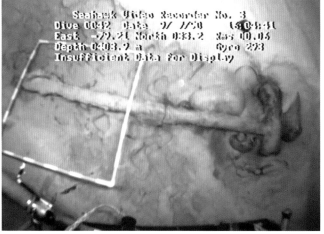

Fig. 36 (above left). Extensive ceramics snagged
around anchor A1 at the southeast flank.

Fig. 37 (above right). Anchor A3 at the northeast flank,
seemingly dragged out of context by shrimp trawlers.

Fig. 38 (left). A bronze cauldron in situ alongside a
cluster of olive jars, a juglet and Columbia Plain dish.

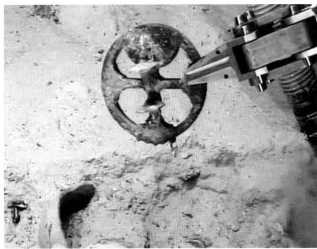

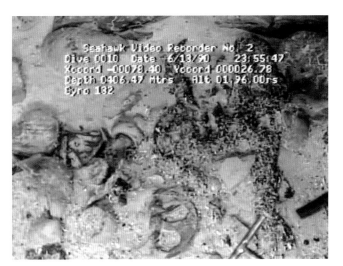
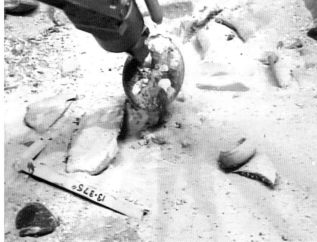

Figs. 39-42. Two bronze astrolabes in situ *and being recovered.*

Fig. 43. A gold bar in situ *in the stern.*
Note the marine-bored ballast alongside.

Fig. 44. Two gold bars in situ *in the stern.*

Fig. 45. A basalt metate grinding stone in situ in the stern.

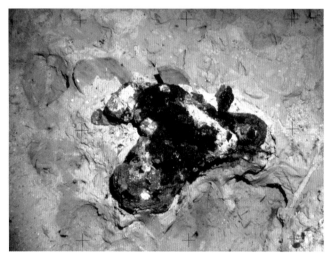

Fig. 46. A cluster of encrusted iron cannonballs in the southeast starboard bow quadrant.

4. The Site

The Tortugas shipwreck lies at a depth of 394.5-406.4m on a northwest to southeast orientation, the keel line extending along a 150° axis (Fig. 11). When discovered the site was dominated by a low-lying mound of amorphous ballast stones, whose main nucleus extended across an area measuring 10.0 x 4.8m (Figs. 10, 25, 33). The total wreckage covers 19.2m long and 15.6m wide. Despite the historical description of four iron cannon required for the *Buen Jesús y Nuestra Señora del Rosario* (Kingsley, 2013), no such ordnance was present on the site.

The exposure of the heavily deteriorated rudder (coordinates 83.5/33.0) signifies the presence of the stern to the northwest (Figs. 67-71).[6] The presence of one concreted iron anchor, A1, to the southwest (mid-shank coordinates 72.7/15.9) reveals the location of the bows (Fig. 36), with

the anchor seemingly originally lashed to the ship's port flank at the time of sinking. The shank from a second anchor, A2, underlies it. A third anchor at the north end of the site (A3, mid-shank coordinates 78.7/33.2), seems to be out of context and may have been displaced by bottom trawler activities (Fig. 37). A fourth large anchor was salvaged in 1972 prior to the present project (Marx, 2009: 57) and its present location is unknown.

5. Artifact Distributions

Although the wreck is technically coherent because the hull is articulated and largely concealed by an overlying veneer of ballast, the cargo and domestic wares have been subjected to post-depositional scrambling. Based on a count of the distribution of all finds, just 25.2% overlay the main ballast and hull nucleus, while 74.8% were scattered closely around its perimeter. Subdividing the site into quadrants, as a whole the finds were equally distributed (50.4% in the northern aft half, 49.6% in the southern forward half). However, just 34.9% occupied the portside eastern half of the site and 65.1% the western starboard half (Fig. 20). This would seem to indicate that the ship settled listing to starboard. The furthest displaced artifacts are an olive jar deposited 16.2m due south of the southern edge of the main ballast nucleus (coordinates 76.9/1.4) and an astrolabe dispersed 16.4m south of the southernmost ballast edge (coordinates 76.9/1.3).

The *botijas* (olive jars) were the most conspicuous artifact features on the site and extended across an area 32.8m north/south and 21.5m east/west (Figs. 14, 29-35). Just 26.4% of the total olive jars overlay the main ballast and hull area and 73.6% lay outside their perimeter (Fig. 15). Of the latter, the majority (74.2%) were clustered along the starboard western edge of the wreck. The northwestern site quadrant contained 45.8% of the total olive jars deposited beyond the main ballast and hull area; 28.3% overlay the southwestern site quadrant; 24.2% the southeastern quadrant; and just 1.7% the northeastern quadrant.

The densest clusters of olive jars were recorded within the northeast ballast mound, just outside the southeast edge of the ballast and, more extensively and continuously, on a northwest to southeast axis along the northeastern starboard flank. The above statistics do not reflect balanced cargo stowage. Assuming that the foodstuffs packaged in these ceramic vessels were originally stowed evenly in the hold above the ballast, this class of container has been extensively displaced. The suggested ship's list to starboard may partly explain this pattern, but does not satisfactorily rationalize the low quantity overlying the central ballast mound. The scattering effect is best interpreted as a result of bottom trawling, which has decentralized and swept the olive jars off the pronounced ballast mound. Once rolled to slightly lower depths, the vessels became inundated with sediments in an environment more conducive to long-term preservation.

The distribution of domestic pottery (kitchen and table-wares) displayed a comparable multivariate distribution pattern that supports the above hypotheses (Fig 16). Just 21.2% of the total ceramic wares used by the crew and passengers overlay the central ballast and hull mound. Outside this zone, once again the greatest presence lay within the northwest quadrant (61.2%), followed by 16.4% in each of the northeastern and southwestern quadrants and 5.5% to the southeast. A significant 77.6% of the total remains were clustered in the northern half of the wreck, which corresponds to the original location of the galley structure.

The gold bars, silver coins and even the beads exhibited highly comparable cluster patterns, which mirror the domestic pottery deposition but with a greater depositional focus on the stern (Fig. 43-44). The gold bars were exclusively concentrated in a 7.3m-long and 4.5m-wide section between the sternpost and aft area corresponding to the presumed galley/cabins position, where 61.6% overlay the hull remains (Fig. 17). This pattern is the only anomaly on the Tortugas wreck, where the majority of finds were otherwise outliers beyond the main ballast and hull nucleus. Their general original positions seem to have been retained due to the relatively small size and density of the gold bars.

The silver coins again displayed a significant concentration in the stern area, but otherwise with a perplexing, unbalanced pattern (Fig. 17). Just 9.3% of the silver coins overlay the main ballast mound. The majority, accounting for 61.7%, was recorded in the northwest quadrant. While none overlay the ballast zone to the southeast, beyond its perimeter 28.1% of the total coins were distributed within this quadrant. Just 6.4% was present to the northeast and 3.8% in the southwest quadrant. Two particularly dense clusters were documented: a concentration of 278 coins in the southeast (coordinates 71.7/25.1) and 607 coins in seven clusters in the northwest quadrant across an area of 3.9 x 3.8m (coordinates 84.0-87.7/30.8-33.9). The dense representation in the northwest quadrant again seems to reflect the dual pattern of the ship listing and depositing much of its contents to starboard and the apparent stowage of the silver coins in proximity to the galley cabin.

As would be expected for lighter material more easily dispersed by currents and trawlers, the beads recorded on the Tortugas shipwreck are more evenly distributed across the site (Fig. 18). A minority of 22.5% overlay the ballast mound. The majority, accounting for 45.4% of the total, were once again present in the northwest quadrant, 29.9%

Fig. 47. A section of strakes, frames and ceiling planking exposed towards the starboard stern.

Fig. 48. A section of strakes and frames along the portside stern.

Fig. 49. A section of strakes and frames in the stern.

Fig. 50. Detail of strakes and frames along the portside stern (coordinates 80.12/25.09).

Figs. 51-52. Excavation of strakes, frames and ceiling planks in the stern.

lay to the southeast, 17.6% to the northeast and 7.0% in the southwest quadrant. Thus, the material was almost equally split between starboard and portside (52.4% west of the keel line).

In conclusion, the archaeological data favors the interpretation that the Tortugas *navio* struck the seabed stern first, snapping the rudder, which broke away to starboard. The vessel then settled to starboard. As the upper hull structure deteriorated, the bulk of the ship's cargo and domestic wares stored in the galley correspondingly spilled most extensively westward. The concentrations of the gold bars, silver coins and domestic ceramic wares reflect the general position of the otherwise decomposed galley structure. As the heaviest single artifact on the wreck, the position of a basalt grinding stone *metate* at coordinates 82.0/26.7, plus its *mano* pestle at coordinates 80.6/28.0 (Figs. 19, 45), offers the best general indicators of the galley's original position. A major anomaly on the Tortugas wreck was the identification of a single galley brick; the absence of extensive brick material required to insulate the hearth remains unexplained.

Objects typically identifiable with the galley cabin, including an inkwell (coordinates 87.0/27.5), bronze mortar (coordinates 83.2/27.3) and one of the astrolabes (coordinates 78.6/27.0), also clustered closely around the stern area (Fig. 19). However, several diagnostic elements of the domestic assemblage and valuables have scattered southwards: a gold chain was recorded at the central northern edge of the ballast mound (coordinates 83.79/24.5), while a copper cooking cauldron was identified 6m south of the southern tip of the ballast mound (coordinates 76.19/11.74) and a second astrolabe was even further dispersed 16.4m south of the southern site edge (coordinates 76.9/1.3).

The wreck's 64 pieces of tortoise shell display a divergent configuration, whereby all examples lay offsite northwest of the sternpost with just one example to its southeast (coordinate 83.6-86.2/34.3-34.6 and 78.5/31.3; Fig. 19). The only obvious artifact pattern seemingly reflecting storage in the forward bow half of the hold is a concentration of concreted iron cannonballs recorded along the western edge of the southwest quadrant (coordinates 80.4-85.5/15.5-23.3).

6. The Hull & Ballast

A small area of the Tortugas ship's hull was examined, focused on the stern third of the vessel at the northern end of the site discovered partly exposed above sediments (Fig. 11). The stem was also uncovered with the objective of determining the ship's length, and the ends of the abraded starboard frames exposed. Whereas the wreck was typically excavated to a depth of 50-75cm, the sediments around the stem and sternpost were trenched to depths

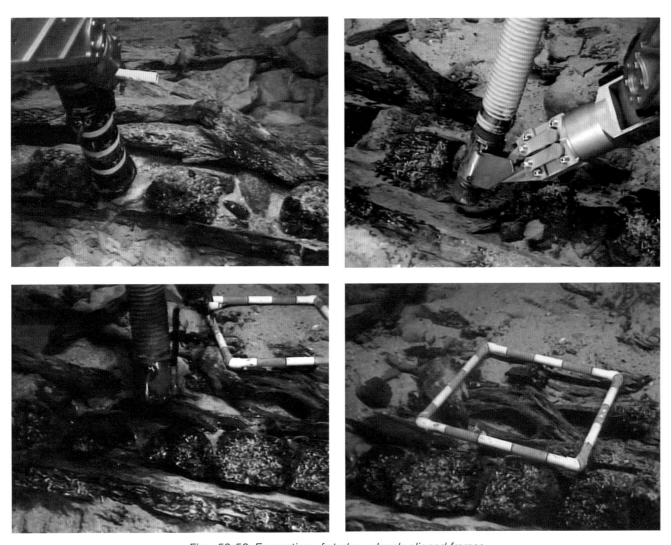

*Figs. 53-56. Excavation of strakes, closely aligned frames
(some with curved sides), ceiling planks and a floor timber in the stern.*

of 0.75-1.0m. The upper level of the pump well retaining shaft was also cleared. In total, less than an estimated one-quarter of the total hull was examined beneath its overlying veneer of ballast. These stones were tightly clustered and it is highly unlikely that any material culture other than the smallest of artifacts and sherds had been vertically displaced through this sealing layer.

The majority of the ballast mound is positioned towards the southeast two-thirds of the visible site, reflecting the requisite structural tapering of the lower hull towards the stern. The weight of the sterncastle/quarterdeck structure would have readily compensated for the lack of ballast in this part of the ship (Moore, 1991). The bows are positioned to the south. The ballast continues all the way up to the stempost.

Samples of the Tortugas ship's ballast stones were examined visually by Dr. Stephen Pollock of the Department of Geosciences, University of Southern Maine, USA,

followed by x-ray diffractometer analysis of six samples. The following rock forms were identified (Fig. 21), of which sandstone (TOR-90-01103-BL) was the prevalent form within the hull:

1. Chert Nodule (TOR-90-00342-BL). Laminated and probably derived from a limestone as a chert nodule, but the surface suggests it was a cobble. In addition to the laminate it has a granular quartz core with a small vug at the center with drusy quartz crystals. There are at least two fossil remnants, which are suggestive of corals.
2. Granite (two samples). TOR-90-00341-BL is a relatively unweathered, fine-grained biotite muscovite granite, and TOR-90-01098-BL is a deeply weathered, fine-grained muscovite granite. The feldspars are the most deeply weathered and much of the small sample appears to be just quartz and muscovite, but there is a small area that illustrates an equigranular granitic texture.

Figs. 57-58. Marine borers, calcareous tubes and related hull decomposition.

3. Basalt (two samples). Two samples, relatively fresh and unweathered. TOR-90-00338-BL is a typical dark gray to gray black very fine-grained microcrystalline basalt that x-ray diffractometer analysis indicates contains a calcium rich plagioclase feldspar, either labradorite or a sodian anorthite, and the pyroxene augite. TOR-90-00339-BL is a gray-black to black very coarse-grained basalt. The sample appears to be somewhat glassy, mostly due to the luster of the rectangular-shaped, calcium-rich plagioclase feldspar grains. The black 'glassy' grains are probably pyroxene. Minor olivine may be present.

4. Sandstone (TOR-90-01103A-BL and TOR-90-01103B-BL). Well-sorted, fine-grained arenites (a sandstone with less than 15% mud matrix). The small black grains are probably rock fragments. Both are texturally similar and seemingly originally derived from the same geologic formation. Marine boring organisms likely produced the borings in TOR-90-01103A-BL. Remnant shell material appears to be present in at least one

cavity. Sample TOR-90-01103B-BL is thinly bedded with either orange shale/mud laminations or shale/mud chips. No fossils were observed. X-ray diffractometer analysis indicates that the sandstone is composed of quartz and magnesium rich calcite. TOR-90-01103B-BL exhibits an isoclinal fold, which appears to be real based on the textural contrast of the laminations and is not a liesegang ring (secondary nested rings caused by rhythmic precipitation in a fluid saturated rock).

5. Quartz Sandstone (two samples). TOR-90-00340-BL appears to be a uniformly textured, fine-grained quartz arenite or quartzite. Rounded grain surfaces are not readily apparent; rather the grains appear as interlocking grains. The former would be typical of an unmetamorphosed quartz sandstone, and the latter a metamorphosed quartz sandstone. The grains are not uniformly elongated, which is more common in quartzites. TOR-90-01104-BL is an elliptical iron stained cobble, its grain size very fine and similar to the weathered surface of TOR-90-00340-BL.

6. Oolitic Limestone (TOR-90-01100-BL). A relatively extensively weathered, fine-grained oolitic limestone. Small spherical to oval oolitic grains are common. Small shell fragments or peloidal grains may also be present. A pellet or peloidal grain is an indurated fecal pellet. X-ray diffractometer analysis reveals magnesium rich calcite. This rock may be local: there are modern oolites on carbonate banks and platforms in the Caribbean.

The scientific analysis has not led to a positive identification of the ballast's provenance. In light of the high-volume transport of heavy iron goods and wine stored in *botijas* to Cumana in Venezuela by the *Buen Jesús y Nuestra Señora del Rosario*, and a postulated return cargo of low density tobacco (cf. Kingsley, 2013), it may be hypothesized that additional ballast would have been required in Venezuela.

In addition to continuous, articulated strakes, frames and ceiling planking (Figs. 47-56), major structural elements preserved *in situ* include a wood-lined pump well retaining shaft (Figs. 76-84), several deck stanchion steppes (one *in situ* at coordinates 80.97/27.73, 4.6m forward of the sternpost where the hull starts to widen away from the sternpost, and another with a tapered end located loose on the surface on the portside bow 3.2m northeast of the stempost at coordinates 75.23/20.38; Figs. 100-102), what appears to be the stump of the main mast still stepped into the keelson just forward of the pump well, and the top of the stempost (with a scarf and associated forward plank hoods butting into the vertical rabbet; Figs. 72-75). The heavily degraded rudder has snapped off to the starboard side of the sternpost, where it lies in association with at

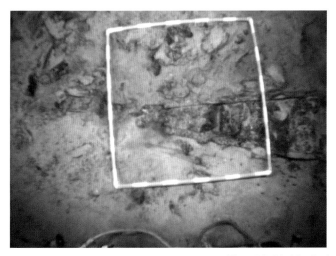
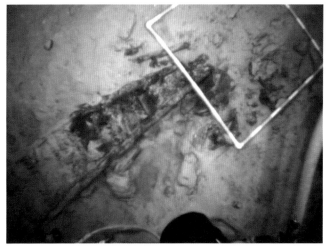

Figs. 59-60. Vertical view of the sternpost.

Figs. 61-64. Detail of the sternpost and tail frames before and during excavation.

Figs. 65-66. Three hooding ends rabetted into the sternpost. Note the dense marine bore tube cover on the upper surface.

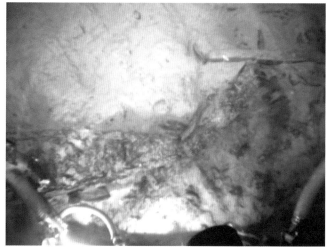

Fig. 67. Vertical view of the sternpost with the rudder broken off to starboard and a long timber possibly identifiable as a spar or part of the ship's tiller.

least one iron gudgeon (Figs. 67-71). Immediately to its east lies a long timber with chamfered edges, potentially either a spar or part of the tiller assembly (Figs. 68-69). One floor and a futtock lie loose on the wreck's surface (Fig. 103).

The area of most intensive focus due to the naturally exposed character of its upper surfaces was the stern (Figs. 59-66). As across several areas of the site, prior to excavation this zone was covered with large amounts of marine-bored and degraded fragments of articulated wooden structural components and highly decayed loose pieces of small planking. The marine borers were so effective on the Tortugas wreck that possibly xylophagous rather than lithophagous organisms also extensively attacked and gribbled much of the soft ballast stones.

The sternpost was located interconnected to the hull. The stern terminates at a 10.8cm sided post, which widens forward to 28.1cm. A second tail frame measured 18.7 x 12.5cm. Three hooding ends, the upper line 5.4cm thick, are visible rabeted into the sternpost (Figs. 59-66). At the opposite end of the hull the upper strake flanking

the portside stempost, which was exposed for a length of approximately 1.2m, is 6.9cm thick (Figs. 72-75).[7] After the Sonardyne navigation and recording system was calibrated for an accuracy of +/- 10cm, the distance from the *in situ* sternpost to where the keel started to rise to form the lower stempost in the bows was measured at 17.4m (Fig. 12). This dimension provides the maximum total length of the Tortugas ship's keel. Drawing a center-line between each post provides a preserved midship width at the lower turn-of-the-bilge (maximum wreck preservation elevation) of 4.6m.

At a distance of 7.8m forward of the sternpost the uppermost perimeter of the bilge pump well's wooden framed retaining shaft *arca* (103.7 x 76.3cm) was exposed, which proved to be built of 14.5cm wide and 2.5cm thick planks installed on their sides (Figs. 76-80). Two overlying retaining planks were exposed in one trench section (Figs. 83-84). The retaining shaft is centrally placed in the hull overlying the keelson (Fig. 11), which measures close to 28cm wide at this point and displays what resembles a mortise for the mast step just aft of the pump. Beneath a light cover of small ballast stones and olive jar sherds a second layer comprising small lengths of planking, presumably decayed shaft shuttering, was encountered within the well (Figs. 81-82). The underlying sump was not exposed. To portside of the pump and keelson are two ceiling planks: the first (CP1) is 27cm wide and secured 25cm east of the keelson; the second (CP2) lies 25cm east of CP1 and is again 27cm wide (Figs. 87-89).

Wood-framed retaining shafts prevented pump sumps from becoming clogged by ballast stones and bilge debris and were typically constructed over one or two sumps leading into the bilge on either side of the mast step

(Waddell, 1985: 256). In light of Philip II's edict of 1552 that required new ships to have two pumps to improve safety at sea, the Tortugas ship would have been expected to have been built with a similar dual pump arrangement on either side of the mast step akin to the Emanuel Point I wreck (Smith *et al.*, 1995: 28-30). This seems not to have been the case.

Structurally the Tortugas pump shaft closely resembles the Basque whaler *San Juan* lost in Red Bay, Canada, in 1565 (Waddell, 1985: 253), although two-thirds of this ship's retaining shaft was constructed to the side of the mast step. Three types of pumps were relied on between the 15th century and the early modern era: the burr pump system, which was based on a foot valve and spear from at least *c.* 1556 to the end of the 16th century; the common suction pump utilized from at least 1433 into the 19th century; and the chain pump. Of these, the Tortugas structure may have operated using the latter type of mechanism. Chain pumps rotated manually using a wheel, usually by foot, were first referred to by Sir Walter Raleigh as an improvement introduced into the English navy in the second half of the 16th century when pumps incorporated blocks of wood as valves to which rags were attached. This technology was commonly described in ship's treatises of the late 16th and 17th centuries as a chain full of burrs (wooden valves or disks) that rotated around a wheel and was considered the best type of pump because they discharged the most water (Oertling, 1984: 29, 32, 43-4, 73, 75-7, 81-2).

The possibility that the Tortugas mechanism operated using a chain pump is based on the excavation of a wooden disk 1.6m aft of the pump well (coordinates 80.22/27.26) that may be remains of a chain and valve assembly (Fig. 85). An adjacent horseshoe-shaped section of iron also resembles a type of sprocket that could have been embedded in a wooden drive wheel from a chain pump (Fig. 86). If this identification is correct, the Tortugas shipwreck's pump device would represent a particularly early archaeologically attested example, predating the parts from the Portuguese frigate *Santo Antonio de Tanna*, which sank off Mombassa in 1697 and is associated with a chain pump relying on horseshoe-shaped sprocket and s-shaped chain links (Oertling, 1984: 81, 83, 85).

Several sections of interconnected strakes, frames and ceiling planks were excavated on the Tortugas wreck. Some 6.3m forward of the sternpost (Figs. 90-91), the outermost exposed section of the starboard hull (coordinates 81.83/26.79) featured a strake and ceiling planking, both 6.2cm thick, and closely aligned frames with sided thicknesses of 14.1-15.6cm and molded heights of 10.3-13.1cm (from north to south). In many frames the outer surface

Fig. 68. The rudder broken to starboard alongside a possible spar or part of the ship's tiller.

Fig. 69. Detail of the surface rudder structure and possible spar/ship's tiller behind.

was left naturally rounded and thus retained 90° of the external curvature of a tree trunk/branch (Fig. 90).

At a distance of 4.8m forward of the sternpost (coordinates 82.74/27.59), the outermost exposed starboard section of hull featured a strake 5.2cm thick, 6.2cm thick ceiling planking and closely aligned frames of 15.0cm sided thickness and 10.3cm molded height spaced 2.2cm apart (Figs. 92-93). About 3m due north of the sternpost (coordinates 83.77/36.42), two planks lay interconnected, but otherwise disarticulated from the hull, and would seem to represent strakes with butt joints, each about 15cm wide and both covered with an unidentified coating of organic resinous waterproofing (Figs. 94-95). A similar sealant was observed on inner strake edges along the starboard stern (coordinates 83.47/29.08). Midship, and some 6.0m forward of the sternpost, two 25cm-wide ceiling planks were exposed.

Figs. 70-71. Detail of the badly decomposed rudder, collapsed to starboard immediately north of the sternpost (right), with one iron gudgeon in situ (bottom left).

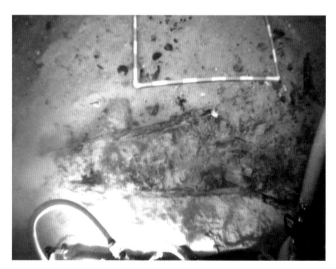

Fig. 72. Vertical view of the stempost area.

A section of the uppermost midship portside hull (coordinates 78.46/28.51) was excavated beneath ballast stones 6.0m forward of the sternpost comprising the uppermost two strakes, seven frames and one ceiling plank (Figs. 96-99). From south to north the central three frames are sided 18.8cm, 21.3cm and 18.8cm and molded 13.7cm and 13.1cm. Two tightly abut one another with less than 1cm space between (and a third frame to the east is similarly spaced). The two western frames are spaced 16.3cm and 15.0cm apart. This unequal framing pattern seems to be a misleading result of uneven preservation: the continuation of this section of hull to the east shows the end of an additional frame broken away at a lower elevation, but otherwise tightly set next to adjacent frames. The uppermost strake in this section of hull is 16.3cm wide and 6.6cm thick, while the ceiling plank is 23.6cm wide and 9.4cm thick.

7. Site Formation

In terms of overall site formation the Tortugas shipwreck is an interesting counterpoint to various wrecks of comparable date, nationality and geographical location. The closest parallels are ballast heaps within the shallow waters of Florida sealing in place substantial hull remains. Even though the Tortugas ship's artifact assemblages have been comprehensively swept to the sides of the central ballast mound, seemingly by shrimp trawler activities, the wreck's material culture is significantly better preserved than regional shallow-water sites.

The Emanuel Point I shipwreck in Pensacola Bay, the earliest shipwreck identified in Florida, represents the coherent remains of part of the fleet of Tristán de Luna, which arrived in Pensacola from Mexico in 1559. The wreck derives from a large vessel with a keel length of 23.6m estimated to have been 29.5m long with a beam of 9.5m, depth of hold of 4.5m and around 400 *toneladas* cargo capacity. The articulated hull extends across an area of 36m and includes the keel, keelson, stem, two gunport covers, as well as the well-preserved lower bow of the ship and a significant section of the collapsed starboard bow. Articulated floors and futtocks, partly covered with ceiling planking, run forward to the stem. A total of 17 athwart ship frames were noted in the lower bow, including seven floors and ten first futtocks. The collapsed starboard side contains the remains of 11 first futtocks and one second futtock. Planking continues uninterrupted on the starboard side for up to 16 strakes, while at least five strakes survive to port side.

Although the Emanuel Point I hull has been examined in far greater detail than the Tortugas site, with the stern protruding beyond the ballast, the white oak rudder collapsed immediately to starboard, and pump sumps preserved *in situ*, both formations are strikingly similar. The Pensacola Bay site exemplifies the optimum level of preservation to be anticipated by any future excavation of the largely untouched Tortugas hull. The survival of the pump well and stump of the main mast *in situ* on the Tortugas site presents additional structural features for study that do not survive at Emanuel Point.

The excellent preservation of the hull dated to 1559 in just 3-4m depth has been explained by the site's shelter from storm waves, currents and erosion within a low saline bay, rather than in the open waters of the Gulf of Mexico. The ship seems to have been transformed into an artificial reef that for generations has attracted sea life, resulting in a densely packed layer of oyster shells that shielded and effectively 'capped' the site (Smith *et al.*, 1998: 1), unlike the Tortugas wreck left exposed to the impact of shrimping fleets.

Even though extensive and varied material culture was recovered from the earlier dated site, it is notably less numerous than on the Tortugas wreck, presumably explained by salvage and higher current dynamism. Sediments in and around the Emanuel Point I hull yielded a rich variety of plant remains and animal bones, stone, lead and iron ammunition, metallic galley wares and ceramics. The pottery assemblage, for instance, consists of 2,012 *botija* sherds, red to green-glazed El Morro ware (128 sherds), maiolica (59 sherds) and glazed redwares (Smith *et al.*, 1998: 119; Mullins, 1998: 136; Williams, 1998: 140). These are numerically far more restricted than the collection of at least 209 intact olive jars and rims (plus over one thousand sherds) and 2,304 kitchen and tableware rims, handles, bases and sherds, including 1,474 tin-glazed maiolica tablewares from Tortugas.

Lying at a depth of 6m on the edge of Hawk Channel, 3.2km off Marathon in the Florida Keys, the 'Mystery Wreck' comprises a comparable compact and consolidated mound of square-shaped cut igneous ballast stones, probably granite, overlying a coral reef. Exposed sections of the hull include stern timbers, the bow assembly and midship timbers. Stern timbers comprised the eroded sternpost, three closely spaced tail-frames and remains of both port and starboard garboard strakes. Remains of the bow include the forward end of the keel and two small, curved disarticulated bow frames.

Midship timbers represent the vessel's keelson, two floors, a rider, a fragment of ceiling plank and seemingly a small section of the pump-box. The ship's keel is approximately 19m long, while the ballast extends beyond the exposed ship remains across an area of 22 x 15m. This ship was possibly an *aviso* or dispatch vessel lost during the first half of the 17th century. The hull associated with this

Figs. 73-75. The stempost area under excavation.

Fig. 76. Vertical view of the uppermost perimeter of the bilge pump well's wood-framed retaining shaft before excavation, overlying the keelson. Ceiling plank CP1 is visible immediately east of the pump box.

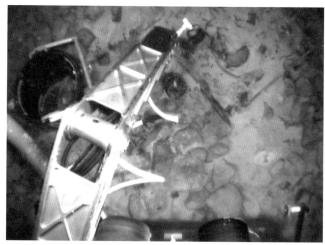

Fig. 77. Vertical view of the bilge pump well's wood-framed retaining shaft during excavation.

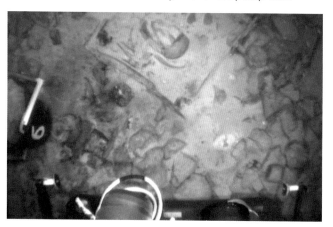

Fig. 78. Vertical view of broken olive jars embedded in the upper stratum of the bilge pump well's wood-framed retaining shaft.

Fig. 79. Side view of the bilge pump well's wood-framed retaining shaft before excavation.

Fig. 80. The bilge pump well's wood-framed retaining shaft before excavation.

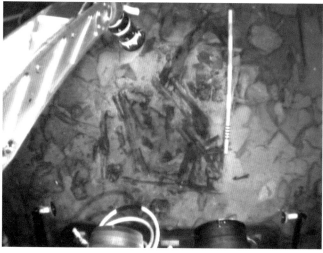

Fig. 81. Vertical view of thin plank sections, remains of shaft shuttering, in a second layer underlying the olive jar fragments within the bilge pump well's wood-framed retaining shaft.

Fig. 82. Detail of wooden shuttering beneath the olive jar fragments within the bilge pump well's retaining shaft.

Figs. 83-84 (top right and middle left). The double layer of side-edged planks used to build the bilge pump well's retaining shaft.

Fig. 85. A wooden disk aft of the pump well, possibly remains of a chain and valve pump assembly.

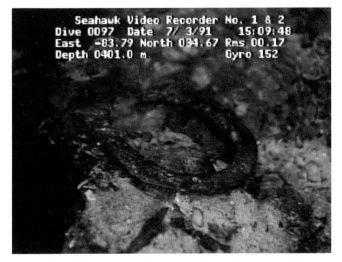

Fig. 86. A horseshoe-shaped section of iron resembling a sprocket from a wooden chain pump drive wheel.

Fig. 87. The keelson and possible mast step assembly (left) with ceiling plank CP1 to the east.

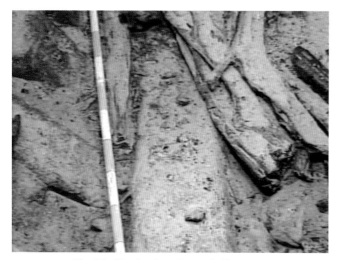

Fig. 88. The keelson towards the stern.

Fig. 89. Ceiling plank CP1 and CP2 east of the pump well.

*Figs. 90-91. Section of a starboard strake, ceiling plank and frames
6.3m forward of the sternpost (coordinates 81.83/26.79).*

ballast mound is far less intact than at the Emanuel Point I and Tortugas sites, and its ceramic assemblage contains just three olive jar necks and 90 potsherds, including four *botija* rims (McKinnon and Scott-Ireton, 2006; Smith *et al.*, 2006).

All three shipwrecks cited above reveal the importance of sealing layers for preserving underlying sand and mud inundated wooden hulls in anaerobic environments. With its notoriously thick and ever-shifting sands, the Florida Keys may be considered especially conducive to hull preservation, irrespective of date, exemplified by 324 76-85cm-long cement barrels with a minimum estimated weight of 644 tons that pinned down a 20m-long hull at Loggerhead Reef off the westernmost Dry Tortugas island. The 'Barrel Wreck' dates broadly to *c.* 1840-55 and is most probably the schooner *John Howell* burnt off the Dry Tortugas islands in 1847 (Gould and Conlin, 1999).

The 9m-long section of lower hull strakes and frames from the *Atocha*'s stern is a final example of hull remains well preserved by being sealed by a durable overload, in this case more than 30 wooden chests containing over 100,000 silver coins and 115 gold bars, 1,041 silver ingots, over 750 piece of silverware and 200 copper ingots (Mathewson, 1986: 106, 115). The combination of deep sediment cover and overlying material culture was also sufficient to preserve the ceramics to an equal level as the Tortugas collection (cf. Marken, 1994). Too little is known of the seemingly Spanish colonial site FOJE-UW-9 in shallow waters off the Fort Jefferson National Monument on the Tortugas Islands to compare preservation levels (Johnson, 1982).

While the hull of the 300-ton Spanish *San Martín* lost *c.* 1618 between Florida's Sebastian Inlet and Jupiter Inlet was well preserved in sand-inundated sediments (Moore and Muir, 1987), cargo did not survive. By contrast, the

Figs. 92-93. Starboard strakes, ceiling planks and frames 4.8m forward of the sternpost (coordinates 82.74/27.59).

Figs. 94-95. Two planks 3m east of the sternpost (coordinates 83.77/36.42) coated with a resinous layer of waterproofing.

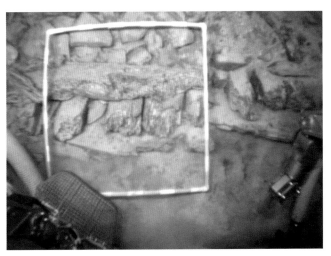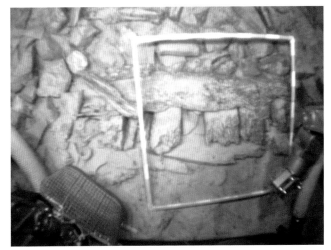

Figs. 96-97. A section of two strakes, seven frames and one ceiling plank along the portside hull, 6.0m forward of the sternpost (coordinates 78.46/28.51).

Figs. 98-99. A section of strake, frames and ceiling planking along the portside hull (coordinates 78.46/28.51).

rocky seabed where the Spanish galleon *Nuestra Señora de la Concepción* sunk off Hispaniola in 1641 may not have facilitated the preservation of the hull, but significant non-contextual artifacts have been recovered (Borrell, 1983).

The study of the 367m-deep mid-19th century Jacksonville 'Blue China' shipwreck off Florida, where over three-quarters of the cargo had been destroyed, demonstrates the susceptibility of cargos such as on the Tortugas site to off-shore shrimp trawler impacts (Gerth *et al.*, 2011: 198-202).

8. Conclusion

The 'Tortugas Deep-sea A' shipwreck was the world's first archaeological excavation conducted solely using robotic technology. A Remotely-Operated Vehicle was custom-tooled with equipment suitable for sensitive archaeological excavation, recording and recovery methodologies. The combined package enabled 16,903 artifacts of widely varying medium to be examined comprehensively at a depth of 405m. The safe recovery of human teeth, 565 seeds and tiny pearls and beads testifies to the system's success.

The site's formation was characterized by a central ballast mound contextualized with extensive material culture, although the majority of artifacts were not technically *in situ*. Some 75% of the finds were deposited outside the ballast mound's perimeter, with a strong emphasis to the west suggestive of the hull's collapse to starboard. The relocation of anchor A3 off the portside sternpost and an astrolabe plotted 16.4m south of the ballast edge further reflects significant post-depositional site interference. Since the Tortugas shipwreck first came to consciousness after artifacts were snagged in a trawler's nets, and because the region has been renowned as a focus of southern North America's shrimp fisheries since 1949, the site's integrity has undoubtedly witnessed multiple impacts.

Despite this anthropogenic disturbance the Tortugas wreck remained a continuous and coherent cultural entity with intact ceramic wares and considerable elements of its domestic assemblage preserved from olive jars to leather shoe fragments. The heavily gribbled planking condition is best explained not by marine boring activity, which even tunneled into the sandstone ballast, but by the stiff mud's less ideal wreck preservation capacity than sand-inundated environments.

The limited human remains suggest that the ship's company largely took its chances in the open sea at the time of sinking. The absence of the four iron cannon on the wreck's surface – historically documented for the *Buen Jesús y Nuestra Señora del Rosario* (Contratación 1172, N.2, R.1) – reflects the possibility that some shipboard objects may have been jettisoned. The ship's anchors on the seabed, however, are anomalous in this regard. The presence of a single hearth brick from the galley structure, and the lack of rigging, are additional notable anomalies.

The wreck's 17.4m keel length corresponds to the dimensions of a Spanish ship with a 30 *codos*-long keel and thus an overall breadth of 10 *codos* and a total length of around 36 *codos* (20.7m) and 106 tons (conversions based on Spanish *Ordenanzas* regulations for shipbuilding of 1618: Rodríguez Mendoza, 2008: 179, table 11; Fernández-González, 2009: 12). These dimensions, considered alongside the wreck's Venezuelan pearl cargo, ship magnitudes and outward-bound destinations of the historically attested 1622 Tierra Firme fleet, indicate that the most plausible identification for the wreck is the 117-ton *Buen Jesús y Nuestra Señora del Rosario. Contratación* 1172, N.2, R.1 specifies that this merchant vessel was built in Portugal, but it is believed to have been Spanish operated by its owner, Juan de la Torre (cf. Kingsley, 2013).

The presence seemingly of just one pump centrally overlying the keelson reinforces the non-Spanish characterization of the Tortugas ship. Following the 1608 *Ordenanzas*

Figs. 100-101. A stepped stanchion along the portside bow (coordinates 75.23/20.38).

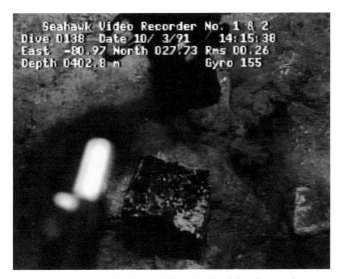

Fig. 102. A deck stanchion in situ 4.6m forward of the sternpost (coordinates 80.97/27.73).

Fig. 103. A futtock under excavation.

regulations, Spanish ships involved in the Indies trade were legally bound to be constructed with two pumps, one functional and one spare. Accordingly, "The judge of la Casa will force every owner or master of Nao of the Armada or Fleet to take two pumps, one as a spare; if this rule is not followed, the ship cannot be dispatched" (*Ordenanzas* 1608, Libro IX, Título XXVIII, Ley 11). The presence of a single rather than dual pump system overlying the keel would not have been permissible for Spanish merchant vessels, but seemingly would have been acceptable for a Portuguese vessel built and included in the *flota* system when Portugal was annexed into the Spanish empire between 1581 and 1640.

The identification of both endposts, the rudder, bilge pump well and stanchions indicate that important structural features await future fieldwork. The survival of extensive artifact assemblages, unparalleled in volume on other early 17th-century Spanish sites, however, remains the most significant characteristic of the Tortugas shipwreck.

Notes

1. The significant volume of gold bars, silver coins and pearls discovered on the Tortugas shipwreck, coupled with Seahawk's status as a publicly-traded company, inevitably led to an abrupt rise in stock value and trading activity. In turn, in 1991 this attracted the attention of the US Securities and Exchange Commission (SEC). The Tortugas wreck was investigated based on false rumors that the site was a fabrication (the underwater photographs were considered too well lit to have been taken at a depth of 400m) and that the gold bars were modern forgeries. The federal trial began in October 1997 and in November the jury voted in favor of a complete vindication of Seahawk's directors.

In the meantime the company's directors had chosen to resign to safeguard its interests. The new directors went on to sell the entire collection and archive. In January 2004 both returned to the market place at an auction held in Beverly Hills, where Greg Stemm bought back all the surviving materials – including the artifacts and precious underwater video archive, the basis of the current scientific Tortugas publications – for Odyssey Marine Exploration. Some 8,501 Tortugas artifacts today remain in Odyssey's permanent collection in Tampa, Florida, where they are kept for ongoing research (cf. Vesilind, P.J., *Lost Gold of the Republic*, Shipwreck Heritage Press, Tampa, 2005: 87, 90, 93, 96, 221-22). The dispersal and transfer of archival material to different parties has in some cases complicated assembly of aspects of the Tortugas reports.

2. This site has been classified as the 'Tortugas Deep-sea A' on the possibility that additional shipwrecks will be discovered in adjoining deep waters in the future.

3. See: http://www.epa.gov/gmpo/about/facts.html.

4. Shivlani, M., *Development of the Dry Tortugas Ecological Reserve: Characterization of the Commercial Fishery* (no date).

5. See: http://www.fishwatch.gov/seafood_profiles/species/shrimp/species_ pages/pink_shrimp.htm.

6. The coordinates cited in this report are localized on-site measurements based on the creation of an electronic recording grid, illustrated graphically on all distribution maps in this report.

7. The hull dimensions provided in this report are not derived from direct ROV measurements, which were not undertaken in 1990-91. Instead, they are based on imprecise measurements taken by comparing features to surveying scale rods set immediately next to planking. Analysis of the Tortugas hull, based on black and white vertical photomosaic imagery, is ongoing.

Bibliography

Astley, J. and Stemm, G., *The Deep-Sea Tortugas Shipwreck, Florida: Technology* (OME Papers 25, 2013).

Borrell, P.J., *Historia y Rescate del Galeon Nuestra Señora de la Concepcion* (Museo de las Casas Reales, Santo Domingo, 1983).

Fernández-González, F., *The Spanish Regulations for Shipbuilding (Ordenanzas) of the Seventeenth Century* (Naval History Symposium, US Naval Academy, Annapolis, MD, 10-11 September, 2009).

Gerth, E., Cunningham Dobson, N. and Kingsley, S., 'The Jacksonville 'Blue China' Shipwreck (Site BA02): A Mid-19th Century American Coastal Schooner off Florida'. In G. Stemm and S. Kingsley (eds.), *Ocean Odyssey 2. Underwater Heritage Management & Deep-Sea Shipwrecks in the English Channel & Atlantic Ocean* (Oxford, 2011), 143-220.

Gould, R.A. and Conlin, D.L., 'Archaeology of the Barrel Wreck, Loggerhead Reef, Dry Tortugas National Park, Florida,' *International Journal of Nautical Archaeology* 28.3 (1999), 201-28.

Ingalls, A.E., Aller, R.C., Lee, C. and Wakeham, S.G., 'Organic Matter Diagenesis in Shallow Water Carbonate Sediments', *Geochimica et Cosmochimica Acta* 68.21 (2004), 4363-79.

Johnson, R.E., *Underwater Archaeological Investigations at FOJE-UW-9 Conducted in Summer, 1982 at Fort Jefferson National Monument, Dry Tortugas, Florida* (Southeast Archeological Center, National Park Service, Tallahassee, Florida, 1982).

Kingsley, S., *The Identity and Maritime History of the Deep-Sea Tortugas Shipwreck* (OME Papers 26, 2013).

Marken, M.W., *Pottery from Spanish Shipwrecks 1500-1800* (University Press of Florida, 1994).

Marx, R., 'Deep Sea Treasure Hunting', *Wreck Diving Magazine* 18 (2009), 54-61.

Mathewson, D., *Treasure of the Atocha* (Houston, 1986).

McKinnon, J.F. and Scott-Ireton, D.A., 'Florida's Mystery Wreck', *International Journal of Nautical Archaeology* 35.2 (2006), 187-94.

Moore, D. and Muir, B., 'The Archaeology of *San Martin*', *Seafarers Journal of Maritime Heritage* 1 (1987), 188-94.

Moore, D., *Preliminary Site Analysis. Tortugas Site, 12 July 1990* (Seahawk, 1991, unpublished).

Mullins, D., 'More than Just El Morro'. In R.C. Smith, J.R. Bratten, J. Cozzi and K. Plaskett, *The Emanuel Point Ship Archaeological Investigations 1997-1998* (Report of Investigations No. 68 Archaeology Institute University of West Florida, 1998), 135-39.

Oertling, T.J., *The History and Development of Ships' Bilge Pumps, 1500-1840* (MA Thesis, Texas A&M University, 1984).

Rodríguez Mendoza, B.M., *Standardization of Spanish Shipbuilding: Ordenanzas para la Fábrica de Navíos de Guerra y Mercante – 1607, 1613, 1618* (MA Thesis, Texas A&M University, 2008).

Rudloe, J. and Rudloe, A., *Shrimp. The Endless Quest for Pink Gold* (Upper Saddle River, New Jersey, 2010).

Smith, R.C., Bratten, J.R., Cozzi, J. and Plaskett, K., *The Emanuel Point Ship Archaeological Investigations 1997-1998* (Report of Investigations No. 68 Archaeology Institute University of West Florida, 1998).

Smith, R.C., Scott-Ireton, D., McKinnon, J., Beckwith, S., Altmeier, B. and MacLaughlin, L., *Archaeological and*

Biological Examination of "The Mystery Wreck" (8MO143) off Vaca Key, Monroe County, Florida (Report Submitted to the Florida Keys National Marine Sanctuary in Fulfillment of a NOAA Maritime Heritage Program Minigrant, 2006).

Smith, R.C., Spirek, J., Bratten, J. and Scott-Ireton, D., *The Emanuel Point Ship: Archaeological Investigations, 1992-1995, Preliminary Report* (Bureau of Archaeological Research, Division of Historical Resources, Florida Department of State, 1995).

Stiles, M.L., Harrould-Kolieb, E., Faure, P., Ylitalo-Ward, H. and Hirshfield, M.F., *Deep Sea Trawl Fisheries of the Southeast US and Gulf of Mexico: Rock Shrimp, Royal Red shrimp, Calico Scallops* (OCEANA, 2007).

Van Dresser, E., 'Pink Gold Strike in the Gulf', *Popular Mechanics* (July 1950), 124-26, 130.

Waddell, P.J.A., 'The Pump and Pump Well of a 16th Century Galleon', *International Journal of Nautical Archaeology* 14.3 (1985), 243-59.

Walter, D.J., Lambert, D.N. and Young, D.C., 'Sediment Facies Determination Using Acoustic Techniques in a Shallow-water Carbonate Environment, Dry Tortugas, Florida', *Marine Geology* 182.1-2 (2002), 161-77.

Williams, C., 'Analysis of Tin-glazed Ceramics from the Emanuel Point Ship Second Campaign'. In R.C. Smith, J.R. Bratten, J. Cozzi and K. Plaskett, *The Emanuel Point Ship Archaeological Investigations 1997-1998* (Report of Investigations No. 68 Archaeology Institute University of West Florida, 1998), 140-45.

3

The Deep-Sea Tortugas Shipwreck, Florida:
A Spanish-Operated *Navio* of the 1622
Tierra Firme Fleet. Part 2, the Artifacts

Greg Stemm, Ellen Gerth
Odyssey Marine Exploration, Tampa, Florida, USA

Jenette Flow
Pasco-Hernando Community College, New Port Richey, Florida, USA

Claudio Lozano Guerra-Librero
Stratigraphy Area, Faculty of Experimental Sciences, University of Huelva, Spain

Sean Kingsley
Wreck Watch Int., London, UK

The 405m-deep Tortugas shipwreck excavated in 1990 and 1991 off the Florida Keys by Seahawk Deep Ocean Technology of Tampa, Florida, contained an extensive collection of 16,903 artifacts. These were recorded and recovered solely using the Remotely-Operated Vehicle Merlin. The Tortugas project was the world's first scientific deep-sea shipwreck excavation. The most plausible identification for this ship is the Portuguese-built and Spanish-operated 117-ton *Buen Jesús y Nuestra Señora del Rosario* that sailed with the Tierra Firme fleet for Nueva Cordoba (Cumana) on the Pearl Coast in modern Venezuela before attempting to return to Spain in September 1622.

This report presents the wreck's cargo, domestic assemblage and navigational equipment. The inter-relationship between valuable commodities (gold bars, silver coins, pearls), low-value goods (trade beads) and the domestic assemblage (extensive ceramic tablewares, olive jars, tortoise shell combs, glass bottles, drop spindles, a sundial, faunal remains) makes the Tortugas site an important index of colonial trade with the Americas early in the reign of King Philip IV and towards the end of Spain's Golden Age. The wreck's archaeology reflects Seville and the Casa de Contratacíon's political and economic control over small *flota* vessels. The Tortugas ship enables the material culture from a small Spanish-operated merchantman to be compared to high level state and royal socio-economics typified by the galleons *Nuestra Señora de Atocha* and *Santa Margarita* from the same 1622 fleet.

1. Introduction

Following the discovery of the Tortugas shipwreck in 1989 at a depth of 405m off the Florida Keys, the cargo and domestic assemblage were comprehensively recorded and recovered between 1990 and 1991 using pioneering remote technology developed around the Remotely-Operated Vehicle (ROV) Merlin. The collection of 16,903 artifacts is highly diverse in medium. In terms of greatest numerical order the largest assemblages comprise:

- Pearls: 6,639
- Ceramics (rims/bases/handles/sherds): 3,935 (2,304 table/kitchen wares, 1,631 olive jars)
- Ballast: 1,658
- Lead musket shot: 1,186
- Silver coins: 1,184
- Seeds: 565
- Beads (glass, stone, clay, wood, palm nut, bone/ivory): 258
- Animal bones: 165
- Unidentified concretions: 145
- Glass wares: 127
- Gold bars and bits: 39

Many of these assemblages compare closely to the material culture of other sites excavated on land and underwater.

Volume only reveals one dimension of the ship's colorful, and in some cases unexpected, character. A one-handle Portuguese jug is an anomaly amongst the otherwise Seville focused ceramic tablewares (Kingsley *et al.*, 2012: 17, fig. 22). How exactly the single recovered agate bead from India ended up on the Tortugas wreck is intriguing. Did the owner of this gem also carry the high-status ivory sundial manufactured in Nuremberg, but which was actually functionally useless so far from the West? The three astrolabes are perhaps unexpectedly numerous for such a small merchant vessel.

The collection of tortoise shell contains what seem to be 'blank' scutes and semi-worked examples that hint at the on-site craftsmanship of lice combs and cases by an industrious crew member. Three jadeite artifacts, including a labret mouth adornment, raise speculation about whether a native of South America or Mesoamerica accompanied the ship to Spain and, if so, for what purpose? The evidence of a cat, rats and a parrot on board provide a unique insight into shipboard life and a rare form of cargo transport, and showcases the success of the deep-sea excavation in extracting maximum data from the wreck using nuanced recovery systems (cf. Astley and Stemm, 2013).

What is missing from the shipwreck is equally as illuminating as the eclectic nature of the assemblages. Does the very small number of human bones accurately reflect the decision of the ship's company to have jumped ship at the time of sinking? Despite the presence of iron cannonballs and lead shot, no cannon or musket parts were recovered. Finally, the volume of olive jars are indicative of the transport of shipboard supplies, which leaves unresolved the question of precisely what cargo the Tortugas ship was transporting.

The distribution of the material culture across the wreck site and related patterns have been presented elsewhere (Stemm *et al.*, 2013). The assemblages are discussed below beginning with the ceramics and progressing to the glass wares, gold bars, bits and jewelry, silver coins, pearls, trade beads and buttons, navigational equipment (anchors, astrolabes, ship's bell, sounding lead), followed by an analysis of the tortoise shell, miscellaneous metallic, stone and organic artifacts, human and animal bones, and concluding with the seeds. The most significant classes will be examined in greater detail in separate papers. How the artifacts reflect the date, identification, status and itinerary of the Tortugas ship is also treated individually (Kingsley, 2012).

2. *Botijas* ('Olive Jars')

The most conspicuous class of artifact covering the surface of the Tortugas shipwreck were intact and broken olive jars.

During the excavation a policy of total ceramic recovery was implemented, which yielded 86 intact olive jars plus 123 individual rims alongside 1,344 sherds (Figs. 1-12). The ship was thus transporting a minimum of 209 olive jars that were relatively evenly distributed across the site (cf. Stemm *et al.*, 2013: 20-21, fig. 15). The descriptive term 'olive jar' is a misnomer because these vessels were packaged with a wide variety of liquid and solid foodstuffs. However, 'olive jar' has become a generic name for this ceramic form today and is used in this report as a convenient term.

The question of the provenance of the Tortugas ship's ceramic vessels was addressed in 2011 by chemical analysis of a sample of fabrics using Inductively-Coupled Plasma Spectrometry (ICPS) to identify chemical fingerprints. ICPS investigates whether ceramics derive from the same clay source by examining atomic emissions for all the major chemical elements, plus a range of trace elements. This method has the advantage of straightforward calibration, consistent accuracy, precision of results and ready availability as a technique (cf. Hughes, 2008: 120-31). Previous projects using ICPS and neutron activation analysis (NAA) have defined the chemical characteristics of Seville-produced pottery, which were compared to the Tortugas results. The representative selection from the wreck consisted of 57 examples, including principally olive jars, maiolica, Morisco wares, redwares, and Tortugas colonoware cooking vessels (cf. Hughes, forthcoming; Kingsley *et al.*, 2012; section 3 below).

The majority of the Tortugas olive jars adhere to the generic Middle Style A form (Goggin, 1968: 283). The collection also includes seven small globular jars defined as Middle Style B form, as well as two small carrot-shaped jars classified as Middle Style C. Two intact flat-bottomed large vessels are represented within the assemblage.

In terms of a site-specific classification, the following typology is applicable to the Tortugas shipwreck:

- Tortugas Type 1 (87.2% of the total *botija* assemblage; Figs. 1, 7): the prevalent jar type characterized by the classic shape of a tall body with rounded shoulder surmounted by a high-set, short rim inclining relatively smoothly to a gently rounded base. The type's dimensions vary from: H. 43.5-56.5cm, Diam. 17.9-34.1cm, circumference 87.4-107cm, rim H. 2.1-4.5cm, volume 14.2-22.5 liters, weight 5.9-9.9kg, color range from light red (7.5YR 6/6) to pink (2.5YR 8/3), reddish yellow (7.5YR 6/8) and very pale brown (10YR 7/4). Inductively-coupled Plasma Spectrometry (ICPS) analysis suggests production for this type in the region of Cordoba (Hughes, forthcoming).
- Tortugas Type 2 (8.1% of the total; Figs. 1, 8): a small,

compact globular jar, almost anatomically circular, with a continuously rounded base, body and shoulder. The style displays a more pronounced neck and higher rim than Type 1. Its dimensions are surprisingly diverse: H. 27.0-34.0cm, Diam. 23.7-25.8cm, circumference 49.8-78.5cm, rim H. 2.5-4.0cm, volume 3.7-8.1 liters, weight 1.9-3.6kg, color range from very pale brown (10YR 7/3) to pink (7.5YR 8/4), yellowish red (5YR 5/8) and reddish yellow (5YR 6/6). ICPS analysis indicates that this *botija* type bears the chemical signature of Seville clays (Hughes, forthcoming).

- Tortugas Type 3 (2.3% of the total assemblage; Fig. 5): a carrot-shaped vessel, far more narrow than the above series, with a slender body, more v-shaped in profile, leading to a more pointed toe. The simply rounded rim, surmounting a short neck, is far wider in relation to the vessel's diameter than the above types, equating to half the size of the jar's width. H. 33.0cm, Diam. 15.9cm, circumference 49.8cm, rim H. 2.1cm, rim Diam. 8.5cm, volume 2.8 liters, weight 1.8kg, reddish yellow (7YR 5/8).

- Tortugas Type 4 (2.3% of the total assemblage; Fig. 9): anatomically similar to the neck and upper body shape of Tortugas Type 1, but clearly differentiated by an everted neck and short, slender rim. The shoulder is

bulbous before assuming a vertical profile along the lower third of the vessel and terminating at a flat base. Type 4 is covered with closely aligned body ribbing. Functionally its slender rim and neck and flat base make this vessel perhaps better suited to use as kitchen or galley ware, rather than as an archetypal transport jar. H. 43.5cm, Diam. 31.2cm, circumference 99.6cm, rim H. 2.1cm, rim Diam. 11.9cm, volume 20.8 liters, weight 6.4kg, reddish yellow (7.5YR 8/6). ICPS analysis suggests that Tortugas Type 4 *botijas* derived from Seville (Hughes, forthcoming).

The Tortugas jars' clay fabrics contain small flecks of gold colored mica, along with sand temper. Spalling is extensive in the walls, indicating that the jars were fired when not thoroughly dry and/or that the clay was improperly or insufficiently wedged. Traces of rilling, or throwing rings, and small pieces of clay within the vessels' interiors, indicate that the jars were thrown in upright positions. Evidence of green glaze is apparent on the interior and dripped onto the exterior of a minority of sherds.

Avery's analysis of the Tortugas wreck collection (1997: 103-104, 106, fig. 15) demonstrated that the rim profiles of Type 1 are angular, while the Type 2 rim shape is rounded. The rims from the traditional Type 1 form display

Fig. 1. Large Type 1 and small Type 2 olive jars (botijas) *from the Tortugas shipwreck.*

Fig. 2. A Type 1 olive jar being prepared for
recovery using the limpet suction device.

Fig. 3. A Type 1 olive jar being recovered
using the limpet suction device.

Fig. 4. A Type 2 olive jar being recovered
using the limpet suction device.

Fig. 5. A Type 3 olive jar in situ.

Fig. 6. A Type 1 olive jar being placed in a
foam-lined 4Plex storage unit to await surface recovery.

a wide overhang above the neck, while Type 2 rims from
globular jars are narrower with less overhang. On average,
Type 1 olive jar rims have an interior throat diameter of
4.89cm, a lip diameter of 5.81cm and a maximum diameter of 9.43cm. The average Type 2 rim dimensions are
4.67cm for the interior throat diameter, 6.30cm lip diameter and 8.56cm maximum diameter (Avery, 1997: 123).

Tortugas Types 1-3 are identical to the three main
varieties present on the wreck of the *San Antonio*, lost off
Bermuda in 1621, just a year before the loss of the Tortugas wreck. The *Atocha* of 1622 was transporting Types
1-4 and, as expected, is thus a direct typological match for
the Tortugas wreck's *botija* assemblage (cf. Marken, 1994:
65-71). The more unusual flat-bottomed Tortugas Type
4 jar was visually reported from the site of the *San Antonio* and documented on both the *Atocha* and *Santa Ana*

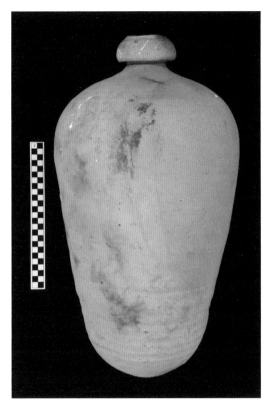

Fig. 7. A Tortugas Type 1 olive jar.

Fig. 8. A Tortugas Type 2 olive jar.

Maria, wrecked in 1627 off Castletownsend, Ireland (Marken, 1994: 81). Type 4 is an archaeological marker that on current evidence seems to be restricted to shipwrecks of the early 17th-century, although the basic shape had been in evolution in Valencia, Spain, since the 14th century (Marti and Pascual, 1995: 169, fig. 15.8, no. 2).

Graffito incisions present on either the shoulder or rim of some jars appear to have been made, with one exception, prior to firing. One *botija* is incised with a Jerusalem cross on the shoulder, while another displays a post-firing pecked design on the shoulder. Motifs were impressed into the wet clay on the mouths of some jars. Several are identical to marks present amongst the *Atocha botija* assemblage (Marken, 1994: fig. 4.22, B). Small parallel cuts on and near the rims probably result from vessel reuse.

The elaborate cross style on a Tortugas *botija* is paralleled on jars from the wreck of the *San Martin* of 1618 and from the Santo Domingo Monastery at La Antigua in Guatemala. The impressed circular incision present on the rim of another Tortugas jar occurs in at least five styles on 11 olive jars from the Santo Domingo Monastery, ten dated between the late 16th century and *c*. 1641. This form of mark has also been recognized at the colonial port of Bodegas on Lake Izabal in northeast Guatemala (Carruthers, 2003: 46, 48, fig. 7b, fig. 9). A circular mark impressed onto the rim of a *botija* deposited into Pit 4 at

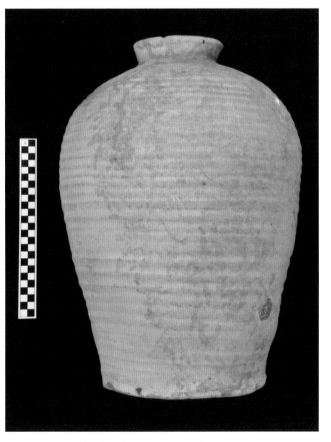

Fig. 9. A Tortugas Type 4 olive jar.

Jamestown, Virginia, shortly after 1610 (Kelso *et al.*, 1999: 39), is also similar to the Tortugas material.

It is seemingly chronologically significant that no *botijas* identified at the Santo Domingo Monastery in Guatemala from contexts post-dating 1641 featured impressed or stamped rim marks. Instead, of the 113 marked olive jars excavated 111 were recorded on early Middle Style Type A rims, suggesting these particular sets of makers' marks were restricted to the period *c.* 1583-1641 (Carruthers, 2003: 52-3). Olive jar collections of the early 18th century lack comparable marks, indicating that the practice had ceased by this time (Marken, 1994: 72). The various motifs may be interpreted as producers' marks.

During the ship's descent onto the seafloor, or soon after deposition, the pressure exerted on the olive jars forced their cork seals to implode: 72 intact and fragmentary cork stoppers were found inside some vessels. Complete examples were tapered and measured 5.1-5.85cm on the upper plane, 4.51-5.08cm on the lower plane and were 1.55-2.29cm thick (Avery, 1997: 123). Resin was detected within some jar interiors demonstrating sealant by coating the edges of conical-shaped corks with pitch. A similar sealant method was used on the *Atocha* and *Margarita*, where intact corks were attached to the rim with *pez* or pitch presumably to seal the jar's mouth (James, 1988: 56-7).

The interior lining of a few sherds was coated with a chalky red stain, which has been interpreted by visual observation alone possibly as red ocher, a product listed amongst ships provisions for carpenters (cf. *Nautical Instruction*, 1587). Alternatively, it may constitute cochineal listed as cargo on ships returning to Europe from the Indies (cf. *The Spanish Rule of Trade to the Indies*, 1702). Olive jar fragments stained red on the interiors, associated with the *San Antonio* sunk en route from Havana to Spain in 1621, similarly suggest that these vessels contained a dyestuff bound for Spanish markets (James, 1988: 61)

Despite the catch-all misnomer 'olive jars' for the material culture in question, in reality Spanish merchants seemingly did not differentiate between either shapes or contents to define jar names, but referred to them by size, including (Pleguezuelo-Hernandez, 1993):

• *Botija de arroba y media* (16.5 liters)
• *Botija de arroba y cuarta* (13.87 liters)
• *Botija de arroba/botija perulera* (11.5 liters)
• *Botija de media arroba* (5.7 liters)
• *Botija de cuarto de arroba/botija de aguda* (2.87 liters)

The volume of *botijas* on the Tortugas wreck is relatively limited and they are unlikely to have served as cargo. Instead, colonial Spain pursued an unwavering policy of stocking all ships with sufficient supplies for entire round trips to the Americas and home. Eight months of food and four months of water were loaded in Seville, typically sufficient surplus to mitigate against unexpected bad weather. Ships often returned with surplus foods, although stocks were commonly replenished at Havana (De la Fuente, 2008 and section 13 below). *Botijas* of all sizes were used for storing a multitude of foodstuffs: wine, oil, vinegar, honey, as well as solids such as rice, almonds, hazelnuts, raisins, capers and olives (Pleguezuelo-Hernandez, 1993). Although recovered from the ROV's SeRF system, and not from jar interiors, it is likely that many of the seeds and pits from almonds, plums, peaches, olives, hazelnuts and grape from the Tortugas shipwreck were originally *botija* contents. The site produced just one fragment of a possible wooden barrel.

In the early 17th century stocking outward-bound ships to the Americas with staple foodstuffs absorbed 26% of total ship preparation costs. The mainstay of the diet was biscuit (1.5lbs a day) and wine (half an *azumbre*/2 pints a day) (Avery, 1997: 165-6). Foodstuffs outgoing to the Indies included wine, olive oil, vinegar, raisins, almonds, figs, olives in brine, fish, rice, flour, *garbanzos* (chickpeas), honey, lard, eggplants and capers, as well as non-consumables such as medicine, turpentine, gunpowder and pitch, all packaged in ceramic pots (Lister and Lister, 1987: 128).

On the basis of current evidence Spanish fleets sailing to the Americas relied seemingly exclusively on containers manufactured in southern Spain. The single anomaly to this pattern was the localized production of Spanish olive jars along the Moquegua Valley in southern Peru, where 130 wine *hacienda* sites have been recorded, including a 17th-century kiln at Locumbilla, developed to satisfy specialized demands linked to regional silver-mining centers (Rice, 1996).

Amongst the exported products of mainland Spain, two olive jar clay fabric types have been identified: a red-firing clay derived from islands in the Guadalquivir River or from pits in the meadows of Triana or Tablada and, secondly, a light firing calcareous clay from the banks of the Guadalquivir (Avery, 1997: 130). A Seville provenance has been confirmed by the excavation of hundreds of olive jars excavated beneath 17th and 18th-century dwellings in the city, where factory rejects were installed beneath floors as humidifiers intended to draw in moisture to help counter the local climate. An origin for these recycled seconds west of Seville in nearby Aljarafe, the delta of the Guadalquivir, or most distant of all at Cazalla in the mountains north of Seville, has been postulated (Lister and Lister, 1987: 136). The Inductively-coupled Plasma Spectrometry analysis of the Tortugas *botijas* points to two sources for this collection, Seville and Cordoba (Hughes, forthcoming).

In terms of diffusion, *botijas* traveled far and wide wherever Spanish merchants, clergymen and immigrants roamed. They are the most common form of earthenware excavated from Spanish colonial sites in the New World (Deagan 1987: 28), widely distributed throughout the Caribbean, Mexico and Central America, and also frequently encountered along the Atlantic coast and occasionally in the American Southwest. Other than within Florida, olive jars are uncommon in the interior of the Southeast (Beck *et al.*, 2006: 70).

Functional settlement contexts vary relatively widely across the Americas. Olive jar sherds occur at the Berry site along the upper Catawba River in western North Carolina, which served as the capital of the late 16th-century Native American chiefdom of Joara and of Fort Juan, the most important of a succession of Spanish fortifications constructed by the soldiers of the Spanish explorer Juan Pardo during his expeditions across the Carolinas and Eastern Tennessee (Worth, 1994: 2; Beck *et al.*, 2006: 65). *Botijas* were also used by English colonists at Fort Raleigh on Roanoke Island in North Carolina from *c.* 1585 and 1587 (Skowronek and Walker, 1993: 65, fig. 2). Their abundance in Virginia at British Jamestown again reflects the willingness of a militarily hostile population to embrace foreign cultural culinary habits (cf. Malios and Straube, 2000: 18, 19). Examples contemporary with the Tortugas wreck occur in Virginia at the British plantation of Martin's Hundred (Noël Hume and Noël Hume, 2001: 329, fig. 33.4).

Further afield, *botijas* were relied on in the Spanish colony of Puerto Real (McEwan, 1986: 44). These jars were similarly abundant on ecclesiastical and missionary sites, such as Mission San Martin de Timucua (Fig Springs) in Columbia County and Mission San Luis de Talimali near Tallahassee (Deagan, 1972: 34-5; McEwan, 1991: 48, 50). Some 585 *botijas* have been studied from the Santo Domingo Monastery at Antigua, Guatemala (Carruthers, 2003). Olive jars dating to the 17th and 18th centuries reached northwest Europe in large volumes, having been recorded on 110 sites in Britain and Ireland. Examples are also numerous in the Low Countries and penetrated Scandinavia (Hurst, 1995: 46). At perhaps the greatest cultural extreme, *botija* fragments of *c.* 1600 have been excavated in small numbers at Nagasaki, Japan (Kawaguchi, 2011).

3. Ceramic Kitchen & Tablewares

The Tortugas shipwreck ceramic assemblage contains a major collection of 2,304 kitchen and tableware rims, handles, bases and sherds (RBHS), the most extensive associated with the 1622 Tierra Firme fleet scientifically

Fig. 10. Olive jars, a Blue-on-Blue Seville maiolica dish and Blue Morisco ware jug in situ.

Fig. 11. Olive jars and a Seville White ware dish in situ.

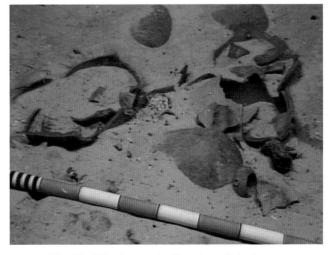

Fig. 12. Olive jars and a San Juan Polychrome Mexican juglet in situ (at center).

excavated to date. These derive from 22 types of pottery forms (1,390 tin-glazed maiolica sherds, 84 blue-painted wares tablewares, 279 Tortugas colonoware kitchen vessels, 218 unglazed coarse redwares and 333 glazed coarse redwares; Figs. 10-19).

All are currently identified as of Spanish origin centered on Seville with the minor exceptions of a San Juan Polychrome maiolica juglet, one Columbia Plain bowl subform of possible New World origin and one Portuguese jug. In addition, the kitchenware cooking pots and pans solely comprise highly coarse colonoware that could be South American, Mesoamerica or circum-Caribbean products. The ICPS analysis identified the closest match, based on available samples, in the Valley of Mexico (Hughes, forthcoming). In this report this material is referred to as Tortugas colonoware.

In the below analysis, the Tortugas colonoware (Types 10-11; Fig. 19) is excluded from the quantification because they constitute the exclusive kitchenwares used for cooking and are not tablewares functionally comparable to the rest of the assemblage. Sherds are also omitted from the below statistics (based on rim, base and handle counts: RBH) due to wide differences in vessel fragmentation rates caused by variances in body vessel sizes and thicknesses, which can heavily skew count-based results.

Quantification indicates that the tin-glazed maiolica products represent the most numerous tableware category, accounting for a combined 82.4% of the assemblage by RBH count. The Tortugas tablewares may be sub-divided into the following categories following current classifications (pers. comm. Alexjandra Gutíerrez, April 2011), even though the pottery is predominantly of Seville manufacture probably centered on Triana. The prevailing 'Morisco' classification used by ceramicists is misleading for the Tortugas wreck because Seville's Morisco Muslim community was expelled in 1610 (Pike, 1972: 163, 168), over a decade prior to the ship's voyage in 1622, and thus cannot have crafted these wares, even if there they originally inspired some styles. ICPS analysis of the Tortugas pottery implemented to help determine the assemblage's provenance is published in full elsewhere (Hughes, forthcoming).

The tableware types and volumes comprise:

1. *Seville Wares*
   - Blue-on-Blue Seville: 48.4% (Type 1; Fig. 13)
   - Blue-on-White Talavera-Style: 13.5% (Type 2; Figs. 14, 41)
   - White Seville: 6.0% (Type 4; Fig. 16)
   - Andalusia Polychrome: 2.3% (Type 5; Fig. 16)
   - Blue-on-White Seville: 0.9% (Type 8; Fig. 17)

2. *'Morisco' Wares*
   - Columbia Plain: 6.5% (Type 3; Fig. 15)
   - Decorated Linear Blue Morisco: 2.8% (Type 6; Fig. 17)
   - Mottled Blue Morisco: 1.4% (Type 7; Fig. 17)

3. *Others*
   - San Juan Polychrome: 0.5% (Type 9; Fig. 12)
   - Unglazed Coarse Redwares: 11.2% (Types 12-19A; Fig. 18)
   - Glazed Coarse Redwares: 6.0% (Type 19B-22; Fig. 18)

Unglazed coarse redwares represent 11.2% of all the ship's tablewares (Types 12-19A) and glazed coarse wares 6.0% (Types 19B-22). The latter two categories contain mixed forms not dominated by any single product (Fig. 18). A further three classes of coarse wares sharing an identical fabric were common on the shipwreck, one form of cooking pots and one cooking pan variety of Tortugas colonoware (Types 10-11; Fig. 19), accounting for 12.1% of the total combined kitchen and tablewares and seemingly serving exclusively as the onboard cooking vessels.

Counts of intact, or predominantly intact vessels, in addition to unique rim or base fragments, reveal that a minimum of 60 tin-glazed tablewares were onboard the Tortugas ship when it sank: 35 dishes, 11 bowls, four cups, five jugs and five juglets. The 70 other maiolica rim fragments in the collection are too small or indistinct to ascertain whether they derive from the same or different vessels.

The most conspicuous tablewares are 17 Blue-on-Blue Seville maiolica dishes (Type 1: 48.4% of all tablewares; Fig. 13), which incorporate ten different motifs painted across the rims, primarily schematized swirling floral variants. The interior base medallions feature 11 forms of star, fruit and, most common, six sub-forms of floral motifs with outward radiating petals. The same decorative scheme appears on shallow bowl bases. Dish dimensions vary from H. 3.1-4.2cm, Diam. 18.1-21.3cm and rim Th. 0.5cm. This maiolica style was also present in four shallow bowl bases featuring the same decorative scheme (Type 1B). Comparable Blue-on-Blue Seville majolica is attested on the 1622 wreck of the *Atocha* off Florida Keys and further afield in the Convento de San Francisco in the Dominican Republic (Goggin, 1968: 137, fig. 12b). The decorative rim style has been recovered in Seville (Lister and Lister, 1987: 159, fig. 102) and was probably originally inspired by the Chinese ceramic symbol of the lotus flower (cf. Pijl-Ketel, 1982: 276).

Imitating Chinese blue-on-white Wanli porcelain, the Blue-on-White Talavera-Style dishes (Type 2, 13.6% of the total fine wares; Figs. 14, 41) display the most graphic

Fig. 13. Blue-on-Blue Seville maiolica brimmed dishes (Tortugas Type 1).

Fig. 14. Blue-on-White Talavera-style maiolica dishes (Tortugas Type 2).

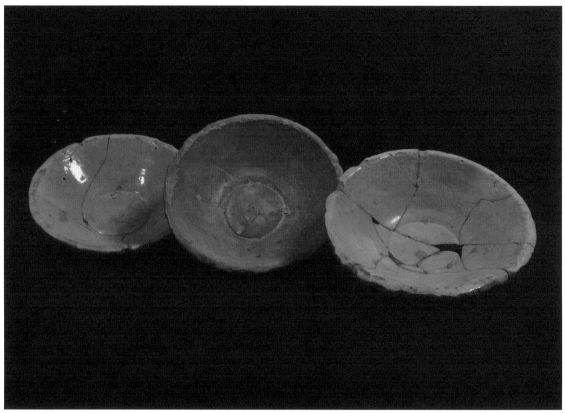

Fig. 15. Columbia Plain maiolica dishes (Tortugas Type 3).

Fig. 16. Andalusia Polychrome juglets (Tortugas Type 5) and White Seville ware bowls (Tortugas Type 4).

Fig. 17. Linear Blue Morisco ware jugs (Tortugas Type 6, back row), a mottled Blue Morisco ware cup (Tortugas Type 6), a Blue-on-White Seville ware bowl and a Blue-on-White Seville ware juglet (both Tortugas Type 8) (front, left to right).

Fig. 18. A half-dipped green glaze juglet, a one-handle Portuguese redware jug, a green glazed large coarse redware jug, and a glazed coarse ware juglet (from left to right).

Fig. 19. South American, Mesoamerican or circum-Caribbean Tortugas colonoware cooking pot and pan fragments (Tortugas Types 10-11).

decorative schemes within the Tortugas collection. Type 2A imitates kraakware rims with vertical diaper registers and classical base motifs, such as a bird sitting on a rock in a garden landscape. An additional set is adorned with heraldic or religious motifs, such as two crossed keys surmounted by a cross (Fig. 41) and two dish fragments inscribed with the letters 'CAR' 'MO', potentially part of the ecclesiastical name Carmel. Identical dish styles excavated at the Carthusian monastery at Jérez de la Frontera, Spain, inscribed on their interior bases with the monogram 'AM' for Ave Maria, would have been appropriate for ecclesiastical use (Lister and Lister, 1987: 150, fig. 92). While such religiously inspired dishes, and a Catholic pendant and clay figurine of the Virgin Mary excavated from the Tortugas shipwreck (Fig. 69), could have been used by members of the crew, it would not have been unexpected to find a clergyman on the ship traveling between a monastery on the Spanish Main and the Spanish homeland.

Due to the thick and heavy nature of their production, the seven Columbia Plain *platos* dishes (Type 3B, H. 4.8-5.7cm, Diam. 19.5-19.8cm, rim Th. 0.9-1.1cm; Fig. 15) and three *escudilla* bowls (Type 3C, H. 5.9-6.2cm, Diam. 13.0cm, rim Th. 0.65-0.7cm) proved to be the best preserved vessel form on the Tortugas shipwreck, even

though they account for just 6.5% of the site's tablewares. This is one of the few categories of Spanish colonial pottery whose origin in Seville is archaeologically verifiable. A workshop and kiln excavated in the famous potters quarter of Triana in Seville (Gerrard *et al.*, 1995: 284) is also a likely origin for part of the Tortugas ship's Blue-on-Blue Seville maiolica. A group of intact Columbia Plain plates have allegedly been recovered from a well in Seville (Lister and Lister, 1974: 20).

In addition to the conspicuous presence of Columbia Plain dishes on the *Atocha* (Marken, 1994: 154, 156-7, figs. 5.9, 5.10, pl. 18), four decades earlier the ceramic component of tablewares recorded on the Spanish Armada shipwreck *La Trinidad Valencera* off Ireland was largely unchanged morphologically. In general, the distribution of this ceramic form closely follows the routes of the Seville-based *flotas* and has been hypothesized to be cheap, standardized 'official issue' of the Casa de Contratacíon (Martin, 1979a: 284-6). The favored use of sturdy Columbia Plain dishes and bowls on fleet ships is further exemplified by the Emanuel Point I wreck from the *flota* of Tristán de Luna, which was lost during a hurricane in 1559 during the first European attempt to colonize Florida (Williams, 1998: 141), and by its frequency as the most common tableware on the St. John's wreck sunk off the Little Bahama Bank soon after 1554 (Malcom, 1996).

The tablewares are completed by a vibrant set of two-handled Andalusia Polychrome juglets, one version painted with a dark blue fruit motif on a lighter blue surface, the second with blue and yellow floral motifs overlying a brownish cream background (Type 5, H. 9.6cm to mid-neck, body Diam. 9.8cm, body Th. 0.57cm; Fig. 16). This form comprises 2.3% of the tablewares and presumably was best suited to the pouring of oil at table. Though well preserved on the wreck, decorated linear Blue Morisco ware two and one-handled jugs and mottled Blue Morisco ware cups represent just 4.2% of the Tortugas tablewares (Types 6-7, Fig. 17). Blue-on-White Seville bowls and juglets (Type 8, Fig. 17), and one San Juan Polychrome juglet, comprise just 0.9% and 0.5% respectively.

To what degree do the Tortugas ship's tablewares conform to recognized patterns with a suggested orientation around official issue Columbia Plain products? The ship's profile notably differs to the majority of Spanish wrecks dated between *c.* 1550-1625 through the numerical dominance of Seville Blue-on-Blue wares. ICPS analysis, however, does reflect a strong gravitation in and around Seville for the tablewares as a whole, but with several minor anomalies. Analyses clarified that the types fell into two major chemical groups (Hughes, forthcoming), which correspond to Seville wares and 'Morisco' wares respectively (as defined by Lister and Lister, 1987).

The first group contains the Blue-on-Blue Seville products, which are chemically similar to the Blue-on-White Talaveran style wares. Assigning Talaveran maiolica to its place of production is complicated by its imitation in Seville (Deagan, 1987: 64-5). Chemical analysis of the Tortugas shipwreck's Blue-on-White Talavera style pottery, however, confirms manufacture in Seville and not Talavera. Andalusian Polychrome juglets proved to be chemically part of the same Seville wares group. Two Seville White Wares again fitted chemically with the Blue-on-White Talavera pottery originating in Seville (Hughes, forthcoming).

'Morisco' wares formed the second major clay chemical group, which was higher in lime (calcium oxide) and lower in the percentage of clay-related chemical elements, indicative of a higher percentage of quartz sand temper relative to the Seville wares. Four Columbia Plain white wares dishes and bowls examined contained three different paste chemical compositions: one had the chemical signature of Seville, one seemingly the signature of New World ceramics, and the other two formed part of a previously unreported group containing high levels of magnesium present as the clay mineral montmorillonite (up to around 11% magnesium oxide in the paste, compared to 2-3% present in Seville

pottery) originating in a rural Andalusian context 24km west of Seville, close to the Rio Guadiamar. Combined with suggested evidence of bowl manufacture at Mata da Machada, Lisbon, *c.* 1550-70 (Casimiro, 2011: 144, fig. 71), and possibly in dish form in Mexico in the first half of the 16th century (Lister and Lister, 1974: 24, fig. 3a), far wider colonial imitation must now be considered for Columbia Plain products.

As well decorated and diverse as the tablewares used for dining on the Tortugas shipwreck appear to be, notably no pewter vessels were excavated. This trend seems to reflect the social hierarchy of the 1622 fleet, where gold, silver and pewter tablewares are associated with the *Atocha* and *Margarita* (Mathewson, 1986: 136-7, C-10, C-12, C-30, C-31; Malcom, 1998a). The reliance on ceramic tablewares on the Tortugas ship is an index of its comparatively humble status.

4. Glass Wares

A total of 127 fragments of glass were excavated from the Tortugas shipwreck, including square-sectioned case bottles, a form of vial with an everted rim and a vase or wine glass. By far the most conspicuous class derived from a minimum of two rims and eight bases from square-sectioned case bottles produced in three sizes. The bases are all medium olive green in color and contain air bubbles (Fig. 20). Glass rim and neck sherds were recovered still attached to 14 lead screw collars and caps that originally sealed some of the Tortugas ship's bottle mouths (Fig. 21). A combination of data suggests a minimum presence of 16 square-sectioned bottles on the ship.

The square-sectioned glass bottle rims vary in size from an external diameter of 3.1cm (TOR-90-00163-GL) to 4.6cm (TOR-90-00160-GL) with thicknesses of 0.1cm and 0.3cm respectively. The base diameters provide a clearer reflection of the bottle series' three different sizes, which fall within the parameters of 4.3 x 3.6cm, 6.0 x 5.9cm to 6.4 x 6.3cm, and 9.4 x 8.1cm to 10.3 x 9.9cm.

The two-piece permanent lead collars and caps that originally closed the bottles' mouths possess everted sides and a horizontal shoulder surmounted by a short vertical mouth. Each collar, 1.4-1.9cm high, is subdivided into two seamless elements: at top a narrow screw thread (W. 1.5-1.9cm, Th. 0.2cm) consisting of three convex external edges between two inner recessed threads for receipt of a lead cap, and below the main section (max W. 2.1-3.3cm, bottom W. 1.9-2.9cm, Th. 0.2-0.4cm) that originally covered and protected the glass bottle neck and rim. The two zones are separated by a horizontal ledge, furrowed on the lower edge. The bottom edge of the inner diameter, reflecting the

Fig. 20. Base fragments from green
glass square-sectioned bottles.

Fig. 21. Lead screw collars and caps from the
tops of square-sectioned glass bottles.

bottle's neck diameter, ranges from 1.2-1.7cm. The collar was a permanent component cast over the bottle.

The cap designed to screw onto the underlying collar is 1.8cm high and surmounted by a ring (H. 0.8cm, W. 1.1cm, Th. 0.3cm) comprising an upper section wider than the lower one (W. 2.2cm, Th. 0.2cm), separated by a thickened ridge. A single-link crude chain (L. 3.7cm, Th. 0.3cm) extending through the ring was presumably originally attached between cap and collar to prevent the former from getting lost (pers. comm. Bill Lindsey, 4 September 2012).

The square-sectioned bases derive from what would become termed case bottles in later decades that were common throughout Europe and the Americas. The term derives from the fact that square-sided bottles were particularly developed for packing in wooden cases with compartments (cellarets) for oceanic voyages (pers. comm. Beverly Straube, 11 September 2012). Such bottles

primarily contained spirits, which were essential in the 17th century when natural water supplies were considered infectious and alcohol was taken for medicinal purposes (McNaulty, 1971: 98, 100). However, as with most bottles of the era, after being emptied the bottles were often reused for different products (Malcom, 1990; pers. comm. Bill Lindsey, 21 October 2011), which may have been the case on the return voyage of the Tortugas ship.

The Tortugas bases are part of a square-molded bottle type that was seemingly first produced in Germany in the last quarter of the 16th century. Similar bottles dating from 1570-1600 were also manufactured in the glasshouses of Bohemia and Belgium (Van Den Bossche, 2001: 308). The typically green glass form was subsequently introduced into the Rotterdam area of the Netherlands, which began manufacture on a large scale in the 17th century as the country evolved into Europe's major shipping center. The industrialization of glass production, combined with the rapid growth in the standard of living and a burgeoning middle class, provided the demand and means to support the production of an increasingly large glass bottle industry that replaced the more common earthenware and metal vessels (McNaulty, 1971: 91-2, 103).

These bottle forms are common in North America on sites of multiple nationalities. Dozens of square-sectioned bottles have been excavated from the site of Mathews Manor, an early 17th-century English mansion on the James River in present-day Newport News, Virginia. At least one example retains part of a threaded pewter collar (Hume, 1974: 69). Pewter neck and bottle caps also circulated in 17th-century English Jamestown (McNaulty, 1971: 104, 106). The bottle style has been excavated in large numbers at the William Harwood and subsequent structure, the Fort and the John Boyse Homestead, covering the period *c.* 1619-45. The Harwood and post-Harwood farmstead of *c.* 1623-45 was home to at least 108 case bottles (Noël Hume and Noël Hume, 2001: 339-41). Early examples were located in Well 3 at the Reverend Richard Buck Site, Virginia, which was filled in between 1630 and 1645 (Mallios, 1999: 32-3, fig. 32).

Square bottles were equally popular on 17th-century shipwrecks of varied nationality, ranging from the Swedish warship *Vasa* lost in Stockholm harbor in 1628 (McNaulty, 1971: 107) to the *Virginia Merchant*, bound from Plymouth in England to Jamestown in Virginia and sunk off Bermuda in 1661 (Berg and Berg, 1991: 63; pers. comm. Ivor Noël Hume, 25 October 2011). One intact bottle, one neck and 25 square bases from green glass case bottles in two sizes, 11 x 11cm and 10 x 8.5cm, were found on the Dutch East Indiaman *Vergulde Draeck* wrecked off Western Australia in 1656 (Green, 1977: 224-5).

Pewter and lead bottleneck reinforcements of the Tortugas shipwreck form are similarly common on wrecks, such as the Dutch East Indiaman *Batavia* lost off Western Australia in 1629 (Green, 1989: 173), and the VOC *Lastdrager* sunk off Yell, Scotland, in 1653, where they were associated with square-based green glass bottles believed to have held spirits (Sténuit, 1974: 241, fig. 21). Some 26 examples were found on the VOC's *Vergulde Draeck* (Green, 1977: 215-7). The Jutholmen shipwreck of *c.* 1700 in the archipelago of Stockholm, Sweden, contained one pewter screw cap associated with fragments of a square case bottle (Ingelman-Sundberg, 1976: 57, 64).

Especially significant for the case of the Tortugas shipwreck are identical glass bottle bases and lead bottle caps, with reconstructed bottle heights varying widely from 6.6-21.3cm and 300-1,500ml liquid capacity, associated with the lower hull of the *Atocha*. As on the Tortugas wreck, square-sectioned bottles proved to be most common amongst the *Atocha* glasswares. The *Margarita* site also contained a number of bottle closures comparable to the Tortugas wreck, evidence that identical products were aboard this ship (Malcom, 1990). As part of the same Spanish fleet lost in the Florida Keys during the hurricane of September 1622, this parallel evidence may start to question the common assumption that square bottles were largely of Dutch or English manufacture. In light of the fleet's near-total cultural preference for goods made in Seville, epitomized by the ceramic record, this subject requires further research. In reality, very little has been written about the wider European straight-sided and square-sectioned bottles that preceded the emergence of globular forms *c.* 1650 (Noël Hume and Noël Hume, 2001: 340, note 273).

Similar glasswares have been excavated from other Spanish shipwrecks. An intact square-sectioned green bottle was stocked on the Spanish galleon *Nuestra Señora de la Concepción*, sunk off Hispaniola in 1641 (Borrell, 1983: 112). Pewter caps from square-sectioned bottles were recovered from the *San Martin*, the Almiranta of the Honduras fleet en route from Havana to Spain in 1618, and were still in use a century later on the 1715 fleet wrecked off Florida (Deagan, 1987: 133). On the basis of this evidence, it is reasonable to propose that one line of lead-capped square bottles conceivably may have been manufactured in Spain, mirroring in glass the overwhelming dominance of Seville wares amongst the ceramics.

Glass production thrived in Spain since the Roman period and is documented throughout the medieval and colonial periods. Glass was produced at Almería, Castril and María in southeast Spain by the 13th century, while Catalonia (especially Barcelona) was renowned for its craftsmanship as early as 1324, when an edict prohibited the establishment of glass factories inside the city limits. Jeronimo Paulo wrote in 1491 that its glassware compared favorably to Venice and was extensively exported to Rome (Barber, 1917: 8, 11, 15).

Following the artistic patronage of Ferdinand and Isabella (r. 1479-1504), Catalonia held annual glass fairs in the 16th century and the region's production peaked following the migration of Venetian glassblowers from Murano (where they had been virtually imprisoned by the State in the 16th century) across Europe. Glass vessels for pouring wine, water and oil were common in 16th-century households under the names of *gerro*, *aiguamanil* and *setrill* (Frothingham, 1963: 36, 38; Deagan, 1987: 127-8).

A major reason underlying the superiority of Spanish glass was the abundance of high quality *barilla*, a marine plant used in glassmaking. One year before the loss of the Tortugas shipwreck, James Howell (1754: 51-2) described the properties of this wondrous raw material and its processing and sale for "one hundred Crowns a Tun" in southern Spain in a letter dated 27 March 1621.

Utilitarian glasswares (bottles, vials, flasks, tumblers) were produced throughout Spain during the colonial period, and bottles and vials comprise the major part of Spanish colonial archaeological glass collections. An origin in southern Spain's thriving glassworks, particularly Andalusia, has been proposed for these products (Deagan, 1987: 127-8), which would be logical given Seville's function as the hub of the Americas fleet supplies.

Spanish square-sectioned green bottles, frequently associated with pewter caps, first appear on archaeological sites in deposits dated to the first half of the 17th century and are the earliest types of Spanish bottles documented in the circum-Caribbean area. They were blown with rounded, sloping shoulders and straight, non-tapering sides, as were all square-sectioned straight-sided 'case' bottles at this time. Spanish examples are frequently defined by bubble- and striation-filled metal (Deagan, 1987: 131-3).

Seville glassmen and vendors established furnaces and sales rooms throughout the 16th and 17th centuries in a street called El Vidrio, where tablewares, stained glass church windows and ornamental wares were manufactured. The name of one master craftsman, Juan Rodríguez, is listed in records dated to 1557. Originating in the Castillian glass center of Cadalso, Rodríguez settled in Seville and applied for permission to set up a furnace, sponsored by three glassblowers and a merchant. The only other glass center in the region seems to have been at Cala in the Huelva province (Frothingham, 1963: 57-8).

The chances that the Tortugas shipwreck's square glass bottles and lead caps originated in Spain are perhaps

Fig. 22. A selection of the 27 gold bars recovered from the Tortugas shipwreck.

enhanced by iconographic evidence in still life paintings of the first half of the 17th century. Square-sectioned glass bottles with pewter caps are depicted in Juan van der Hamen y Léon of 'Madrid's *Still Life With Sweets* of 1622, early 1620s *Serving Table*, and *Still Life with Fruit and Glassware* dated to 1629, while *Still Life With Sweets* includes an uncapped square glass bottle painted by Blas de Ledesma, who worked in Grenada and Malaga from 1602 to at least 1652 (Jordan, 1985: 65, 67, 103, 127, 130, 141, fig. 2.3, pls. 13, 14, 20). Awareness and use of the Tortugas shipwreck type of square glass bottle in the Sevillian School of Art and urban society is reflected by a bottle of red wine closed with a pewter collar and cap in Pedro de Camprobin's *Still Life with Chestnuts, Olives and Wine* of 1663 (Jordan and Cherry, 1995: 113). These compositions drew on local life and customs and permit graphic insights into southern Spain's dining rooms in the first half of the 17th century.

5. Gold Bars, Bits & Jewelry

A. Gold Bars & Bits

As the most highly coveted product of the New World the presence of 27 gold bars and 12 gold bits amongst the Tortugas assemblages is unsurprising on a ship of the 1622 Tierra Firme fleet (Figs. 22-28). The material may be interpreted as payment received for outward-bound private consignments shipped to the Americas from Seville (cf. Kingsley, 2013). An additional seven pieces of jewelry, two coins, a 12m-long chain and an emerald finger ring complete the gold collection (Figs. 29-33). The gold bars were clustered in two areas of the wreck: off the north/northwest stern zone and east/west between midship and the stern (Stemm *et al.*, 2013: 21, fig. 17). Specific types were also nucleated. Examples stamped 'EN RADA' were centrally clustered, deposited east to west, while the thinner 'SARGOSA' bars were concentrated off the stern.

The gold bars vary substantially in states of completeness. From a catalogue of 25 examples, only three were intact, four were preserved for three-quarters of their original length, seven for half of their length, four for one-quarter length or less and seven were bits. The lengths of the differently preserved bits and bars vary from 1.2-25.4cm and weights from 2.50gms to 1.224kg and purity stamps from 20 to 22 karats. 'SARGOSA PECARTA' stamps occur on eight bars, 'EN RADA' on seven bars and 'SEBATN ESPANOL' on just one example. *Quinto* tax stamps and karat purity indicators are presented on all bars (Figs. 22-28).

Three intact gold bars display the following dimensions and features:

- 90-1A-000227: an intact small gold bar, unusually symmetrical and incorporating smooth edges, with gently rounded ends, L. 14.3cm, W. 2.4cm, 418.7gms. Four royal seal/*quinto* tax stamps along the bottom surface, each set facing the end to which each is closest. Two creviced depressions on the bottom surface (3.1 x 0.8cm and 3.3 x 0.4cm) reflect the presence of an uneven mold or uneven casting.
- 90-1A-000476: squared off at one end and rounded at the other, with an assayer's bite in the bottom right edge, L. 25.4cm, max W. 2.6cm, W. of squared off end 1.2cm, 646.2gms. Covered with 17 stamps comprising 12 royal seal/*quinto* tax stamps, four purity marks with the numerals XXI surmounted by three solid dots signifying 21¾ karats purity, and one SARGOSA PECARTA stamp within a rectangular frame. The bar's sides are uneven and non-linear (Fig. 23).

- 90-1A-000571: both ends are curved, one blunted to a square edge, the other distorted by the removal of the edge for an assayer's bite, L. 22.4cm, max W. 2.2cm, 396.6gms. The lower surface is densely covered with 12 stamps oriented from the blunted end facing downwards: seven small curved sections of two royal seals/*quinto* tax stamps, two SARGOSA PECARTA stamps in a rectangular frame and three XXI Roman numerals signifying 21 karat purity.

All the various impressed marks stamped on the bottom surface of the bars, confirming the payment of the 20% royal *quinto* tax, plus numerals and characters signifying the purity of the gold, were struck into the molten bars after casting. Purity was marked in Roman numerals (such as XXI for 21 karat purity) set in rectangular frames; above appeared solid dots enclosed by smaller rectangular frame denoting fractional values (one dot for one-quarter karat, two dots for a half, etc). The word 'EN RADA' appears with several co-joined letters (P and L, A and E, and R and A and N). Other stamps read 'SARGOSA PECARTA' and 'SEBATN ESPANOL'.

These stamps represent abbreviated names of the Antioquía foundries of the Colombia mines where this colonial gold was extracted and cast. The 'SARGOSA PECARTA' gold bars derived from Zaragoza, which started operations in 1582, while 'SEBATN ESPANOL' signifies extraction at the seemingly small San Sebastian mines of Timaná (Craig and Richards, 2003: 77). The 'EN RADA' gold is an abbreviation of 'Peñarenda', a wealthy family that owned gold mine concessions in various parts of the New World, including seemingly Colombia and Mexico (pers.

*Fig. 23. An intact gold finger bar covered with 17 stamps: 12 royal seal/*quinto* tax stamps, four 21¾ karat purity marks, and one 'SARGOSA PECARTA' stamp (L. 25.4cm, 646.2gms, TOR-90-1A-000476).*

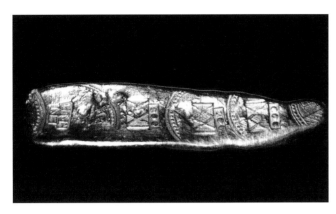

Fig. 24. Half of a gold finger bar with nine stamps: five quinto *tax stamps, three 21¾ karat purity stamps, and one 'EN RADA' stamp (L. 13.1cm, 426gms, TOR-90-1A-000766).*

Fig. 25. The central section of a gold finger bar, stamped with 21¼ karat purity mark (L. 7.9cm, 192.5gms, TOR-90-1A-000414).

Fig. 26. Detail of an 'EN RADA' stamp on gold finger bar TOR-90-1A-000766.

comm. John de Bry, 6 March 2012). Different mines seem to have processed the bars in minor contrasting styles. The 'SARGOSA PECARTA' stamped bars exhibit tapered, almost pointed ends, and an assayer's bite cut from the end of the bar. On the 'EN RADA' bars, which incorporate blunt, almost squared off ends, the assayer's bite is found at the end's center.

The Tortugas type of Spanish gold finger bar (and cut bits) was already in circulation on the Los Mimbres ship, wrecked between 1521 and 1536 on the northwest edge of Little Bahama Banks, 88km across the Strait of Florida off Palm Beach (Craig and Richards, 2003: 19). The single gold bar recovered from the group of Spanish ships lost off Padre Island in 1554, from which a section of metal had been cut off as in the Tortugas collection, is thinner and taller than the Tortugas bars, with a more curved upper surface. The stamp 'AVS' signifying gold occurs on the curved upper edge of the Padre Island example (Barto Arnold and Weddle, 1978: 275, fig. 49), not on the underside as appear on the Tortugas gold bars.

Finger bars of identical shape covered with almost circular tax stamps and squared off sections comparable to the Tortugas products foundered on a Spanish wreck of *c.* 1595 off Bermuda (Peterson, 1975: 43). The Tortugas 'SARGOSA PECARTA', 'EN RADA' and 'SEBATN ESPANOL' stamps are all represented on identical gold bars recovered from the *Atocha* (alongside another five named mines), but have not been identified on the *Margarita*. The bar form remained largely unchanged on the wreck of the *Nuestra Señora de las Maravillas*, sunk in the Bahama Channel in 1656, although the absence of EN RADA stamps suggests that the source of this alluvial gold was exhausted by this date (Mathewson, 1986: pl. C-6; Craig and Richards, 2003: 19, 21, 30, 75, 91).

An important contribution of the Tortugas assemblage is evidence of production and function. The collection mainly comprises half and quarter examples, which have been cut for convenient use. These breakage patterns display little functional rationale. An estimate of the required weight and size was simply sliced off as demanded. Obsessive repeat stamping on intact bars demonstrates that such fragmentation was a functional expectation. Efforts were consistently made to preserve a segment of the tax stamp on every piece to confirm that the king's tax had been honored. The presence of even slight royal tax marks on smaller bar fragments would have lent reassurance during exchange and commerce regarding the validity and respectability of a merchant.

Residual gold originating from bars might eventually be converted into improvised coinage, exemplified by three gold bits on the Tortugas wreck (Diam. 0.8cm, Th.

0.1-0.2cm, 0.46-1.46 grams; Fig. 28). Each incorporates four small dots across the surface recognizable as traces of *quinto* stamp sections. The larger bit contains the authentic amount of gold required for a half *escudo* coin. The two smaller bits were suitable as quarter *escudos*. Therefore, it may be assumed that these bits served as improvised or 'homemade' legal coinage. Not only were they marked for legal tender, but the value was in keeping with everyday commerce.

B. Jewelry

A 461-gram gold chain composed of six individual strands crafted with plain oval links, gathered and held together with a gold ring, was recovered off the extreme north/northwest stern area of the wreck (coordinates 83.89/34.97; 90-1A-002457, Fig. 31). Each strand is approximately 2.0m long and contains respectively 770, 762, 762, 766, 761 and 762 links. One link subjected to chemical analysis by Honeywell Materials Testing Lab in Clearwater, Florida, identified the metal as 21-karat purity.

These chains are familiar from other Spanish colonial shipwrecks. The *San Diego* sunk off the Philippines in 1600 produced a braided gold necklace or neck chain comprised of 22 strands braided in chevrons from which probably originally hung a pendant (Provoyeur, 1994: 258). Substantial gold chains from a few inches to 3.6m in length weighing 2.9kg have been recovered from the *Atocha* (Mathewson, 1986: C-13, C-16), at least two 22-karat examples from the *Concepción* lost off the Dominican Republic in 1641 (Grissim, 1980; Borrell, 1983: 107) and from the 1715 fleet off Fort Pierce and Vero Beach, Florida (Burgess and Clausen, 1982: pl. 2-3). Eight sections of gold chain from the Vero Beach site measured between 20.4cm to over 2.04m in length, five were of plain simple link form (four with 3mm diameter links and 53 links per 10cm, and the fifth with 2mm diameter links and 90 links per 10 cm), while four-petaled floral motifs were added to three full chains (thickest diameter 5mm with 44 links per 10cm (Clausen, 1965: 23). A 162.5cm-long, 479gms gold chain composed of six strands of fine flattened rectangular links, with a single scalloped gold ring and clasp in the form of four wire loops, was salvaged from the *Nuestra Señora de Esperanza*, a Spanish galleon of 650 tons lost in Mystery Bay, Gulf of Mexico, in 1658.[1]

The chain's function remains a matter of conjecture: it may have comprised jewelry or, being intrinsically valuable, could have served as a portable 'money belt'. Such chains were used for both ceremonial purposes, as conspicuous displays of wealth and were bestowed as diplomatic gifts throughout the 17th century. These symbols of status

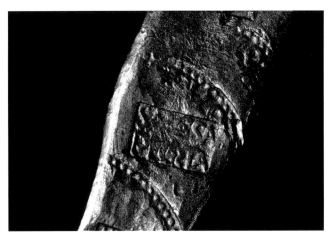

Fig. 27. Detail of a 'SARGOSA PECARTA' stamp on a gold finger bar.

Fig. 28. Twelve gold bar ends and bits recovered from the Tortugas shipwreck.

and wealth appear in 17th-century paintings across Europe from Rembrandt's *Self Portrait with a Gold Chain* of 1633 to Diego Velázquez's majestic full-length portrait of Philip IV (1605–1665), King of Spain of *c.* 1624 (Metropolitan Museum of Art, 14.40.639) and his *Portrait of an Old Gentleman with a Gold Chain and Cross of the Order*. Velázquez himself was gifted a gold chain for his Portrait of Innocent X painted *c.* 1650 (Galleria Doria-Pamphilj, Rome; Armstrong, 2004: 78).

A 1702 edition of *Spanish Rule of Trade to the West Indies* discussed different usage of gold chains whereby:

"Soldiers wounded in the King's Service, are to be allowed some advance of their pay, or a free gift; such as perform any extraordinary action, to be rewarded with gold chains, from 50 ducats value to 200, with a certificate containing the cause why it was bestoyed on them, that upon occasion they may be further rewarded."

The heavy Tortugas chain is of plain design and may have served a purely decorative purpose or had been a convenient means of shipping gold in non-currency form. If the latter, the gold chain would parallel the *Margarita*, where the weights of the largest links were analogous to half and one *escudos* gold coins (pers. comm. Jim Sinclair, 3 September 2012).

A gold finger ring with a single emerald inset (90-1 A-0000073, Figs. 29-30), identified as Colombian in origin, is sufficiently large to have belonged to a man or to have fitted over the gloves of a lady. A similar example was recovered from the *Atocha* (Mathewson, 1986: C-18). Seven miscellaneous gold jewelry stems for bead necklaces or from a rosary were excavated (Fig. 32). A fragment of a badly eroded drilled pearl, estimated at measuring

approximately 5-8mm in diameter, encircles the stem of one example. Both the ring and gold stems were presumably personal jewelry rather than cargo.

6. Silver Coins

A significant assemblage of 1,184 silver cob coins in various degrees of degradation was recovered from the Tortugas shipwreck (Figs. 34-39). In the usual process of producing cob coins, silver with the requisite fineness of 92-98% purity was hammered into crude sheets with slight variances in thickness. Pieces of the bar were subsequently cut to approximate size, weighed and the edges clipped until the blanks fell within authorized weight requirements.

These planchets were then reheated or annealed, placed between dies and struck to imprint the crowned Shield of the House of Habsburg on the obverse and a cross with the Lions of Léon and Castles of Castile in the four quadrants of the cross on the reverse. Coins produced in the

Denomination	Mexico	Potosi	Bogota/ Cartagena or Old World	Unknown	Total
8 *reales*	335	212	6	9	562 (53.5%)
4 *reales*	157	67	4	4	232 (22.1%)
2 *reales*	66	45	2	6	119 (11.3%)
1 *reale*	104	31	1	1	137 (13.0%)
½ *reale*	1	--	--	--	1 (0.1%)
Unknown	--	--	--	133	---
Total	663 (56.0%)	355 (29.9%)	13 (1.1%)	153 (13.0%)	

Table 1. Tortugas shipwreck silver coins by quantity, denomination and mint (1999 analysis of 1,184 coins).

Denomination	Mexico	Potosi	Unknown Plus Assume Potosi	Bogota/ Cartagena or Old World	Unknown	Total
8 *reales*	199	34	66	3	41	343 (75.9%)
4 *reales*	28	9	17	2	3	59 (13.1%)
2 *reales*	5	3	11	1	1	21 (4.6%)
1 *reale*	23	2	4	0	0	29 (6.4%)
Unknown	60	4	32	1	98	195
Total	315 (48.6%)	52 (8.0%)	130 (20.1%)	7 (1.1%)	144 (22.2%)	

Table 2. Tortugas shipwreck silver coins by quantity, denomination and mint (2011 analysis of 648 coins).

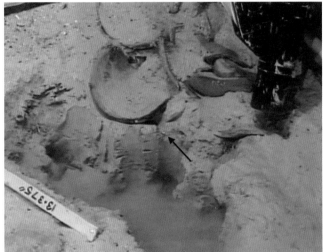

Figs. 29-30. A gold ring with an emerald inlay and
in situ *on the shipwreck below a cluster of olive jars.*

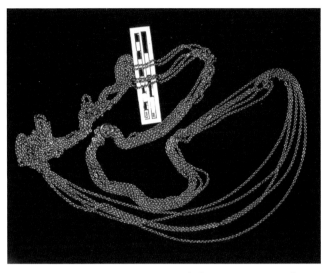

Fig. 31. A 461gms gold chain (TOR-90-1A-002457)
composed of six individual strands of plain oval links.

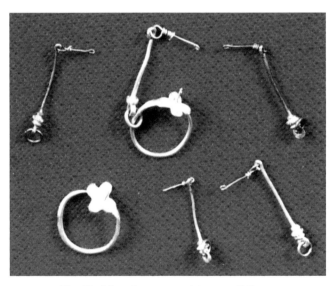

Fig. 32. Miscellaneous gold rosary fittings,
one incorporating a fragment of pearl.

Fig. 33. Two pre-1580 Spanish
peninsular coins (weights 6gms).

South American mints at Potosi, La Plata, Lima, Bogota and Cartagena featured a Greek cross. Issues from the Mexico mint held a cross whose four extensions ended in an orb. The resultant image was frequently off center, and because both sides were imprinted simultaneously the image is often more pronounced on one side. Since the thickness of the coin also varied, the strike may be clearer from one point to another over the surface. Cob coins were thus never round or even.

Silver coins were recovered from most parts of the Tortugas shipwreck site, but with a heavy concentration in the stern, and tended to be scattered, lying individually rather than in large concreted clumps (cf. Stemm *et al.*, 2013: 21, fig. 17). The average weight of coins identified as 8 *reales* coins after cleaning and electrolysis was 8.99gms, with a total overall range of 1.53-22.5gms. The official standardized weight for 8 *reales*, as minted, was 27.47gms. Considerable weight was seemingly lost due to prolonged immersion and corrosion in saltwater (and during the cleaning and treatment process).

From the sample of 1,184 silver Tortugas wreck coins initially examined, (excluding 'Unknown' examples) 53.5% of the assemblage comprised 8 *reales*, 22.1%

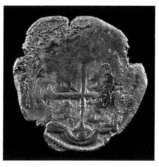

Fig. 34. Mexico City mint; 1 reale *denomination (TOR-90-00763-CN). Obverse: the small framed pomegranate symbolizing New Granada, upper-center, clearly depicted. Reverse: a cross whose four extensions each end in an orb, indicative of the Mexico City mint, quarters the lions of Léon and castles of Castile. Diam. 2.0cm, Grade 3.*

Fig. 35. Mexico City mint; 4 reales *denomination (TOR-90-00382-CN). Obverse: mintmark 'oM' to left of shield, above assayer initial 'D.' Kings' ordinal III clearly visible at the 6:00 position. Reverse: lions of Léon and castles of Castile, quartered by an orbed cross and surrounded by a curving quatrefoil. Diam. 3.1cm, Grade 3.*

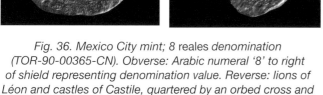

Fig. 36. Mexico City mint; 8 reales *denomination (TOR-90-00365-CN). Obverse: Arabic numeral '8' to right of shield representing denomination value. Reverse: lions of Léon and castles of Castile, quartered by an orbed cross and surrounded by a curving quatrefoil. Diam. 3.3cm, Grade 3.*

Fig. 37. Potosi mint; 2 reales *denomination (TOR-90-00762-CN). Obverse: crowned Habsburg shield; mintmark 'P' above 'Q' for assayer Agustín de la Quadra (1613-16). Reverse: lions of Léon and castles of Castile, quartered by a Greek cross and surrounded by a curving quatrefoil. Diam. 2.4cm, Grade 3.*

Fig. 38. Potosi mint; 8 reales *denomination (TOR-90-00402-CN). Obverse: crowned Habsburg shield with mintmark 'P' to left, above the initial 'B' signifying assayer Juan de Ballesteros Narváez. Reverse: the lions of Léon and castles of Castile, quartered by a Greek cross and surrounded by a curving quatrefoil. A Philip II era issue that would have been struck c. 1577-98. Diam. 3.8cm, Grade 3.*

Fig. 39. Unidentified mint; 8 reales *denomination (TOR-90-00517-CN). Obverse: eroded. Reverse: lions of Léon and castles of Castile quartered by a Greek cross surrounded by a curving quatrefoil; partial date of '162-' at 11:00 position. The elaborate open-mouthed lions and rendering of the castles suggest production in one of the Nuevo Reino de Granada mints or a Spanish peninsular mint. Diam. 3.5cm, Grade 3.*

Fig. 40. A silver ingot, not stamped and probably contraband (Diam. 8.9cm, 280gms TOR-90-01060-IT).

Fig. 41. A three-pronged silver fork with a key stamped into the head (L. 12.7cm) placed on a Blue-on-White Talavera style dish (TOR 90-1A-000577).

4 *reales*, 11.3% 2 *reales*, 13.0% 1 *reales* and 0.1% ½ *reales*. Two coins were of the *c.* pre-1572 pillar design (Flow, 1999: 87-8). Most common were 8 *reales* issues minted in Mexico (335 coins; Fig. 36). A further 212 8 *reales* issues derived from Potosi (Fig. 38). Third most common were 157 4 *reales* from Mexico (Fig. 35), followed by 104 1 *reale* from Mexico (Fig. 34). In total, 56.0% of the silver coins originated in Mexico, 29.9% in Potosi and 1.1% in Bogota/Cartagena or an Old World mint (Table 1).

A reanalysis by Carol Tedesco in 2011 of a sample of 648 Tortugas shipwreck coins retained by Odyssey

Marine Exploration in Tampa yielded differing data (Tedesco, 2013). The quantification produced slightly differing results caused by the smaller sample size and availability for study of badly deteriorated issues (Table 2). The material was still dominated by the Mexico mint (48.6%), but the Potosi coins accounted for a far lower 8.0%, while the Bogota/Cartagena or Old World examples were identical (1.1%). Unknown denominations accounted for an extensive 42.2% of the collection. Due to the superior volume of coins available for analysis in 1999, the statistics derived from that study are considered the optimum data set for the Tortugas shipwreck.

The 2011 reanalysis contributed greater complexity to the understanding of the assemblage. Nine Tortugas coins were identifiable as Philip II (r. 1554-98) period issues. Two coins retain the partial dates of '162-', while a third reads '16--'. Some 30 of the 315 Mexico City mint coins examined incorporated visible assayer's initials, in chronological order: 'O' for Bernardo de Oñate and Luis de Oñate, *c.* 1572-89; 'A' for Antonio de Morales, *c.* 1608-10; and an assayer 'D' confirmed from 1618 through post-1622 shipwrecks (Fig. 35). Of the 52 Potosi mint coins examined, 30 have a visible assayer's initial: 'R' type attributable to assayer Alonso de Rincón, *c.* 1574-76 and Baltasar Ramos Leceta, *c.* 1590-1612; 'B' for Juan de Ballesteros Narváez, intermittently *c.* 1577-1615, and also Hernando Ballesteros substituting for Juan de Ballesteros (Fig. 38); 'Q' for Agustín de la Quadra, 1613-16 (Fig. 37); 'M' for Juan Muñoz, 1616-17; 'T' for Juan Ximénez de Tapia, 1618 through post-1622 shipwrecks. Seven of the coins originated from one of the New World mints of Santa Fe de Bogotá, Cartagena or from a Spanish Peninsular mint (Tedesco, 2013).

Other than the parallel sets of ceramics, pearls, gold bars and astrolabes on the Tortugas shipwreck and in the *Atocha* and *Margarita* collections, the 2011 coin reanalysis established certain evidence for a numismatic link between all three wrecks, confirming that the Tortugas ship sailed with the 1622 Tierra Firme fleet. There are no mints, timeframes or assayers represented in the Tortugas coin assemblage that have not been documented on the *Atocha* and *Margarita*. On all three wrecks assayer 'D' is the final assayer to represent the Mexico City mint, assayer 'T' is the final assayer from the Potosi mint and assayer 'A' is the only operative to represent the mints of Nuevo Reino de Granada. Each of these officers held their posts immediately prior to and after 1622, when the Spanish fleet sank off the Florida Keys (Tedesco, 2013).

In addition to the coins, a 12.7cm-long silver fork with a key motif stamped into its head (Fig. 41) and one single crude silver disc ingot were recovered near the pump well (coordinates 79.26/26.70; 90-1A-000779, Diam. 8.9cm,

280gms; Fig. 40). This ingot form has a long history from its appearance on the Padre Island Spanish shipwrecks of 1554, where some of the *planchas* carried stamps indicating mining districts and others indicating that the *quinto* tax was paid in Mexico (Barto Arnold and Weddle, 1978: 276-7, 279). The form with a hemispherical, porous base prevailed in both silver and gold on the 1715 fleet sunk off Vero Beach, Florida (six silver discs of 11.4-24.1cm diameter, 1.3-3.8cm thickness, weighing 1lb 3 ounces to 271lbs, 90% silver), but whereas the gold examples were stamped on the upper surfaces, only the largest silver example was marked (Clausen, 1965: 15-16). The absence of any marks across the surfaces of the Tortugas wreck ingot points towards its transport as contraband.

7. Pearls

A total of 6,639 pearls scattered across the site was recovered from the Tortugas wreck through the use of the project's SeRF sieve system (Figs. 42-43). When recovered from the dredged sediments many were a dark gun-metal gray color, but after conservation reverted to a range of colors and lustrous finishes. Pearl shapes include round, pear, egg, drop, button, baroque and blister, as defined by the Gemological Institute of America, and vary in color from white to cream, rose, pink, silver, yellow, blue and black. Some 636 of the pearls are drilled. From a sample of 6,494 well-preserved pearls, the sizes range from 1-10mm and five classes were identified:

- Large (7-10mm): 95 (1.5%)
- Medium/large (5.5-6.0mm): 114 (1.7%)
- Medium (3.5-5.0mm): 2,837 (43.7%)
- Small (2.0-3.0mm): 1,752 (27.0%)
- Minimal (1.0-1.5mm): 1,696 (26.1%)

Despite the heyday of exploitation having long ceased by 1622, the Venezuelan oyster beds were still visited in hope and some success in the first quarter of the 17th century. Three ships from the 1622 Tierra Firme fleet visited these waters: the 115-ton *Santa Ana* sailed for Margarita Island, the 110-ton *San Francisco* for Cumana, while the 117-ton *Buen Jesús y Nuestra Señora del Rosario* headed to Nueva Cordoba, the antiquated name for Cumana. The destination of two additional vessels, the 100-ton *Nuestra Señora del Rosario* and the 180-ton *Nuestra Señora de los Reyes*, is listed generally as 'Venezuela' (Chaunu and Chaunu, 1956: 26-7).

As the earliest source of wealth imported by colonial Spain from the Americas, more than gold and silver the pearl trade symbolizes Spain's non-sustainable exploitation of regional economies in the New World. The islands of

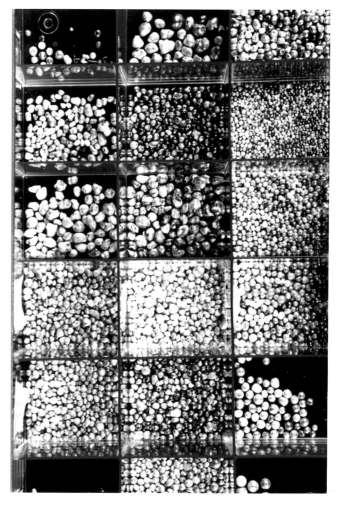

Fig. 42. Some of the 6,639 eastern Venezuelan pearls from the Tortugas wreck sorted according to size and shape.

Fig. 43. Drilled Venezuelan pearls from the Tortugas wreck.

Coche, Cubagua and Margarita off the eastern coast of Venezuela and mainland Cumana were the source of Spain's richest pearl beds throughout the 16th and 17th-century colonial exploitation of the Americas. Although Columbus was the first European to realize the economic potential of Cubagua during his third voyage of 1498, when he bartered hawk bells, beads and sugar with the Arawaks of eastern Venezuela's Paria Peninsula for more than six marks (about 1.4kg) of pearls, he never personally landed amidst the fabled source of this wealth (Romero *et al.*, 1999: 59, 60; Romero, 2003: 1014, 1016; Warsh, 2009: 16, 22).

On the back of his reports, *capitulaciones* (contracts) were swiftly secured and already in 1499 different voyages by Alonso de Ojeda and Peralonso Niño traded 44.2kg of pearls. By the turn of the 16th century the Crown had declared the pearl trade a royal monopoly subjected to a 50% *quinto* taxation. Clay and straw hut *rancherías* emerged on Cubagua, where the natives exchanged pearls for wine, linen shirts, wheat bread, firearms and European goods (Romero, 2003: 1016).

The two decades spanning 1508-20 witnessed the peak exploitation of the *Costa de las Perlas* – the Pearl Coast. To maximize extraction Spain ceased relying on the local Guayqueri divers from Margarita (Warsh, 2009: 32) and, instead, in 1508 paid as high as 150 gold *pesos* per person for large numbers of Lucayan Indians from the Bahamas (Romero *et al.*, 1999: 62). Renowned as the finest free divers (formerly for conch shells), the Lucayans could dive to 30m, making the average 13m-deep pearl beds easily accessible. Such was the hyper-exploitation of the Cubagua region's resources that by 1518 the Bahamas' Lucayan presence had been entirely denuded of its estimated 60,000 population for slaves (Romero, 2003: 1017).

In 1509 the Spanish government encouraged increased production and trade in pearls by reducing the tax from 50% to 20% of gross production. Inspired by the clamor for this luxury product, in 1528 Nueva Cádiz (Cumana) become the first European city in South America, populated by 223 Europeans and 700 natives, a frontier town plagued by administrative corruption, drinking, gambling, murder, adultery and the rape of native women. Between 1530 and 1535 the island fisheries of eastern Venezuela were exploited to the maximum (Mackenzie *et al.*, 2003: 1; Romero, 2003: 1017).

The oyster beds were already becoming severely depleted by 1528 and due to ever-diminishing returns Cubagua began to be depopulated in 1533 in favor of newly discovered beds on the South American coast, such as Cabo de La Vela and Rio Hacha off the Guajira Peninsula. By 1537 the Crown was informed that no pearls had been obtained from the Pearl Islands for a year and a half. Two years later

a maximum of 50 people remained on Cubagua, whose buildings were destroyed in a hurricane in 1541 (Romero, 2003: 1018).

The decline in oyster stocks was caused directly by an ever-expanding drive towards productivity, seemingly resulting in deeper dives from larger boats. By 1628 'canoe' owners employed crews of at least 12 African slaves, an African captain, a Spanish pilot and an overseer. The craft dived from were by now effectively significant boats described as lateen-rigged frigates. A Spanish visitor to Cabo de la Vela in 1653 witnessed pearl boats manned by two Spanish captains and 20-30 slaves (Warsh, 2009: 53).

The volume of pearls harvested from the Pearl Coast was colossal, even though records suggest that only one pearl was found for every 1,000 oysters collected (Romero *et al.*, 1999: 68). In the space of just one or two weeks, six divers working from a single boat could recover around 35,000 oysters in the heyday of resource availability. Based on tax records the total weight of pearls procured from the Cubagua region between 1515 and 1542 achieved a minimum of 11,326kg or 566,300 carats from 113,260,000 oysters (Romero, 2003: 1019). To meet this demand each diver would have needed to harvest 196,321 oysters per month or 2,355,857 oysters annually (Romero *et al.*, 1999: 69). Between 1513 and 1540 an estimated 120 million pearls were fished up from the Pearl Coast (Warsh, 2009: 21). Shipments could be impressive: one of the largest cargos destined for Spain listed in June 1533 carried at least 340kg of pearls (Mackenize, 2003: 10).

Despite the Crown's vigorous attempts to tightly control the Caribbean trade, it fought an unsuccessful battle. Even though Seville's Casa de Contratación served as the official clearing house for the administration of the pearl trade with the Indies, where shipments to merchants, individuals and the royal *quinto* needed to be registered, pearls easily escaped centralized attempts to channel them into the imperial House of Trade (Warsh, 2009: 26).

Historical accounts estimated that over half of the total pearls harvested were never declared. Vast volumes were used at source as currency (Romero *et al.*, 1999: 67-8), even to purchase slaves delivered to the fisheries. Many Spaniards avoided the peninsular markets by offloading their wares in the smuggler-friendly Atlantic islands (Warsh, 2009: 31, 82). The complex web of exchange models through which the Pearl Coast products reached Seville, and increasingly Lisbon, Venice, London and Amsterdam, demands the question of whether 6,639 pearls were being transported on the Tortugas shipwreck through official trade or as contraband?

The size of the Tortugas pearl shipment is considerable, and despite the close proximity of the *almiranta, capitana* and its officials within the 1622 fleet cargos could not be guaranteed to be contraband free. Bearing in mind Charles V's former prohibition of pearl drilling in 1532 to curtail the production of pearl jewelry on the islands (Warsh, 2009: 29), and the fact that a considerable 636 pearls on the Tortugas ship are drilled (Fig. 43), the specter of contraband cannot be excluded. Their interpretation as smuggled goods is perhaps favored in light of the discovery of a lead box containing 16,184 pearls on the wreck of the *Margarita*, which were categorically not listed on the ship's manifest (Tedesco, 2010a: 21), as would have been compulsory for material subjected to the royal *quinto*.

The Tortugas shipwreck's pearl cargo – the first to be scientifically excavated – is both rare and symbolic of the final decades of an ill-managed colonial industry. Apart from thousands of pearls recovered off Bermuda from the *San Pedro* of 1596 (Marken, 1994: 21-2), from the *Margarita* of 1622, the *Nuestra Señora de Guadalupe* and the *Conde de Tolosa* lost in 1724, no comparable consignments have been identified underwater.

The Tortugas pearls reflect the end of the line – one of history's earliest examples of hyper-exploitation resulting in the depletion of species, changes in ecosystem structure, displacement and extermination of local human populations and their culture. Before the establishment of the silver mines at Potosi in Peru in 1545 and Zacatecas in Mexico in 1547, pearl exports from the American continent exceeded the value of all other exports combined. The depletion of the oyster beds along the Pearl Coast is considered to be the first documented case of unsustainable natural resource depletion by Europeans in the American continent (Romero *et al.*, 1999: 70-1). These massive harvest overkills caused irreparable damage to societies and species, from which the Caribbean pearl fisheries never fully recovered (Warsh, 2009: 22, 45).

8. Trade Beads & Buttons

A total of 258 intact and fragmentary beads manufactured from glass, stone, clay, wood, palm nut and bone/ivory were recovered from the Tortugas shipwreck (around 34% glass, 17% cut crystal, 14% ceramic, 35% organic; Figs. 44-46). The majority of the glass beads are monochrome faceted examples used by European colonists as gifts and for bartering amongst the indigenous peoples of the New World. While 16th and 17th-century Spain largely used beads in rosaries and not as accessories, they rigorously exploited the indigenous cultures' perceived value of these wares (Francis, 2009a: 8).

Beads were already deemed essential for gifts and exchange when Columbus arrived in the Caribbean in

1492, and continued to serve an important role throughout the conquest and settlement of the New World (Smith, 1983: 147; Francis, 2009e: 86). A strong bead-making tradition pre-existed before Spain's arrival, especially in Mesoamerica, the Andes, and amongst the Native Americans of North America. Spain, however, substituted indigenous production with a continuous flow of relatively cheap glass beads, assuming total control over sourcing and imports.

A. Glass & Ceramic Beads & Buttons

The glass trade beads (Fig. 44) include eight white, blue and red faceted and ground Chevron beads of both five and seven-layer glass in three different sizes (maximum L. 2.5cm, W. 1.2cm; Kidd IIIm and IIIm1: bead typology is as defined by Kidd and Kidd, 1970). These drawn beads of compound construction consist of multi-layered glass, which present an appealing star pattern when viewed from each end (Deagan, 1987: 164). 'Faceted' Chevrons are common amongst the earliest New World assemblages, yet prevail into the 1620s and originate in Venice and Holland (Francis, 2009c: 74).

Most abundant amongst the Tortugas glass bead assemblage are 45 monochrome faceted Venetian glass beads, barrel or spherical in shape (Kidd If; Diam. 0.3cm, L. 0.2-0.3cm, holes Diam. maximum 0.1cm). The majority are translucent cobalt blue, while others range from turquoise to light brown, amber and deep red. Most exhibit three to five randomly spaced facets, while two red beads feature 13 and 17 facets. The red color, in particular, is quite unusual and was highly desired (Frantis, 2009d: 82; pers. comm. Marvin Smith, 7 December 2011). A dark navy blue spherical bead with three irregularly placed facets (Kidd If) retains a small fragment of its original metal stringing wire within the central bore.

Referred to today as 'charlottes', these products are considered to have been the most expensive class of small faceted beads, which could be threaded onto necklaces but were often used in embroidery (Smith *et al.*, 1994: 39; Francis, 2009b: 63). The Tortugas examples, however, appear too large for the latter purpose (pers. comm. Marvin Smith, 28 February 2012). By 1630 Spain had seemingly stopped importing charlottes, possibly due to their relatively high cost or simply because they had gone out of fashion (pers. comm. Marvin Smith, 23 August, 2012). The Tortugas examples are thus significant exemplars dated towards the end of the period of production.

The bead assemblage includes one half of a translucent turquoise blue-bodied spherical eye bead (TOR-90-01142-GL, L. 0.7cm, Diam. 0.5cm), with a 1.5mm-wide longitudinal white stripe running parallel to the bore and a small red and white dot in the middle (similar to Kidd IIh1). The color is typical of Ichtuknee Plain beads, distinguished by bubbles termed longitudinal 'spun sugar striations' (Pendleton *et al.*, 2009: 42). The Tortugas example appears representative of the Class I, Series A, Sunburst Variety 2 (Smith, 1982: 123-24). Classifiable as an '*a speo*' finished complex bead ('by the spit' as opposed to on an iron pan: Pendleton *et al.*, 2009: 42), such wares were produced by the Paternostri Venetian beadmaker's guild.

An additional spherical-shaped opaque turquoise blue/green bead (Kidd IIa40) with a 'striated' or 'spun sugar' appearance is represented within the Tortugas assemblage (TOR-90-00348-GL, W. 0.3cm, L. 0.2cm, hole Diam. 0.1cm). Finished by the '*a speo*' method, these products are again Venetian Paternostri beads, although manufacture in France by Italian glassworkers has also been proposed (Francis, 2009c: 75, 78).

The smallest beads in the glass assemblage are tiny ring-shaped seed beads also known as 'rocailles', which range in color from turquoise blue (Kidd IIa41) to a darker cobalt blue (Kidd IIa56; Diam. 0.1cm, L. 0.1cm, hole Diam. 0.05cm). Seed bead refers to small examples typically produced of drawn glass finished by tumbling (stirring the

cut segments over heat, *a ferarazza*: Pendleton *et al.* 2009: 53) that were frequently used in beadwork. Whether these beads were shipped in bulk or strung before shipping is unclear, although the latter would have held the advantage of making these beads easier to handle and divide.

The collection includes 40 intact and seven fragmentary clear quartz cut crystal beads (mainly Diam. 1.3cm, Th. 0.9cm, hole Diam. 0.1cm), similar to examples originally referred to as 'Florida Cut Crystal' (as defined by Goggin and later by Fairbanks, 1968: 13-16), based on examples recovered from 16th-century Native American sites in Florida (Deagan, 1987: 180-1; Francis, 2009g: 117). The examples display between 24 and 40 facets ground into their surface.

Faceted cut crystal beads were largely produced from the end of the 13th century in the major cutting centers of Venice and Paris. However, it has been suggested that poorer quality examples, including those recovered from the *Atocha* and *Margarita*, originated in Spain (Francis, 2009g: 118). Castille has recently been proposed as the source of cut crystal beads excavated on St. Catherines Island, Georgia (Thomas, 2011: x), and could perhaps be the source of the Tortugas examples.

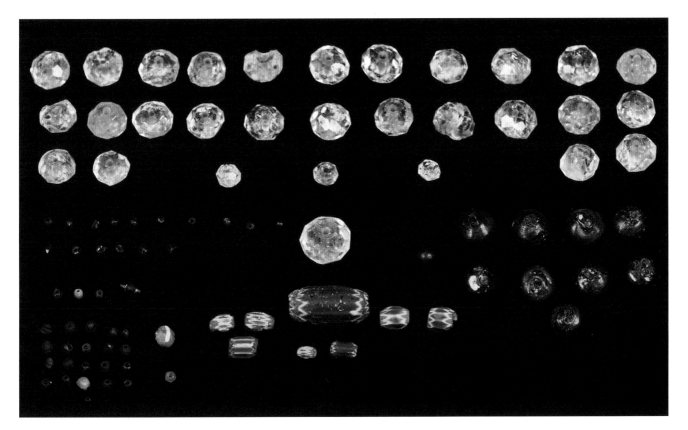

Fig. 44. Mineral beads: cut crystal (back three rows and center); glass beads: amber, light brown, deep red, cobalt, navy and turquoise blue faceted examples ('charlottes'), opaque turquoise blue/green bead, turquoise half of an 'eye' bead; blue seed beads (middle left and lower left); five and seven-layer Chevrons (center); black bead; and black glass buttons (right).

*Fig. 45. Cylindrical, barrel-shaped and conical ceramic
beads with an incised lattice design (Diams. 0.8-1.2cm).*

A single mineral bead (FS 90-1A-000680.57, Diam.
1.0cm, L. 0.9cm), believed to be carnelian or agate, features an equatorial edge cut in two rows of six unevenly
sized and smoothed facets to form a total of 12 surfaces.
For millennia this rock form was mined along the Narmada
River in central India and cut locally at lapidary centers
such as Limudra. Cambay (modern Khambhat in western
India) earned a reputation as a major bead-making center by at least 1630 and probably several decades earlier
(Francis, 2009g: 119). Certainly carnelian and agate beads
were already reaching Spain in Portuguese hulls by the early
16th century and were a form of exotica that Columbus
transported to the New World on his first journey (Deagan,
1987: 182).

The Tortugas wreck also contained 40 ceramic beads,
half of which are undecorated, cylindrical, badly eroded and
porous (Fig. 45). The other 20 barrel-shaped and conical
examples are decorated with an incised lattice design across
the body and incised double or single lines encircling the
ends (Diam. 0.8-1.2cm, L. 0.7-0.8cm, hole Diam. 0.1cm).
At least three beads exhibit tiny flecks of gold on their surfaces, perhaps remains of original gold leaf veneer. Such
beads are generally identified as European trade products
(pers. comm. Richard Patterson, 2 March 2012), which are
poorly documented within Spanish-contact North American assemblages, suggesting limited use in the New World.

In addition to beads, glass buttons were popular colonial
trade products amongst the New World Indians (Bradley,
1987: 158). Examples were frequently used less as garment
fasteners than as clothes' ornamentation (Koch, 1977: 73).
The Tortugas assemblage includes nine small opaque black
buttons (Diam. 1.2cm) with two small holes for iron wire

eye attachment. Glass buttons were uncommon items in
Spanish commerce, and are largely intimately associated
with Dutch merchant trade with the Native Americans of
North America.

B. Organic Beads

The 26 intact and 12 fragmentary carved wood beads of
undetermined species from the Tortugas wreck (Fig. 46) are
largely of simple spherical design (W. 0.9-1.2cm, L. 0.9-
1.2cm, hole Diam. 0.2-0.3cm). Larger spherical examples
with a hollow interior (five intact and 15 fragments) appear
to have been produced from a palm nut (W. 0.9-1.2cm, L.
0.9-1.2cm, hole Diam. 0.2-0.3cm).

Several beads are more intricately carved barrel and
conical examples with rows of raised ribbing at both ends
(Diam. 1.5cm, L. 1.7cm, hole Diam. 0.2cm). Similar
examples strung on a rosary with a gold medallion recovered from the *Atocha* have been identified as ebony (*Atocha*
database inv. A86.1127).

The Tortugas assemblage includes 27 largely intact
and eight fragments of undecorated small spherical beads,
which bear some resemblance to ivory, bone or possibly
a seed product (Diam. 0.8cm, H. 0.7cm, hole Diam. 0.2
cm). These round beads are mainly brown with cream-col-
ored eroded patches, and are again comparable to examples
from the *Atocha*, which are thought to be ivory or bone
rosary beads (Malcolm, 1993: 7). The smallest organic
bead examples recovered from the Tortugas wreck (Diam.
0.4cm, L. 0.3cm, hole Diam. 0.1cm) resemble examples
produced from seeds.

Some of the Tortugas wreck's organic beads produced
from palm nuts appear similar to those described by John
Esquemeling in his *Buccaneers of America* of 1684. Citing
the various palm species on the island of Hispaniola, he
referred to the "Palma a Chapelet" (rosary-palm), whose
hard, small seed was "very fit for making rosaries or beads
to say prayers upon" (Esquemeling, 1684: 36). A total of
261 whole or fragmentary palm seeds, some seemingly
bored, were recovered from the Tortugas wreck (see section
14); their function aboard ship is difficult to determine
unless they were raw material intended for future rosary
bead production in Spain.

C. Distribution & Function

The significant assemblage of beads and buttons on the Tortugas ship may be interpreted largely as residual cheap trade
goods cargo intended for bartering or gift giving to grease
the wheels of commerce amongst the native populations of
South America. Given the presence of pearls on the vessel
and its plausible identification as the *Buen Jesús y Nuestra
Señora del Rosario*, which sailed to Cumana, the beads were

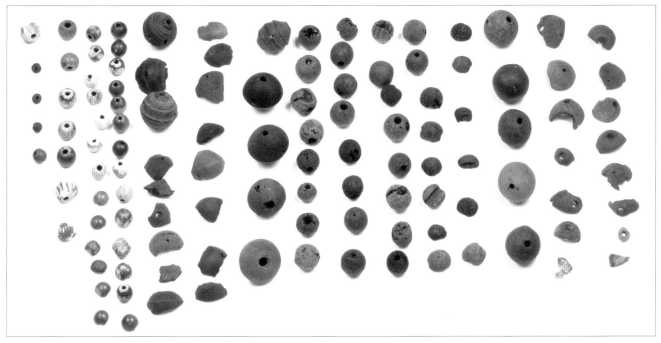

Fig. 46. Organic beads (left to right): smallest beads in the assemblage, possibly produced from seeds (column 1); carved spherical wood and bone (or possibly ivory) beads (columns 2-4); incised beads of unknown organic material (columns 1 and 2); ribbed barrel and conical-shaped wooden (ebony) rosary beads (column 5 and 7); carved ebony beads, possibly from/for an abacus (column 7); wood and palm nut beads (and bead fragments), the larger examples likely intended as rosary beads (columns 8-15).

probably at least partly intended for use along the east and west coast of Venezuela. The palm nut and possible ivory or bone beads are exceptions seemingly under export to Spain for rosary production, although some may have originated from crew or passengers' personal rosaries.

Few comparative assemblages have been published from South America. The geography and character of exploitation are best assessed through collections excavated west of Venezuela. The Tortugas bead repertoire is strongly represented amongst Spanish and Spanish-influenced sites. Chevron beads were common on Spanish colonial sites in the Americas between the early 16th century and the early 17th century, and were especially popular in Mexico and Peru (Smith and Good, 1982: 7-8; Deagan, 1987: 165; Mitchen and Leader, 1988: 44, 47). Examples reached the Franciscan mission site at Tipu in western Belize, which was occupied from the 1540s into the early 17th century (Smith *et al.*, 1994: 31, 36). A dozen early Chevron beads have been recovered from the Governor Martin site in Tallahassee, Florida, a native Apalachee settlement (Anhaica) occupied in 1539-40 by Hernando De Soto and his army (Ewen and Hann, 1998: 15-16, 85, 98). Chevrons also circulated beyond the sphere of Spanish colonial influence, such as 96 examples from 17th-century English Jamestown in Virginia (Lapham, 2001: 6; pers. comm. Beverly Straube, 11 September 2012).

Charlottes are one of the largest bead groups recovered from Tipu in Belize (mid-16th to early 17th-century), where faceted examples constitute 16.2% of the assemblage (Smith *et al.*, 1984: 38-9; Francis, 2009b: 63). Examples in turquoise, blue and red have been found at Spanish Nombre Di Dios, one of the first European settlements on the Panama Isthmus occupied from 1510-96 (pers. comm. Richard Patterson, 1 March 2012). The type is represented in the 16th-17th century Spanish Mission of Santa Catalina de Guale on St. Catherines Island, Georgia, predominantly within the cemetery, where one Native American burial contained over 900 faceted cobalt blue beads (Blair, 2009: 160-1).

Given the distinctive qualities of crystal beads, they are not thought to have functioned significantly within the mainstream New World trade orbit (Fairbanks, 1968: 14-15; Deagan, 1987: 180-1). The Tortugas wreck examples are thus seemingly of higher status than the rest of the ship's bead assemblage, a point highlighted by the personal belongings of Queen Isabella, the wife of Philip II (r. 1554-98), who owned earrings adorned with prized rock crystal and a girdle decorated with 32 crystals (Deagan, 1987: 180; Francis, 2009g: 118).

Just half a dozen cut crystal examples amongst the 69,000 glass trade beads were excavated from the Franciscan Mission of Santa Catalina de Guale on St. Catherines

Island in Georgia (Pendleton *et al.*, 2009: 50; Thomas, 2011: vii, x), which served as the northernmost Spanish settlement along the Eastern seaboard for a century until 1680. This pattern reflects the comparative rarity of these products. Cut crystal beads and pendants, however, were common in the Mission San Luis de Talimali in modern Tallahassee, capital of the missions in western Florida and home to the largest Christianized Apalachee population in America *c.* 1656-1704 (McEwan and Poe, 1994: 90; pers. comm. Marvin Smith, 1 December 2011), where a significant deposit was located within with the Chief's house, the site's sole Apalachee structure.

Southeastern Indians believed that crystal possessed unique mystical properties and examples have been discovered amongst shamans' belongings.[2] Further west, cut crystal beads reached the large Cherokee mound centers of the Upper Little Tennessee River in the 16th century, where the early Spanish explorers Hernando de Soto (1540) and Juan Pardo (1567) first made European contact (Badger and Clayton, 1985: 114). These beads are thought to have functioned as exotic Spanish gifts to the Indians (Deagan, 1987: 181). Crystal beads also occur on shipwrecks dated between 1550 and 1625, including the *Margarita* (Deagan, 1987: 180; Francis, 2009g: 118; pers. comm. Corey Malcom, 4 November 2011).

The glass buttons are an anomaly within the pattern of Spanish control and exploitation of European beads in the Americas. The Dutch seem to have dominated the trade in these wares, exchanging them as gifts with Indian tribes since the late 16th century. They occur in the Northeast on Dutch-contact sites occupied by the Onondaga Iroquois (Bradley, 1987: 158; pers. comm. Marvin Smith, 19 December 2011), and are associated with Dutch colonial trade objects in western New York State on Seneca sites of the first half of the 17th century (Baart, 1987: 6). Few wire eye buttons have been recovered in 16th and 17th-century Spanish contexts and none from pre-1550 Florida or the Caribbean (Deagan, 2002: 161-2). Their rarity opens up the possibility that they served as fastenings for clothing belonging to a passenger onboard the Tortugas ship.

In summary, multivariate statuses and to some degree functions may be proposed for the Tortugas wreck's beads. The majority are recognizable from Spanish-contact sites and were seemingly being transported for trade, barter and gift giving along at least the coast of Venezuela (Chevrons, charlottes, turquoise, eye, striated and seed beads: 23% of the total assemblage). Alongside these, Venetian and French wares are more rare products of greater social hierarchical value, including cut crystal beads possibly manufactured in Spain (18.5% of the beads), a carnelian or agate bead from central India (<0.5%), and evidence of gilt-covered

ceramic wares (16%). The ivory or bone beads (10%) and some palm nut products (16%) may have originated from the crew and passengers' rosaries. Finally, the glass buttons (3.5% of the bead assemblage) closely resemble Dutch commodities and may have been dress-related rather than commercial cargo.

9. Navigational Equipment

A. Anchors

Limited navigational equipment was identified during the Tortugas shipwreck excavation, the largest of which were the site's three iron anchors (excluding a fourth large example snagged by a steel cable dragged between two shrimp boats during a prior salvage attempt in 1972: Marx, 2009: 57). Anchor A1 lies to the southeast of the site (coordinates 72.6/16.8, L. 2.5m, arm W. 1.3m; Figs. 47-48) and thus remains close to the bows, where it was presumably catted unused on the ship's port flank at the time of sinking. Its arms are rounded, albeit slightly angular, and terminate with well-defined palms, which occupy half the arm's length. The shank is oriented on a 18° axis with the arms facing north. Solidly adhering to the anchor's heavily concreted surfaces and clustered around them were eight intact olive jars on the southern side of the anchor shank as well as a wooden plank just below the sand displaying a nail hole and diagonal scarf.

One intact *botija* and fragments of at least three more jars were uncovered in shallow mud in front of the intact anchor arms alongside a one-handle half-dipped jug (TOR-90-00016-CS). A1's arms literally rest on top of an olive jar rim. A gold bar was discovered next to the anchor during the site metal detector survey (coordinates 73.01/15.56). A further extensive linear concretion underlying and perpendicular to A1's lower shank extending westwards is a third anchor on the site, A2 (and thus a fourth in total from the wreck).

Anchor A3, by contrast, lies amongst loose mud sediments with its arms and lower shank on a 14° southwest/northeast axis at the northeastern, stern flank of the site and seems to be out of context, perhaps having been displaced from the bows by bottom trawler impacts (coordinates 79.3/33.3; Figs. 49-50). Although broken at its midpoint, the shank is 2.30m long and has a maximum concreted thickness of about 13cm. The east-facing palms are broken off. One intact and two broken olive jars lay to the sides of the arms, while a Blue-on-White Talavera-style dish was located between the eastern arm and shank juncture. The ring (L. 37.5cm) survives at the end of the shank. The broken arms (current L. 67cm) were evidently originally curved rather than v-shaped.

Figs. 47-48. Anchor A1 at the southeast flank of the site contextualized with Type 1 olive jars.

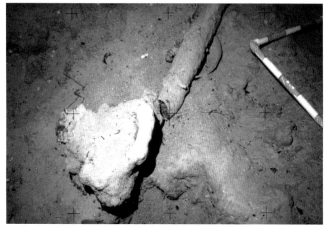

Figs. 49-50. Anchor A3 at the northeast flank of the site.

Ten comparable iron anchors were recovered from the *Atocha* and *Margarita*, whose construction contracts listed six anchors for each ship (Mathewson, 1986: 38-9). Many feature arms that are v-shaped and with a diagnostic stepped anatomy that are dissimilar to Tortugas anchor A1 (bearing in mind the presence of thick concretion on the latter, which was not recovered for study). However, the *Margarita*'s kedge anchor (L. 1.65m, ring Diam. 0.22m, arm L. 0.52m, palm L. 0.27m), whose crown bore the date of 1618 and a foundry mark, was distinctly rounded like A1. One published v-shaped *Atocha/Margarita* anchor (inv. 52898, L. 2.02m, arm L. 0.85m, palm L. 0.45m) features a round section for the stock and square section for the arms; the palm is triangular.[3]

Tortugas anchor A1 seems to be transitional between these stepped/v-shaped and rounded examples. In all *Atocha, Margarita* and Tortugas anchors related to the 1622 fleet the flukes occupy just over 50% of the total arm length. As in the case of a *Margarita* stream anchor still associated with its wooden stock, identified as rosewood, palm and *lapacho* (Mathewson, 1986: 38-9), and a white oak stock from the 1554 Padre Island Spanish fleet (Barto

Arnold and Weddle, 1978: 230), the Tortugas anchors would have been equipped with wooden stocks.

The interpretation of a concretion with 24cm-long links (inv. 52899) associated with a *Margarita* anchor as anchor chain is not confirmed at Tortugas or by contemporary shipwrecks worldwide. Instead, rope cable retained its traditional function. Double chains encrusted onto the crown and arms of a large iron anchor from the 1554 Spanish fleet lost off Padre Island, Texas, were probably intended to hold the main stay or other major rigging in place. Rope was found wrapped around its crown (Barto Arnold and Weddle, 1978: 322). The Emanuel Point I wreck's rope was made from hemp or *Canabis sativa* and was probably supplied from the Iberian region of Navarre (Burns, 1998: 78). A 6-7m length of 0.13m diameter hemp cable (four main strands laid left-handed along a heart rope) found on the wreck of the Spanish Armada transport *La Trinidad Valencera*, lost off Donegal, Ireland, in 1588, as well as a short length of similar cable wrapped around the shank of the southern anchor (Martin, 1979b: 32), confirm the traditional use of cable on Spanish vessels of the period.

Comparisons between the above Spanish anchors of 1622 with the 1544 Padre Island fleet suggests an evolution in design from examples with v-shaped arms towards open rounded arms by the second quarter of the 17th century. The seven anchors recovered from the 1544 fleet wrecked off Texas display v-shaped arms with average angles of 57.4° (Barto Arnold and Weddle, 1978: 229), which essentially fits the general proposition that before *c.* 1550 the angle between the fluke, crown and shank tended to be around 45° and around 60° after that date (Tinniswood, 1945: 85). The 3.15m-long Emanuel Point I Spanish wreck of 1559 retains an identical v-shaped morphology of approximately 65° with arm lengths of 1.25m and fluke lengths of 0.60m (Burns, 1998: 72-5).

Despite the opening up of the arm angle on two wrought-iron anchors from the Spanish Armada transport *La Trinidad Valencera* (L. 4.57m and 4.80m, total arm W. 2.44m and 2.74m), which closely mirrors those from the *Santa Maria de la Rosa* from the same 1588 Armada, its arm angle remains distinctly more v-shaped than Tortugas A1. Another example associated with the *Gran Grifon* measured 4.15m in length, while three examples salvaged from the *San Juan de Sicilia* off Tobermory, Mull, measured 5.48m, 4.57m, and 3.05m in length (Martin, 1979b: 31). With its very lightly rounded arms that display angular tendencies with long palms taking up almost half the length of the arms, the Tortugas A1 anchor is similar to the *Vasa*'s port bower anchor (Cederlund, 2006: 467).

Unlike the far larger *Atocha* and *Margarita* galleons equipped with six anchors, the Tortugas ship almost certainly carried four main examples, as registered for the *Santa María de Yciar* of 1554 and counseled in 1575 by Escalante de Mendoza (one sheet and three bowers, each weighing 10 *quintales* or about 460 kgf) (Barto Arnold and Weddle, 1978: 224; Castro *et al.*, 2010: 21). Four were specified for the *Buen Jesús y Nuestra Señora del Rosario* of 1622 (*Contratación* 1172, N.2, R.1), which is believed to equate to the Tortugas wreck. At 2.3m and 2.5m in length the Tortugas anchors are notably shorter than all of the 1554 and 1588 anchors listed above, although closer to the size of the *Margarita*'s kedge anchor and another of 2.02m. A1 and A2 evidently were not bowers and most likely functioned as kedge or stream breaking mechanisms.

B. Astrolabes

Surprisingly for the modest size of the Tortugas ship, two bronze astrolabes recovered in the stern half of the ship near the pump well (coordinates 78.6/27.0) and a third from the southern extremity of the site (coordinates 76.9/1.3) were available to its captain (Figs. 51-54). The forerunner to the sextant, the astrolabe was widely utilized in the 16th and 17th centuries as a navigational device to measure the angle of a celestial body in the sky and hence to determine latitude in conjunction with declination charts and tables. The device was developed for shipboard use by the Portuguese in the mid-15th century (Brigadier, 2002: 30). With solar tables and an accurate instrument with which to measure the height of the sun at meridian passage, latitude could be computed without reliance on viewing the Pole Star.

The earliest recorded use of a sea astrolabe was by the Portuguese Diogo d'Azambuja in 1481 on a voyage down the west coast of Africa. Early astrolabes were large wooden instruments (Vasco de Gama's measured 0.61m diameter) suspended from a frame. Smaller brass instruments replaced the earlier wooden variety in the 16th century to become essential parts of navigational assemblages. A 1635 directive (Phillips, 1986: 130) required that:

> "each pilot was to carry with him four compass needles, fixed and well conditioned with the lodestone; six hourglasses (ampolletas), each of one half hour; a sailing chart for the voyage, marked with compass points; an astrolabe weighting over ten pounds; a forestaff with three scales marked for the sun and stars; 150 brazas (825 feet) of sounding line, fine and thin and well-tarred; and three lead weights (escandallos) of six, ten, and fifteen pounds each."

Suspended by a ring from the thumb, the instrument was held at arm's length and the center alidade rotated so that the sun or specific star could be sighted through a hole in the vertical plates. The altitude of the object was read by noting the number to which the alidade pointed on a scale

Fig. 51. Bronze astrolabe TOR-90-00007-CU (Diam. 18.6cm, 3.08kg).

Figs. 52-53. Bronze astrolabe TOR-90-00006-CU (Diam. 18.5cm, 3.1kg) with the armillary sphere of the Armazéns Reais royal warehouse incised onto the front face, the official symbol of the administration of King Dom Manuel I of Portugal 1495-1521.

Fig. 54. Bronze astrolabe
TOR-90-00008-CU (Diam. 17.3cm, 2.54kg).

of degrees engraved around the perimeter of the device. A book of tables was consulted to interpret the reading and to estimate latitude. Astrolabes went out of use after the mid-17th century, and finds of subsequent date are rare. Some 65 examples are listed in Simpson's *The Mariner's Astrolabe* (1987), but the updated total currently stands at 81 (Garcia, 2008: 249-50). A catalogue of the three Tortugas shipwreck astrolabes is presented below and derives heavily from the published work of Gustavo Adolfo Garcia (2005: 75-82; 2008: 263-5), who personally examined and recorded the Tortugas examples as part of his doctoral research:

• TOR-90-00007-CU (Fig. 51): the best preserved astrolabe from the Tortugas shipwreck (Diam. 18.6cm, top Th. 2.3cm, bottom Th. 2.4cm, weight 3.08kg). A typical example of a Type Ia Iberian astrolabe manufactured during the first half of the 17th century.[4] A substantial section of the alidade, 14.8cm long, remains secured in position by remains of the axis pin. Parts of the sighting vanes also survive, although they are broken beneath the observation pinholes. The suspension ring is absent. No scales of limb or other marks are distinguishable due to extensive surface erosion.

• TOR-90-00006-CU (Figs. 52-53): a Type 1a instrument and the most remarkable astrolabe in the collection (maximum Diam. 18.5cm, minimum Diam. 17.1cm, maximum Th. 2.6cm, 3.126kg). An unusual feature of this instrument is an exceptionally clear image of an armillary sphere set on the front face of the bottom ballast. Only one other archaeologically attested astrolabe dated to 1593 and recovered off

Cuba shares this attribute. The armillary sphere was the official symbol of the administration of Dom Manuel I, king of Portugal from 1495 to 1521. Hence, it is theorized that this mark may have been stamped on instruments coming from the Armazéns Reais, the Portuguese royal warehouse. The suspension ring of the Tortugas astrolabe is absent, but a section of the alidade survives. The instrument's diameter is more typical of Iberian astrolabes of this period.

• TOR-90-00008-CU (Fig. 54): the cast brass wheel of a Type 1a astrolabe (Diam. 17.3cm, top Th. 2.1cm, bottom Th. 2.3cm, approx. 2.54kg), fairly well preserved. Parts of the axis pin are present and the brass alidade was recovered separately. Other than the pin the suspension ring is similarly absent. As with its two counterparts this astrolabe is a typical Iberian instrument dating to the first half of the 17th century. Most of the original surface is eroded, but the upper spoke exhibits pairs of thin parallel lines on the lower quadrant typical of similar examples.

While the site of the *Margarita* yielded one astrolabe, five comparable examples were recovered from the wreck of the *Atocha* (Malcom, 1998b), one of which derives from the same manufacturer as one of the three examples used on the *Nossa Senhora dos Mártires* sunk down the River Tagus in 1606 (Brigadier, 2002: 43-7). A comparable cast example inscribed with the date '1616' was recovered from the Rincón wreck. Similarly dated and designed astrolabes found on shipwrecks dated from 1555/6 to 1645 and located off Cuba, Manila, Malaysia, Cape Verde, Florida Keys (America), Canada and Portugal have been catalogued (Garcia, 2005: 35, 45-95). The Dutch East Indiaman *Batavia*, lost off Western Australia in 1629 (Green, 1989: 84-9), carried four astrolabes. Despite its small size and status, the Tortugas *navio* was thus surprisingly well stocked with this sophisticated class of navigation equipment.

C. Ship's Bell

A bronze bell (TOR-90-00010-CU, H. 27.2cm, maximum Diam. 21.8cm, H. of canon ring 7.2cm, W. of cannon ring 9.3cm, Th. of canon ring 1.6cm, 4.1kg; Figs. 55-56) was the first artifact recovered from the Tortugas wreck site. The bell was found with a gaping hole on one side, without its clapper and is heavily patinated and degraded greenish blue with copper chloride corrosion products. No decorative symbols or inscriptions are visible, just three ridges set three-quarters down the body. The shoulder is surmounted by a single suspension canon ring subdivided into three sub-triangular spaces suitable for lifting with a single hand. One side of the bell is extensively broken and missing.

Figs. 55-56. Bronze bell (H. 27.2cm, TOR-90-00010-CU).

Ship's bells were utilized mainly to identify the passage of time during the day, marking the half hours, changes of watch and time for prayers and dinner. The sounding of the bell also warned of danger, fire, fog or an enemy ship (Wede, 1972: 4; cf. Cunningham Dobson, 2011: 89-90). The Tortugas bell would almost certainly have been the last sound that rang out wildly as the ship sank in the hurricane of 5 September 1622.

The basic shape of the Tortugas bell mirrors an example recovered from the wreck of the *Concepción* (Hispaniola, 1641) with its gently tapered bottom, again featuring a series of narrow ridges three-quarters down. This example, however, has a traditional single vertical canon without a tripartite division (Borrell, 1983: 106). An identical canon form, however, occurs on the bell from the 16th-century Spanish-operated Western Ledge wreck off Bermuda (Watts, 1993: 118), while a 35.5cm-high silver example from the *Atocha* is identical in all respects other than metal medium, and may have been an unusual ruse to ship contraband.[5] The same tripartite canon is paralleled by a bronze bell from the 1715 fleet (Wagner, 1967: 96). The canon shape with the tripartite apertures prevailed in use over centuries and was still utilized on the bell from *L'Astrolabe* wrecked off the Solomon Islands as late as 1788 (Wede, 1972: 58-9).

Fig. 57. Lead coastal sounding weight (L. 17.9cm, 2.9kg, TOR-90-00022-LD).

D. Sounding Lead

A single mildly triangular sounding lead (TOR-90-00022-LD, L. 17.9cm, base W. 5.6cm, rope hole Diam. 5.6cm, base recess Diam. 2.4cm, base recess H. 0.4cm, 2.9kg; Fig. 57) was recovered from coordinates 73.22/25.25 east of midship. The basic elongated shape remained highly conservative throughout the 16th and 17th centuries. Sounding leads generally either incorporated a mild triangular shape with outward angled sides and rounded summits pierced by a single hole, as with the Tortugas artifact, or had near-parallel sides with flattened summits (sometimes with multi-chamfered edges).

This generic style of equipment was relied on to determine the depth of water between the keel and seabed. Those with an arming hole recessed into the base, as on the Tortugas example, could be used not just to measure water depths, but to ascertain sediment compositions. The earliest sounding lead was first illustrated in Lucas Janszoon Wagenaer's _Spieghel der Zeevaerdt_ (1584), although the basic shape, largely unchanged, was widely exploited across the Mediterranean Sea by the Roman period (Oleson, 2008). Leads varied extensively in weight according to the depths in which use was intended. Deep-water examples set at the end of a 200 fathom-long line (360m) weighed over 14 pounds or 6.36kg. Coastal leads for sounding depths up to 20 fathoms (36m) typically weighed 7-14 pounds or 3.18-6.36kg (Swanick, 2005: 98-9). At 2.9kg the Tortugas sounding lead is distinctively a lightweight coastal device.

The Tortugas version was already in use, albeit with chamfered sides (H. 23cm), on the early 16th-century Molasses wreck off the Turks and Caicos Islands (Keith _et al._, 1984: 56, fig. 12). The form is again represented amongst the suite of eight both cylindrical and triangular examples of 2.55-7.2kg on the wreck of the VOC _Batavia_, sunk off Western Australia in 1629 (Green, 1989: 94).

Notably, two examples from the _Atocha_ or _Margarita_ that also feature a tallow recess in the base (inv. M83 912 and M 2821) are far more paralleled-sided than the Tortugas sounding lead. Another cylindrical 6.4kg example has been excavated from the Portuguese-owned 'Wanli' ship lost off Malaysia _c._ 1625 (Sjostrand and Idrus, 2007: 41), while a 6.55kg example associated with the VOC _Lastdrager_ off Yell, Scotland, in 1653, is again notably parallel-sided (Sténuit, 1974: 231-2). The three deep-sea leads associated with the _Vergulde Draeck_ of 1656 are all cylindrical (Green, 1977: 290). Yet another parallel-sided example is a 5.3kg sounding lead from _La Belle_ of 1686 (L. 33.1cm, 5.3kg). A cylindrical version is associated with the wreck of the 38-gun Royal Navy ship _Dragon_, lost off the Casquets, Channel Isles, in 1712 (Bound and Gosset, 1998: 154,

fig. 6). However, two triangular sounding leads with chamfered edges from the 1715 Spanish fleet off Florida (Clausen, 1965: pl. 1d) suggest that shape cannot be judged an obvious index of chronology or conditioned by suitability for depth.

10. Tortoise Shell

A collection of 64 pieces of cut tortoise shell recorded on the Tortugas site (the thin, epidermal plates that overlie the bones of the shell of the hawksbill turtle, _Eretmochelys imbricata_) possibly reflects a formerly unreported aspect of 17th-century Spanish shipboard life. Alongside one intact and two broken lice combs, plus two excavated cases, the majority of the assemblage comprises partly worked shell and apparent processing waste (Figs. 58-59). The combined data indicate that lice combs may have been crafted on the ship during its final homeward voyage.

The intact comb (TOR-90-00025-OC, L. 12.3cm, W. 5.7cm, Th. 0.3cm, teeth L. and Th. Side A 2.1cm and 0.1cm, teeth L. and Th. Side B 2.2cm and 0.2cm), missing just one of its large teeth, incorporates two rows of teeth on opposite sides, one finer and one coarser. The rectangular case is carved from a single piece of mottled brown, amber and golden yellow tortoise shell (TOR-90-00024-OC, L. 12.2cm, W. 7.2cm, Th. 0.3cm). A geometric incised decoration on both sides of the case consists of parallel lines forming a rectangle. From each right angle of the rectangle an incised line extends outward and intersects with another incised line, which then frames the case, forming an exterior rectangle. The case exhibits surface crackling. Drilled holes are present at each end.

The material used in the shipwreck's combs and the raw unused scutes has been visually identified as tortoiseshell (pers. comm. Anne Meylan, 15 February 2012) and subsequently confirmed by DNA analysis (pers. comm. Brian Shamblin, 6 April 2012). The hawksbill has been historically highly valued for the horn-like scales or plates (scutes) covering its bony shell (Goode, 1884: 149; Witzell, 1983: ii). Although greatly diminished in numbers through overexploitation (Spotila, 2004: 114-5), the Atlantic species of the hawksbill turtle, _Eretmochelys imbricata_, inhabits a large region spanning the southern coast of Florida and the states bordering the Gulf of Mexico, extending southward into the West Indies, northeastward to Bermuda and as far south as Guiana and Brazil (Aspinall, 1912: 141). Smaller than the loggerhead or green turtle, a mature hawksbill normally weighing up to 54kg may produce 1.3-1.8kg of tortoise shell (Parsons, 1972: 44).

A symbol of luxury since time immemorial in many cultures, European treasure ships returning from the New World were commonly laden with tortoise shell (Witzell,

Fig. 58. Unworked Hawksbill sea turtle shell and partly worked shell comb cases, processing waste and two fragmentary combs, possible evidence of at least comb case craftsmanship on the Tortugas ship during its homeward-bound voyage.

Fig. 59. Lice combs and cases from Hawksbill sea turtle shells: comb fragment TOR-90-00026-OC (L. 3.4cm), one half case TOR-90-00027A-OC (L. 12.3cm), one half case TOR-90-00027B-OC (L. 11.1cm), intact case TOR-90-00024-OC (L. 12.2), and intact comb TOR-90-00025-OC (L. 12.3cm) (from left to right).

1983: 49), much of which seemingly originated in the West Indies, where the hawksbill once flourished (Fish, 2011: 6-17). Exploited throughout the 17th century and later, its shell was procured extensively for the production of snuff and pill boxes, spectacles, hair combs and as inlay for fine furniture (Pearson and Hoffman, 1995: 203). Rather than high-quality trade goods, the five individual tortoiseshell combs and cases recovered from the Tortugas shipwreck are seemingly less exotic objects crafted from raw material derived largely from the insular Caribbean and along the coast of Central America (pers. comm. Brian Shamblin, 4 September 2012). Such combs functioned as critical delousing and grooming kits for lice-infested passengers and sailors whose cramped and unsanitary living quarters and limited water supply for washing were ideal breeding grounds for such vermin (Fine, 2006: 42).

Additionally, on a second fragmentary bone lice comb from the Tortugas wreck one side contains larger teeth, while finer teeth are visible on the other side. This arrangement typifies lice combs (pers. Comm. Corey Malcolm, 29 September 2011). The small size of this comb suggests that it was a 'nit' comb intended for removing lice eggs or nits, much like the small examples found on the 19th-century American Civil War Ironclad *Cairo* lost in the Yazoo River, Mississippi (Bass, 2004: 276, 283).

The fine, narrowly-spaced tines on one side of the Tortugas combs would have allowed the owner to look for and remove both louse eggs and adult lice from head hair and beards; the regular teeth on the other side of the comb were designed for hair combing and grooming (cf. Bass, 2004: 283). Lice combs renowned for thwarting these bloodsucking creatures have been relied on for hundreds of years and are still considered effective today (Eldridge and Edman, 2000: 109).

Pediculus humanus humanus live in the seams of clothing and attach themselves to the body only when feeding, while head lice thrive in the hair, particularly the back and sides of the head. The problem of lice even inspired a 16th-century belief that the condition inexplicably disappeared at a line of longitude approximately 100 leagues west of the Azores. At the same meridian, eastbound sailors would become afflicted with lice. The legend's root may actually relate to the increase in temperature and removal of clothing associated with tropical climates and, correspondingly, greater lice density in colder climates where heavier clothes were worn (Schowalter, 2009: 375).

While itchy lice bites on the body and head often became infected from excessive scratching, 'ship fever', better known as typhus fever and occurring between a few hours and up to two weeks after the vermin's bite, was more serious. Symptoms included high fever, chills and fatigue,

combined with splotchy skin and a foul odor emitted by the victim. This contagious disease was known to kill more than half of afflicted sailors (Cofer, 1912: 13). Lice-borne typhus killed more passengers on 19th-century Atlantic crossings than any other disease (Bass, 2004: 283).

Early seafarers may not have been particularly knowledgeable about hygiene, or have been aware that lice transmitted a potentially lethal disease, but grooming for bodily comfort and aesthetics was certainly important. Related delousing combs crafted of tortoiseshell, bone, ivory, horn and wood have been recovered from shipwrecks spanning centuries, as well as described in abundant historical sources.

The 11th-century Serçe Limani vessel off southwest Turkey is one of the earliest wrecks that has yielded such combs, in this case associated with scissors, razors and knives from a barber's kit (Bass, 2004: 283-4). The anaerobic mud and silt environment in which the *Mary Rose* sank in 1545 produced the remains of bedding and clothing impregnated with traces of lice infestation (Konstam, 1999: 11) – rare physical evidence of the parasites that habitually plagued seafaring communities. The *Mary Rose* also contained a number of delousing combs, some located in the barber-surgeon's cabin (accompanied by razors) and others discovered individually in personal chests in decorated leather cases in the main deck (Marsden, 2003: 120, fig. 12.12).

Other shipwrecks carrying similar lice combs ranged from the medieval Culip VI wreck off Spain to the *Vasa* sank in 1628, the Dutch East Indiamen *Kennemerland* lost off Scotland in 1664 (Price and Muckelroy, 1979: 319), the Vergulde Draeck of 1656, the 1697 Portuguese warship *Santo Antonio de Tanna* (Piercy, 1978: 305), and *La Belle* lost in Matargorda Bay, Texas, in 1686 (Bruseth and Turner, 2005: 3-4).

Lice combs were recovered from the Spanish armada ship *La Trinidad Valencera* lost off Ireland in 1588 and from the 1622 *Margarita* (Fine, 2006: 42), which bears a resemblance to the intact tortoise shell comb recovered from the Tortugas site. An ivory lice comb was also recovered from the *Nuestra Señora del Populo*, a dispatch or war scout ship that sailed with the 1733 Spanish Plate fleet and foundered in a hurricane in Biscayne National Park, Florida (Weller, 1990: 14).

For personal grooming and hair adornment, Europeans had a long history of fashioning combs out of bone, ivory, tortoise shell and wood, a custom they transmitted into the New World. The trade goods en route to New Amsterdam on the 1657 Dutch vessel *De Wasbleecker* included an inventory of almost 300 combs and 65 comb cases. The Seneca people modeled their bone combs on these imported Dutch forms, but while European combs were largely intended for hygiene, amongst the indigenous peoples they became status symbols associated with luxury and wealth (Loren, 2008: 106).

The evidence for comb and case production on the Tortugas ship on its homeward voyage may have been functionally linked with the capture of both land and sea turtles for consumption, a recognized source of nutrition. According to the Englishman Thomas Gage during his missionary work in the Americas between 1614/15 and 1637, at Cartagena "All these ships make their provision for Spain of tortoise meat. They cut the tortoises in long thin slices… and dry it in the wind after they have well salted it, and so it serveth the mariners in all their voyages to Spain, and they eat it boiled with a little garlic, and I have heard them say that to them it tasted as well as any veal" (Thompson, 1958: 334). Antonio Vázquez de Espinosa confirmed that tortoises could also be purchased at Havana in the 1620s (Clark, 1942: 103).

Similar consumption, followed by functional reuse of the shell for comb production, may have been practiced by a crew member on the Tortugas vessel in the idle hours. The scale of activity seems to have been small-scale and individualistic, unlike the shipment of four boxes of hawksbill turtle shell on the *Nuevo Constante*, wrecked off Louisiana in 1766 en route from Mexico to Spain, where 5.1kg from the two boxes of lost *carei* (91kg) were found in excavations. The tortoise shells were roughly square to rectangular (upper size limits of 36 square inches) and exhibited cut edges, but otherwise had received minimal processing with no effort to trim the shell (Pearson and Hoffman, 1995: 203-204). By contrast, the Tortugas shell seems to have been prepared for working.

11. Miscellaneous Metallic, Stone & Organic Artifacts

A. Cooking & Food Preparation

An intriguing collection of both recognizable and unusual artifacts excavated from the Tortugas shipwreck contributes to the constructible image of shipboard life in the Americas trade in the waning years of the Golden Age of Spanish colonial seafaring. The two sets of bronze mortars (TOR-90-00004-BZ and 90-1A-000554, coordinates 83.25/27.32, H. 10.9cm, maximum Diam. 15.2cm, Diam. at base 10.3cm, rim Th. 0.6-0.9cm, 2.8kg; Fig. 60) and pestles (TOR-90-00005-BZ and 90-1A-000499, coordinates 84.30/29.09, L. 23.6cm, W. grinding end 4.7cm, W. handle 2.1cm, 0.9kg, Fig. 61) located 1.4m apart, just beyond the hull in the starboard stern, are of familiar form used on vessels of multiple nationalities. The

Fig. 60. Bronze mortar for grinding herbs and food preparation or related to medicinal use (H. 10.9cm, TOR-90-0004-BZ).

Fig. 61. Bronze pestle (L. 23.6cm, TOR-90-00005-BZ).

Tortugas mortars are mold decorated externally with what resemble human faces or zoomorphic figures.

Such mortars were manufactured with little stylistic change between *c.* 1600 and the mid-18th century and have been recorded on Dutch East India vessels typified by the *Mauritius* wreck (1609; L'Hour and Richez, 1989: 182), *Batavia* (1629; Green, 1989: 95), *Vergulde Draeck* (1656; Green, 1973: 285) and the *Hollandia* (Scilly Isles, 1743; Marsden, 1975: 290) inscribed 'AMOR VINCIT OMNIA ANNO' ('Love Conquers All') followed by the date of production (the mortars were a minimum of two years old at the date of loss, and in the case of the *Hollandia* a remarkable 50 years old), in these instances suggesting production as wedding presents (Green, 1977: 174). Comparable non-inscribed bronze mortars were used on the Spanish merchantmen *San Diego* (Philippines, 1600; Veyrat, 1994: 177-8), the Portuguese *Nossa Senhora dos Mártires* (Lisbon, Portugal, 1606; Brigadier, 2002: 120-1), the *Atocha* (Florida Keys, 1622; Mathewson, 1986: 100) and amongst

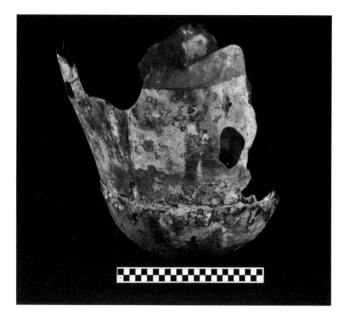

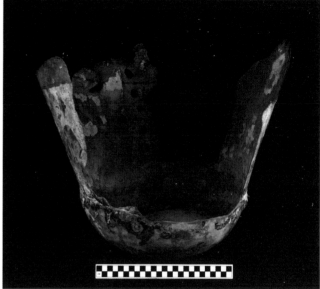

Figs. 62-63. Copper cauldron
(H. 44.5cm, TOR-90-00246-CU).

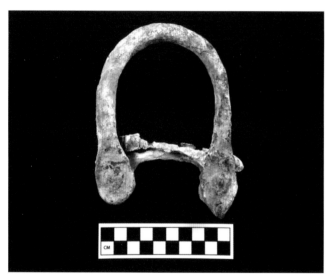

Fig. 64. Bronze cauldron handle
(H. 14.4cm, TOR-90-00161-CU).

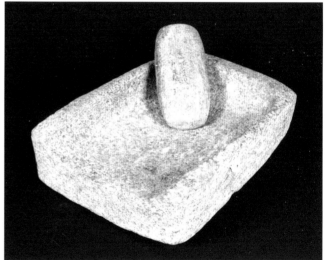

Fig. 65. A granite mano *and* metate
(L. 33cm) excavated from the stern.

assemblages from the 1715 Spanish fleet lost off the Cabin Site, Florida (Marx, 1973: 97). An identical pestle on the Emanuel I ship of 1559 further points towards conservatism in production (Smith *et al.*, 1998: 102).

These utensils are commonly interpreted as surgeon's mortars, undoubtedly due to their depiction in paintings such as *Interior of a Dutch Pharmacy* by the School of Terborgh dated to 1665 and in *The Surgery* by Gerard Thomas, 1663-1720 (Green, 1977: 174). However, these objects enjoyed an equally broader function for basic food preparation. The precise Tortugas type of bronze mortar is extremely common in still life works by the Seville school in the Golden Age, typified by Diego Velázquez's *Kitchen*

Scene with Christ in the House of Martha and Mary of 1618, *Christ at Emmaus* of *c.* 1620 and *Two Young Men at a Table,* assigned a date of 1623-24 (Jordan, 1985: 78, 87-8. fig. 3.7, pl. 8; Jordan and Cherry, 1995: 38, 41). The same object is represented in Francisco López Caro's *Boy in a Kitchen*, painted in the 1620s, and Giovanni Ruoppolo's riotous mid-17th century *Kitchen Still Life* (Jordan and Cherry, 1995: 90, 101).

The origin of the Tortugas wreck's bronze mortars and pestles is unverifiable, but certainly as early as 1549 a letter written in Seville reveals that a metal mortar weighing 9lbs cost 1½ *real* per pound and a pestle 2 *reales* (Barto Arnold and Weddle, 1978: 73-4). Since the record is concerned with how "To transport the containers from Triana to the apothecary shop" (in this instance perhaps revealing usage for grinding medicinal herbs), production within Seville may be hypothesized.

The lower third of a large copper cauldron with a gently rounded base and inclined sides (TOR-90-00246-CU, H. 44.5cm, maximum Diam. 51.7cm, Th. top sheet 0.2cm, Th. bottom sheet 0.6cm; Figs. 62-63) was recorded in grid area 76.19/11.74, 6.0m south of the ballast pile. The surviving vessel is crafted of two sections of copper interconnected using 21 copper rivets set horizontally 6.5cm apart (center to center) and ranging in diameter from 2.2-2.7cm. A resinous pitch embedded in the base suggests that this pot comprised part of a boatswain's stores, used to melt pitch with which to secure the leaking hull and running repairs, rather use for cooking within the galley.

The far earlier Emanuel Point I ship's kettle dated to 1559 displays similar base riveting, although this example has parallel sides (Smith *et al.* 1998: 98). An intact example snagged by fishermen from the Gnalic shipwreck *Gagiana*, based in Dubrovnik and lost off Croatia in 1583, may represent a closer parallel (pers. comm. Filipe Castro, 30 August 2012). From a rounded base its upper half is funnel-shaped and two handles are set vertically just below the rim. Its interior was still filled with tar.[6]

A bronze cauldron handle (TOR-90-00161-CU, H. 14.4cm, W. 11.0cm, Th. 1.3cm; Fig. 64) with its attachment flange, interconnected by a single 2.0 x 1.7cm rivet at each lower handle lug, may derive from one of the Tortugas ship's cooking cauldrons. Both the above artifacts contrast markedly to a three-legged iron cooking pot associated with the *Atocha* (database inv. M82 3975), but is identical to the base of another cooking vessel from the same site (*Atocha* database inv. 86.98.1119/3457).

A basalt *mano* pestle (L. 25.0cm, W. 11.0cm, Th. 5.5cm) and *metate* grinding stone (H. 11.0cm, L. 44.0cm, W. 33.0cm) were excavated in close proximity at coordinates 80.63/28.04 and 82.02/26.70, respectively north of the pump well and just outside the starboard stern hull remains, thus close to the original location of the decomposed galley structure (Fig. 65). This standard domestic equipment was used for grinding corn flour. A three-legged *metate* from the *Nuestra Señora de la Concepción*, wrecked off Hispaniola in 1641 (Borrell, 1983: 30), a four-legged example from the Praia dos Ingleses 1 wreck of 1687 off Santa Catarina Island, Brazil (Noelli, 2009: 101, fig. 5), and a three-legged basalt example of a type of 1766 that was common in Mexico, plus nine fragments of *manos*, from the wreck of the *Nuevo Constante*, Louisiana (Pearson and Hoffman, 1995: 164-5), reveal comparable shipboard food preparation. The need to grind flour became increasingly

Fig. 66. Some 1,190 lead musket shot were recovered from the Tortugas wreck (Diams. 0.7-1.9cm).

Fig. 67. Flints probably used to light fires on the Tortugas ship (L. 2.7cm, Th. 0.8cm).

central from the 1570s with the replacement of hardtack for maize used to make cassava bread (Super, 1984: 60).

B. Artillery

An anomaly on the Tortugas wreck was the presence of 14 cannonballs (Diams. 6.5-9.0cm) clustered exclusively to starboard outside the hull and ballast zone between midship and the bows, but no cannon. Dated to 22 March 1622, *Contratación* 1172, N.2, R.1 records that at departure from the Guadalquivir river for Tierra Firme the *Buen Jesús y Nuestra Señora del Rosario* was expected to transport four iron cannon and 12 muskets. In their absence on the site the likelihood that these guns were jettisoned during the fateful hurricane of 5 September seems high. Around 1,190 examples of lead shot were also recovered from the wreck (Diams. 0.7-1.9cm; Fig. 66), although in a parallel picture to the cannonballs no muskets or related wooden barrels were identified.

Fig. 68. A brass figurative medallion depicting the Virgin Mary and Jesus on one side, and a single figure plus the inscription 'SANTA CATARI--' and 'ROMA' on the reverse (H. 2.9cm, TOR-90-00256-ML).

Fig. 69. The head and fragmentary torso of a clay figurine depicting the Virgin Mary (L. 9.3cm, TOR-90-00345-CS).

The Tortugas wreck site contained several flints (L. 2.7cm, Th. 0.8cm) of a type superficially comparable to those used at a later date to ignite pistols' powder charges (Harding, 1999: 191; Fig. 67). The presence of such small arms, first developed in France in the first quarter of the 17th century, would be especially early in a 1622 context. The flintlock is generally dated from *c.* 1625 (Garigen, 1991: 1, 18), several years after the sinking of the 1622 fleet, and only became popular in the second half of the 17th century. No flints were recorded on the Emanuel Point I ship lost in 1559 (cf. Smith *et al.*, 1998). One of the Tortugas flints shows some sophistication (Fig. 67, far right), but early wedge gunflints were essentially 'do it yourself' types (as defined by de Lotbiniere, 1984: 207).

In light of the absence of gunflints on either of the far more heavily armed 1622 *Atocha* or *Margarita* fleet ships (pers. comm. Jim Sinclair, 1 September 2012), the function of the Tortugas flints remains unclear and may be related to fire lighting. Snaphaunce pistols, however, did rely on a cock with a pair of jaws that held a wedge-shaped piece of flint and were in use by 1560, as was the Spanish 'Miquellet' design developed in the reign of Philip II (1556-98), whose popularity peaked in the first quarter of the 17th century (Given, 1994: 20, 22-23; Kinard, 2003: 17-18).

C. Personal Belongings

Religious artifacts are poorly represented on the Tortugas wreck and other than probable rosary beads are restricted to a figurative rosary pendant and a section of a clay figurine. The highly degraded brass rosary pendant (TOR-90-002560ML, H. 2.9cm, W. 1.6cm, Th. 0.2cm; Fig. 68) depicts the Virgin Mary holding Jesus on one side attended by a second female, and reverse another religious figure presumably identified by the overlying inscription, partly legible as 'SANTA CATERI--- and ROMA', holding an unidentifiable object with a sword to her right. This medallion probably represents St. Catherine of Siena, a 14th-century Dominican nun who had a vision of a mystical marriage with Jesus in the presence of Mary (pers. comm. Beverly Straube, 31 August 2012).

Such pendants in cupreous or precious metal form featuring saintly imagery are extremely common on shipwrecks across the colonial period, crafted of gold on the *Atocha* (hanging from a rosary comprised of carved ebony beads) and present within the 1715 Spanish fleet off the Florida Keys (Wagner, 1967: 78-9). Amongst numerous examples, bronze oval-shaped equivalents comparable to the Tortugas site went down off the Philippines in 1600 on the Spanish merchant vessel *San Diego*, showing the Immaculate Conception scene (Virgin Mary, probably

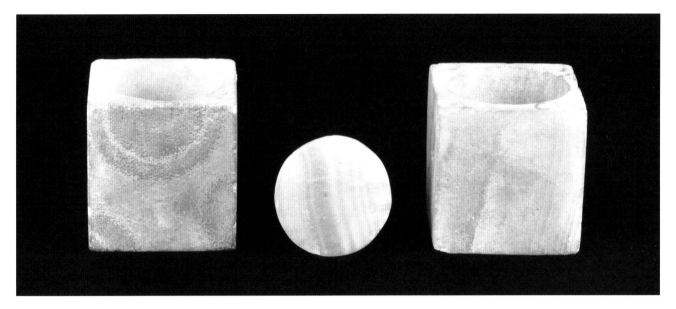

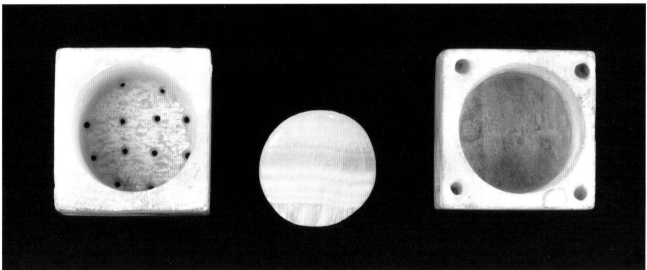

*Figs. 70-71. Onyx powder shaker (H. 5.8cm, TOR-90-00033-SN), lid
(Diam. 4.5cm, TOR-90-00034-SN) and inkwell (H. 5.8cm, TOR-90-00014-SN).*

assuming the form of St. Francis), while another double-sided medallion adorned with St. Francis of Assisi and St. Antony of Padua was recovered from the Genoese ship *Santo Christo de Castello* sunk in 1667 off Mullion Cove, Cornwall (McBride *et al.*, 1975: 246). These religious artifacts were common across the colonies from English Jamestown to the Portuguese Fort Jesus at Mombasa, Kenya, in the late 17th century (Kirkman, 1974: pl. 44; Provoyeur, 1994: 278; Kelso, 2006: 188).

A comparable brass example associated with 22 black glass beads from the Dutch East Indiaman *Vergulde Draeck* lost off Western Australia in 1656 further suggests these objects were common in rosaries (Green, 1977: 223). There is no reason to consider the Tortugas pendant as anything more significant than a belonging of one of the ship's non-ecclesiastical passengers or crew. The reference to Rome hints that the owner may have coveted this souvenir as produced in the capital city of the Catholic Church.

A second religious artifact from the Tortugas wreck appears to be an incomplete and unglazed ceramic figure featuring the head and torso of the Virgin Mary holding something in her arms, presumably the Christ child (TOR-90-00345-CS, L. 9.3cm, H. 7.4cm, W. 4.2cm; Fig. 69). If this artifact depicts the standing Virgin Mary, then the remaining object would seem to represent about one-third of the original figurine. Some of the highly eroded facial features can be observed, including the forehead, eye sockets and the outline and folds of draped garments covering the head and upper torso. The degraded condition of the artifact leaves much to speculation.

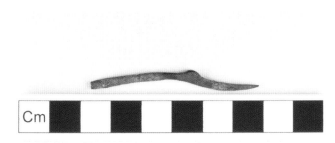

Fig. 72. A possible bronze writing stylus
(L. 5.5cm, TOR-90-00234-CU).

Fig. 73. Brass box/furniture appliqué
(L. 1.3cm, TOR-90-00297-OC).

Fig. 74. Part of a bronze furniture or lamp suspension
element. Fragment A (left: L. 5.9cm, TOR-90-00255A-CU),
fragment B (top right: Diam. 3.5cm, TOR-90-00255B-CU),
fragment C (bottom right: H. 3.2cm, TOR-90-00255C-CU).

A grayish ridged band running along the top of the figure's head and shoulder may represent a mold seam, and as such would be suggestive of a European origin (pers. comm. Byron Sudbury, 28 August 2012). The figure resembles pipeclay (white ball clay) figurines made in the Netherlands in the 15th and 16th centuries, whose iconography focused on the Virgin Mary, the Christ child and the female virgin saints (Gilchrist, 2012: 156). A Mary and Child found in the Overijssel Province of the Netherlands in a context dating to *c.* 1525-75 is one such early parallel (pers. comm. Beverly Straube, 28 August 2012). The Tortugas example, however, does not seem to typify Dutch manufacture (pers. comm. Don Duco, 11 September 2012). The reddish tint of the Tortugas example may represent iron-stained pipeclay. Alternatively, the clay could be earthenware material. Accurate differentiation is impossible without chemical analysis.

The production of white pipeclay figurines is considered to have been a sideline for pipe-making centers that flourished in England, the Rhineland and the Netherlands in the 17th century (Hurry and Grulich, 2012: 8). Traces of the paint that originally decorated figures' dress are still visible on one example (Gilchrist, 2012: 156) and the Tortugas example may have been similarly decorated. The discovery of these figurine types in urban domestic contexts suggests that they were objects of personal devotion thought to be popular amongst women praying for help to manage conception, pregnancy and childbirth. Such figurines were acquired as souvenirs and gifts perhaps purchased during pilgrimages (Hurry and Grulich, 2012: 8; Gilchrist, 2012: 156; Wesler, 2012: 230).

More contemporary to the Tortugas Virgin Mary figurine is the head of a white pipeclay figurine recovered from the St. John's site, an English Farmhouse built in St. Mary's City, Maryland, in 1638. Produced in a two-part mold, the head may represent a cherub, angel or the infant Jesus. Figurines of similar material have been found on sites in New York, Rhode Island, Virginia and Jamaica in the Caribbean, as well as in the Netherlands, Germany and the United Kingdom (Hurry and Grulich, 2012, 1-2).

While the Tortugas figurine would have been suitable for personal devotion, its appropriateness aboard ship was bolstered by the Virgin Mary's religious status as the protector of mariners, *Stella Maris*, the 'Star of the Sea' (Hall, 2004: 17). In the 9th century the French-born monk Paschasius Radbertus described Mary as the 'Star of the Sea', a guide to be followed on the way to Christ "lest we capsize amid the storm-tossed waves of the sea."

Also known as the North Star, *Stella Maris* was the most important celestial body for sailors. Mariners typically sang *Ave Maria* at sundown to protect against the perils of the night and very possibly to welcome the arrival of Polaris, Mary's North Star (Hall, 2004: 46). Most Spanish sailors wore amulets of the Virgin Mary or their favorite saint around their necks to seek protection (Anderson, 2002: 231). For similar protective reasons Christopher Columbus' flagship was named the *Santa Maria* (Hall, 2004: 45-8).

Over a century later, Spanish mariners continued to embrace the cover of Mary's protective mantle. An ivory Virgin Mary and Child is associated with the 1601 Manila galleon *Santa Margarita* sunk at Rota in the Northern Marianas Islands, while a small bronze figure derives from the *Margarita* of the 1622 Tierra Firme fleet (pers. comm. Corey Malcom, 28 August 2012).

Unsurprisingly given the detailed book-keeping practiced by Spain in its long-distance maritime trade, evidence for literacy on the Tortugas ship is present in the form of an onyx set of inkwell, shaker and several bronze styli (Figs. 70-71). The inkwell (TOR-90-00014-SN, H. 5.8cm, W. 5.7cm, coordinates 87.05/27.51) located 5.2m west of the stern starboard planking is crafted of onyx and consists of a square cube featuring a central ink reservoir (Depth 4.3cm) and four holes on the upper edges to hold pens (Diams. 0.7cm). A circular lid (TOR-90-00034-SN, Diam. 4.5cm, Th. 0.6cm) enabled the well to be closed when not in use. The onyx shaker (TOR-90-00033-SN, H. 5.8cm, W. 5.8cm) also has a central reservoir (Depth 4.0cm), but in this example is pierced with 12 holes (Diams. 0.2cm) designed to allow powder to be dispersed over parchment and dry ink.

This style of inkwell, seemingly in bronze and with geometrically decorated sides, is depicted in Francisco de Zurbaran's *Visit of San Bruno to Urbano II* painted in 1655, and an exact bronze parallel was excavated from the Spanish ship the *San Diego* (Philippines, 1600; Veyrat, 1994: 181). A hardy stone version impervious to humid, salty environments was a sound choice for shipboard use. At least one shaft and tip of a bronze styli was excavated from the Tortugas wreck (Fig. 72).

Additional miscellaneous metallic artifacts include an applique from a brass box or piece of furniture (TOR-90-00297-OC, fragment L. 1.3cm, Th. 0.05cm; Fig. 73), three sections of bronze from a furniture fitting or lamp suspension element (TOR-90-00255A-CU; L. 5.9cm, Diam. 1.9cm, ring role internal Diam. 0.4cm; TOR-90-00255B-CU, H. 1.2cm, Diam. 3.5cm, internal hole Diam. 1.0cm; TOR-90-00255C-CU, H. 3.2cm, Diam. 3.8cm, hole 1.2 x 1.0cm; Fig. 74), and a possible bronze vessel handle or canvas sail seam ripper (TOR-90-00242-CU, L. 3.4cm, central barb W. 0.3cm, Th. 0.3cm; Fig. 75). A section of pewter or lead with a v-shaped termination

Fig. 75. A possible bronze vessel handle or sail seam ripper (L. 3.4cm, TOR-90-00242-CU).

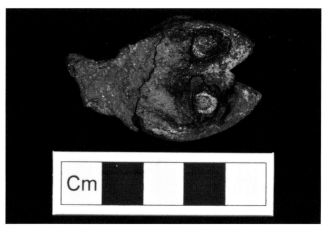
Fig. 76. A probable pewter sword hanger (L. 4.8cm, TOR-90-00080-ML).

Fig. 77. A wooden drop spindle for spinning fibers (L. 31.6cm, TOR-90-00042-CS).

Fig. 78. A wooden drop spindle for spinning fibers (L. 24.4cm, TOR-90-00043-CS).

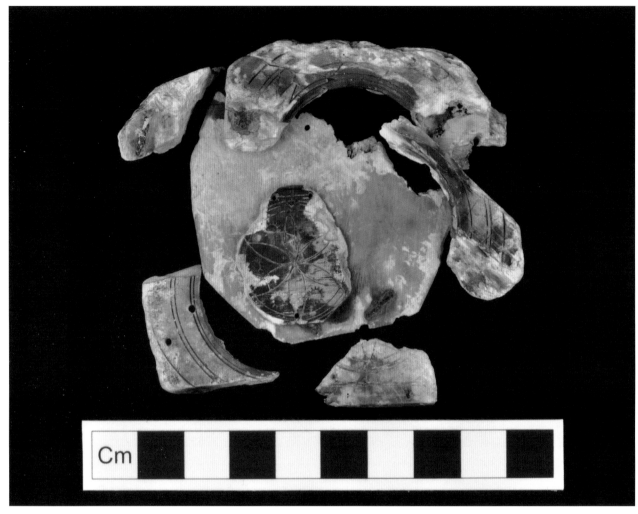

Fig. 79. Sections of an ivory octagonal diptych sundial manufactured in Nuremberg. Estimated external Diam. 6.1cm (TOR-90-00293-OC).

Fig. 80. Ten fragments of felt and leather from one or two shoes.

Fig. 81. Bone or ivory probable syringe joints (L. 0.7cm) perhaps suggest a consignment of medical instruments on the Tortugas ship.

Fig. 82. An unidentified South American or circum-Caribbean ceramic object (L. 1.8cm, TOR-90-00074-CS).

Fig. 83. An unidentified South American or circum-Caribbean ceramic object (L. 1.6cm, TOR-90-00075-CS).

Fig. 84. Pipe stem fragments from probable South American or circum-Caribbean colonoware and one white clay tobacco pipe stem (Diam. stem 0.7-1.2cm).

and pierced with two rivets, within which small pieces of leather are preserved (TOR-90-00080-ML, L. 4.8cm, W. 2.9cm, Th. 1.2cm; Fig. 76), may have functioned as a possible sword hanger attached to a waist belt on the basis of parallels from the *Atocha* (pers. comm. Corey Malcom, 28 November 2011), although examples manufactured in this metal medium are otherwise unknown.

Further organic artifacts include two thin elongated pieces of wood, circular in section, identifiable as hand-held drop spindles or spinning rods used to spin various fibers into thread (TOR-90-00042-CS, L. 31.6cm, Th. at center 1.8cm, Th. right tip 0.6cm, Th. left tip 0.2cm; TOR-90-00043-CS, L. 24.5cm, Th. at center 1.5cm, Th. right tip 0.8cm, Th. left tip 0.6cm; Figs. 77-78). Comparative evidence from Prehispanic Mesoamerica, described in the *Codex Mendoza* as *malacatl*, indicates that women used a wooden spindle fitted with a ceramic disk or whorl, in conjunction with a small ceramic bowl to support the spindle as it twirled, to spin cotton thread in the conquest period (Smith and Hirth, 1988: 349).

Wooden spindles of comparable form from medieval Coppergate, York, were used to spin wool with a top-loaded spindle by hip spinning, and the warp was spun with a bottom-loaded spindle by the drop-and-spin method (Walton Rogers, 1997: 1734, 1745-9). The traditional process of spinning using this tool has been described and illustrated in detail for modern rural Indian Peru (McRobb, 1980: 58-62). Considering that spinning was a traditional gendered activity, these artifacts point towards the presence of a low-status woman (Villanueva, 1985: 17, 19) – presumably a slave – on the Tortugas shipwreck.

Six sections of worked ivory are an extraordinary discovery on the Tortugas ship (TOR-90-00293-OC; lower horizontal leaf: estimated external Diam. 6.1cm; base Diam. 6.3cm, base Th. 0.3cm, base octagonal edges L. 2.8cm, base hole Diam. 0.1cm; base raised box edges: maximum W. 2.6cm, Th. 1.2cm, hole Diams. 0.1cm, incised bands 0.4cm apart; upper vertical leaf: star motif

Fig. 85. Two greenstone slate whetstones (L. 16.5cm, Th. 0.5cm & L. 16.0cm, Th. 0.4cm; 90-1A-10240015 & 90-1A-000567).

decorated leaf W. 2.9cm, Th. 0.2cm, hole Diams. 0.07cm, total W. central star motif 2.2cm, L. each ray 1.1cm, adjoining sun/moon motifs Diams. 0.4cm).

These fragments derive from the upper vertical and lower horizontal leaves of a portable octagonal sundial diptych with sides interconnected with cuprous wire and originally closed with a brass hinge (Fig. 79). The upper plane of the horizontal box leaf that once contained a compass is simply adorned with three bands of dual lines, on one fragment pierced with two holes. The octagonal base was originally secured to the overlying box sections with a three-part bronze hinge composed of two central linear pins on either side of a central hexagonal bolt. It is also pierced at center for securing in place a string gnomon and is incised on the outside edge with one set of dual lines.

The star-decorated ivory plaque was originally set in the center of the upper vertical leaf's exterior surface. Also octagonal, it is covered with a star design subdivided into six rays with curved edges. Between the external edges of each is a single sun motif (six in total). Outside these symbols at the plaque edge are three incised lines. A similar dual incised line extends longitudinally through the center of the star symbol. The sundial's overall decorative scheme is crude.

Two holes pierce the upper vertical leaf on one edge; on the opposite surface these are surrounded by cupreous stains from a three-part bronze hinge similar to that on the base plaque. This indicates that this point corresponds with the lower plaque edge joined to the underlying horizontal

leaf. A single hole on the opposite edge of the vertical leaf accommodated the gnomon.

This form of portable sundial is rare on colonial Spanish shipwrecks, but three examples have been identified at Site PB-3 on Pedro Bank, Jamaica, associated with a 30m-long ballast pile, 21 iron cannon, Middle Style B olive jar sherds and two silver coins, one minted in Lima dated to 1686, the other produced at Potosí in the second half of the 17th century. These dates suggest this site may be one of four Spanish vessels bound for Havana in 1691 (Hoyt, 1984: 102, 106). The Pedro Bank sundials are identical to the Tortugas example.[7] Their gnomons were set at 42°, the line of latitude for either Boston and Madrid, and it is suggested that these finds functioned as minor trade items manufactured in the New World for sale in Spain (Hoyt, 1984: 105, 106, fig. 7B). Such a hypothesis seems unlikely (see below).

Several portable ivory sundials from a heavily looted early 17th-century wreck at Mijoka, Croatia, accompanied a ship transporting raw materials from production centers such as Nuremberg and Murano between Venice, the Adriatic and eastern Mediterranean ports.[8] An octagonal ivory sundial identical to the Tortugas example excavated at Castle Cornet, Guernsey, pre-dates 1690, while a further example in the National Maritime Museum is marked as manufactured by Bloud of Dieppe, France (Burns, 1984: 339-40). The wreck of the Dutch East India Company ship *Vergulde Draeck*, lost off Western Australia in 1656, contained six portable ivory sundials (Green, 1977: 427).

The Tortugas sundial seems to be the earliest octagonal example attested on a shipwreck, and was almost certainly manufactured in the great mathematical tool production center of Nuremberg in Germany under the control of six dominant 'compass-maker' families between *c.* 1550 and 1730: Troschel, Ducher, Karner, Lesel, Miller and Reinmann (Gouk, 1992: 35). The use of ivory in such great quantities was unusual for dials, but was the specialty of Nuremberg's compassmakers (Higton, 2001: 50).

The star and sun motifs on the upper leaf of the Tortugas dial are stylistic identical to decorative schemes unique to Nuremberg (Gouk, 1988: 118, nos. 18 and 24). The multiple holes may be *Elevatio Poli* or *Polhoehe* (height or angular elevation of the pole star, Polaris), which correspond to different latitudes so the sundial could work in varied European cities. The star and sun symbols on the diptych's outer vertical surface seem to be part of a lunar volvelle designed to convert time at night from the shadow cast by moonlight to a corresponding solar time (Lloyd, 1992: 17-18, 24).

Between the 15th and 17th centuries the 24-hour day and sundial helped the devout keep to prayer schedules, while universal portable sundials worked at multiple latitudes to cater for merchants, pilgrims and long-distance travelers (Schechner, 2001: 120, 197, 201, 211-2). The science of sundials not only saved pious souls, but was considered necessary to preserve the market economy and society. As the English mathematician William Leybourn wrote in the preface to Thomas Stirrup's *Horometria: Or, the compleat diallist* of 1659, "What is more necessary in a well ordered Common-wealth [than dialing]? what action can be performed in due season without it? or what man can appoint any business with another, and not prefix a time, without the losse of that which cannot be re-gained, and ought therefore to most be prized?" The Tortugas wreck's sundial signifies the presence of a well-appointed merchant on the ship, if it was not the personal property of the captain.

Ten fragments of worked leather from one or two shoes were excavated from the Tortugas shipwreck, including soles and heel sections (Fig. 80). While the fragments – largely interior shoe remains (L. 3.0-10.5cm, W. 1.4-5.2cm, Th. 0.1-0.6cm, average stiches 0.3 x 0.1cm and three stitches per cm) – may be leather, badly degraded or delaminated waterlogged leather can give the appearance of wool felt, which is similar in structure. The use of felt in shoe soles was not uncommon in 17th-century and later footwear, such as examples recovered from the English warship HMS *De Braak* wrecked in Delaware Bay off northeast America in 1798. The footware from this English warship included sock-linings (false insoles). These were made from wool hat

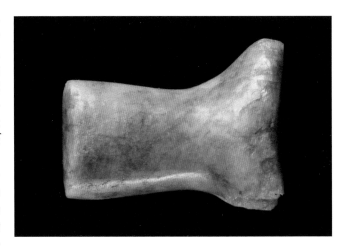

Fig. 86. A probable plagioclase feldspar South American or circum-Caribbean labret (lip ornament) (L. 1.8cm, TOR-90-00343-SN).

felt for added warmth and insulation (pers. comm. D.A. Saguto, 5 March 2012).

The Tortugas wreck presents a shoe styling with a continuous outsole toe to heel, covering a low 'spring' (wedge-shaped) heel built up of multiple leather lifts (layers). This shoe type relied on stitching rather than wooden pegging, which is more closely associated with stacked leather heels that became increasingly common in the mid-to-late second quarter of the 17th century (pers. comm. D.A. Saguto, 5 March 2012). In the alternate method, by contrast, heels were built up by pegging several layers of leather at a time (Goubitz, 2007: 81). The large diamond-section stitching holes visible on most of the Tortugas shoe fragments reflect the use of a stout diamond-section awl (tool), more commonly associated with Continental European shoemaking schools than with English shoemakers, who preferred oval-section awls (pers. comm. D.A. Saguto, 5 March 2012).

A set of four intact and eight fragmentary carved wooden beads are spherical in form with beveled or slanted angles (L. 1.9cm, Diam. 1.9cm, W. 1.8cm, hole Diam. 0.2-0.3cm; Fig. 46). In addition to the holes at each end of the bead, smaller holes are visible on the body. The bead shape is similar to abacus beads, and as such may have been intended for use in an abacus counter, a tool used for performing arithmetic processes since ancient times and today still widely used by merchants in many parts of the world, particularly Africa and Asia.

A series of 13 probably bone, but possibly ivory, small cylindrical hollow objects, all seemingly unused (L. 0.7cm, W. 0.8cm, Diam. of hole 0.5cm; Fig. 81), seem to be spare joints for an undetermined form of utensil or instrument, potentially medical, such as enema syringes.

Two worked ceramic artifacts defy identification (TOR-90-00074-CS, L. 1.8cm, W. of base 0.7cm, W. at top 0.4cm, handle L. 0.9cm, handle Th. 0.2cm, 0.8gms; TOR-90-00075-CS, L. 1.6cm, base Diam. 0.8cm, W. at top 0.4cm, handle L. 0.9cm, handle Th. 0.2cm, 0.7gms; Figs. 82-83). Both are solid cylinders of clay with flaring bases to which a single handle extends upwards to mid-body, while three crude lines and striations have been incised along the lower two-thirds of the object. Two additional incised lines are present on the summit of TOR-90-00074-CS.

In style, these objects resemble miniature thunder-mugs/servidors, candlestick holders or possibly flagons that have been suggested to have served as gaming pieces. A few board pieces were found at Castillo De San Marcos at St. Augustine, Florida (pers. comm. James Levy, 2 December 2011). The crude decoration is reminiscent of North American 'Fort Walton Punctuation' motifs (pers. comm. Marie Prentice, 1 December 2011). However, an origin anywhere in South American, Mesoamerica or in the Caribbean is more likely. A rich tradition of miniatures production, often used as children's toys, existed in colonial Mexico. Their use as thimbles for sewing has also been proposed, although the objects' opening width seems to prohibit such an option. The tiny size of these objects may point towards a different function, and stringing on a necklace or bracelet has been proposed. The cessation of decoration half way down both objects may suggest a practical use as vials for small spouted bottles, the loop being intended to take a string to prevent them being parted from the vessel (pers. comm. Ivor Noël Hume, 16 August 2012). Alternatively they may have been vessel stoppers.

Eight fragments of tobacco pipe stems (Diam. stem 0.7-1.2cm, Diam. inner hole 0.3-0.5cm; Fig. 84) derive from one iron-stained white clay tobacco pipe of possible European or Euro-American manufacture and six Native American earthenware tobacco pipes (pers. comm. Byron Sudbury, 7 March 2012). They are identified as personal belongings of the ship's company, and the six examples attributed a New World origin represent unusual evidence for tobacco trade and use in the first quarter of the 17th century. Cuba and Venezuela are their most likely source of production (Sudbury, forthcoming).

Arguably the least expected artifacts associated with the Tortugas wreck are three jadeite or greenstone objects. Two of the objects are elongated oblong and pendant-like (90-1A-000567 and 90-1A-10240015, L. 16.5cm, W. 3.0cm, Th. 0.5cm; Fig. 85), each with a shaped blade and a carved terminal, one of which features a more elaborate floral motif and a recessed (though not pierced) central drilled hole.[9] The third artifact is small, roughly T-shaped

and seemingly crafted of polished plagioclase feldspar with hints of white and brown (TOR-90-00343-SN, H. 1.8cm, W. 1.3cm, Th. 1.0cm, protruding T-bar 0.9 x 0.8cm; Fig. 86). The shape and the finish suggest the object is a labret (lip ornament).

The blade-like artifacts closely resemble celts, objects of both religious and economic significance amongst the indigenous people of pre-Columbian Mesoamerica, which were exchanged or reworked into statues, jewelry and other precious objects (Grande and Augustyn, 2009: 211). Celts were often worn vertically as pendants, dangling from belts or masks, or worn horizontally as pectorals. A similar, but plain oblong celt-like greenstone object was recovered from the *Margarita;* double drill holes in its center suggest it was worn horizontally as a pectoral ornament (Tedesco, 2010b: 18). Current thinking suggests that the Tortugas examples served more mundanely as whetstones due to the presence of distinct surface wear.

All three artifacts are of almost certain Mesoamerican origins, where jadeite and other physically similar greenstones have deep cultural roots. The Spanish term for jade, *piedra de yjada,* translates as 'stone of the loins', a name inspired by observations of how the native population used jade for therapeutic purposes when mixed in powdered form with water as a cure for internal disorders (Gasco and Voorhies, 1989: 59).[10] In turn, Spaniards attributed to jade the power to cure kidney pain and other healing either when worn as jewelry or placed next to an affected area (Grande and Augustyn, 2009: 211).

Mesoamerica was the main source of jade in the New World, with the dominant sources concentrated in Guatemala, particularly the central Motagua Valley, where appropriate geological conditions exist and several ancient jade-working sites have been recorded along the Upper Rio El Tambor drainage area (Helferich, 2012: 200; Taube *et al.,* 2005). The 16th-century *Codex Mendoza* lists seven provinces as paying tribute to Spain partly in greenstone that is believed to have originated largely in the Motagua Valley, Polochic Valley, Sierra de Santa Cruz, Altos de Cuchumatanes, Sierra de las Minas and Sierra de Chuacus, all in Guatemala (Gasco and Voorhies, 1989: 59, 61-2).

The Tortugas ship would have encountered little difficulty acquiring jadeite and greenstone objects in the main ports of South America and Mesoamerica, but the principal question remains for what reason this Spanish-operated vessel was transporting them? Three interpretations seem feasible: the objects were curiosities being shipped as souvenirs, they had been procured for their curative properties, or they belonged to a Native American Indian onboard the merchant vessel. The last two options seem most logical, and combined with the presence of two unparalleled possible Native American or Caribbean Indian ceramic beads or pendants, and two indigenous wooden weaving spindles, the presence of a female Indian onboard the Tortugas ship cannot be excluded. The labret is so small that it arguably only makes sense as a facial adornment. A Spaniard certainly would never wear one and presumably would have preferred a larger object if it was desired for its curative properties, whether intact or reduced to powdered form. On the other hand, a large greenstone paperweight found in addition to one greenstone celt and another amulet on the *Margarita* (Tedesco, 2010b: 18-19) may reflect a broader trade pattern.

12. Human Bones
The human skeletal material from the Tortugas shipwreck was restricted to a small number of teeth recovered in the ROV's SeRF system. Some upper and lower molars exhibit a discolored, tartar-like substance near the base and two adult molars have cavities. Wear evidence varies from none (a tooth had not erupted) to molars with smoothed cusps and pinhole penetrations through the enamel. Several specimens are represented only by enamel caps, the root and interior of the tooth being completely decomposed.

Separating the teeth by wear creates two groups with type distributions, indicating a minimum number of individuals (MNI) in each (Tables 3-4). The teeth represent at least one child and one adult. Judging from the amount of wear on the teeth, and consulting dentition charts for ages of eruption, the child was ten years old (+/- 30 months).

Type	Child	Adult	Unknown
Incisors	0	1 (L)	----
Canines	0	2 (1U, 1L)	----
Bicuspids	4 (?)	0	----
Molars	7 (3U, 4L)	2 (L, L)	1 (L)

Table 3. Distribution of teeth by probable age of individual.

13. Animal Bones

A. The Sample
A collection of 165 animal bones excavated from the Tortugas shipwreck was reanalyzed by Dr. Philip Armitage in 2011 (Figs. 87-88). His study concluded that the majority of the assemblage was poorly/moderately well preserved with substantial evidence of post-depositional attritional damage from seabed sedimentary disturbance and, in some cases, corrosion caused by prolonged exposure to seawater (cf. Armitage, 2013).

Accounting for 40.0% of the bones, pig predominated over cattle and sheep/goat (13.9%), reflecting the high frequency of this animal in Spanish mariners' diet within the Americas fleets. The inclusion of teeth suggests that live pigs were carried on board the Tortugas ship to supply fresh meat during the trans-Atlantic crossing, a common practice testified in historical accounts. Domestic *Gallus gallus* fowl bones represented 6.2% of the faunal sample. Measurements point towards the consumption of scrawny, bantam-sized birds. One possible turkey bone was identified.

Comprising 32.3% of the Tortugas assemblage, *Rattus rattus,* from at least five black rats were highly represented. Rodent tooth gnawing marks were also identified on a chicken humerus (TOR-90-00214-BN), reflecting scavenging by a shipboard rat.

Unexpected faunal remains consisted of the right and left lower jawbones (TOR-90-00193-BN) from an adult cat (Fig. 88) and, most remarkably, a tarsometatarsus (TOR-90-00170-BN) and a femur (TOR-90-00217-BN) from a parrot. *Pionus* are indigenous to the Caribbean, Central American and northern South American mainland regions. Transport as commercial exotica plausibly explains the parrot's shipboard presence (possibly within a larger caged consignment). The opportunity to purchase these birds would have been possible when the Tierra Firme fleet entered the ports of Portobello (Panama) and Cartagena (Columbia). Former evidence of the trade in small parrot species is scarce, and physical evidence almost non-existent (Armitage, 2013; Cooper and Armitage, forthcoming).

B. Flota Meat Provisions
Outward-bound Atlantic fleets transported livestock to the colonies in the Americas or for slaughtering during the voyage. Although a Spanish law of 1621 prohibited livestock carriage on warships, merchant vessels continued to load hoofed and winged animals, prized amongst the myriad stocks taken to sea in the centuries before ice or refrigeration (Fish, 2011: 406-407). Sailors, soldiers and low status passengers subsisted on a mundane diet almost exclusively comprising dried and salted meat and fish, beans and chickpeas. Hard biscuit was standard fare, the most important sustenance for energy served with a little vinegar as relish and sometimes some butter and cheese, plus the customary rations of wine. Fish acquired during the voyage broke the monotony (Peterson, 1975: 85; Phillips, 1986: 168-9).

Inv. No.	Type	Condition
90-1A-000397.00	Human molar, crown, neck & section of root intact	Very little wear on the four cusps. Two roots indicate a tooth from the lower jaw. Probably a second molar.
90-1A-000397.001	Human bicuspid or premolar, crown, neck & section of root intact	Very similar in wear & size to 90-1A-002066.1189. A tiny facet on one cusp; otherwise little wear. Position is undetermined.
90-000434.118	Mostly intact right lower first bicuspid or premolar	No wear facets
90-1A-000474.114	Human molar crown, small section of root & neck intact	Cavities on both the mesial & distal occlusal surface, one of which penetrates the enamel. Five cusps & oblong shape suggest this was a lower molar. Cusps worn smooth, but discernible. Position undetermined.
90-1A-000474.115	Enamel of a human molar, cusps in Y-5 pattern	Little wear, but has discolored to black
90-1A-0000485.8	Enamel of a human molar, three cusps	Little wear; enamel discolored to black
90-1A-000524.116	Enamel cap of human molar, three cusps	Little to no wear
90-1A-000558.449	Mostly intact human molar with two roots from the lower jaw. Very large tooth, 13mm long, 10mm wide	Extreme wear; the cusps are discernible but smooth; the enamel worn through at three points. Mesial & distal occlusal surfaces have cavities that do not penetrate the enamel
90-1A-000628.1808	Crown, neck & small amount of root of human incisor	Not shovel shaped, enamel worn through on the cusp
90-1A-000680.70	Human first or second molar from lower (left?) jaw, cusps in Y5 pattern	Wear has produced a facet on one cusp, no discernible wear other side
90-1A-000876.071	Crown only of human premolar (or molar?)	No wear facets; stained overall
90-1A-000876.72	Human second molar (right?). Oblong shape & suggestion of three roots indicate upper tooth	Crown intact, small amount of cementum at the neck. Very little wear on four cusps
90-1A-000980.70	Human canine tooth; cingulum indicates upper position, curvature & groove on root flat surface indicate from mouth right side	Mostly intact, only root top broken; some evidence of wear
90-1A-02066.1189	Human bicuspid or premolar, crown & neck intact	Grayish white enamel; cementum is gray, ivory & tan. Tooth not yet erupted
90-1A-002066.1190	Human canine (very similar to 90-1A-00980.70). Crown & neck intact, small part of root present	Cusp worn flat, pinhole penetration through the enamel. No cingulum apparent suggesting from the lower jaw
90-1A-002507.209	Human lower molar crown & some parts of neck. Cusps in +5 pattern, position undetermined	Very little wear
90-1A-002507.211	Human bottom molar, five cusps in Y5 pattern	Crown, neck & part of root intact; no wear
90-1A-00524.117	Crown of a human molar?	Broken & deeply pitted on the surface; impossible to determine the original shape.

Table 4. Condition of human teeth recovered from the Tortugas shipwreck.

While provisions varied little in the 16th and 17th centuries, by the mid-17th century the recommended rations had reduced in proportion. The anonymous *Diálogo* of 1635 cited six ounces of salted meat or fish as the basic ration, the former of which often took the form of bacon or salt pork. This allowance compared unfavorably to the 1560 fleet that permitted half a pound per person. When available, 12 ounces of fresh beef replaced the six ounce salted meat ration. The 1647-51 Indies fleet consumed similar official rations enhanced by 12 ounces of pigs' feet (Phillips, 1986: 168).

Given the obvious preference for fresh produce, *flotas* were habitually provisioned with New World livestock on the homeward leg to Spain. A 1573 order instructed that it was at Havana, the convergence point for returning fleets of New Spain and Tierra Firme, where fleet ships should "take on water, firewood, and meat… and supply all ships properly, so that they do not suffer shortages during the trip" (De la Fuente, 2008: 53).

After returning to Spain from the Americas in 1622, the monk Antonio Vázquez de Espinosa confirmed that at Havana the fleet ships "outfit themselves and take on the supplies necessary to pass through the Bahamas Channel and sail to Spain." Espinosa's testimony from the time of the Tortugas ship's sinking clarifies that all the dietary supplies required by its crew were readily available in Cuba. Havana was built on a deep lagoon and provided an "abundance of meat, fish, turtles, tortoises, corn, manioc, and flour", while plantations of bananas, coconut palms, plums, pineapples, oranges, lemons and vegetables were cultivated in the hinterland (Clark, 1942: 103). In short, the city lived and died by the Carrera, from where it was a 65-day journey to Spain, compared to 115 days from Cartagena, the main north coast port of Tierra Firme (Macleod, 1986: 353). Spanish officials had such confidence in the New World environment that certainly in the 1570s they only provisioned ships with meat for outward journeys (Super, 1984: 61).

The transport of live animals, as attested archaeologically on the Tortugas ship for at least some pigs and chickens, fits with colorful historical sources. The tortoise shell from the hawksbill sea turtle excavated from the Tortugas wreck could also have been sourced in Havana and exploited as welcome by-product after meeting the crew's dietary needs. Thomas Gage, an English Dominican who lived in Mexico and Guatemala between 1625 and 1637, observed at Cartagena (Thompson, 1958: 334) how:

Fig. 87. Animal bones recovered from the Tortugas shipwreck.

"… as hog's flesh there is held to be so nourishing, so likewise no other meat is more than it and tortoises, wherewith all the ships make their provision for Spain… They also take into their ships some fowls for the masters' and captains' tables, and live hogs, which would seem to be enough to breed some infection in the ship, had they not care to wash often the place where such unclean beasts lie. In the ship where I was passenger, was killed every week one for the masters', pilots', and passengers' table."

Spanish Manila galleons sailing across the Pacific Ocean similarly carried egg-laying hens, roosters and pigs, the latter of which were eaten by the officers and passengers, and the leftovers thrown into the stewpot for consumption by the crew (Fish, 2011: 406). The 17th-century Italian traveler Giovanni Francesco Gemelli Careri described livestock taken aboard the Spanish galleon *San Jose* during its stop at Albay in the Philippines, where the mayor gifted the ship's captain 20 pigs plus 500 chickens (Fish, 2011: 401, 407).

Closer to the geographical route of the Tortugas ship, Jonathan Dickinson was caught in a storm while tacking from Cuba to Florida in 1696. During the drama, "Our hogs and sheep were washed away and swam on shore, except one of the hogs which remained in the vessel" (Andrews and Andrews, 1985: 5). These passages conjure up images of the squalid and cramped conditions aboard fleet ships and other merchant vessels, and of human lives closely intertwined with the hoofed animals that provided their sustenance.

The Tortugas shipwreck's faunal assemblage closely mirrors the 986 identifiable bones from the *Atocha*. Excluding the marine fish species on the grounds that this material likely includes a predominance of intrusive bone, the 543 identifiable edible species from the *Atocha* comprised sheep/goat (32.4%), pig (30.0%), cattle (11.9%), sheep/goat/pig (8.1%), sheep/goat/deer (5.7%), land tortoise (5.5%), chicken (1.7%), deer (1.3%), sheep (0.9%), sheep/deer (0.9%), goat (0.7%) and turkey (0.7%) (tabulated from Chapin, 1990: 36-8). The variety of species compares closely to the Tortugas ship with the single exception of a higher representation of land tortoise and the presence of deer, which may reflect the higher social status of the *Atocha* galleon and its passengers' access to veal as specified in 1570s *libro de raciones* (cf. Super, 1984: 60).

The animal bones on the earlier dated St. John's wreck of Spanish identity, lost off the Little Bahama Bank soon after 1554, include an adult pig and cow (Malcom, 1996). Pig, bone and white-tailed deer are attested on the Spanish-operated Western Ledge Reef wreck lost off Bermuda in the last quarter of the 16th-century (Franklin, 1993: 80).

Fig. 88. Animal bones, including the jawbone from the ship's cat (far right), recovered from the Tortugas shipwreck.

Chicken, pig, cow, sheep/goat were represented within the assemblage of 339 bones on the Emanuel I wreck (Smith *et al.*, 1995: 75-81). The faunal remains from the *San Diego*, a Spanish galleon that sank in 1600 off the western Philippines, reveal that the ship carried chickens, pigs and cattle for its crew of 450 men, with some meat stored in 13 'dragon jars' (Cuevas, 1996: 201; Fish, 2011: 407).

A further significant counterpoint to the Tortugas' wreck's faunal assemblage are the animal bones excavated from middens at Nueva Cadiz on the island of Cubagua on the Pearl Coast, where the *Buen Jesús y Nuestra Señora del Rosario* sailed in 1622. The island's main period of *ranchería* occupation dated from *c.* 1516-45. Not surprisingly for a far-flung colonial 'desert island', sea food was most highly represented, followed by mammals and birds, of which local deer and rabbit predominated. Pig followed by chicken was the most significant domesticated species (Wing, 1961: 163-4). The eastern Venezuelan colonial pattern of indigenous consumption was thus a far cry from *flota* supplies.

C. Black Rats

The evidence for rats on the Tortugas ship is not unexpected, but helps illuminate an infamous problem experienced by mariners in 1622. Having departed from the Honduran port of Trujillo aboard the *Nuestra Señora de la Candelaria*, the Spanish Carmelite monk Antonio Vázquez de Espinosa vividly recounted the invasion that overtook the ship. While transferring dyestuffs at Havana, rats were found to have devoured flour, hard tack, chickpeas, beans and meat. Over one thousand rats were allegedly killed on the *Candelaria* in port, but at sea the crew discovered a few thousand more infesting the ship from bow to stern, which ruthlessly consumed several tons of food, gnawing through sacks, boxes, jars, casks and stoppers (Peterson, 1975: 232, 241-2; Phillips, 1986: 157). They overran the storage holds, below the quarterdeck and plundered the stern salon, the cabins and even the pilot's seat. The vermin took four quintels of bread from the priest's cabin, plus the biscuits stored under the hatchway. Ham and sides of bacon hanging in the stern store chest were also heartily consumed (Galeanon, 1985: 197).

Thirsty passengers found drowned rats floating in barrels of water. All that remained in the hencoop were bones and feathers. Caged parrots were defenseless against the rodent army (see above for a unique point of archaeological convergence on the Tortugas wreck). Equipped with clubs and knives, the *Candelaria*'s sailors kept watch over the remaining food day and night, eventually killing over 3,000 rats before the fleet reached home (Galeanon, 1985: 197; Phillips, 1986: 157).

The rat bones associated with the Tortugas shipwreck contribute to our understanding of shipboard conditions at sea during the 1622 fleet's return to Spain. The problem, of course, was neither new, nor unique: excavation of the 1559 Emanuel I wreck recovered 206 bones from both young and adult *Rattus rattus*, as well as two from house mice (Smith *et al.*, 1995: 78-82).

14. Seeds

A. Sample

A total of 565 intact seeds and fragments derived from the ROV's SeRF system was recovered, examined and catalogued from the Tortugas site (Table 5; Figs. 89-93). The species type identifications were reconfirmed in 2012 by Victor Vankus, Southern Region Native Plant Coordinator, USDA Forest Service, National Seed Laboratory, Georgia. These provide little more than a flavor of the site's total archaeobotanical collection. Following the pattern of plant and food remains deposition observed on the Emanuel Point shipwrecks (Lawrence, 2010: 79), more substantial material is likely to be preserved among and under the ballast stones in the lower hull, which was not excavated on the Tortugas site. Positive identification was not always feasible given the fragmentary condition of much of the Tortugas material.

A number of seeds belong to the *Prunus* genus of plants, including intact specimens of peach (*Prunus persica*, L. 2.5cm) and the cherry family (Diam. 0.4cm). Also present are endocarp that appear to be almonds, *Prunus dulcis*, as well as fragments of plum seeds that are flatter in shape than peach (pers. comm. Victor Vankus, March 2012). Peaches, in particular, were amongst the earliest fruits shipped to the Americas by Spain and introduced into Mexico in the early 16th century; less than 50 years after Cortez conquered the country, peach trees were common regionally (Hedrick, 1917: 39-40). Historical records indicate that the peach was procured for cultivation at the failed Luna colony in Pensacola in 1559, and that peach trees were brought to Florida by the Spanish to St. Augustine not long after (Lawrence, 2010: 13, 40-1).

The presence of fruit and nuts aboard the Tortugas ship is not surprising in light of the devastating effects of the disease now known to be scurvy. While sailors had only limited knowledge about this fatal disease, by at least 1620 the condition was understood to be connected to diet and sea travel (Drymon, 2008: 114-5). Sailors were conscious that fresh provisions were somehow linked to the prevention of sickness (Phillips, 1986: 173), and fruits and nuts were considered especially beneficial for long journeys. Recognizing their nutritional value, these hearty edibles

Type	No. Whole	No. Fragments	Total No.
Almond (*Prunus dulcis*)	5	4	9
Burr (*Xanthium strumarium*)	1	0	1
Coconut (*Cocos nucifera*)	4	12	16
Grape (*Vitis vinifera*)	1	0	1
Hazelnut/filbert (*Corylus Americana*)	1	25	26
Melon (?) (*Cucurbitaceae*)	1	0	1
Olive (*Olea*)	98	77	175
Palm (round) (*Arecaceae*)	104	38	142
Palm (ribbed) (*Arecaceae*)	2	117	119
Cherry (?) (*Prunus cerasus*)	5	2	7
Squash (*Cucurbitaceae*)	1	0	1
Unidentified	22	45	67
TOTAL	245	320	565

Table 5. Seed types and volumes recovered from the Tortugas shipwreck.

were often added to official provisions, enhancing an otherwise bland diet (Smith *et al.* 1995: 94; Konstam, 2004, 35).

In addition, sugar, raisins and nuts were thought to hold curative properties. Almonds are cited in Habsburg-period provision lists as comprising special foodtsuffs transported for the sick, wounded and for highest-ranking fleet officials (Phillips, 1986: 97). The *Nuestra Señora de la Concepcion* was provisioned with almonds on its 1552 voyage from Seville to New Spain (Veyrat, 1994: 168). For the 1629 fleet in which Martin de Arana's six galleons first sailed to the Indies, 1,500lbs of almonds were listed among the *dietas* (special foods) retained for the original 3,000-man fleet (Phillips, 1986: 178).

The most prevalent seed type recovered from the Tortugas wreck was a hard, round, woody palm nut from one of the species in the *Arecaceae* palm family, most examples of which were intact (Diam. 2.4cm). These may have functioned as raw material for carving beads (carved and drilled examples of this nut type on the Tortugas shipwreck are discussed in the beads category: see section 8 above). Certainly in the late 17th century this raw material was used for palm-crafted rosaries, examples of which are associated with the *Atocha*. Two intact and many fragmented examples of a second type of palm nut were also recorded. Four intact coconuts and several broken coconut endocarp shell fragments were also recovered (Th. 0.4cm).

The olives pits can be subdivided generally into two sizes, the smaller approximately 1cm in diameter and the larger approximately 1.5cm in length (with maximum lengths for some examples of 2.0cm), suggesting the consumption on the Tortugas ship of two types of shipboard olives. One intact hazelnut was recovered (L. 2.0cm), alongside further fragments, as well as a single grape seed. One example of a burr (*Xanthium strumarium*, Diam. 0.4cm) could have been matted into the hair of either a

human or animal host or could have attached itself unnoticed to clothing or other material.

One seed has been classified as squash (L. 2.1cm) and another identified tentatively as melon (closely resembling a mature watermelon seed), but may have been a variety of squash as well. These seeds could have come aboard the ship in numerous ways: as food for the crew and passengers, on animals, as dunnage, fuel, stomach/intestinal contents, embedded in hooves, in or on cargo, or matted in hair, fur, feathers or clothing.

B. Parallels

The archaeobotanical material from the Tortugas shipwreck is largely typical of Spanish shipboard collections, which are otherwise more eclectic. The approximately 54 macrobotanical types recovered from the Emanuel Point II shipwreck (Florida, 1559) ranged from common hazelnuts, grape seeds, palm, cherry, almond and plum to a wide variety of remains mainly unattested on the Tortugas wreck: persimmon (*Diospyros virginiana*), English walnut (*Juglans regia*), apple or pear *(Malus* sp. or *Pyrus* sp.), black cherry (*Prunus serotina*), mustard family for flavoring food (*Brassicaceae*) and coriander (*Coriandrum sativum*). Additional seeds unique to the Emanuel Point I site were sapote (*Pouteria* sp.), New World papaya (*Carica papaya*) and a single fragment of coconut shell (*Cocos nucifera*) (Lawrence, 2010: 35-37, 39-44, 46).

The recovery of 175 olive pits from the Tortugas wreck, and 400 from the Emanuel Point I shipwreck (Lawrence, 2010: 81), obviously reflects the centrality of olives and olive oil in the Spanish diet. Included in the Emanuel Point I sample are cherry seeds, hazelnuts and almonds. Olive pits, almond shells and hazelnuts were similarly excavated from the 1554 *San Estéban* lost off Padre Island, Texas (Smith *et al.*, 1995: 92, 94).

Fig. 89. Seeds recovered from the Tortugas wreck using the SeRF system.

The Iberian vessel wrecked off Western Ledge Reef, Bermuda, in the last quarter of the 16th century contained an exotic assemblage reflecting New World food consumption and exploitation. The common olive pits and plum/cherry were accompanied by Jerusalem artichoke, pumpkin, American chestnut, one fragment of coconut, liquorice, English walnut and sweet almond (Franklin, 1993: 77-8). Further afield off Malaysia 150 hazelnuts, 30 peach pips and coconut were identified on the Spanish ship *San Diego* (Veyrat, 1994: 171). Nine different species of seeds were recovered from the *Atocha*, including samples which are similar to the seeds and nuts carried aboard the Tortugas ship: pumpkin/squash (*Cucurbita pepo*), hazelnut (*Corylus* sp), Mediterranean olive (*Olea Europa*), and Royal Palm (*Roystonea* sp) (Malcom, 1993: 8).

Two sets of atypical data emerge as particularly significant from the Tortugas shipwreck. Palm nuts account for 46.2% of the sample and seemingly reflect their con-

sumption for food and recycling in Spain for rosary bead production. The four intact and 12 coconut shell fragments seem a high representation compared to the single example recorded on both the Emanuel I and Western Ledge Reef sites.

Coconuts were first recorded in the Americas by Oviedo *c.* 1524 on Cocos Island on the shores of the Bay of Panama, and at Burica Point, and by 1580 were also documented at Motín along the central Pacific coast of Mexico between Colima and Zacatula. Fray Alonso Ponce commented on the profusion of coconut palms near Colima in 1587, where their woody shells were turned into drinking vessels for export to Spain (Bruman, 1945: 213).

The coconut was not indigenous to Panama and Mexico, but was washed there naturally from the Pacific islands, especially the Philippines, by the Equatorial Countercurrent (Bruman, 1945: 214-5; Salvaggio, 1992: 336). The product had become so commercially successful by 1610

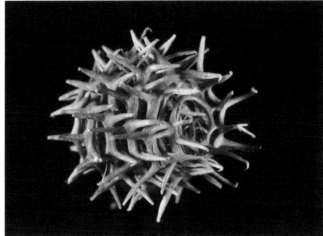

that on 29 March a decree of Luis de Velasco, the Viceroy of New Spain, sought to curtail Filipino immigrants making wine from coconut palms in the Colima area (Bruman, 1945: 215):

> "There is so great an abundance of these palms in the towns that in one of them alone there are sixty taverns where the wine is sold. The wine is cheap and strong, and the natives use it to such excess that it costs them their health and their lives. The sale of Castilian wine is hindered in these provinces by the excessive use of palm wine, and the royal treasury is thereby deprived of its rightful amount of tax money… The manufacture and sale of *vino de cocos* is therefore prohibited."

The ruling had little effect, and the trade was thriving so widely in 1619 that the naval officer Sebastián de Pineda proposed repatriating the native Indians back to the Philippines from Colima (Bruman, 1945: 215-6). The coconuts on the Tortugas ship may have originated in Mexico and been shipped intra-regionally into the Gulf of Mexico, possibly Havana, where they entered this merchantman as a source of nutrition and possible vessel production.

15. Conclusion

The Tortugas shipwreck's significance lies in its status as a small *navio* operating at the opposite commercial spectrum as the *Atocha* and *Margarita* lost in the same Tierra Firme fleet off the Florida Keys in September 1622. The ship is most plausibly identified as the Portuguese-built and Spanish-operated *Buen Jesús y Nuestra Señora del Rosario* (Kingsley, 2013). Although the three sites share many cultural features – including olive jar types, tablewares, Tortugas kitchen colonowares, gold bars, silver coins, astrolabes, pearls, rosary beads, glass bottles, bronze mortars and pestles, animal bone, seeds and even Native American greenstone exotica – the Tortugas ship was not transporting gold,

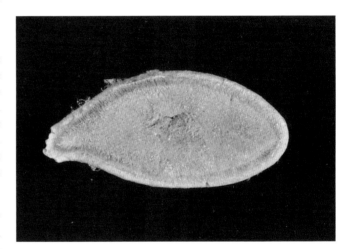

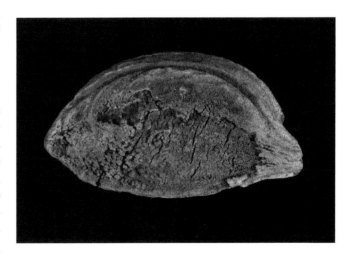

Figs. 90-93. Seeds recovered from the Tortugas wreck using the SeRF system: a ribbed palm nut, burr, pumpkin/squash and plum (top left to bottom).

silver and copper en masse. Differences rather than similarities are some of the wreck's most enduring characteristics.

The Tortugas ship contained at least 209 *botijas* produced in two sources in Cordoba and Seville, which are interpreted as ship's stores rather than cargo. Sources indicate that the *Buen Jesús y Nuestra Señora del Rosario* was licenced at Seville in March 1622 to carry 2,500 jars, but finally transported a reduced 1,400 jars of wine on behalf of various merchants (cf. AGI *Contratación* 3041 and *Contratación* 1172, N.2, R.1). The small quantity of olive jars excavated from the wreck accounts for just 8.4% of its authorized capacity and is best explained as containing foodstuffs intended for consumption by the crew and passengers on the return journey to Spain. Perhaps some of the site's olives, grapes (wine), hazelnuts, almonds, cherry and nuts derived from spilled *botija* interiors. Based on the geographic movements of the *Buen Jesús*, tobacco – now completed decomposed – has been proposed as the Tortugas ship's primary cargo (Kingsley, 2013).

The ship combined valuable goods and exotica alongside humble personal belongings. The 27 gold bars originating in the Colombian mines of Zaragoza and San Sebastian, some operated by the Peñaranda family, and the 1,184 silver coins largely minted in Mexico (56%) and Potosi, Bolivia (30%), may be interpreted as payment for the outward-bound cargos sold by and consigned to Juan de la Torre. The 6,639 pearls would have been picked up in eastern Venezuela at Cumana, the *Buen Jesús's* outward-bound destination in 1622 (Chaunu and Chaunu, 1956: 26-7).

Although historical sources decried the severe depletion of the Pearl Coast's oyster beds in the second half of the 17th century, the archaeology of the Tortugas ship demonstrates that profitable stocks could still be secured, especially if shipped as contraband, as the evidence implies. The three astrolabes, gold rosary stems, onyx inkwell and shaker, and elaborate ivory diptych sundial manufactured in Nuremberg complete the picture of a well-appointed *navio* with influential commercial prowess.

A fascinating counterpoint to the owner and captain's adventurous spirit in traveling beyond the Spanish safe havens of Mexico and Cuba to eastern Venezuela, a sea lane that was being increasingly blitzed by Dutch and English privateers in the first quarter of the 17th century, is the near-total cultural monopolization of the ceramic olive jars and tablewares by Andalusian products. Other than one Portuguese jug, a Columbia Plain bowl of possible New World manufacture, one San Juan Polychrome juglet from Mexico and South American, Mesoamerican or circum-Caribbean colonoware relied on exclusively for cooking, 99.8% of the 2,025 tablewares derived from Seville and a

rural location 24km west of Seville, close to the Rio Guadiamar. Unlike the *Atocha* and *Margarita*, no high-end gold, silver or even pewter tablewares were attested on the Tortugas site. A Spanish source is similarly not impossible for the ship's square-sectioned green glass bottles.

As home to the all-powerful Casa de la Contratacíon, Seville's monopoly over the Tortugas ship's stores is logical (albeit not mirrored strictly on contemporary English and Dutch merchant vessels), although the dominance of Blue-on-Blue Seville wares over Columbia Plain is unexpected. The major exception to this trend is the monopolization of the cooking wares by the Tortugas colonoware, a feature shared by the *Atocha*. In light of the clear cultural bias towards Andalusian ceramic repertoires, and dismissing the improbable assumption that the cooking pot assemblages from both ships broke simultaneously en route to the Americas, demanding replacement in South America or the Caribbean, this divergent pattern remains anomalous. According to contemporary documents, the *Buen Jesús y Nuestra Señora del Rosario* was crewed by ten sailors and a licensed pilot, supported by eight cabin boys and three pageboys (Kingsley, 2013). How many additional passengers accompanied them is unknown, although the ivory sundial, gold chain and gold rosary fittings may point to at least one wealthy individual. The personnel were mixed in age and nationality: the excavated human teeth derive from both a child and an adult, while the two drop-spindles are fiber spinning tools typically used by women. The two Native American ceramic pendant-like artifacts from the wreck and three greenstone whetstones and labret hint at her ethnicity as being Native South American or Mesoamerican.

While the woman weaved cotton, and a member of the crew idled away the quiet hours cutting lice combs and cases from Hawksbill tortoise shell, a caged consignment of blue-headed parrots squawked in the captain's cabin and the ship's cat looked on as a ferocious hurricane bore down on the unforgiving Florida Keys. On the basis of the highly limited human remains, the majority of the ship's company may have chosen to take their chances in the open sea as disaster struck and the bell sounded its final fury.

Acknowledgements

This archaeological report has been a long time in gestation and has benefited from a wide team of personnel from technicians and engineers to archaeologists and scholars. First and foremost, the project – the world's first full-scale deep-sea shipwreck excavation – would have been impossible without the vision of Seahawk co-founder John Morris and Project Managers Gordon Richardson and John Astley, who designed and assembled with Greg Stemm the entire suite of technology and scientific package required for deep-sea archaeology (including customization of the ship, the four point mooring system and the ROV system incorporating the venturi dredge for excavating sediment, the limpet suction device for recovering artifacts and a sediment filtration system attached to the rear of the ROV). Even by 21st-century standards the success of this technology to record the positions of almost 17,000 objects and document them graphically at a depth of 405m with very little systems loss of time to interruption was remarkable.

Great appreciation is also extended to David Moore and his assistant Heather Gibbs, who diligently directed the procurement of archaeological data in the field and interfaced with the ROV team to achieve pioneering results. Jenette Flow supervised years of intensive post-excavation study and management of the Tortugas collection with the assistance of David Morris, who oversaw the conservation of the collection. The diligence and creativity of the team on the ship was paramount to the project's success, including Captains Dale Wilson and Harvey Hawkins and ROV technicians Sandy Delgarno, Bill Garden, Vince Trotta and Russell Macdonald. Significant contributions to the development of the ROV technology and tooling were made by Graham Hawkes, Sylvia Earle and John Edwards of Deep Ocean Engineering, as well as by Dr. James Cooke, Scott Stemm, Steve Dabagian, Jan Ricks, David Six and Tim Ricks, who ran the RV *Seahawk* and its search system, including the Phantom ROVs, and discovered the Tortugas site.

This report – an 'excavation' of the excavation initially conducted by Seahawk Deep Ocean Technology – was brought to reality under the auspices of Odyssey Marine Exploration, which owns the intellectual property rights to 8,501 Tortugas shipwreck artifacts and retains and curates the Tortugas collection in Tampa, Florida. Odyssey's management and personnel have supported this study and publication project with great enthusiasm and we are sincerely grateful to: Mark Gordon, Laura Barton, Alice Copeland, Eric Tate and Melissa Dolce (reports design). Special thanks are extended to John Oppermann and his team at Odyssey's ARC laboratory at Tampa: John has bent over backwards to accommodate this project and make resources available at every turn, supported by the energy and commitment of Fred Van de Walle (Conservation Manager), Alan Bosel (collection photography, slides digitization), Chad Morris (cataloguing and sampling), Gerri Graca (video conversion, research material procurement), Mark Sullivan (Spanish historical sources supply and translation management) and Mark Mussett (map production, fish species identification). The authors also sincerely thank Dr. Juan Antonio Morales González from the Investigation group of Coastal Geology and Water Resources of the University of Huelva.

This report benefits substantially from summaries of specialists' reports on Tortugas shipwreck assemblages to be published separately: Philip Armitage, Curator, Brixham Heritage Museum, UK (animal bones); Michael Hughes (Inductively-Coupled Plasma Spectrometry analysis of pottery); Byron Sudbury, Clay Tobacco Pipe Specialist, Consultant and Sr. Research Scientist at J.S. Enterprises (the tobacco pipes); and Carol Tedesco, Key West (the silver coins).

The authors are especially grateful to numerous specialists and colleagues who generously offered their expertise relevant to assemblages recovered from the Tortugas shipwreck: Tânia Casimiro, Instituto de Arqueologia e Paleociências das Universidades Nova de Lisboa e do Algarve, Portugal; Ann S. Cordell, Staff Archaeologist, Florida Museum of Natural History, Gainesville; Kathleen Deagan, Distinguished Research Curator Emerita of Historical Archaeology, Florida Museum of Natural History, Gainesville; Susan D. DeFrance, Associate Professor of Anthropology and Chair, University of Florida Department of Anthropology; John de Bry, Director, Center for Historical Archaeology, Florida; Don Duco, Curator, Pijpenkabinet, Netherlands; Charles Ewen, Director, Phelps Archaeology Laboratory, East Carolina University; Alejandra Gutiérrez, Department of Archaeology, University of Durham; Robert Hunter, historical archaeologist, ceramic specialist and Editor, *Ceramics in America*; Silas Hurry, Curator of Collections and Archaeological Laboratory, Historic St. Mary's City, Maryland; William F. Keegan, Curator of Caribbean Archaeology, Florida Museum of Natural History, Gainesville; Elise V. LeCompte, Registrar and Asst. Dept. Chair, Department of Natural History, Florida Museum of Natural History; James Levy, Former Historic Conservator, Florida Bureau of Archaeological Research, Division of Historical Resources; Bill Lindsey, SHA/BLM Historic Glass Bottle ID and Information Website; Corey Malcom, Director of Archaeology, Mel Fisher Maritime Heritage Society, Key West; Jamie May, Senior Staff Archaeologist, Jamestown Rediscovery, Virginia; Melissa Memory, Chief of Cultural Resources, Everglades and Dry Tortugas National Parks; Susan Milbrath, Curator of Latin American Art and Archaeology, Florida Museum of Natural History, Gainesville; Anne Meylan, Research Administrator, Fish and Wildlife Research Institute, Fish and Wildlife Conservation Commission, St. Petersburg, Florida; Ivor Noël Hume, Former Chief Archaeologist, Colonial Williamsburg, Virginia; Richard Patterson, Trade Bead Historian; Stephen Pollock, Professor of Geosciences, University of Southern Maine; Marie Prentice, Senior Archaeologist,

Florida Bureau of Archaeological Research, Division of Historical Resources; Prudence M. Rice, Distinguished Professor Emerita, Department of Anthropology, Southern Illinois University Carbondale; D.A. Saguto, Colonial Williamsburg Foundation, Virginia; Brian Shamblin, Postdoctoral Research Associate, Warnell School of Forestry and Natural Resources, University of Georgia, Athens; Russell Skowronek, Professor of History and Anthropology, University of Texas-Pan American; Marvin Smith, Professor of Anthropology, Department of Sociology, Anthropology, and Criminal Justice, Valdosta State University; Roger Smith, State Underwater Archaeologist, Florida Bureau of Archaeological Research, Division of Historical Resources; Beverly Straube, Senior Archaeological Curator, Jamestown Rediscovery, Virginia; Claire Tindal, Historic Conservator, Florida Bureau of Archaeological Research, Division of Historical Resources; Victor Vankus, Southern Region Native Plant Coordinator, USDA Forest Service National Seed Laboratory; Richard Vernon, Supervisory Museum Curator, National Park Service, Southeast Archeological Center, Tallahassee; Molly Warsh, Assistant Professor of History, Texas A&M University; all the staff of the Archivo General de Indias in Seville.

The authors also extend sincere gratitude to colleagues who generously found the time from their busy schedules to read and comment on the Tortugas Reports: Filipe Castro, Frederick R. Mayer Faculty Professor II of Nautical Archaeology, Nautical Archaeology Program, Texas A&M University; Ivor Noël Hume; Miguel San Claudio Santa Cruz, Archeonauta, Spain; James J. Sinclair, Principal Investigator, SeaRex Inc., Florida; Russell Skowronek, Professor of History and Anthropology, the University of Texas-Pan American; Roger Smith, State Underwater Archaeologist, Bureau of Archaeological Research, Florida; and Beverly Straube, Senior Archaeological Curator, Jamestown Rediscovery, Virginia. All errors are our own.

Finally, we would like to take this opportunity to thank those people who provided so much support for the project but are no longer with us, including Mendel Peterson, Sir John Rawlins, Peter Throckmorton and Jack Painter.

Notes

1. Christie's Auction 7748, 21 October 1993, New York: http://www.christies.com/LotFinder/lot_details. aspx?intObjectID=2455842.
2. See Mission San Luis de Talimali, US Department of the Interior, NPS, 9: http://www.nps.gov/nhl/designations/samples/fl/San%20Luis%20de%20Talimali.pdf.
3. Dimensions taken from artifacts at: http://www.historicshipwrecks.com.
4. Types of astrolabes are as defined by Waters and Stimson: cf. Garcia, 2008: 250.
5. See: the auction catalogue for *Gold and Silver of the Atocha and Santa Margarita* (Christie's New York, 14-15 June, 1988).
6. See: http://inadiscover.com/blogs/gnalic-project.
7. See: http://ina.tamu.edu/pedrobank/pedrobank.htm.
8. Zmaic, V., 'Post Medieval Shipwreck from the Early 17th Century at the Mijoka Shallows off the Island of Murter': http://icua.hr/en/archaeologyprojects/114-novovjekovni-brodolom-s-poetka-17st-na-pliini-mijoka-kod-murtera.
9. The description of the greenstone objects 90-1A-000567 and F24001.0015 is based on one drawing. The artifacts are no longer in the Tortugas collection maintained by Odyssey Marine Exploration in Tampa, Florida.
10. See: Howard, Kim Be, Jadeite (Canadian Institute of Gemmology, Vancouver, no date).

Bibliography

Anderson, J.W., *Daily Life During the Spanish Inquisition* (Westport, Conn., 2002).

Andrews, E.W. and Andrews, C.M., *Jonathan Dickinson's Journal or, God's Protecting Providence. Being the Narrative of a Journey from Port Royal in Jamaica to Philadelphia between August 23, 1696 and April 1, 1697* (Port Salerno, Florida, 1985).

Armitage, P.L., *The Deep-Sea Tortugas Shipwreck, Florida: the Animal Bones* (OME Papers, 2013).

Armstrong, W., *Velazquez: A Study of His Life and Art* (Whitefish, Montana, 2004).

Aspinall, A.E., *The British West Indies: their History, Resources and Progress* (London, 1912).

Astley, J. and Stemm, G., *The Deep-Sea Tortugas Shipwreck, Florida: Technology* (OME Papers 25, 2013).

Avery, G., *Pots as Packaging: the Spanish Olive Jar and Andalusian Transatlantic Commercial Activity, 16th-18th Centuries* (PhD. Thesis, University of Florida, 1997).

Baart, J.M., 'Dutch Material Civilization: Daily Life Between 1650-1776. Evidence from Archaeology'. In R.H. Blackburn and N.A. Kelley (eds.), *New World Dutch Studies Dutch Arts and Culture in Colonial America 1609-1776* (Albany Institute of History and Art, 1987), 1-11.

Badger, R.R. and Clayton, L.A., *Alabama and the Borderlands from Prehistory to Statehood* (University of Alabama Press, 1985).

Barber, E.A., *Spanish Glass in the Collection of the Hispanic Society of America* (London, 1917).

Barto Arnold, J. and Weddle, R., *The Nautical Archaeology*

of Padre Island. The Spanish Shipwrecks of 1554 (New York, 1978).

Bass, G.F., 'Personal Effects'. In S. Matthews, J.R. Steffy and F.H. van Doornick, Jr., *Serçe Limani. An Eleventh-Century Shipwreck, Vol. 1. The Ship and its Anchorage, Crew, and Passengers* (Texas A&M Press, 2004), 275-87.

Beck, R.A., Moore, D.G. and Rodning, C.B., 'Identifying Fort San Juan: A Sixteenth-Century Spanish Occupation at the Berry Site, North Carolina', *Southeastern Archaeology* 25.1 (2006), 65-77.

Berg, D. and Berg, D., *Bermuda Shipwrecks: a Vacationing Diver's Guide to Bermuda's Shipwrecks* (New York, 1991).

Blair, E.H., 'The Distribution of Beads from St. Catherines Island'. In *The Beads of St. Catherines Island* (Anthropological Papers of the American Museum of Natural History 89, 2009), 135-66.

Borrell, P.J., *Historia y Rescate del Galeon Nuestra Señora de la Concepcion* (Museo de las Casas Reales, Santo Domingo, 1983).

Bound, M. and Gosset, P., 'The Dragon, 1712'. In M. Bound (ed.), *Excavating Ships of War* (Oswestry, 1998), 149-58.

Bradley, J.W., *Evolution of the Onondaga Iroquois: Accommodating Change 1500-1655* (Syracuse University Press, 1987).

Brigadier, S.R., *The Artifact Assemblage from the Pepper Wreck: an Early Seventeenth Century Portuguese East-Indiaman that Wrecked in the Tagus River* (MA Thesis, Texas A&M University, 2002).

Bruman, H.J., 'Early Coconut Culture in Western Mexico', *Hispanic American Historical Review* 25.2 (1945), 212-23.

Bruseth, J.E. and Turner, T.S., *From a Watery Grave: the Discovery and Excavation of La Salle's Shipwreck, La Belle* (Texas A&M University Press, 2005).

Burgess, R.F. and Clausen, C.J., *Florida's Golden Galleons. The Search for the 1715 Spanish Treasure Fleet* (Port Salerno, FL, 1982).

Burns, J.M., 'The Anchor and Related Rigging Components'. In R.C. Smith, J.R. Bratten, J. Cozzi and K. Plaskett, *The Emanuel Point Ship Archaeological Investigations 1997-1998* (Report of Investigations No. 68 Archaeology Institute University of West Florida, 1998), 72-9.

Burns, R.B., 'The Pedro Bank Sundial', *International Journal of Nautical Archaeology* 13.4 (1984), 339-40.

Carruthers, C., 'Spanish *Botijas* or Olive Jars from the Santo Domingo Monastery, La Antigua Guatemala', *Historical Archaeology* 37.4 (2003), 40-55.

Casimiro, T.M., *Portuguese Faience in England and Ireland* (BAR Int. Series 2301, Oxford, 2011).

Castro, F., Fonseca, N. and Wells, A., 'Outfitting the Pep-per Wreck', *Historical Archaeology* 44.2 (2010), 14-34.

Cederlund, C.O., Vasa I. *The Archaeology of a Swedish Warship of 1628* (Oxford, 2006).

Chaunu, H. and Chaunu, P., *Séville et l'Atlantique (1504-1650). Première partie: partie statistique. Le movement des navires et des merchandised entre l'Espagne et l'Amérique de 1504-1650. Tome V. Le traffic de 1621-1650* (Paris, 1956).

Clausen, C.J., *A 1715 Spanish Treasure Ship* (University of Florida, Gainesville, 1965).

Clark, C.U. (tr.), *Antonio Vázquez de Espinosa. Compendium and Description of the West Indies* (Washington, 1942).

Cofer, L.E., 'A Word to Ship Captains About Quarantine', *Public Health Bulletin* 55 (1912), 3-19.

Craig, A.K. and Richards, E.J., *Spanish Treasure Bars from New World Shipwrecks, Volume One* (West Palm Beach, Florida. 2003).

Cuevas, M.A., 'The *San Diego* Wreck Site off Fortune Island, Philippines', *Indo-Pacific Prehistory Association Bulletin* 14 (1996), 197-202.

Cunningham Dobson, N., '*La Marquise de Tourny* (Site 33c): A Mid-18th Century Armed Privateer of Bordeaux'. In G. Stemm and S. Kingsley (eds.), *Ocean Odyssey 2. Underwater Heritage Management & Deep-Sea Shipwrecks in the English Channel & Atlantic Ocean* (Oxford, 2011), 69-108.

Deagan, K.A., 'Fig Springs: The Mid-Seventeenth Century in North Central Florida', *Historical Archaeology* 6 (1972), 23-46.

Deagan, K., *Artifacts of the Spanish Colonies of Florida and the Caribbean, 1500-1800. Volume 1: Ceramics, Glassware and Beads* (Washington, 1987).

Deagan, K., *Artifacts of the Spanish Colonies: Florida and the Caribbean, 1500-1800. Volume 2: Portable, Personal Possessions* (Washington, 2002).

Drymon, M.M., *Disguised as the Devil. A History of Lyme Disease and Witch Accusations* (Wythe Avenue Press, 2008).

Eldridge, B.E. and Edman, J.D., *Medical Entomology* (Dordrecht, 2000).

Ewen, C.R. and Hann, J.H., *Hernando De Soto Among the Apalachee. The Archaeology of the Winter Encampment* (University Press of Florida, 1998).

Fairbanks, C.H., 'Early Spanish Colonial Beads'. In S. South (ed.), *The Conference on Historic Site Archaeology Papers 1967 - Volume 2, Part 1* (South Carolina Institute of Archaeology and Anthropology, University of South Carolina, 1968), 3-21.

Fine, J.C., *Treasures of the Spanish Main. Shipwrecked Galleons in the New World* (Guildford, Connecticut, 2006).

Fish, S., *The Manila-Acapulco Galleons: the Treasure Ships of the Pacific with an Annotated List of the Transpacific*

Galleons 1565-1815 (Central Milton Keynes, 2011).

Flow, J., *Tortugas Deep Water Shipwreck. Interim Report* (Tampa, 1999, unpublished).

Francis, P., Jr., 'Beads in the Spanish Colonial Empire'. In *The Beads of St. Catherines Island* (Anthropological Papers of the American Museum of Natural History 89, 2009a), 7-12.

Francis, P. Jr., 'The Glass beads of the Margariteri of Venice'. In *The Beads of St. Catherines Island* (Anthropological Papers of the American Museum of Natural History 89, 2009b), 59-64.

Francis, P., Jr., 'The Glass Beads of the Paternostri of the Netherlands and France'. In *The Beads of St. Catherines Island* (Anthropological Papers of the American Museum of Natural History 89, 2009c), 73-80.

Francis, P. Fr., 'The Glass Beads of China'. In *The Beads of St. Catherines Island* (Anthropological Papers of the American Museum of Natural History, 2009d), 81-84.

Francis, P. Jr., 'The Glass Beads of Spain'. In *The Beads of St. Catherines Island* (Anthropological Papers of the American Museum of Natural History 89, 2009e), 85-95.

Francis, P. Jr., 'Glass Beads of Other Manufacturing Centers'. In *The Beads of St. Catherines Island* (Anthropological Papers of the American Museum of Natural History 89, 2009f), 97-100.

Francis, P. Jr., 'Imported Beads of Hard Stone'. In *The Beads of St. Catherines Island* (Anthropological Papers of the American Museum of Natural History 89, 2009g), 117-22.

Franklin, M., 'Description of Artifacts assemblage Archaeologically Recovered from Western Ledge Reef Wreck, Bermuda', *Bermuda Journal of Archaeology and Maritime History* 5 (1993), 70-83.

Frothingham, A.W., *Spanish Glass* (London, 1963).

Fuente, A., de la, *Havana and the Atlantic in the Sixteenth Century* (University of North Carolina Press, 2008).

Galeano, E., *Genesis: Memory of Fire (Volume 1)* (Nation Books, 1985).

Garcia, G.A., *The Rincón Astrolabe Shipwreck* (MA Thesis, Texas A&M University, 2005).

Garcia, G., 'Nautical Astrolabes'. In F. Vieira de Castro and K. Custer (eds.), *Edge of Empire* (Caleidoscópio, 2008), 249-74.

Garigen, L.L., *Description and Analysis of Flintlock Pistols Recovered from a Seventeenth-Century Shipwreck on Pedro Bank, Jamaica* (MA Thesis, Texas A&M University, 1991).

Gasco, J. and Voorhies, B., 'The Ultimate Tribute: the Role of the Soconusco as an Aztec Tributary'. In B. Voorhies (ed.), *Ancient Trade and Tribute. Economies of the Soconusco Region of Mesoamerica* (University of Utah Press, 1989), 48-94.

Gerrard, C.M., Gutiérrez, A., Hurst, J.C. and Vince, A.G., 'A Guide to Spanish Medieval Pottery'. In C.M. Gerrard, A. Gutiérrez, A. and A.G. Vince (eds.), *Spanish Medieval Ceramics in Spain and the British Isles* (BAR Int. S610, Oxford, 1995), 281-95.

Gilchrist, R., *Medieval Life: Archaeology and the Life Course* (Woodbridge, 2012).

Given, B.J., *A Most Pernicious Thing. Gun Trading and Native Warfare in the Early Contact Period* (Carleton University Press, 1994).

Goggin, J.M., *Spanish Majolica in the New World. Types of the Sixteenth to Eighteenth Centuries* (Yale University Press, New Haven, 1968).

Goode, G.B., *The Fishery and Fisheries Industry of the United States* (Washington, 1884).

Goubitz, O., *Stepping through Time. Archaeological Footwear from Prehistoric Times until 1800* (Stichting Promotie Archaelogie, 2007).

Gouk, P., *The Ivory Sundials of Nuremberg 1500-1700* (Cambridge, 1988).

Gouk, P., 'Nuremberg Diptych Sundials'. In S.A. Lloyd, *Ivory Diptych Sundials 1570-1750* (Harvard University Press, 1992), 33-98.

Grande, L., and Augustyn, A., *Gems and Gemstones. Timeless Natural Beauty of the Mineral World* (University of Chicago Press, 2009).

Green, J.N, 'The Wreck of the Dutch East Indiaman the *Vergulde Draeck*, 1656', *International Journal of Nautical Archaeology* 2.2 (1973), 267-89.

Green, J., *The Loss of the Verenigde Oostindische Compagnie Jacht Vergulde Draeck, Western Australia 1656. Part i* (BAR Suppl S36(i), Oxford, 1977).

Green, J.N., *The Loss of the Verenigde Oostindische Compagnie Retourschip* Batavia, *Western Australia 1629* (BAR Int. S489, Oxford, 1989).

Grissim, J., *The Lost Treasure of the* Concepción (New York, 1980).

Hall, L. B., *Mary, Mother and Warrior. The Virgin in Spain and the Americas* (University of Texas Press, 2004).

Harding, D.F., *Smallarms of the East India Company 1600-1856. Volume III. Ammunition and Performance* (London, 1999).

Hedrick, U.P., *The Peaches of New York* (Albany, 1917).

Helferich, G., *Stone of Kings. In Search of the Lost Stone of the Maya* (Guilford, Conn., 2012).

Higton, H., *Sundials. An Illustrated History of Portable Dials* (London, 2001).

Howell. J., *Epistolae Ho-Elianae: Familiar Letters Domestic and Foreign…* (London, 1754).

Hoyt, S.D., 'The Archaeological Survey of Pedro Bank, Jamaica 1981-1983', *International Journal of Nautical*

Archaeology 13.2 (1984), 99-111.

Hughes, M.J., 'Scientific Analysis'. In I.M. Betts, 'Spanish Tin-glazed Tiles from Woking Palace and other Sites in South-east England', *Surrey Archaeological Collections* 94 (2008), 66-7.

Hughes, M.J., *The Chemical Analysis by Plasma Spectrometry (ICPS) of Pottery from the Tortugas Shipwreck (Florida Keys, 1622)* (OME Papers, forthcoming).

Hume, I.N., *The Guide to Artifacts of Colonial America* (New York, 1974).

Hurry, S.D. and Grulich, A.D., *Putti, Kings and the Mother of God* (2012, unpublished).

Hurst, J.G., 'Post-Medieval Pottery from Seville Imported into North-West Europe'. In D.R. Hook and D.R.M. Gaimster (eds.), *Trade and Discovery: the Scientific Study of Artefacts from Post-Medieval Europe and Beyond* (London, 1995), 45-54.

Ingelman-Sundberg, C., 'Preliminary Report on Finds from the Jutholmen Wreck', *International Journal of Nautical Archaeology* 5.1 (1976), 57-71.

James, S.R., 'A Reassessment of the Chronological and Typological Framework of the Spanish Olive Jar', *Historical Archaeology* 22 .1 (1988), 43-66.

Jordan, W.B., *Spanish Still Life in the Golden Age, 1600-1650* (Kimbell Art Museum, Fort Worth, 1985).

Jordan, W.B. and Cherry, P., *Spanish Still Life from Velázquez to Goya* (London, 1995).

Kawaguchi, Y., 'The Newly Found Olive Jars in Japan and their Historical Significance', *Sokendai Review of Cultural and Social Studies* 7 (2011), 123-32.

Keith, D. H., Duff, J.A., James, S.R., Oertling, T.J. and Simmons, J.J., 'The Molasses Reef Wreck, Turks and Caicos Islands, B.W.I.: a Preliminary Report', *International Journal of Nautical Archaeology* 13.1 (1984), 45-63.

Kelso, W.M., *Jamestown. The Buried Truth* (University of Virginia Press, 2006).

Kelso, W.M., Lucketti, N.M. and Straube, B., *Jamestown Rediscovery V* (Association for the Preservation of Virginia Antiquities, 1999).

Kidd, K.E. and Kidd, M.A., 'A Classification System for Glass Beads for the Use of Field Archaeologists'. In *Canadian Historic Sites Occasional Papers in Archaeology and History* 1 (Ottawa, 1970).

Kinard, J., *Pistols. An Illustrated History of their Impact* (Santa Barbara, 2003).

Kingsley, S., *The Identity and Maritime History of the Deep-Sea Tortugas Shipwreck* (OME Papers 28, 2013).

Kingsley, S., Gerth, E. and Hughes, M., 'Ceramics from the Tortugas Shipwreck. A Spanish-Operated *Navio* of the 1622 Tierra Firme Fleet', *Ceramics In America* (forthcoming, 2012).

Kirkman, J., *Fort Jesus. A Portuguese Fortress on the East African Coast* (Oxford, 1974).

Koch, R.P., *Dress Clothing of the Plains Indians* (University of Oklahoma Press, 1977).

Konstam, A., *The History of Shipwrecks* (Lyons Press, 1999).

Konstam, A., *Spanish Galleon 1530-1690* (Oxford, 2004).

Lapham, H.A., 'More Than "A Few Blew Beads": the Glass and Stone Beads from Jamestown Rediscovery's 1994-1997 Excavations', *The Journal of the Jamestown Rediscovery Center* 1 (2001), 11-14.

Lawrence, C.L.R., *An Analysis of Plant Remains from the Emanuel Point Shipwrecks* (MA Thesis, Department of Anthropology College of Arts and Sciences, University of West Florida, 2010).

L'Hour, M. and Richez, F., *Le Mauritius. La mémoire engloutie* (Casterman, 1989).

Lister, F.C. and Lister, R.H., 'Maiolica in Colonial Spanish America', *Historical Archaeology* 8 (1974), 17-52.

Lister, F.C. and Lister, R.H., *Andalusian Ceramics in Spain and New Spain: a Cultural Register from the Third Century BC to 1700* (University of Arizona Press, Tucson, 1987).

Lloyd, S.A., *Ivory Diptych Sundials 1570-1750* (Harvard University Press, 1992).

Loren, D.D.P., *In Contact. Bodies and Spaces in the Sixteenth- and Seventeenth-Century Eastern Woodlands* (Lanham, MD, 2008).

Lotbiniere, S. de, 'Gunflint Recognition', *International Journal of Nautical Archaeology* 13.3 (1984), 206-209.

Mackenzie, C.L., Troccoli, L. and León, L.B., 'History of the Atlantic Pearl-Oyster, *Pinctata imbricata*, Industry in Venezuela and Colombia, with Biological and Ecological Observations', *Marine Fisheries Review* 65.1 (2003), 1-20.

Malcom, C., 'Glass from *Nuestra Señora de Atocha*', *Astrolabe: Journal of the Mel Fisher Maritime Heritage Society* 6.1 (1990).

Malcom, C., 'The Flotation of Waterlogged Organics: the *Atocha* Example', *Astrolabe: Journal of the Mel Fisher Maritime Heritage Society* 8.1 (1993), 2-7.

Malcom, C., *St. John's Bahamas Shipwreck Project. Interim Report I: the Excavation and Artifacts 1991-1995* (Key West, 1996).

Malcom, C., 'Pewter from the *Nuestra Señora de Atocha*', *The Navigator: Newsletter of the Mel Fisher Maritime Heritage Society* 13.11-12 (1998a).

Malcom, C., 'The Mariner's Astrolabe', *The Navigator: Newsletter of the Mel Fisher Maritime Heritage Society* 13.5 (1998b).

Mallios, S., *Archaeological Excavations at 44JC568, The Reverend Richard Buck Site* (Association for the Preservation of Virginia Antiquities, 1999).

Mallios S. and Straube, B., *Interim Report on the APVA Excavations at Jamestown, Virginia* (Association for the Preservation of American Antiquities, October 2000).

Marken, M.W., *Pottery from Spanish Shipwrecks 1500-1800* (University Press of Florida, 1994).

Marsden, P., 'The Dutch East Indiaman *Hollandia* Wrecked on the Isles of Scilly in 1743. Archaeological Report', *International Journal of Nautical Archaeology* 4.2 (1975), 278-97.

Mardsen, P., *Sealed by Time. The Loss and Recovery of the Mary Rose* (Trowbridge, 2003).

Marti, J. and Pascual, J., 'Tradición e Innovación en el Repertorio de la Cerámica Valenciana Bajomedieaval'. In C.M. Gerrard, A. Gutiérrez, A. and A.G. Vince (eds.), *Spanish Medieval Ceramics in Spain and the British Isles* (BAR Int. S610, Oxford, 1995), 159-75.

Martin, C.J.M., 'Spanish Armada Pottery', *International Journal of Nautical Archaeology* 8.4 (1979a), 279-302.

Martin, C.J.M., 'La *Trinidad Valencera*: an Armada Invasion Transport Lost off Donegal. Interim Site Report, 1971-76', *International Journal of Nautical Archaeology* 8.1 (1979b), 13-38.

Marx, R.F., *The Lure of Sunken Treasure* (New York, 1973).

Marx, R., 'Deep Sea Treasure Hunting', *Wreck Diving Magazine* 18 (2009), 54-61.

Mathewson, D., *Treasure of the* Atocha (Houston, 1986).

McBride, P., Larn, R. and Davis, R., 'A Mid-17th Century Merchant Ship found near Mullion Cove. 3rd Interim Report on the *Santo Christo de Castello, 1667*', *International Journal of Nautical Archaeology* 4.2 (1975), 237-52.

McEwen, B.G., 'Domestic Adaptation at Puerto Real, Haiti', *Historical Archaeology* 20.1 (1986), 44-9.

McEwan, B.G., 'San Luis de Talimali: the Archaeology of Spanish-Indian Relations at a Florida Mission', *Historical Archaeology* 25.3 (1991), 36-60.

McEwan, B.G. and Poe, C.B., 'Excavations at Fort San Luis', *Florida Anthropologist* 47.2 (1994), 90-106.

McNaulty, R.H., 'Common Beverage Bottles: their Production, Use and Forms in the 17th and 18th Century Netherlands' (Part I),' *Journal of Glass Studies* 13 (1971) 91-119.

McRobb, J.H., *A Contemporary Peruvian Weaving Technique on the Continuous Warp Loom: Learning and Instruction in a Non-Literate Society* (MA Thesis, University British Columbia, 1980).

Mitchen, J.M. and Leader, J.M., 'Early Sixteenth Century Beads from the Tatum Mound, Citrus County, Florida: Data and Interpretations', *Florida Anthropologist* 41.1 (1988), 42-60.

Noël Hume, I.N. and Noël Hume, A.N., *The Archaeology of Martin's Hundred. Part II: Artifacts Catalogue* (Williamsburg, Virginia, 2001).

Noelli, F.S., Viana, A. and Moura, M.L., 'Praia dos Ingleses 1: Arqueologia Subaquática na Ilha de Santa Catarina Brasil (2004/2005/2009)', *Revista do Museu de Arqueologia e Etnologia, São Paulo* 10 (2009), 92-107.

Oleson, J.P., 'Testing the Waters: The Role of Sounding-Weights in Ancient Mediterranean Navigation.' In R.L. Hohlfelder (ed.), *The Maritime World of Ancient Rome* (University of Michigan Press, Ann Arbor, 2008), 119-76.

Parsons, J.J., 'The Hawksbill Turtle and the Tortoise Shell Trade', *Études de géographie tropicale offertes à Pierre Gourou* (1972), 44-60.

Pearson, C.E. and Hoffman, P.E., *The Last Voyage of* El Nuevo Constante. *The Wreck and Recovery of an Eighteenth-Century Spanish Ship off the Louisiana Coast* (Louisiana State University Press, 1995).

Pendleton, L.S.A., Blair, E.H. and Powell, E., 'The Bead Assemblage from St Catherines Island'. In *The Beads of St. Catherines Island* (Anthropological Papers of the American Museum of Natural History 89, 2009), 35-50.

Peterson, M., *The Funnel of Gold* (Boston, 1975).

Phillips, C.A., *Six Galleons for the King of Spain* (Johns Hopkins University Press, 1986).

Piercy, R.C.M., 'Mombasa Wreck Excavation. Second Preliminary Report, 1978', *International Journal of Nautical Archaeology* 7.4 (1978), 301-19.

Pike, R., *Aristocrats and Traders. Sevillian Society in the Sixteenth Century* (Cornell University Press, Ithica, 1972).

Pleguezuelo-Hernandez, A., 'Seville Coarsewares, 1350-1650: a Preliminary Typological Survey', *Medieval Ceramics* 17 (1993), 39-50.

Price, R. and Muckelroy, K., 'The Kennemerland Site. The Fifth Season, 1978. An Interim Report', *International Journal of Nautical Archaeology* 8.4 (1979), 311-20.

Provoyeur, P., 'Les arts de la table, les bijoux et les objets de dévotion'. In Carré, D., Desroches, J.-P. and Goddio, F., *Le San Diego. Un trésor sous la mer* (Paris, 1994), 258-98.

Rice, P.M., 'Peru's Colonial Wine Industry and its European Background', *Antiquity* 70 (1996), 785-800.

Romero, A., 'Death and Taxes: the Case of the Depletion of Pearl Oyster Beds in Sixteenth-Century Venezuela', *Conservation Biology* 17.4 (2003), 1013-23.

Romero, A., Chilbert, S. and Eisenhart, M.G., 'Cubagua's Pearl-Oyster Beds: the First Depletion of a Natural Resource Caused by Europeans in the American Continent', *Journal of Political Ecology* 6 (1999), 57-78.

Salvaggio, J.E., 'Fauna, Flora, Fowl, and Fruit: Effects of the Columbian Exchange on the Allergic Response of

New and Old World Inhabitants', *Allergy Proceedings* 13.6 (1992), 335-44.

Schechner, S., 'The Material Culture of Astronomy in Daily Life: Sundials, Science, and Social Change', *Journal for the History of Astronomy* 32 (2001), 189-222.

Schowalter, T.D., *Insect Ecology. An Ecosystem Approach* (San Diego, 2009).

Sjostrand, S and Syed Idrus, L.L., *The Wanli Shipwreck and its Ceramic Cargo* (Department of Museums, Malaysia, 2007).

Skowronek, R.K., Walker, J.W., 'European Ceramics and the Elusive "Cittie of Raleigh"', *Historical Archaeology* 27.1 (1993), 58-69.

Smith, M., 'Chronology from Glass Beads: the Spanish Period in the Southeast, 1530-1670'. In C.F. Hayes (ed.), *Proceedings of the 1982 Glass Bead Trade Conference* (Rochester Museum & Science Center, New York, 1983), 147-58.

Smith, M.E. and Hirth, K.G., 'The Development of Prehispanic Cotton-Spinning Technology in Western Morelos, Mexico', *Journal of Field Archaeology* 15 (1988). 349-58.

Smith, M.T. and Good, M.E., *Early Sixteenth Century Glass Beads in the Spanish Colonial Trade* (Greenland, Mississippi, 1982).

Smith, M.T., Graham, E. and Pendergest, D.M., 'European Beads from Spanish-Colonial Lamanai and Tipu, Belize', *Beads Journal of the Society of Bead Researcher* 6 (1994), 21-47.

Smith, R.C., Bratten, J.R., Cozzi, J. and Plaskett, K., *The Emanuel Point Ship Archaeological Investigations 1997-1998* (Report of Investigations No. 68 Archaeology Institute University of West Florida, 1998).

Smith, R.C., Spirek, J., Bratten, J. and Scott-Ireton, D., *The Emanuel Point Ship: Archaeological Investigations, 1992-1995, Preliminary Report* (Bureau of Archaeological Research, Division of Historical Resources, Florida Department of State, 1995).

Spotila, J.R., *Sea Turtles* (Johns Hopkins University Press, 2004).

Stemm, G., Gerth, E., Flow, J., Lozano Guerra-Librero, C. and Kingsley, S., *The Deep-Sea Tortugas Shipwreck, Florida: A Spanish-Operated Navio of the 1622 Tierra Firme Fleet. Part 1, the Site* (OME Papers 26, Tampa, 2013).

Sténuit, R., 'Early Relics of the VOC Trade from Shetland. The Wreck of the Flute Lastdrager Lost off Yell, 1653', *International Journal of Nautical Archaeology* 3.2 (1974), 213-56.

Stone, D.Z., 'Jade and Jade objects in PreColumbian Costa Rica'. In F.W. Lange (ed.), *Precolumbian Jade. New Geo-*

logical and Cultural Interpretations (University of Utah Press, 1993), 141-48.

Sudbury, J. B., *Clay Tobacco Pipes Recovered from the 1622 Tortugas Shipwreck* (OME Papers, forthcoming).

Super, J.C., 'Spanish Diet in the Atlantic Crossing, the 1570s', *Terrae Incognitae* 16 (1984), 57-70.

Swanick, L.A., *An Analysis of Navigational Instruments in the Age of Exploration: 15th Century to Mid-17th Century* (MA Thesis, Texas A&M University, 2005).

Taube, K., Hruby, Z. and Romero, L., *Jadeite Sources and Ancient Workshops: Archaeological Reconnaissance in the Upper Río El Tambor, Guatemala* (FAMSI, 2005).

Tedesco, C., 'The Lost Treasures of the Santa Margarita', *X-Ray Magazine* 34 (2010a), 20-1.

Tedesco, C., 'Stones of Green and Other Treasures', *X-Ray Magazine* 36 (2010b), 16-20.

Tedesco, C., *The Deep-Sea Tortugas Shipwreck, Florida (1622): the Silver Coins* (OME Papers, Tampa, 2013).

Thomas, D.H., *St. Catherines: An Island in Time* (The University of Georgia Press, 2011).

Thompson, J.E.S., *Thomas Gage's Travels in the New World* (University of Oklahoma Press, 1958).

Tinniswood, J.T., 'Anchors and Accessories, 1340-1640', *Mariner's Mirror* 31 (1945), 84-105.

Van den Bossche, W., *Antique Glass Bottles. Their History and Evolution (1500-1850)* (Woodbridge, 2001).

Van der Pijl-Ketel, *The Ceramic Load of the 'Witte Leeuw' 1613* (Rijksmuseum, Amsterdam, 1982).

Veyrat, E., 'Chronique d'une vie oubliée'. In D. Carré, J.-P. Desroches and F. Goddio, F., *Le San Diego. Un trésor sous la mer* (Paris, 1994), 160-83.

Villanueva, M.A., 'From Calpixqui to Corregidor: Appropriation of Women's Cotton Textile Production in Early Colonial Mexico', *Latin America Perspectives* 12.1 (1985), 17-40.

Wagner, K., *Pieces of Eight. Recovering the Riches of a Lost Spanish Treasure Fleet* (Norwich, 1967).

Walton Rogers, P., *The Archaeology of York. Volume 17: the Small Finds. Textile Production at 16-22 Coppergate* (York, 1997).

Warsh, M.A., *Adorning Empire: a History of the Early Modern Pearl Trade, 1492-1688* (PhD Thesis, Johns Hopkins University, Baltimore, 2009).

Watts, G.P., 'The Western Ledge Reef Wreck: a Preliminary Report on Investigation of the Remains of a 16th-century Shipwreck in Bermuda', *International Journal of Nautical Archaeology* 22.2 (1993), 103-24.

Wede, K., *The Ship's Bell. Its History and Romance* (New York, 1972).

Weller, R., *Famous Shipwrecks of the Florida Keys* (Birmingham, 1990).

Wesler, K.W., *An Archaeology of Religion* (University Press of America, Lanham, MD., 2012).

Williams, C., 'Analysis of Tin-glazed Ceramics from the Emanuel Point Ship Second Campaign'. In R.C. Smith, J.R. Bratten, J. Cozzi and K. Plaskett, *The Emanuel Point Ship Archaeological Investigations 1997-1998* (Report of Investigations No. 68 Archaeology Institute University of West Florida, 1998), 140-45.

Wing, E.S., 'Animals Remains Excavated at the Spanish Site of Nueva Cadiz on Cubagua Island, Venezuela', *Nieuwe West-Indische Gids* 2 (1961), 162-5.

Witzell, W.N., *Synopsis of Biological Data on the Hawksbill Turtle* Eretmochelys imbricata *(Linnaeus, 1766)* (Food and Agricultural Organization Fisheries Synopsis No. 137, 1983).

Worth, J.R., *Exploration and Trade in the Deep Frontier of Spanish Florida: Possible Sources for 16th-Century Spanish Artifacts in Western North Carolina* (Paper Presented at the 51st Annual Southeastern Archaeological Conference, Lexington, Kentucky, 1994).

4

The Identity & Maritime History of the Deep-Sea Tortugas Shipwreck

Sean Kingsley

Wreck Watch Int., London, UK

From 1990-91 Seahawk Deep Ocean Technology of Tampa, Florida, conducted the world's first comprehensive deep-sea shipwreck excavation on a small *navio* from the Tierra Firme Spanish fleet lost off the Florida Keys on 5 September 1622. Archival documentation does not specify the names of all this fleet's ships. The fate of the smaller merchant vessels not connected to the transport of royal taxes or consignments are particularly neglected. A combination of historical and archaeological research suggests that the best fit identification for the deep-sea Tortugas shipwreck is the Portuguese-built and Spanish-operated 117-ton *Buen Jesús y Nuestra Señora del Rosario.*

The outward-bound final destination of this *navio* to Nueva Cordoba, Cumana along northeast Venezuela's Pearl Coast, would explain the consignment of pearls associated with the wreck. The recorded length of the Tortugas ship's keel also corresponds to the size of the *Buen Jesús* as specified in its outbound manifest based on Spanish *Ordenanzas* shipbuilding regulations. Cumana was particularly renowned in the 1620s for the cultivation of high value tobacco, and it is proposed that the *Buen Jesús* may have been transporting a significant cargo of this plant to Seville when disaster struck.

1. The 1622 Tierra Firme Fleet

Establishing the identity of the deep-sea Tortugas wreck is compounded by complex methodological problems. First and foremost, contemporary accounts of the 24-hour hurricane that enveloped the Florida Keys on 4-5 September 1622 concentrated on the fate of the major 'treasure' ships in the Tierra Firme fleet. References to the smaller, less valuable merchant vessels that were not transporting Crown property received cursory coverage. In addition, the same ship is often cited under multiple different names or just by the name of the owner or captain, some of whom do not match listed personnel. On occasions, a ship and owner/captain's name seems to be conflated. Multiple vessels also carried the same name.

The sources concur, however, on the basic timeframe of events and the climatic conditions preceding the tragedy. Historical documents, notably *A True Relation of that Which Lately Hapned to the Great Spanish Fleet, and Galeons of Terra Firma in America* (1623), and primary documentation collated by Martín Fernández de Navarette (1971, Tomo XII, 1371, fols 128-35), confirm that the Tierra Firme fleet set sail from Portobello on 22 July 1622 and reached Cartagena on 27 July (AGI *Contratación* 5116; Fig. 15). On 3 August the ships continued towards Havana, where they dropped anchor on 22 August to prepare for the home voyage to Spain (Fig. 16). The following day the fleet general ordered every ship to register its gold, silver, bullion, merchandise and other commodities in the account books with a view to sailing on 28 August.

To discuss the optimum date of departure, the Governor of Havana called a council with the General commanding the soldiers, the Admiral of the Armada, the Captain General of the Fleet and his Admiral, the Supervisor of the Treasury. Despite prevailing fair weather, the collective wisdom favored remaining in port pending the lunar conjunction, expected on 5 September, which "did commonly in those parts bring clouds and obfuscation of ayre, which would not vanish without tempests, and turbulent winds" (*A True Relation*, 1623).

Behind schedule and well into hurricane season, 28 ships with their "Admirall", eight galleons, three *pinaces* (presumably *pataches*, small fleet dispatch ships) and "other attendants upon the Fleet, with their consorts" eventually weighed anchor at sunrise on Sunday 4 September. Rather than head directly for the Bahama Channel, the fleet spent the day tacking in front of Havana, monitoring whether the lunar conjunction was likely to improve conditions.

By Monday 5 September the fleet was underway at the worst possible time: the weather window had indeed changed and the incoming winds turned to the northeast. A storm was brewing and the ships wound up their mainsails, tied them fast to the yards and continued solely under the power of their mizzen sails. The wind strengthened and started to whistle, the clouds thickened and the horizon

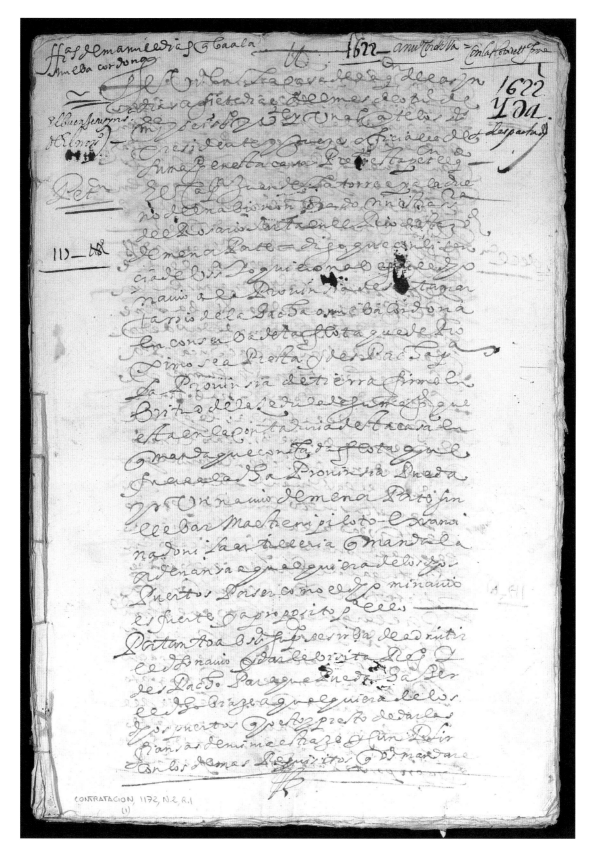

Fig. 1. Section of the Spanish manifest of the Buen Jesús y Nuestra Señora del Rosario, *identified as the merchant vessel lost in September 1622 at the Tortugas shipwreck site off the Florida Keys. Photo: Archivo General de Indias,* Contratación 1172, N.2, R.1.

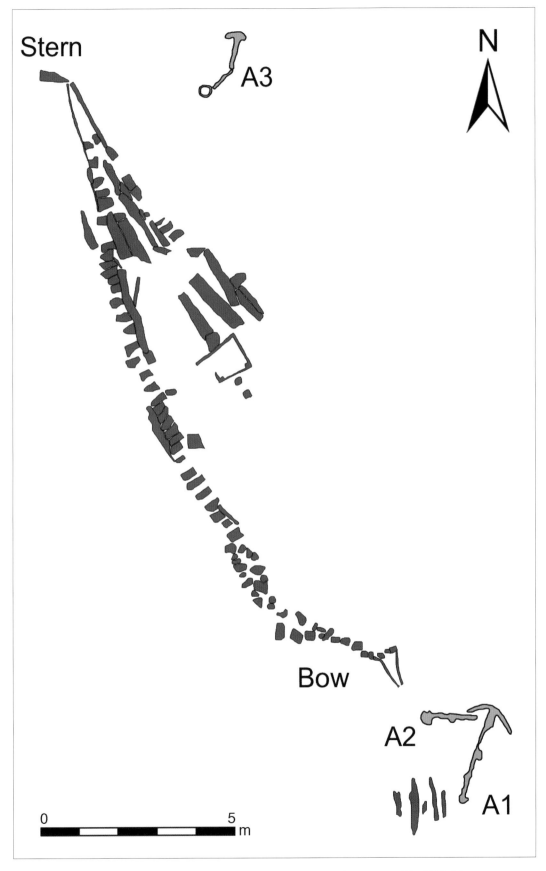

Fig. 2. Plan of the Tortugas shipwreck hull as partly excavated in 1990-91.

turned overcast. At sunrise the fleet was very close to the Tortugas Islands and 'Bajos de los Martires' when the hurricane hit (Fig. 17).

The air became so dark that the fleet ships lost sight of one another. Before midday (*A True Relation*, 1623):

> "all the Galeons were dissipated and dissevered, and the most part of the Fleet for their better passage went before the wind, tooke a course to save themselves as well they could: In which violence they were driven from one another, and the wind continued so impetuous, that it not only unloosened their tacklings and sayles, but brake asunder their fore-masts, and rent their maine yards in shivers, so they had not shift but to beare no sayle at all, or crosse the wind as they could."

The waves continued to roll, and then the wind turned to the south, rain started to fall and the seas ran very high.

Another source places the time when the hurricane struck at 7am (AGI *Contratacion* Gen. 1144). The ships remained victims of the elements and incapable of steering under sail until 3pm, a condition that forced the 630-ton *Santa Margarita*'s mainmast to snap and its rudder to break. The storm continued to rage until the morning of Tuesday 6 September, leaving behind a trail of devastation. The surviving ships headed back to Havana for repairs and to survey the damage, limping into port between 10-14 September. On Monday 12 September only 10 ships had returned safely to port, seven merchant vessels and three galleons, all dismasted and full of water (including the *capitana* of the fleet, *Nuestra Señora del Rosario, Santa Ana la Real* and the *Nuestra Señora de la Candelaria*). Sources loosely report that five galleons, 11 other ships, plus "some others" from the Tierra Firme fleet eventually reached Havana safely (AGI *Mexico* 29, N. 101, Doc. 3).

On all eight wrecks scattered across more than 80km of the Florida Keys as far east as the Marquesas Keys, around 550 people, including 121 priests, drowned (Lyon, 1989: 68; Mathewson, 1986: 24). The gold, silver, pearls, indigo, cochineal, tobacco and other products lost were valued at 4,000,000 *pesos*. The wrecked *Atocha* and *Margarita* alone were transporting a registered million and a half *pesos* each, of which 254,000 *pesos* belonged to the king (AGI *Contratacion* 5116).

The total number of ships lost on the Florida Keys varies within historical documentation between seven and nine. The sunken treasure ships included the *Atocha, Margarita* and the *Nuestra Señora del Rosario,* which was entirely salvaged soon after in a cay near the Tortugas islands. Nearby to the *Rosario* a fleet *patache* sank in the shallows.

Of the remaining casualties the historical testimony is frustratingly limited, presumably because these ships sank in deep water during the hurricane, where their movements went largely unobserved. *A True Relation* merely states that two "Ships of the Fleet" were lost "before they could approach the shore". A 'Communication from Don Luis de Cordoba to Crown Havana', dated 10 December 1622 (AGI *Santo Domingo* 132; cf. Lyon, 1989), also referred to "two moderate-sized ships of the convoy, which capsized in the force of the weather." The same generalization eventually circulated in London's *News of the Week* for 26 May 1623, which reported that "In the same hour, with the same tempest, and almost at the same place" as the loss of the *Atocha* and *Margarita*, "two ships of the fleet were swallowed in the sea, and perished before they could reach shore." These deep-water casualties are strong candidates for the Tortugas shipwreck.

The only historical source that specified names for this lost group merely stated that "Also three merchant *naos* were lost, that of Juan de la Torre Ayala, of Gaspar Gonzales de los Reyes and of Fulano Virgilio; all these sinking completely with no survivors on them" (Navarette, Tomo XII, 1371, fols 128-35).

Lyon's well-researched summary of events (1989: 62-6) concluded that five ships were swept towards the Florida Keys and sank in the shallows: the *Rosario*, the fleet *patache* (tender), a Portuguese slaver, the *Margarita* and the *Atocha*. One further small ship, the *Buen Jésus*, which apparently had lost both masts and its rudder, "fell farther and farther behind the other vessels and was finally lost to sight", while the small *Nuestra Senora de la Consolacíon* struggled along under a close-reefed foresail and abruptly capsized.

Research consulted by Barnette (2003) concurred that the *Nuestra Senora de la Consolacíon* of Captain Gonzalo Perez capsized in deep water and remains undiscovered. Barnette suggests that the Tortugas wreck excavated by Seahawk equates possibly to the *Nuestra Senora de la Merced* of Captain Juan de Campo. Such a correlation is improbable (see Section 2 below), not least because the *Merced* is now believed to be a 'ghost galleon' that did not actually sail with this fleet (Moore, 1991).

2. The Identity of the Tortugas Shipwreck

For the sake of objectivity it must be acknowledged that the Tortugas region of southernmost Florida is a sprawling ship's graveyard, where myriad vessels met their fate and where 241 casualties of all periods have been documented (Murphy and Jonsson, 1993: 144). Some of these date close to the disaster of 1622. A small *patache* carrying mail foundered about 3 leagues off the Dry Tortugas in 1621 en route from Veracruz to Spain; the flagship and the galleon

Espiritu Santo both sank in the Florida Straits in 1623; one of two galleons sent to the Keys to protect salvors working the *Margarita* from attack by Dutch privateers went down 4 leagues to windward of the *Atocha*; a salvage vessel foundered in 1625; two galleons of the Tierra Firme fleet of 1630 carrying supplies from Havana to St. Augustine were wrecked at the head of the Florida Keys; and, finally, a 'relief ship' sailing from New Spain to St. Augustine was lost in 1691 (Marx, 1969: 42-3; Bearss, 1971: 43; Skowronek, 1982: 9; Flow, 1999).

The Tortugas shipwreck's material culture, however, so closely matches sets excavated from the *Atocha* and *Margarita* that there can be no doubt that it comprised part of the fleet returning to Spain that sunk off the Florida Keys on 5-6 September 1622 (Stemm *et al.*, 2013). The Tortugas coin assemblage includes no issues post-dating 1622 and the latest match by mint and assayer those recorded on the *Atocha* and *Margarita* (cf. Tedesco, 2013). Additional sets of artifacts recovered from the *Atocha* are duplicated on the Tortugas site in the form of gold finger bars stamped with identical mint, *quinto* and karat quality production marks, while the four forms of olive jars (including parallel *graffiti* notations), the tablewares (Columbia Plain, Blue-on-Blue Seville maiolica, Blue 'Morisco' ware) and non-Spanish kitchen colonowares clearly originated in the same kilns as the ceramic wares from the *Atocha* (Kingsley *et al.*, 2012). Other parallel artifacts include the astrolabes, beads and a bronze mortar and pestle.

While contemporary historical sources focused on the king's gold and silver lost on the fleet's largest ships, the *Atocha, Margarita* and *Rosario*, references to the fate of the smaller merchant vessels were cursory. No official list of lost merchant vessels has survived into the modern day. Various sources cite the seven or eight ships wrecked off the Florida Keys on 5-6 September 1622 as comprising:

- The *Atocha*.
- The *Margarita*.
- The *Nuestra Señora del Rosario*.
- A *patache*.
- Three to four other vessels (most commonly cited in accounts).

The *Atocha* and *Margarita* discovered and excavated by Mel Fisher and his team are the most celebrated shipwrecks of the Florida Keys and have inspired numerous popular publications and preliminary scientific notes (Mathewson, 1986; Lyon, 1989; Malcom, 1990; 1993; 1998; Smith, 2003; Tedesco, 2010) and an excellent analysis of the ceramic record (Marken, 1994). The lost *Nuestra Señora del Rosario* and *patache* can be safely discounted from the

Fig. 3. The port of Seville c.1590 by Alonso Sanchez Coello, with a detail of a merchant vessel moored along the Guadalquivir river of comparable form to the Tortugas ship.

current investigation. Sources unanimously agree that the *Rosario* galleon ran aground on a cay, largely identified as Tortugas (*A True Relation… 1623*; 'Communication from Marquise of Cadereita… 1623'; 'Communication from General Don Francisco Venegas… 1624'; Navarette, 1971, Tomo XII, 1371, fols 128-35; Marx, 1969: 42; Barnette, 2003: 141-4). The ship's company all survived to report the wreck's location (*A True Relation… 1623*):

> "The Galeon of our *Lady del Rosario*, wherein Captaine Chacurretta was Commander, likewise perished, not without great suspition beforehand: she rann aground, as the Admirall did, so that none of the Ships that came into the Harbour could give an account of her, until a certaine Barke arrived the 22 of September at the Port of Havana with Letters from the said Captaine, which advertised them, that the said Galeon perished in Tortuga, all the company escaping miraculously, who had the fortune to save themselves with convenient victual and necessary supplimemts, keeping firme stations on their chests, masts, and such other things."

The *Rosario* was subsequently located by a salvage operation on 24 September 1622 "grounded on one of the keys". All the crew and passengers were saved and the wooden structure above the waterline burned to expose the treasure within the hull, resulting in the recovery of all the silver and 20 pieces of artillery (AGI *Santo Domingo* 132; Lyon, 1989). Following the salvage of equipment valued at more than 6,000 or 7,000 ducats, another report confirmed that Vargas "began the operation of salvaging the silver, first setting fire to the galleon, to burn it down to water-level. In this way he recovered all the treasure, artillery, and copper which she carried and brought it all back to this port

Ship Name	Shipmaster	Owner	Ship Type	Tonnage	Direction
N.S. de la Candelaria	Pedro de Vargas	Antonio Ruiz Navarrete	Galleon (Havana)	650	Tierra Firme
N.S. de la Consolacion	Gonzalo Perez	Juan de Miranda	Navio (Triana)	180	Tierra Firme
San Diego	Pedro Gutierrez	Antonio Malla de Salcedo	Navio (Indias)	180	Tierra Firme
N.S. del Buen Successo	Gaspar Ochoa	Gaspar Ochoa	Navio (Portugal)	90	Tierra Firme
N.S. del Rosario	Bernabe de Ibarra	Pedro Diaz Franco	Navio (Havana)	100	Venezuela
N.S. de los Reyes	Diego Gallardo	-----	Navio (Seville)	180	Venezuela
N.S. de Guia	Juan Rodriguez de Acosta	-----	Navio (Triana)	100	Rio de la Hacha
Santa Cruz	Martin de Carbuera	Martin de Carbuera	Navio (Havana)	100	Jamaica
Jesus y N.S. del Rosario	Manuel Diaz	Juan de la Torre	Navio (Portugal)	117	Nueva Cordoba
Santa Ana	Sebastian Martin Hidalgo	-----	Navio (Margarita)	115	Margarita
San Francisco	Bartolome Garcia	Pedro Gonzalez	Navio	110	Cumana
N.S. de la O	Diego Guerra	Francisco Diaz Pimienta	Navio (Triana)	90	Cuba
San Antonio (N.S. del Rosario)	Tomas Felipe [Josefe de Licarça]	-----	-----	100	Santa Marta
N.S. de Rosario	Pedro Ortiz de Ibarrola	-----	Felibot (frigate of Havana)	110	Florida
N.S. de Valvaneda	Juan de Urriola	Estevan Blanqueto	Nao (Campeche)	500	Tierra Firme

Table 1. Tierra Firme fleet ships outward-bound to the Americas in April 1622 (Chaunu and Chaunu, 1956: 26-29).

with the people who were saved" ('Communication from General Don Francisco Venegas, Governor and Captain-General of the Island of Cuba and the City of San Christobal of Havana, for the King Our Lord'; Lyon, 1989).

Site FOJE-UW-9 near Loggerhead Key, trial-trenched off the Dry Tortugas in 1982 by the Southeast Archaeological Center (SEAC), the University of South Florida and the FSU Marine Laboratory, is a possible candidate for the *Rosario*. The surface materials include Middle Period Spanish olive jar fragments, glass fragments, a wrought iron swivel gun, a wood fragment, brass fastener, galley tiles, ballast, a buckle and iron fasteners, which, combined with the site's geographical location, is considered to be generally consistent with the documented sinking of the 600-ton *Rosario*, the only large early 17th-century vessel lost in that section of the Dry Tortugas. However, no specific temporal or cultural affiliation has been assigned to FOJE-UW-9 and no ballast pile typifying the wreck of a large ship has been identified (Johnson, 1982: 1, 20, 22, 28-9).

The nearby site FOJE-UW-17 associated with six swivel guns, significant quantities of olive jar fragments, ballast stones and other ferrous material has been assigned a probable 16th or 17th-century Spanish identity. The best guess concerning the site is that it represents a contemporary 1622 salvage vessel that sank in a second hurricane while attempting to salvage the *Rosario* (Johnson, 1982: 25, 28-9, 35-6).

Due to its shallow geographical proximity to the *Rosario* (Marx, 1969: 42), the *patache* (designed to carry dispatches, survey forward of advancing fleets and guard entrances to ports) may also be excluded from attempts to define the deep-sea Tortugas shipwreck. According to a 'Communication from Don Luis de Cordoba to Crown Havana, Dec. 10, 1622' (AGI *Santo Domingo* 132; Lyon, 1989), "the fleet armada *patache*... grounded in Tortuga". Barnette (2003: 141-4) has suggested that this wreck may possibly correspond to the 'Coast Guard Dock Ballast Pile' site.

Fig. 4. The port of Seville c.1590 by Alonso Sanchez Coello, with the Americas fleet preparing to sail. The merchant vessels along the banks of the Guadalquivir river are of comparable form to the Tortugas ship.

No archaeological data link the 19m-long Iberian 'Mystery Wreck', located at a depth of 6m off Marathon in the Florida Keys, with one of the missing 1622 Spanish ships, although the site has been interpreted as the possible remains of an *aviso* or dispatch vessel traveling in the company of other ships in the first half of the 17th century. Material culture recovered from the 'Mystery Wreck' includes ballast stones, encrusted iron objects, 208 musket balls, 127 grape shot, 34 lead shot, three cannonballs, firebricks, wood, a rudder gudgeon, a piece of melted copper, one piece of bone, lead sheathing, a broken *mano* (grinding stone), an anchor and anchor ring, olive jar body sherds and four olive-jar necks (McKinnon and Scott-Ireton, 2006: 187, 193; Smith *et al.*, 2006: 19).

The three or four additional losses associated with the Tierra Firme fleet of September 1622 outside the major large silver galleon group of the *Atocha, Margarita* and the *Rosario* are generally cited in disparate contemporary sources as being associated with:

- Juan de la Torre Ayala.
- Gaspar Gonzales de los Reyes.
- Fulano Virgilio.
- Navarette also mentions a Portuguese frigate (excluded because the Tortugas ship was a merchantman) and a *nao vizcaína* (from Biscay) of Pedro de Vargas (presumably the 650-ton *Nuestra Señora de la Candelaria*, actually lost off San Lucar, Spain, outward bound: Chaunu and Chaunu, 1956: 26-7; Moore, 1991).

Chaunu and Chaunu's *Séville et l'Atlantique* confirms the name of Juan de la Torre Ayala's ship as the *Buen Jesús y Nuestra Señora del Rosario* (Manuel Diaz master, *navio*, built in Portugal, 117 tons, outward bound to Nueva Cordoba in Venezuela; Table 1). No other ships of the Tierra Firme fleet cited in *Séville et l'Atlantique* were either owned or captained by a Gaspar Gonzales de los Reyes or a Fulano Virgilio. Bearing in mind that names were often confused and conflated, of potential tangential relevance within the Tierra Firme fleet may be a Gonzalo Perez, master of the *Nuestra Señora de la Consolacion*, a Gaspar Ochoa who owned the *Nuestra Señora del Buen Successo* and a Pedro Gonzalez who owned the *San Francisco*. Moore (1991) has also suggested that the name Gaspar Gonzales de los Reyes may have become confused with the actual name of the ship the *Nuestra Señora de los Reyes*. To this pattern of uncertainty is the generic tendency in Spanish history to use 'Fulano' to mean 'Anybody' when an individual's name was unknown (pers. comm. Greg Stemm, 5 October 2012; Claudio Lozano Guerra-Librero, 8 October 2012).

The long-list for the possible identity of the Tortugas wreck based on the outward-bound Tierra Firme fleet listed by Chaunu and Chaunu (1956: 26-9) thus comprises:

- *Buen Jesús y Nuestra Señora del Rosario* (master Manuel Diaz, owner Juan de la Torre, *navio* of Portugal, 117 tons, outward bound to Nueva Cordoba).
- *Nuestra Señora de la Consolacion* (master Gonzalo Perez, owner Juan de Miranda, *navio* of Triana, 180 tons, Tierra Firme).

Codos					
Length	34	36	39	41	45
Keel	28	30	32	34	36
Breadth	9	10	11	12	13
Rake Stern	2	2	2 ¼	2 1/2	3
Rake Stem	4	4	4 ¾	5	6
Depth	4	4 1/2	5	5 1/2	6
Tonnage (*toneladas*)	80 ¾	106 1/8	157*	198	251

* This tonnage is not provided by Fernández-González (2009: 12) and instead derives from Rodríguez Mendoza (2008: 179, table 11).

Table 2. Dimensions established by Ordenanzas of 1618 in codos (from Fernández-González, 2009: 12).

Meters					
Length	19.53	20.68	22.41	23.56	25.86
Keel	16.09	17.24	18.38	19.53	20.68
Breadth	5.17	5.74	6.32	6.89	7.47
Rake Stern	1.14	1.14	1.29	1.43	1.72
Rake Stem	2.29	2.29	2.72	2.87	3.44
Depth	2.29	2.58	2.87	3.16	3.44
Tonnage	80 ¾	106 1/8	157*	198	251

* This tonnage is not provided by Fernández-González (2009: 12) and instead derives from Rodríguez Mendoza (2008: 179, table 11).

Table 3. Dimensions established by Ordenanzas of 1618 in metric equivalent to the codos (one shipbuilder cubit = 57.468cm) (from Fernández-González, 2009: 12).

- *Nuestra Señora del Buen Successo* (master Gaspar Ochoa, owner Gaspar Ochoa, *navio* of Portugal, 90 tons, Tierra Firme).
- *San Francisco* (master Bartolome Garcia, owner Pedro Gonzalez, *navio*, 110 tons, Cumano).
- *Nuestra Señora de los Reyes* (master Diego Gallardo, owner unknown, *navio* of Seville, 180 tons, Venezuela).

The material culture of the Tortugas ship is strongly linked through its ceramic assemblage to Seville. In theory, this might exclude the *Buen Jesús y Nuestra Señora del Rosario,* a *navio* of Portugal. However, this vessel sailed with the *flota* from the Guadalquivir River and thus had clearly visited Seville (AGI *Contratación* 1172, N.2, R1). For this reason this ship cannot be excluded. Whether the *Buen Jesús* commonly operated out of Portugal or was just built there and subsequently relocated to Spain remains undetermined from the historical record.

The presence of 6,639 pearls on the deep-sea Tortugas shipwreck also points to direct or indirect commerce with Venezuela's northeastern coast. Known Tierra Firme vessels that travelled outward to Venezuela in 1622 included:

- *Buen Jesús y Nuestra Señora del Rosario* (master Manuel Diaz, owner Juan de la Torre, *navio* of Portugal, 117 tons).
- *Nuestra Señora del Rosario* (master Bernabe de Ibarra, owner Pedro Diaz Franco, *navio* of Havana, 100 tons).
- *Nuestra Señora de los Reyes* (master Diego Gallardo, *navio* of Seville, 180 tons).
- *Santa Ana* (master Sebastian Martin Hidalgo, *navio* of Margarita, 115 tons).
- *San Francisco* (master Bartolome Garcia, owner Pedro Gonzalez, *navio*, 110 tons).

Of these outward-bound ships the *Nuestra Señora del Rosario* may be excluded from the long list because it seems to have been local to the Americas and was not involved in a round trip back to Spain. The ship's owner and master did not possess corruptions of names that include permutations of any word in Gaspar Gonzales de los Reyes or Fulano Virgilio, and the *Rosario* was also seemingly too small to correspond to the deep-sea Tortugas wreck (see Section 3 below).

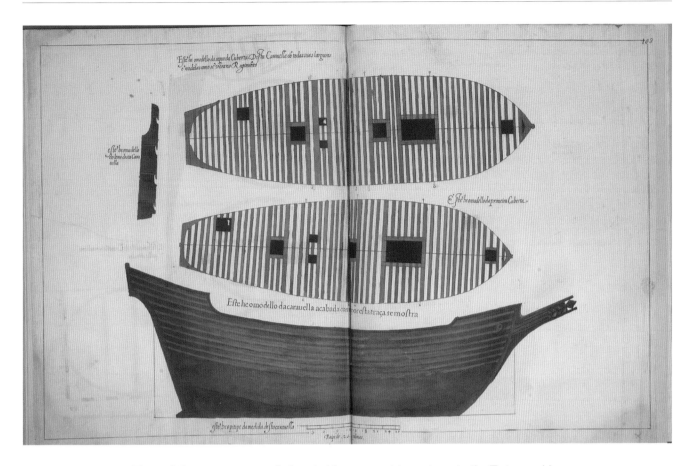

Fig. 5. A Portuguese caravel of probable comparable anatomy to the Tortugas ship, depicted in 1616 in the Livro de Traças de Carpintaria. *Photo: Biblioteca Nacional de Portugal.*

Further, historical sources confirm that three of these ships, the *Nuestra Señora de los Reyes*, the *Nuestra Señora del Rosario* and the *San Francisco* were still active in subsequent years. The *Nuestra Señora de los Reyes* arrived back in Spain in 1623 with other ships in the fleet of the Marquis of Cadereita that survived the storm of 1622 (AGI *Contratación* 171 A, 808, 809 A; AGI *Contratación* 2988; AGI *Contratación* 5777). The *San Francisco* was also documented readied for a voyage with the Tierra Firme fleet to Rio de la Hacha once more on 28 November 1623 with the same master as in the previous year, Bartolome Garcia (AGI *Contratación* 18). The *Nuestra Señora del Rosario* has not been tracked down in post-1622 Spanish manifests and documentation, but since its captain and master appear in sources continuing to trade with the Americas in later years it plausibly survived as well. The *Santa Ana la Real* did not sink off the Florida Keys during the hurricane (*México* 29, N. 101, Doc. 2).

This leaves three ships proposed for a final shortlist, the *Nuestra Señora del Buen Successo* (90 tons), the *Buen Jesús y Nuestra Señora del Rosario* (117 tons) and the *Nuestra Señora de la Consolacion* (180 tons).

3. Ship Magnitudes

The optimum means of correlating one of these vessels to the Tortugas wreck is by determining the Seahawk ship's tonnage. The vessels listed in the outward-bound Tierra Firme fleet of 1622 ranged in age from new to four years old maximum (Chaunu and Chaunu, 1956: 26-9) and thus would have been constructed following the Spanish *Ordenanzas* regulations for shipbuilding of 1618, which relied on the formula of one shipbuilder's cubit to one *codo*, the equivalent of 57.468cm (Tables 2-3).

Based on accepted correlations between tonnage and vessel dimensions, the 90-ton *Nuestra Señora del Buen Successo* would have had a keel length of over 28 *codos* but less than 30 *codos*; the 117-ton *Buen Jesús y Nuestra Señora del Rosario* would have had a keel length of over 30 *codos* but less than 32 *codos;* and the keel of the 180-ton *Nuestra Señora de la Consolacion* would have measured between 32-34 *codos*. While Portuguese ships may not have been constructed to the same *Ordenanzas* formulae, these correlations provide a general means of determining the comparative ship sizes for these Iberian craft.

In 1991 the Tortugas wreck's length was measured by Offshore Project Manager John Astley using the on-site Sonardyne navigation and surveying system (Astley and Stemm, 2013). From the *in situ* lower sternpost to where the keel started to rise to form the lower stempost in the bows measured 17.4m (57ft). The Sonardyne system was calibrated for this specific activity and provided an accuracy of +/- 10cm (pers. comm. John Astley, 6 January 2012). This dimension provides the maximum total length of the Tortugas ship's keel (Fig. 2).

Based on these *in situ* measurements, the Tortugas shipwreck most tightly corresponds to the dimensions of a Spanish *navio* with a keel length closest to 30 *codos* and a 10 *codos* beam (Figs. 3-5), data that most plausibly identify the wreck as the *Buen Jesús y Nuestra Señora del Rosario*. Notably, the owner of this ship, Juan de la Torre, is specifically mentioned in contemporary sources of 1622/23 as having lost a ship in the Florida Keys hurricane. This *navio* was outward-bound to Nueva Cordoba, Cumana on the north coast of Venezuela, which was the center of Spanish pearl harvesting in the colonial era. The presence of 6,639 pearls on the Tortugas wreck again points towards this identification.

The above calculation of the Tortugas ship's proposed dimensions uses the Spanish *codos* for cross-fleet comparisons, even though the *Buen Jesús* is listed as a Portuguese vessel (see Section 4 below). As such it presumably would have been built using the *rumo* as its unit of measurement (Castro, 2008: 69). Nevertheless, the ship may be readily compared to other Spanish craft in the 1622 Tierra Firme fleet for two reasons.

The *Ordenanzas* of 1618 demanded consistency in ship construction for all *flota* ships, specifying that "We order that all the *Navíos* to be fabricated from now on in all our Kingdoms and Lordships be in accordance with these *Ordenanzas* without exceeding one point." Craftsmen that failed to comply with these regulations were subjected to substantial fines: 500 ducats for the fabricator, 100 ducats for the master shipwright and 1,000 ducats and loss of position for the superintendent (Fernández-González, 2009: 8, 17). Secondly, the inspection of the *Buen Jesús*'s suitability for service in the Tierra Firme *flota* specified the vessel's measurments in *codos* (AGI *Contratación* 1172, N.2, R.1), thus facilitating accurate cross-fleet dimensional comparisons using this unit of measurement.

4. *The Buen Jesús y Nuestra Señora del Rosario*

While the homeward-bound manifest for the *Buen Jesús y Nuestra Señora del Rosario* has not been located in the archives, the outward-bound register and manifest – as compiled by the inspector of the ship in port, Juan Zarco de Amaya, witnessed by Pedro de Miranda, Juan de Herrera, Atanasio de Gongora and signed off by Fermín de Ynurrica, Antonio Moreno and Juan de Sandoval – provide key information about the ship's structure, character and itinerary (Fig. 1). The administrative and registration process was lengthy, taking six months to conclude (cf. AGI *Contratación* 1172, N.2, R.1).

The captain of the *Buen Jesús* initially sought permission from Casa de la Contratación officials to sail to the province of Santa Marta-Río de la Hacha-Nueva Córdoba on 9 October 1621 in the company of the fleet being prepared for Tierra Firme. On 23 October the characteristics of the ship were presented to the Casa. Having verified these specifics, three days later the Casa admitted the *Buen Jesús* to the voyage. On 18 February 1622 the Casa acknowledged satisfaction that Juan de la Torre, the ship's owner, was not burdened by any pending debts and thus was legally permitted to travel with the Tierra Firme fleet.

The master and captain of the *Buen Jesús* paid the necessary voyage bonds on 19 February in the form of 10,000 *ducados* and swore to comply with the ordinances of the Casa de la Contratación. On 18 March Manual Diaz confirmed in writing that the ship was prepared to sail and that the inspection of the Casa officials was expected. On 22 March the Casa ordered the *Buen Jesús* to be inspected, at which time the officials granted multiple merchants' cargo transport licenses (AGI *Contratación* 3041). Finally, the ship was inspected in the river of Seville on 29 March and officials granted final clearance for the *Buen Jesús y Nuestra Señora del Rosario* to depart with the Tierra Firme fleet (Figs. 3-4).

The following characteristics relate to the dimensions, crew and itinerary of the *Buen Jesús* (AGI *Contratación* 18; AGI *Contratación* 1172, N.2, R.1):

- Owner: Juan de la Torre Ayala.
- Master: Manuel Diaz.
- Construction: Portugal.
- Tonnage: 117 and three-eighths ton.
- Length (stern to prow): 37 *codos*.
- Keel: could not be measured due to the overlying presence of cargo ("palo de Campeche"), but was estimated at 28 *codos*.
- Breadth: 11 *codos*.
- Depth: 5 ¾ *codos*.
- Departed from the River Guadalquivir with the fleet of General Juan de Lara Morán.
- Route: Santa Marta, Rio de la Hacha and Nueva Cordoba.

Date (1622)	Merchant	No. Wine Jugs	No. Pipes Wine	No. Oil Jugs
22 February	Xpoval de Biedma	1,500	10	
22 February	Gonzalo de Herrera		2	100
22 February	Juan de Céspedes			100 *arrobas* 100 jugs = 200 total?
12 March	Baltasar de León	100		
17 March	Pedro Fernández	200		
25 March	Juan de Neve	100		
25 March	Francisco de Gandía	300		
25 March	José del Bosque	300		

Table 4. Quantities of wine and oil/olive jugs granted for shipment to the Americas on the Buen Jesús y Nuestra Señora del Rosario, *but not transported in their entirety (AGI* Contratación *3041).*

Following the inspection, Captain Zarco confirmed that the ship was in good condition and stipulated that it should carry four anchors and a boat with two sets of oars. In terms of ordnance, the ship was designated as needing to be armed with four iron cannon and its ammunition, a hundred bullets, 12 muskets, gunpowder, lead bullets and two dozen "magpies". The ship was crewed by ten sailors and a licensed pilot, and supported by eight cabin boys and three pageboys. Registered passengers were Francisco Afelio de Gandía, Francisco de la Torre y Ayala, the merchant Juan de Céspedes and Cristóbal de Biedma.

The manifest for the *Buen Jesús's* outward-bound voyage (AGI *Contratación* 1172, N.2, R.1) reveals a complex pattern of multiple consignments transported to different destinations and personnel. A disparity exists between the original volume of commodities cleared for transport on the ship by named merchants (as stipulated in AGI *Contratación* 3041; Table 4) and the physical cargo eventually stowed and shipped (AGI *Contratación* 1172, N.2, R.1). The former document permitted a total of 2,500 jugs of wine to be transported by various merchants on the *Buen Jesús* (Table 4).

However, in the final eventuality just 1,400 commercial wine jars were stowed, albeit alongside extensive additional forms of cargo. This was supplemented by 500 jugs of wine for which Juan de la Torre Ayala only paid tax on 200 in Seville and was compelled to pay further tax on the remainder to the Royal Officials of Cartagena on 27 July 1622 (AGI *Contaduría* 1394). These were intended for use by the crew, with the surplus seemingly expected to be sold in the Americas.

The consignments transported to New Spain by the *Buen Jesús y Nuestra Señora del Rosario* in 1622 included a variety of wine and oil jars, mixed foodstuffs, fabrics, metal items and art works, and consisted in its entirety of (AGI *Contratación* 1172, N.2, R.1):

1. Juan de Neve, a citizen of Seville, loaded fabrics, knives, women's shoes and mattocks. Taxes paid in Seville on 10 March amounted to 6,500 *maravedís (almojarifazgo)* and 1,300 *maravedís (avería)*.

2. Francisco Ajelli de Gandía, a citizen of Seville, loaded 300 wine jugs from Aljarafe (Seville) of his own crop and on his own account and risk, bound for the city of Nueva Cordoba with the fleet of Tierra Firme of General Juan de Lara for delivery of the wine. Taxes paid in Seville on 17 March amounted to 765 *maravedís (almojarifazgo)* and 1,125 *maravedís (avería)*.

3. Juan de la Torre Ayala and Juan de Neve (each owning 50%) loaded iron bound for the city of Nueva Cordoba. Taxes paid in Seville on 9 March amounted to 9,500 *maravedís (almojarifazgo)* and a further 9,500 *maravedís (avería)*.

4. Juan de Céspedes loaded a tapestry with a painting of the souls of purgatory bound for the city of Nueva Cordoba to be collected there by Juan de Lemos, and in his absence by Diego López Aries, citizens of Cartagena, and to be sent later to Captain Antón Suarez at the lagoon of Maracaibo, on whose account and risk the picture was shipped. Taxes paid in Seville on 4 March amounted to 750 *maravedís (almojarifazgo)* and 150 *maravedís (avería)*.

5. Juan de Céspedes loaded packaged food, quince meat, hats, fabrics, raisins, hazelnuts, almonds and chestnuts bound for the city of Nueva Cordoba. The merchandise was consigned to Luis de Lemos, and in his absence to Diego López Aries, and in the absence of both to Gaspar Fernández Rebelo, all citizens of Cartagena. The

recipients were charged with selling the merchandise and sending the profits to Spain on the account of Juan de Céspedes, to whom the merchandise belonged and on whose account and risk it was loaded. Taxes paid in Seville on 4 March amounted to 8,000 *maravedís (almojarifazgo)* and 1,700 *maravedís (avería)*.

(Luis de Lemos, the son of Portuguese parents but living in Seville, was a prominant slave merchant and the owner of two large ships that traveled under permission each year to Rio de la Hacha, mainly carrying clothes from Spain. De Lemos developed commercial contacts across Spain and the Indies, and also had relatives in Nicaragua with whom he traded primarily indigo (Ortega, 2002: 146).)

6. Juan de Céspedes loaded oil, capers and olives bound for the city of Nueva Cordoba. The merchandise was consigned to Luis de Lemos, in his absence to Diego López Aries, and in the absence of both to Gaspar Fernández Rebelo, all citizens of Cartagena, so that the merchandise recipient had to sell it and the profits be sent to Spain on account of Juan de Céspedes, to whom the merchandise belonged and on whose account and risk it was loaded. Taxes paid in Seville on 4 March amounted to 1,700 *maravedís (almojarifazgo)* and 340 *maravedís (avería)*.

7. Juan de Céspedes loaded 400 jugs of wine from Trebujena (Seville) bound for the city of Nueva Cordoba. The merchandise was consigned to Luis de Lemos, in his absence to Diego López Aries, and in the absence of both to Gaspar Fernández Rebelo, all citizens of Cartagena, so that the merchandise's recipient had to sell it and send the profits to Spain on account of Juan de Céspedes, to whom the merchandise belonged and on whose account and risk it was loaded. Taxes paid in Seville on 9 March amounted to 13,220 *maravedís (almojarifazgo)* and 1,768 *maravedís (avería)*.

8. Juan de Céspedes loaded fabrics, ten flasks of brandy/sherry and a chest with women's shoes bound for the city of Nueva Cordoba. The merchandise was consigned to Luis de Lemos, in his absence to Diego López Aries, and in the absence of both to Gaspar Fernández Rebelo, all citizens of Cartagena, so that the merchandise's recipient had to sell it and the profits be sent to Spain on account of Juan de Céspedes, to whom the merchandise belonged and on whose account and risk it was loaded. Taxes paid in Seville on 9 March amounted to 2,500 *maravedís (almojarifazgo)* and 500 *maravedís (avería)*.

9. Xpoval de Biedma loaded on his account and risk 500 jugs of wine from Salteras (Seville) bound for the city of Nueva Cordoba. The wine was to be delivered to Juan de la Torre Ayala, in his absence to Diego Bernal

de Heredia, and in the absence of both to Juan de Peña. Taxes paid in Seville on 18 March amounted to 275 *maravedís (almojarifazgo)* and 2,210 *maravedís (avería)*.

10. Pedro Fernández Hidalgo loaded on his account and risk 200 jugs of wine from Sierras Llanas bound for the river of the Hacha in the province of Tierra Firme with the fleet of General Juan de Lara. Taxes paid in Seville on 18 March amounted to 510 *maravedís (almojarifazgo)* and 894 *maravedís (avería)*.

Despite the availability of a detailed manifest for the final outward-bound voyage of the *Buen Jesús*, the precise history of this ship and its owner and master eludes us. Records for the vessel and/or owner and master prior to 1622 are also not present in the Archivo General de Indias archives. The *Nuestra Señora del Rosario* listed as sailing to and from Venezuela in 1619 with the Tierra Firme fleet of General Fernando de Sousa does not share the same precise ship or master's names (AGI *Contratación* 2196, 2198, 3026). Neither the vessel nor the personnel of 1622 accompanied fleet general Juan de Benavides Bazán to New Spain in 1621 (AGI *Contratación* 1864-1871).

However, both Simón de la Torre and Juan de la Torre, the owner of the *Buen Jesús*, crop up in 1619 loading money onto the *San Francisco de Padua*, the flagship of the Tierra Firme fleet returning to Spain that year (AGI *Contratación* 2195). Sources also indicate that Juan de la Torre traded in slaves: in May 1622 the Casa de la Contratación filed a lawsuit against him for failing to deliver three slaves to Seville picked up in New Spain by the *Magdalena* in 1616.

The implications of the archival data are that Juan de la Torre Ayala was a well-known merchant and ship owner who was familiar with the markets of Venezuela. While he and his family had ventured to the Americas on multiple occasions prior to 1622, this seems to have been the first voyage of the *Buen Jesús y Nuestra Señora del Rosario* to New Spain. The absence of the ship in pre-1622 documentation hints that it was newly built in Portugal and that this trading enterprise was opportunistic in nature, exploiting the established maritime trade route of the Tierra Firme fleet.

5. Nueva Cordoba: the Frontier 'City' of Cumana

The outward-bound manifest of the *Buen Jesús y Nuestra Señora del Rosario* compiled in Seville confirms that nine out of the ship's ten outward-bound consignments were destined for Nueva Cordoba (AGI *Contratación* 1172, N.2, R.1; Chaunu and Chaunu, 1956: 26-7). Even though the manifest cites an antiquated geographical term, the locality concerned was undoubtedly the 'city' bearing this name on Venezuela's Pearl Coast (pers. comm. Mark Sullivan, 29 November 2011), more familiarly known in the early 17th century as Cumana. In New Andalusia the Indian name of Cumana – first discovered by Christopher Columbus during his third voyage of 1498 – superseded the former names of Nueva Toledo and Nuevo Cordoba (Marquez and Ramos Navarro, 1998; Tarver and Frederick, 2005: 25; Von Humboldt *et al.*, 2009: 181).

By the first quarter of the 17th century Nueva Cordoba was the established military headquarters and distributive center of the Pearl Coast fisheries (Fig. 6). As early as 1504 the Crown had ordered the Spanish Governor of Hispaniola, Nicolas de Ovando, to build a fort near Cumana to protect the royal taxation interests against *rescate,* illicit trade, barter and contraband (Warsh, 2009: 16). A Franciscan and Dominican religious monastic presence followed in 1518, and after a Spanish armed expedition landed 300 armed soldiers from five ships in 1521 the local Indians were 'pacified' and Nueva Cordoba founded. Soon after the settlement changed its name to Santa Inez de Cumana (Humbert, 1906: 46, 48).

Following harvesting and securement in locked boxes, the region's highly coveted pearls were stored in coastal warehouses situated at Nueva Cadiz on Cubagua, La Asuncion on Margarita, Cumana and at Rio de la Hacha on the mainland, pending distribution to market (Figs. 7-10). The royal *quinto* was imposed in these key centers for return to Spain (typically *in natura* rather than as converted coin) and from here private cargos were dispatched to other major Spanish Caribbean entrepôts, such as San Juan, Santo Domingo, Puerto de Plata, Cartagena and Havana (Warsh, 2009: 16, 29-31).

According to the monk Antonio Vázquez de Espinosa, who returned to Spain from the Americas in 1622, the city of Cumana in Nueva Andalucia was founded by Captain Gonzalo de Ocampo in 1520, when he arrived to retaliate against the Indians' destruction of the local Franciscan convent and the murder of its friars (Clark, 1942: 52). Spain established the *gobernación* (governance) of Margarita in 1525, comprising the islands of Margarita, Coche and Cubagua, which from 1528 were situated within the province of Venezuela under the jurisdiction of the *audencia* of Santo Domingo. In 1567 the seat of Margarita's *gobernación* was transferred to the City of Asunción (Tarver and Frederick, 2005 34-5). The *gobernación* of Cumana (Nueva Andalusia) was established in 1568 by the conquistador Diego Fernández de Serpa (died 1570) on the site of the former 'city' of Nueva Cordoba, an event that coincided with the re-founding of the town (Lombardi, 1976: 24; Tarver and Frederick, 2005: 35).

Fig. 6. Pearl divers and fishermen on the island of Cubagua, Venezuela, harvesting oysters for Spanish overlords. From Theodor de Bry, Americae Pars Quarta (Frankfurt, 1594, plate XII). Photo: John Carter Brown Archive of Early American Images 09775.

On 22 July 1619 King Philip III appointed Captain Diego de Arroyo y Daza as the new Governor of Nueva Andalusia, which retained its headquarters at Cumana (Marley, 2008: 167). The frontier settlement's status may have improved following the burning of the castle and town of Margarita by Dutch forces in 1620 (Marshall, 1832: 480). By January 1622 sources hint that Cumana was dwindling, perhaps one of the reasons why the Governor of Santa Marta petitioned the king of Spain to send 50 men there for purposes of defense and repopulation in the annual outward-bound 'royal pearl galleon' (AGI *Santa Fe* 50).

By the end of the 17th century the Capuchin order of Aragon had a significant presence at Cumana, alongside three additional civil settlements. Cumana itself consisted of around 100 small thatched buildings built of mud and tree branches and owned by impoverished farmers. The small town of San Balthasar do los Arias (also known as Cumanacoa) comprised 20-25 structures similarly constructed and inhabited by poor Mulattos and Negros, who cultivated tobacco for local consumption. Cocoa cultivation was also carried out in small farms at San Felipe de Austria or Cariaco (Humbert, 1906: 49).

The character of the Spanish fortified headquarters along the Pearl Coast is captured in a later comparative description of the early 19th century (Depons, 1806: 60):

"The city of Cumana, near a hundred leagues east of La Guira, is sufficiently difficult to access to an invading enemy. Situated a cannon shot from the sea, with its harbour

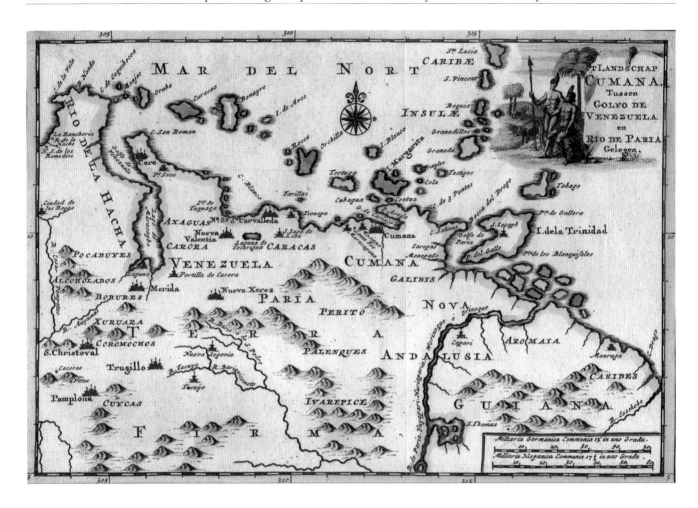

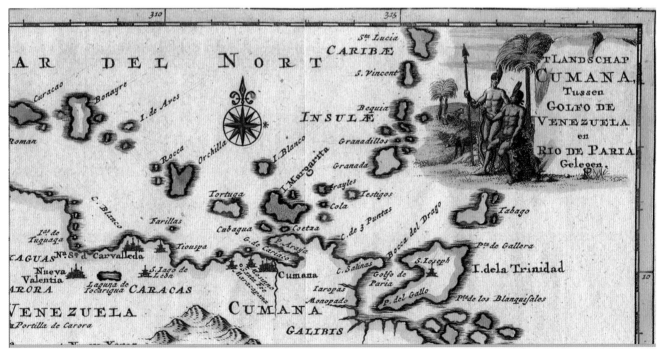

Figs. 7-8. Map of Venezuela showing the Tortugas ship's route between Rio de la Hacha and Cumana (with detail of the Pearl Coast region below) by Pieter van der Aa (Leiden, 1706).

half a league to leeward, it has nothing to fear but attacks under sail, which the distance would render ineffectual. In case of debarkation, a fort, well maintained, situate on a hill in the eastern quarter of the city… The island of Margarita, four leagues to the north of Cumana, is defended by nature, and one company of regular troops… This island derives no attractions from its productions. The ungrateful soil admits no culture except of cotton, and that only in parts least cursed with sterility."

Before he returned to Spain in 1622, Antonio Vázquez de Espinosa described a significant presence at Cumana, which had 200 Spanish residents, plus Negros, Mulattos, Indians and servants. The city included a parish church, a Dominican convent with a few friars and a shrine under the patronage of Our Lady of Carmen, which served as a hospital for the sick. Two Spanish villages existed in its district: San Felipe, 24 leagues inland with 40 residents, and Cumanagoto west of Cumana, opposite the island of Borracha, which had 150 Spanish residents and large numbers of Indians in its hinterland (Clark, 1942: 52-3).

Excavations in 1954, 1955 and 1961 on the nearby island of Cubagua – Nueva Cadiz in the colonial period – provided insights into the regional architecture and town planning (Figs. 12-13). Walls were built of uncut stones, chinked with clay and plastered with lime produced from ground coral. The floors were of simple earth, while the flat roofs were reed plastered with clay. Buildings were arranged in rectangular blocks. The largest houses, plus a church, were situated to the southeast, where the trade winds offered the greatest cooling effect. A monastery was located on a side street and a second church to the island's leeward end. A typical house consisted of four rooms: a living room and bedroom at the front, and a storeroom and kitchen at the back flanked by a walled patio. Some houses possessed masonry stairways indicating original access to a second story. Rectangular hearths were raised 50cm above kitchen floors. In one excavated house a pot full of pearls was discovered (Rouse and Cruxent, 1963: 135-7). Such was the nature of the landscape and economic character of Cumana and its environs when the *Buen Jesús y Nuestra Señora del Rosario* visited in 1622.

Even though Venezuela's oyster fisheries were excessively over-exploited in the first half of the 16th century, resulting in species collapse and crisis, limited volumes of pearls were still harvested in the second half of the 16th century and into the first half of the 17th century. But business was certainly slow. In 1622 the king was informed that the fisheries were badly depleted, so that just one ship was required at Cumana and Margarita annually to collect the royal pearl tax *in natura* (AGI *Contratación* 5173).

Under these circumstances why would the *Buen Jesús y Nuestra Señora del Rosario* have risked venturing beyond the economic core of the main Tierra Firme fleet's geographic circulation to the depleted oyster beds of Cumana? This *navio* certainly was not designated for the conveyance of the royal *quinto* back to Seville in 1622 because the king's pearls were registered for export to Spain onboard the ships of General Tomás de Larraspuru (AGI *Contaduría* 1669).

The most probable explanation is that since pearls were in such short supply significant consignments could only be secured at source, which in addition was the ideal means of negotiating optimum deals. If correct, then the *Buen Jesús* sailed to Cumana speculatively at a time when the availability of the product was a matter of chance. As a 'Letter from Pedro Gómez de Revenga and Pedro Ruiz de Guiçaburuaga to the Casa de la Contratación' written from Margarita on 11 June 1623 explains (AGI *Contratación* 5116):

Fig. 9. 'Occidentalis Americae Partis' from Americae Pars Quarta *showing the Pearl Coast topography of eastern Venezuela (Frankfurt, 1594). Photo: John Carter Brown Archive of Early American Images 09887-2.*

Fig. 10. Satellite view of Cumana in eastern Venezuela, the destination of the Buen Jesús y Nuestra Señora del Rosario *in 1622 and location of the oyster harvesting islands of Margarita, Cubagua, Coche and of the salt marshes of the Araya peninsula.*

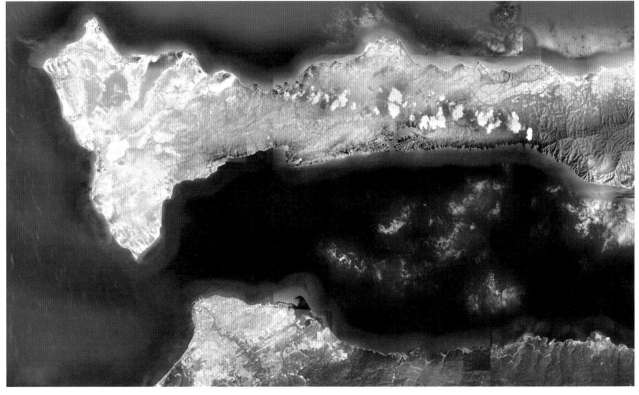

Fig. 11. Satellite view of the bleached saltmarshes and lagoon of the Araya peninsula opposite the mainland of Cumana, Venezuela.

Fig. 12. Aerial view of ruins from the colonial Spanish oyster and pearl harvesting town on the island of Cubagua, Venezuela.

"Your Excellency will consider the sending of pearls from this island to be a new thing because they have not been remitted for so many years, caused by their absence in the fishery. Twelve *marcos,* three ounces and three *ochavas* and two *tomines* of all types have been collected in the Royal Box of our charge of the royal fifth *(quinto real)* of His Majesty these passed years. And although the quantity is so weak because of the large expenses expended by His Majesty, and the great loss of silver in the galleons of the last year did not help the matter, we have encouraged ourselves to make up to His Majesty for this shortage, delivered in this island in a pack covered with cloth and with its key to Captain Pedro de Aguilar y Guzmán, a person named for this effect by General Antonio de Oquendo, directed to Cartagena to the said general so that he should register them in the *capitana* or in the *almiranta* ship to deliver to Your Excellency in the Casa de la Contratación, so that having received the said pearls Your Excellency, by the testimony of the registration that goes with this, the will of His Majesty will be done".

The mercantile character of the Tortugas ship's pearl consignment is not intrinsically transparent. No manifest registrations for 1622 mention cargos of pearls collected at Cumana and Margarita other than the king's *quinto* (AGI *Contratación* 5173; AGI *Santo Domingo* 206). The reality is obscured by an absence of documentation: between June 1622 and June 1623 the accountants of Santa Fe (and possibly Santo Domingo) suffered continuous illness that prevented them from producing accurate accounts (AGI *Santa Fe* 52).

The discovery of a chest of pearls on the wreck of the *Margarita* off the Florida Keys, not listed in the ship's manifest (Tedesco, 2010: 21), proves that this exotic form of jewelry remained in circulation and was almost certainly

exported as contraband. Another reference to the ships of the Marquis of Cadereita suggests that the 1622 fleet was in on the game more widely. In June 1623 royal officials informed the king that one consignment of emeralds and another of pre-drilled pearls originating in Rio de la Hacha – both unregistered – were discovered on Cadereita's ships and that the Casa de Contratación was unsure how to process the contraband (AGI *Contratación* 5173). Though neither Cadereita's vessels, nor the *Margarita,* traded directly with Cumana and Margarita, evidently pearls remained coveted, in circulation and could be secreted onto merchant vessels at source.

In conclusion, the pearls excavated from the deep-sea Tortugas shipwreck fit the maritime history of the *Buen Jesús y Nuestra Señora del Rosario* in 1622. Like the unregistered pearls reported from the ships of the Marquis of Cadereita, and associated with the *Margarita*, some of the Tortugas examples were also pre-drilled, which may hint at an overall impression of contraband. Alternatively, the procurement of royal taxes in 1622 leaves no doubt that surplus pearls could be purchased at Cumana, which would suggest a typical commercial model for their presence on the Tortugas ship. Whichever holds true, perhaps after the *Buen Jesús* joined the main Tierra Firme *flota* it was this merchant vessel that made an early profit by selling a few extra chests to interested parties in the fleet.

6. Rio de la Hacha, Colombia

Located in modern northeastern Colombia, one of the ten consignments listed in the *Buen Jesús's* outward-bound manifest were Pedro Fernández Hidalgo's 200 wine jugs to be delivered to Rio de la Hacha en route east to the final destination at Cumana (Fig. 7). The locality was renowned

Fig. 13. Dense oyster shells strewn across a ruined road between buildings on the island of Cubagua, Venezuala, 16th to 17th century Spanish Nueva Cadiz.

as a clearing house for pearls and slaves, which ultimately caused its downfall at the hands of marauding smugglers and privateers.

In the first few decades following the discovery of oyster beds in northeastern Venezuela, pearls were commonly sold down the line to Rio de la Hacha, which functioned as a regional collecting center inhabited by treasury officials, private contractors and craftsmen. In 1536, for instance, Juan de la Berrera of Seville bought a quarter-share in a Cubaguan pearl-fishing venture and 12 years later sold 400,057 *maravedis* of pearls to the treasurer in Rio (Donkin, 1998: 326-7). Pearl harvesting began in its own right at Rio in 1542, 1,000km west of Venezuela's Pearl Coast (Orche, 2009: 22).

In the mid-16th century Rio de la Hacha possessed around 50 households, but no productive hinterland. Thereafter, the slave trade swiftly took center stage. Sir John Hawkins sold slaves and merchandise at Rio in 1567 for £6,250, and in 1569 another English convoy delivered 260 African slaves at both Rio and Santa Marta (Reiss, 1997: 24). By 1572 the Casa de la Contratación reported that a significant part of the illegal 'negro' slave trade ran to the Indies without registration from the ports of Algarve and Portugal in ships dispatched to Puerto Rico, Cabo de la Vela, Rio de la Hacha and Islas de Barlovento and thence onward to Santo Domingo "and are sold in truck for hides and sugar" (Andrews, 1978: 73).

Sir Francis Drake's men sacked and burned Rio and its *ranchería* in 1595, taking five canoes and over 100 'negros' (Guasco, 2008: 8). English and French corsairs again raided its fisheries in 1598, 1599 and 1603, impoverishing the town. By 1616 Rio de la Hacha's pearl fishery had been silent for five years and was still dormant in 1620 (Andrews, 1978: 127, 164, 222).

Antonio Vázquez de Espinosa's *Compendium and Description of the West Indies* seems to reveal something of a renaissance between this date and 1622, when he returned to Spain (Clark, 1942: 314-5). The friar referred to the city as "one of the best and richest in this State", populated by over 100 Spanish residents and boasting a parish church, two Dominican and Franciscan convents and a hospital. Four heavy bronze cannon and a garrison of soldiers protected a good fort, where the Paymaster and Treasurer of the Royal Patrimony were stationed. Pearl fishing 8-16 leagues offshore towards the Cape of La Vela with "seven boats of Negroes" was once again active. Moreover, de Espinosa was familiar at Rio de la Hacha with "quantities of hides dressed here, brazilwood, guaiacum, and other valuables". Nevertheless, the site's role in the commercial history of the *Buen Jesús y Nuestra Señora del Rosario* in 1622 seems to have been minimal.

7. Venezuelan Tobacco

In light of the interpretation of the 209 olive jars excavated from the Tortugas wreck as containers for ship's stores, rather than a cargo of foodstuffs and liquids, the excavated hull appears to have been improbably empty. What other commodities might the *navio* have carried? Returning to Seville with an empty hold devoid of the riches of the New World would have been unthinkable. In the absence of tangible excavated archaeological data from the comprehensive fieldwork, any supplementary goods are likely to have been organic in nature. If the *Buen Jesús*'s pearls were contraband, the vessel would have had an added reason to stock up with other products at Cumana to justify to Crown regulators its presence in northeast Venezuela. Tobacco may be proposed as a highly likely primary cargo stowed for export to Seville.

Depending on which source is consulted, Venezuela emerges as not especially rich in regional produce, and in the 19th century was remembered as a region that "procured no kind of commercial produce... Cupidity received no other ailment but that derived from the pearls in the environs of Margaretta. Here the pearl fishery was carried on with equal activity and inhumanity; but soon, by means of sacrificing Spaniards and Indians to this murderous occupation, the bank of oysters that produced them was exhausted" (Depons, 1806: 268).

Fig. 14. Aerial view of the Spanish colonial garrison fort on the Araya peninsula, built in the early 17th century to safeguard the abundant salt reserves from Dutch incursions.

Fig. 15. The Tierra Firme port of Cartagena, Colombia, in 'Civitas Carthagena in Indiae occidentalis...', drawn to accompany Walter Bigges' Expeditio Francisci Draki, *published in 1588.*

The early modern proposed agricultural 'sterility' was a far cry from late 16th- and 17th-century reality. In Vázquez de Espinosa's lifetime, prior to his return to Spain in 1622, Indian corn supplies for bread were produced locally "and in this district they grow and harvest a great amount of tobacco, which is the chief staple of the country. They have other crops and native fruits which are highly regarded, and sugarcane and sweet potatoes". The residents also built ranches along the banks of Cumana, where quantities of cattle, pigs and horses were raised between abundant Indian corn and yucca. Excellent fish were available in profusion (Clark, 1942: 52-3).

Cumana's 17th-century fertility was confirmed by the historian José Agustín Oviedo y Baños, born in Sante Fe de Bogotá in 1671, who was familiar with a Venezuela that "abounds in wheat, maize, rice, cotton, tobacco, and sugar, from which dainty and exquisite conserves are made. Also there is found cacao, which in trade brings its inhabitants their greatest wealth". Its forests produced mahogany, dividivi, lignum vitae, brazilwood, jacaranda and cedar, while vanilla plants, Sarsaparilla and indigo were common field crops. Canafistula, tamarind, chinaroot, tacamahac (a remedy for headaches), Carora balsam, and Cumana or Maria oil (an antidote for wounds and a highly prized preventive of muscle spasms) were cultivated for medicinal applications (Johnson Varner, 1987: 7-8).

Venezuela also seemingly possessed tin and copper mines "of great opulence and productivity. His Majesty profited from the considerable amount of metal that was extracted from them and carried to Spain for casting artillery". Oviedo y Baños was similarly impressed by Venezuela's blue-veined, highly fine transparent crystals and woods processed for dyes. "In sum", he concluded, "there is every-

thing that might be desired for the maintenance of human life without any need for the products of neighboring provinces. If the application of its inhabitants were equal to its fertility, and if they knew how to profit from the benefits it offers, it would be the richest province in America" (Johnson Varner, 1987: xv, 7-9). Cocoa production emerged in the 1620s and would remain a profitable export for the next 200 years (Page, 2003: 609).

Although the success of tobacco within Spain began in 1558, widespread commercialization only took place in the early 17th century in Seville, Lisbon and Amsterdam. With insufficient precious metals accessible to cover its debts on the international market, Spain started to lean on tobacco as a staple specialist crop for revenue exchange (Nater, 2006: 93, 98). Caribbean Creole farmers cultivated tobacco on a large scale along the north coast of Venezuela and on Cuba in the last decades of the 16th century and, within a second tier below the high-value products (gold, silver, emeralds and pearls) of the Americas, it swiftly became the dominant commodity exported to Seville (Baud, 1991: 31).

During the 1590s and early 1600s Spanish Cumana and Caracas were transformed into Europe's main tobacco suppliers (Klooster, 2009: 150; Figs. 18-20). Dutch and English traders sailed in growing numbers to Cumana and La Guaira. Tobacco came to Cumana's salvation in 1592 when Sir Walter Raleigh attacked the settlement with six naval vessels: the locals bartered a cargo of tobacco with a Captain Flamenco in exchange for harquebuses, muskets, powder and shot, which enabled them to repel the English privateer (Clark, 1942: 53).

The leading tobacco cultivation center was Nueva Ecija de los Cumanagoto, a small village with 30 *vecinos* situated 12 leagues west of Cumana on the Pearl Coast near

Fig. 16. The Spanish silver fleet assembled at the Tierra Firme port of Havana, Cuba, in the 17th century (English School, 19th century). Photo: Private Collection/Peter Newark American Pictures/The Bridgeman Art Library.

Fig. 17. Detail of the Florida Keys where the Tortugas ship was wrecked in 1622. From 'Occidentalis Americae Partis', published in Americae Pars Quarta *(Frankfurt, 1594). Photo: John Carter Brown Archive of Early American Images 09887-2.*

the mouth of the River Unare, whose output amounted to 30,000lbs in 1603 and which was all bought within the space of three months that year in exchange for contraband (Sluiter, 1948: 182; Klooster, 1998: 31). Two years later Andrés de Rojas described the local producers as "riff-raff who have no other source of income than the tobacco crop that is so esteemed in Flanders and England. I realize they will not reform, for they are people of small account, some of them doing it one year and another lot the next, so that the place is like a fair, by way of which contraband enters and reaches as far as Peru" (Andrews, 1978: 227).

Although the methods of tobacco cultivation were not detailed in contemporary accounts of the West Indies, Antonio Vázquez de Espinosa's description of its production on the nearby island of Trinidad reflects the productive reality in the second quarter of the 17th century (Clark, 1942: 56-7):

"The tobacco is planted in little seedbeds like lettuce, and when it is ready – in November and December on this island – they transplant it along lines or rows, like a bean field or vineyard; and as it keeps growing, they clean out and weed the rows, until it is about a varia high, which point it reaches in about 50 days; thereupon they cap it, i.e., they cut off the crown or topmost shoot, so that it will grow to leaves, and they keep pulling off the branches or shoots which it puts out along with them, so that the leaves will grow and get thick, until it is ripe, which takes another 50 days, and they weed it continually and pick off the caterpillars which usually do

some harm to it. In this way the tobacco leaves grow 4 or 5 palms long, and more, and 2 or 3 across, according to the richness of the soil. After they ripen, they gather and string them and hang them up inside a house, so that there in the shade they may sweat and dry off, which takes 8 or 10 days; then they pull out the central vein and twist them up into ropes or rolls; there are men so expert in this operation that in one day they twist 300 pounds of tobacco and more."

Towards the end of the 16th century northwest Europe was enveloped by an extraordinary market expansion for tobacco. In 1604 King James I criticized the scale and sweeping effects of the new social revolution in *A Counter-Blaste to Tobacco*, as having become "in place of a cure, a point of good fellowship, and he that will refuse to take a pipe of *Tobacco* among his fellowes… is accounted peevish and no good company… Yea the Mistresse cannot in a more mannerly kinde, entertaine her servant, then by giving him out of her faire hand a pipe of *Tobacco*."

According to customhouse Book of Rates, no tobacco imports were registered in England in 1558. By 1610, in contrast, England's tobacco use was valued at £60,000, and a year later a Spanish observer valued the annual national consumption at 100,000lbs worth 400,000 ducats. England's total imports for 1621-22 substantially exceeded 166,000lbs. The Netherlands, France and Germany combined consumed at least as much again. During the lifetime of the *Buen Jesús* tobacco was a highly coveted and costly luxury in a short-lived boom before expanded production led to a crash in the later 1620s and 1630s. At that time prices dropped from 20-40 shillings per pound to just a few pence per pound *c*. 1630, dwindling a few years later to no more than a penny, a low cost that promoted a pan-societal addiction. In reality, England's tobacco was shipped almost entirely directly via the Indies. No more than 6,000lbs of this supposed Spanish royal monopoly actually came from Spanish hands (Andrews, 1978: 225, 229).

Between 1600 and 1625 most tobacco purchases on the Spanish Main were transacted at Cumana. Contemporary documents record that the Tierra Firme ships that sailed there in 1622 departed for Spain largely with cargos of tobacco (AGI *Contaduría* 1652; AGI *Contaduría* 1653). Indeed, the 1622 Americas fleet predominantly exchanged Spanish wine, clothes and gunpowder for the "fruits of the land", specifically tobacco (AGI *Contratación* 5188).

At least two other major tobacco consignments were picked up beyond the Pearl Coast. The ships of the Marquis of Cadereita were topped up in Cartagena with great quantities of this product (AGI *Contratación* 5189). *Flota* administrator Diego del Valle Alvarado and accountant Martin de Urdaniz chronicled that at Cartagena 193,451 *pesos* of eight *reales* were paid by Tierra Firme fleet merchants to the royal officials as Crown tax in return for 14,964 *arrobas* and 22 pounds of tobacco (*Contratación* 5116) – 172 tons in modern equivalents. Both the *Atocha* and the *Rosario* carried shipments of tobacco alongside their riches of gold, silver and copper. Notably, a 'Letter from Diego Pinelo to the Casa de la Contratación. Cartagena, 3 August 1622' (also in AGI *Contratación* 5116) confirms that 3,772 pouches of tobacco were collected by fleet galleons at 'Maracaybo' in northwest Venezuela. Tobacco exports thus played a dominant role in the homeward-bound trade of the 1622 Tierra Firme fleet.

Given appropriate soil and climate, tobacco was easy to cultivate and did not demand the same level of skilled labor as sugar. For young colonies with little capital, labor or business organization, tobacco was an ideal crop. High profits, however, quickly attracted Dutch, English and French envy from Chesapeake Bay to the Amazon in the first quarter of the 17th century and, worryingly, for the Spanish economy, caused a thriving contraband trade to evolve in Venezuela, and later across Trinidad and Guiana. As Sancho de Alquiza, the Governor of Caracas, informed the Crown in 1607, "tobacco has been one of the chief factors causing these coasts to be so much frequented by pirates, by reason of the great demand there has always been for it; and in truck for it they give merchandise that comes cheaper than had it been bought in Spain" (Klooster,

Fig. 18. A tobacco plant illustrated in the Hortus Eystettensis *by Basil Besler (German School, the Stapleton Collection 1613). Photo: Private Collection/The Stapleton Collection/ The Bridgeman Art Library.*

1998: 31). The marketability of tobacco and its political control are proposed to have been a major reason for the *Buen Jesús's* presence at Cumana in 1622.

8. Venezuelan Contraband Trade

Apart from purely commercial objectives, strong political reasons had arisen for Spain to need – and perhaps order – an increased mercantile presence at Cumana in 1622: the Crown was hemorrhaging economically as a result of lost revenues. To no avail local authorities had consistently complained to the Crown, the Council of the Indies and the House of Trade in Seville that since the 1570s Spanish merchants and ships neglected the ports of the Antilles and Tierra Firme east of Cartagena, allowing foreign smugglers and corsairs to infest the coasts. The island of Margarita opposite Cumana was a particularly favored stopping place for French and English corsairs, as well as Portuguese slave-smugglers and, ultimately, Dutch commercial infiltration. Its coastal watering places were natural smugglers' dens.

The scale of the problem was faithfully chronicled by Jerónimo de Torres, the town clerk of La Yaguana in Espanola, in 1577 (Andrews, 1978: 75-7):

Fig. 19. Native Americans picking and smoking tobacco leaves. From André Thevet, La cosmographie vniuerselle ... Tome seconde *(1575). Photo: John Carter Brown Archive of Early American Images 07598-12.*

Fig. 20. African slaves twisting and drying tobacco. From Jean Baptiste Labat, Nouveau voyage aux isles de l'Amerique, ... Tome quatrième *(Paris, 1722). Photo: John Carter Brown Archive of Early American Images 09905-1.*

"Among the settlements and ports most frequented for commerce by the French and Portuguese, the island of Margarita is the first they reach in the Indies, and next the ports of the province of Venezuela and Caracas... and they pass along this coast trading for pearls and gold, going on to Rió de la Hacha and beyond to Cartagena and Nombre de Dios, where they complete their transactions... those that are merchants – Portuguese or French – run from Margarita along the Venezuelan Tierra Firme, doing a quick trade in passing because they prefer hides, sugar and cassia fistula to coin, gold or silver, for they say they get a double profit on such merchandise, one here and the other in their own countries, whereas with money they only get one...

All the settlements of this island, Margarita, the Venezuelan Tierra Firme and the islands of Puerto Rico, Española, Cuba and Jamaica are for the most part maritime, either by the shore or half a league or so away... even when the stock is at some distance they bring it on the hoof and hides and sugar in carts as far as the harbor where the ships lade, and for this purpose they have built houses by the shore where they stow the goods until a ship or bark comes for them; and it is this seaside nature of the merchandise that makes the trade possible and very secret... All the merchandise the inhabitants of these settlements trade with the enemy is delivered in deserted places, as I have said, and as secretly as possible; the territory is unoccupied and few or no people go there, but should anyone notice, all are *vecinos*, all are on the council and all are involved in trade, rich and poor... so that information is never to be found against anyone, nor can they be punished."

By 1604 the Dutch had started surveying the Orinoco River, followed by the Swedes one year later. Initially Spain successfully contained these incursions, but constant war with the Caribs deflected attention away from the Pearl Coast, whose slaves were captured by the English and shipped to St. Vincent. Foreign powers seemed capable of attacking Spain's Venezuelan possessions at will (Tarver and Frederick, 2005: 31-2).

Not just the Dutch and English were profiting from smuggling, but Spanish officials were also in on the take. In 1611 the Governor of Sante Fe de Bogota accused Fernando de Berrio, the Governor of Trinidad, of illegal trade with the Dutch. Berrio claimed that his tobacco had been seized by Dutch troops, but the Crown was able to establish from planters that he had actually exchanged royal tobacco for slaves. Enemy intrusions escalated in 1614, when the Dutch built a fort at Essequibo (modern Suriname) as a base to arm the Caribs. A new, short-lived English settlement followed on the coast near Margarita, but when Sir Walter Raleigh's son attacked the Spanish fort of Santo Tomé down the Orinoco River in January 1618 with 10 ships and 500 troops, killing the Governor of Guayana, Diego Palomeque de Acuña, and also Raleigh's son, the adventurer was accused of insubordination and treason by King James I, imprisoned in the Tower and executed for his Indies misadventures in October 1618 (Whitehead, 1988: 86; Tarver and Frederick, 2005: 31-2).

The presence of the *Buen Jesús y Nuestra Señora del Rosario* and other vessels of the Tierra Firme fleet at Cumana in 1622 was arguably not purely commercial, but also strategic. Spain acutely needed to retain a strong visible presence along the Pearl Coast, where trade is likely to have been encouraged.

Commercial action in Venezuela in 1622 was intimately intertwined with protracted hostilities and leaking treaties in Europe. In 1585 the English were the main regional predators, when a powerful fleet sacked Santo Domingo and Cartagena, launching an 18-year phase of plunder. Between 1585 and 1603, 76 English expeditions traveled to the Caribbean with 235 vessels (of which 74 were private ventures comprising 183 individual voyages). English raiding substantially damaged the lands east of Cartagena, leaving Venezuela's pearl fishery especially vulnerable, so that the Governor of Cumana reported in 1600 that the settlement was "barred from trade and intercourse with all places because no ship or frigate of trade dare not come hither". By 1596 just 43 smuggling vessels from Portugal, Andalucia and the Canaries had visited Margarita and Cumana during the previous ten years (Andrews, 1978: 135, 156, 165, 174).

Contraband trade across Venezuela and the adjacent islands escalated to an unprecedented scale at the turn of the 17th century, ushering in a critically dangerous mercantile era. From *c.* 1596 the Netherlands emerged as the main threat to Spain's monopoly on trade in her dominions, when two Dutch ships sold a purported 80,000 ducats worth of cloth at Margarita. Trade seems to have been particularly poorly protected along the Pearl Coast at the time. Thus, in 1595 Gillis Dorenhovenn, the captain of the Dutch *Zwemmende Leeuw (Swimming Lion)*, sailed to the wilds of South America, where he quietly traded at "Margarita, Cumaná, Manecillas & the Baya river." The goods exported from Zeeland were bartered for "tobacco, sassafras, canafistula, a great number of pearls of different kinds, gold jewelry, and costly leading-strings, gold crucifixes adorned with pearls, garnet, & emerald; earrings and finger-rings, and diverse precious stones, as well as wrought silver & a great number of hides, not to mention a batch of pieces of eight and pieces of four" (van Ittersum, 2007: 7, 21-2).

The Dutch may be credited for plunging the dagger into the heart of the failing pearl fisheries. The oyster beds of Margarita, Cubagua and Araya could only be worked in rotation every three years. With the Araya region less accessible and the Dutch presence magnified, pearl smuggling escalated. Pearl production at Cubagua between December 1600 and May 1601 yielded 40,000 ducats of produce, of which two Dutch smuggling ships carried away 30,000 *pesos* worth. In 1603 Suárez de Amaya reported that the royal *quinto* had dwindled to 3,000 *pesos*, and a year later to 1,600 ducats, a sum that could not even sustain the governor's salary (Sluiter, 1948: 181).

The main commodity sought by the Dutch was neither pearls, nor tobacco, but the region's abundant salt reserves, which were used in butter and cheese and to pickle meat, but were predominantly essential for the nation's herring industry after direct trade routes to Iberia – notably Setúbal

in southern Portugal – dried up following the outbreak of war between the Netherlands and Spain in the 1590s (Klooster, 1998: 26). Salt carriers from the Netherlands invaded the great 13km-long natural saltpan at the western end of Punta de Araya between Margarita and Cumana in 1594 (Jarvis, 2010: 189). The lagoon's gem salt was the finest in the Caribbean (Figs. 10-11, 14), and allegedly in the whole world (Sluiter, 1948: 176). That summer 13-14 ships filled their holds with salt. Eight more arrived in the autumn and 50 more vessels in May 1600, largely *urcas* (hulks) of 200-400 ton capacity. Many were armed and carried privateering papers. By 1603 more than 120 Dutch ships were annually collecting salt at Araya, plus another 30 English, French and Scottish vessels (Jarvis, 2010: 189).

The Dutch ships seizing free salt were comparable in volume to the official Indies fleets dispatched from Seville for Mexico and Portobello (Parry, 1963: 187). Official figures tabulated by Governor Diego Suárez de Amaya between 7 June 1600 and 8 December 1605 amounted to a minimum of 611 Dutch salt ships, plus a further 55 Dutch smuggling vessels in the wider Margarita-Araya-Cumana region. Over the same period just 25 English, four French, two Italian and one Scottish ship were listed (Sluiter, 1948: 178-9). In the reign of King Philip III a Spanish official observed that to the Dutch the saltpans were like mines "as rich as those of Potosí were for His Majesty". The majority of Dutch vessels sailed from the West Frisian towns of Hoorn, Medemblik and Enkhuizen, where the fishing industry thrived (Klooster, 1998: 27).

Antonio Vázquez de Espinosa described the Araya saltpans in 1622 as located three leagues from Cumana and as "the most abundant and the richest in salt to be found in the universe, for under the water lies rock salt in such quantities that if a hundred boats or galleons finish loading there, as has often been seen, and another hundred arrive, there is a cargo for all of them and one notices no diminution in consequence of earlier cargoes" (Clark, 1942: 54) A league and half in circumference, the lagoon lay 700 paces from the sea and was fed from the ocean, so that salt formed continuously in abundance. The produce was so concentrated that foreigners diluted it to make three boatloads out of one.

From 1599 to 1605, Dutch, English and French vessels met little effective Spanish resistance, enabling Dutch ships to challenge the economic control of the Caribbean and to extend their influence over Trinidad, the Guiana coast, Caracas and beyond. Contraband trade and heavy defense commitments in Italy, the Mediterranean, Atlantic and the new front in the East Indies, would lead to such Crown poverty that in 1596 and 1607 Spain's debt payments were suspended. Creditors were instead compelled to accept state bonds. The resulting loss of credit was a major cause of peace with France in 1598 and the Dutch truce of 1609.

Spain retaliated with words, but ultimately with limited actions. Peace with England improved relations in the West Indies in 1604, and a year later Fajardo led an expedition against the Dutch hulks at Araya with 14 galleons and 2,500 men. Twelve Dutch vessels were captured (as well as one French and three English interlopers) and the prisoners killed, drowned trying to escape, put to the sword, hanged or taken prisoner to Lisbon for consignment to the galleys. Following Bautista Antoneli and Pedro Suárez Coronel's inspection of the saltpans the same year, Spain decided that the best means of curtailing Dutch salt smuggling off Cumana would be to fill in the saltpans using a workforce of 500-600 Moriscos shipped in on four galleons and two *pataches* at a cost 162,000 ducats. The proposal was never realized. Instead, in 1605 royal approval was granted for a force of ten vessels totaling 2,300 tons to be built for the permanent defense of the Caribbean (two galleons, four *galeoncetes* of 300 tons each, and four minor craft) carrying 630 soldiers, 580 sailors and 150 cast pieces. The project would cost 224,689 ducats for construction and 271,114 ducats a year for maintenance, but when the coinage arrived from New Spain in 1606 the treasury siphoned it off for alternative purposes. The scheme was suspended (Sluiter, 1948: 177; Andrews, 1978: 201-203).

Ultimately, the main Spanish strategy devised to end the contraband trade was desperate and ill advised. By an ordinance of 26 August 1606, Margarita, Cumana and Caracas, the chief producers of tobacco, were ordered to suspend sowing tobacco seeds for ten years and, in February 1606, Pedro Suárez Coronel, the Governor of Cumana, was instructed to depopulate Cumanagoto, the regional commercial epicenter (Andrews, 1978: 214).

With one regional fire extinguished, others quickly broke out. The prohibition merely enabled the tobacco trade to expand under foreign control, impoverishing the Spanish dominions further. Although all cultivation along the coast of Cumana had stopped, it boomed instead in Trinidad, and in the 'Wild Coast' between Venezuela and northern Brazil from the Orinoco River as far as Maranhao, where the French, Dutch and English built new factories and plantations (Klooster, 1998: 32). Bernardo de Vargas Machuca, the Governor of Margarita, also pointed out in 1609 that the ban was counterproductive because it made the African slaves and pearl fishermen of Margarita restless and unproductive (the inference being that slaves were pacified with cheap tobacco). More immediate political concerns were undoubtedly exerted by the Church, whose yearly levies in excess of 1,000 ducats from tobacco sales were in jeopardy (Baud, 1991: 32; Goodman, 2005: 133).

In 1611 the Governor of Honduras complained about the ruinous condition of his province, as well as conditions in Jamaica. A year later the population of Panama had dwindled by two-thirds due to changes in the pattern of American trade, and Rio de la Hacha pleaded remission of its taxes because it was too poor to pay them. To make matters worse, Caribs from Tobago and further north attacked Cumana (Andrews, 1978: 222).

The uneasy truces within the West Indies came to an end in 1618 with the Thirty Years War in Europe. The Dutch-Spanish truce expired in 1621 within weeks of Philip IV taking the throne. A marked revival of corsair attacks ensued in the Caribbean, and Margarita, Cumana and Punta de Araya bore the brunt of heavy assaults. Privateers raided Margarita in 1618 and the island was ransacked in August 1620. Following Dutch attempts to seize the saltpans in 1621, the Governor of Cumana, Diego de Arroyo Daza, fortified the area in November 1622 (Andrews, 1978: 236, 238; Fig. 14).

According to Antonio Vázquez de Espinosa, King Philip IV ordered a garrison and fort to be built at Santiago de Araya in 1622 for the protection and defense of the salt beds. The new fort held 200 infantry soldiers, a lieutenant under the command of Don Juan de Vargas Machuca, 40 bronze and cast iron cannon, 25 artillerymen and their master gunner, so that "the salt beds are protected and the pirates no longer dare come to them, and so that nest of pirates was broken up" (Clark, 1942: 54). The project was a success and after the soldiers drove off another heavily armed Dutch incursion in January 1623, the Dutch withdrew from Araya and began instead to exploit San Martin in the Leeward Islands, Bonaire, Tortuga and Curaçao off the Venezuelan coast for salt (Andrews, 1978: 238).

9. Conclusion

The collective archaeological evidence for the deep-sea Tortugas shipwreck excavated by Seahawk Deep Ocean Technology (pearls, keel length and 'negative' data indicative of an organic primary cargo), examined against the profile of outward-bound ships in the Tierra Firme *flota* of 1622, suggests that the 117-ton *navio Buen Jesús y Nuestra Señora del Rosario* (master Manuel Diaz, owner Juan de la Torre) best fits the profile for this shipwreck.

The keel measures 17.40m in length maximum, which corresponds to a vessel with a keel length just in excess of 30 *codos* (17.24m and 106 1/8 tons) and a beam of 10 *codos* (5.74m). These parameters seem to discount the other two short-listed possibilities. At 90 tons the *Nuestra Señora del Buen Successo* appears to be too small (28-30 *codos*, 16.09-17.24m) and at 180 tons the *Nuestra Señora de la Consolacion* too large (32-34 *codos*, 18.38-19.53m).

While the outward-bound destination of these two vessels is unspecified in Spanish manifests (AGI *Contratación* 1172 merely states they were heading for Tierra Firme), journey's end for the *Buen Jesús y Nuestra Señora del Rosario* was officially listed as Nueva Cordoba (Cumana), which was the center of Venezuela's celebrated Pearl Coast. The consignment of 6,639 pearls excavated from the Tortugas wreck adds credibility to the proposed identity of the ship.

At first glance the pearl cargo rationalizes the *Buen Jesús*'s presence at Cumana on the east coast of Venezuela. However, 1622 coincided with a critical moment in time for Spain's control over Tierra Firme, and wider political and economic currents may have underlain the ship's voyage to the Pearl Coast. Smuggling plagued Venezuela as contraband tobacco and pearls eroded the Crown's tax revenues. The minimum of a thousand ships that sailed from Amsterdam to America in search of free salt and colossal illicit trade between 1587 and 1602 reflects the enormity of the commercial problem (Sluiter, 1948).

The start of King Philip IV's reign coincided with a profound change in Spain's commercial policy towards the Northern Countries (notably the Netherlands and England) as the fear of a negative balance of payments, whereby deficits would have to be paid off in silver, necessitated a shift towards a more protectionist policy (cf. Nater, 2005: 254). With the end of the 12-year truce signed with the United Provinces in 1621, all trade was officially closed to the rebels. At the time of the *Buen Jesús*'s fateful voyage, Spain was committed to a phase of economic warfare designed to suffocate enemy trade (Aparicio, 2009: 1-2). The *Buen Jesús* was conceivably a pawn that served to help maintain in a small way both a visible presence at Cumana and to guarantee the flow of taxed tobacco to Seville.

The possibility of a major consignment of tobacco on the *Buen Jesús* fits with the maritime history of the 1622 fleet, from which at least the *Atocha* and *Rosario* were transporting the same product. Venezuelan tobacco may also have served as a perfect camouflage to cover the captain's tracks in procuring valuable contraband pearls at Cumana (cf. Rondón, 2009), if this was the case; the pearls found on the *Margarita* are similarly absent from the ship's homeward-bound manifest.

Other secondary cargos were also readily available in Venezuela and may have been picked up at Cumana or Rio de la Hacha. Indigo, cocoa, sugar, ginger, copper, turquiña stone for painters, garnets and other merchandise were all accessible in the Bay of Maracaibo in northwest Venezuela, a transit point en route to and from the Pearl Coast (AGI *Contratación* 5173). Other produce is often proposed for this period, but American cotton can be excluded because this trade did not develop until the 1740s (Thomson, 2008).

Cacao is often envisioned as having taken off by 1622. Pope Pious V proclaimed in 1569 that chocolate mixed with water could be consumed during a ritual fast as a "restorative" and not as actual food. While Dutch pirates were busy throwing a cargo of cacao beans, mistaken for sheep droppings, overboard from a captured Spanish galleon, in 1585 the first official shipment arrived in Seville. Some scholars argue that by the 1620s cacao from the *criollo* variety of the *Theobroma* tree had become Venezuela's primary export (Kim, 2007). The dominant plantations of Caracas emerged in the late 16th century using Indian labor (Klein, 1986: 85); by the early 17th century Caracas is sometimes accepted as having started to export cacao (Piñero, 1994: 34).

In terms of scale, such trade is unlikely to have been significant in 1622 or to have attracted the interests of the *Buen Jesús*. Cacao cultivation accounted for a lowly 0.5% of Caracas's exports in 1607 (compared to 42.9% for tobacco, the leading regional commodity). By 1650, levels had escalated to 50% of the town's exports. The Caraqueños may have realized that local cacao beans could be sold to Indian consumers for profit in the 1620s, but Dutch exports in that decade were minor. The earliest cacao beans exported to Mexico were shipped by the Basque Liendo immigrant family in 1628, whose Caracas estates boasted 12,382 trees by 1653 (Ferry, 1989: 3, 45-6; Klooster, 1998: 182). Before then cacao was used solely for small-scale barter.

Alongside the commercial attractions of pearls and tobacco at Cumana, plus the *Buen Jesús*'s strategic role in 1622, several other products identified on the Tortugas wreck could have been readily collected at journey's end. Both finished tortoiseshell combs and comb cases, plus apparent examples of blanks for cutting and processing, were excavated from the site. All would have been widely available at Cumana.

Ethnohistoric and other documentary sources indicate that turtles were systematically exploited along Venezuela for eggs, meat, oil and carapace in the 16th to 18th centuries and that nesting beaches were renowned off Margarita. The region was home to the green turtle (*Chelonia mydas*), the hawksbill turtle (*Eretmochelys imbricata*), whose translucent carapace plaques have traditionally been used to produce diverse articles and implements, and thirdly the loggerhead turtle (*Caretta caretta*), which was the most common species in eastern Venezuela. At the beginning of the 16th century Fernandez de Oviedo y Valdéz described the nesting of "many gigantic turtles, with as much meat as a six months calf" on Cubagua and the other eastern islands of Venezuela, clearly referring to green turtles. The volume of meat obtained from the marine turtle is relatively large: green turtles can weigh up to 275kg, with its flesh constituting about 40% of its total weight (Antczak *et al.*, 2007: 63-5). 'Tortoises' (presumably including turtles) were also recognized sources of nutrition obtained by Europeans for return voyages (Thompson, 1958: 334). Perhaps similar consumption, followed by functional reuse of the shell for comb production, was practiced by the *Buen Jesús*'s crew.

To complete the possible links between the Tortugas wreck and Venezuela, Philip Armitage's identification of two bones as originating from the blue-headed parrot, *Pionus menstruus* (Armitage, 2013), bring to mind José Agustín Oviedo y Baños's reference to the country in the last quarter of the 17th century, where "The fields are always full of birds, delightful for their beautiful plumage and their melodious songs, as well as their delectable flesh" (Johnson Varner, 1987: 8). Of course both turtles and parrots would have been equally readily available in Havana, the final port of call where fleet ships took on fresh supplies of food, water and firewood for the 115-day long haul back to Spain (Macleod, 1986: 353; de la Fuente, 2008: 13, 53). Such are the reconstructed parameters – probable and tentative – for the deep-sea Tortugas shipwreck.

Acknowledgements

This work stands on broad shoulders and I am acutely aware of the enormous industry and passion that went into the Tortugas shipwreck excavation. In addition to everyone most sincerely acknowledged in OME Papers 27, I would like to applaud Odyssey Marine Exploration for investing purely in the science of this project. Greg Stemm made it a point of honor to publish the Tortugas site, and throughout this long journey he has been hands on supportive from facilitating initiatives to minutely proofreading all texts. Odyssey's Mark Gordon, Laura Barton and John Oppermann agreed to all post-excavation research needs, with Mr. Oppermann's Archaeology, Research and Conservation Laboratory dealing with all requests with good humor and efficiency. It has been a nurturing collaboration.

The proposed identification of the Tortugas ship as the *Buen Jesús y Nuestra Señora del Rosario* and the *navío*'s historical reconstruction would have been impossible without the vision of John Astley – a great mind in deep-sea archaeological technology – and of Tortugas site archaeologist David Moore. For generously reading and commenting on this text I am truly appreciative of the support of Filipe Castro, Frederick R. Mayer Faculty Professor II of Nautical Archaeology, Nautical Archaeology Program, Texas A&M University; Alice Copeland and Ellen Gerth, Odyssey Marine Exploration, Tampa; Claudio Lozano Guerra-Librero, Stratigraphy Area, Faculty of Experimental Sciences, University of Huelva; Russell Skowronek, Professor of History and Anthropology, the University of Texas-Pan American; and Carol Tedesco, Historic Underwater Discoveries, Inc., Key West, Florida.

Bibliography

Andrews, K.R., *The Spanish Caribbean. Trade and Plunder 1530-1630* (Yale University Press, 1978).

Antczak, A., Buitrago, J., Mackowiak de Antczak, M.M. and Guada, H.J., 'A Contribution to the History of Marine Turtles Exploitation in Venezuela'. In *Fifty-Ninth Gulf and Caribbean Fisheries Institute Proceedings* (2007), 63-73.

Aparicio, A.A., 'Portuguese Contraband and the Closure of the Iberian Markets, 1621-1640. The Economic Roots of an Anti-Habsburg Feeling', *E-Journal of Portuguese History* 7.2 (2009), 1-18.

Armitage, P.L., *The Deep-Sea Tortugas Shipwreck, Florida: the Animal Bones* (OME Papers, Tampa, 2013).

Astley, J. and Stemm, G., *The Deep-Sea Tortugas Shipwreck, Florida: Technology* (OME Papers 26, Tampa, 2013).

Barnette, M.C., *Shipwrecks of the Sunken State. Florida's Submerged History* (Association of Underwater Explorers, 2003).

Baud, M., 'A Colonial Counter Economy: Tobacco Production on Española, 1500-1870', *New West Indian Guide* 65 (1991), 27-49.

Bearss, E.C., *Shipwreck Study – the Dry Tortugas* (United States Department of the Interior, National Park Service, 1971).

Castro, F., 'In Search of Unique Iberian Ship Design Concepts', *Historical Archaeology* 42.2 (2008), 63-87.

Chaunu, H. and Chaunu, P., *Séville et l'Atlantique (1504-1650). Première partie: partie statistique. Le movement des navires et des merchandised entre l'Espagne et l'Amérique de 1504-1650. Tome V. Le traffic de 1621-1650* (Paris, 1956).

Clark, C.U. (tr.), *Compendium and Description of the West Indies by Antonio Vázquez de Espinosa* (Washington, 1942).

De la Fuente, A., *Havana and the Atlantic in the Sixteenth Century* (University of North Carolina Press, 2008).

Depons, F., *A Voyage to the Eastern Part of Terra Firma, or the Spanish Main, in South-America, during the Years 1801, 1802, 1803, and 1804. Vol. II* (New York, 1806).

Donkin, R.A., *Beyond Price. Pearls and Pearl-Fishing: Origins to the Age of Discoveries* (Philadelphia: American Philosophical Society, 1998).

Fernández-González, F., *The Spanish Regulations for Shipbuilding (Ordenanzas) of the Seventeenth Century* (Naval History Symposium, US Naval Academy, Annapolis, MD 10-11 September, 2009).

Ferry, R.J., *The Colonial Elite of Early Caracas. Formation and Crisis, 1567-1767* (University of California Press, 1989).

Flow, J., *Tortugas Deep Water Shipwreck. Interim Report July 1999* (Seahawk, Tampa, Unpublished, 1999).

Goodman, J., *Tobacco in History. The Cultures of Dependence* (London, 2005).

Guasco, M., '"Free from the Tyrannous Spanyard"? Englishmen and Africans in Spain's Atlantic World', *Slavery and Abolition* 29.1 (2008), 1-22.

Humbert, J., 'La plus ancienne ville du continent Américain, Cumaná de Vénézuéla', *Journal de la Société des Américanistes* 3.1 (1906), 45-51.

Jarvis, M.J., *In the Eye of all Trade. Bermuda, Bermudians, and the Maritime Atlantic, 1680-1783* (University of North Carolina Press, 2010).

Johnson, R.E., *Underwater Archaeological Investigations at FOJE-UW-9 Conducted in Summer, 1982 at Fort Jefferson National Monument, Dry Tortugas, Florida* (Southeast Archeological Center, National Park Service, Tallahassee, Florida, 1982).

Johnson Varner, J., *The Conquest and Settlement of Venezuela. Don José de Oviedo y Baños* (University of California Press, 1987).

Kim, L., 'Cacao: Impetus for the Creation of an Independent Venezuela', *Emory Endeavors in World History* 1 (2007).

Kingsley, S., Gerth, E. and Hughes, M., 'Ceramics from the Tortugas Shipwreck. A Spanish-Operated Navio of the 1622 Tierra Firme Fleet', *Ceramics In America* (forthcoming, 2012).

Klein, H.S., *African Slavery in Latin America and the Caribbean* (Oxford University Press, 1986).

Klooster, W., *Illicit Riches. Dutch Trade in the Caribbean, 1648-1795* (Leiden, 1998).

Klooster, W., 'Inter-Imperial Smuggling in the Americas, 1600-1800'. In B. Bailyn (ed.), *Soundings in Atlantic History. Latent Structures and Intellectual Currents, 1500-1830* (Harvard University Press, 2009), 141-80.

Lombardi, J.V., *People and Places in Colonial Venezuela* (Indiana University Press, 1976).

Lyon, E., *The Search for the Atocha* (New York, 1989).

Macleod, M.J., 'Spain and America: the Atlantic Trade 1492-1720'. In L. Bethell (ed.), *The Cambridge History of Latin America. Volume I. Colonial Latin America* (Cambridge University Press, 1986), 341-88.

Malcom, C., 'Glass from *Nuestra Señora de Atocha*', *Astrolabe: Journal of the Mel Fisher Maritime Heritage Society* 6.1 (1990).

Malcom, C., 'The Flotation of Waterlogged Organics: the *Atocha* Example', *Astrolabe: Journal of the Mel Fisher Maritime Heritage Society* 8.1 (1993), 2-7.

Malcom, C., 'Pewter from the *Nuestra Señora de Atocha*', *The Navigator: Newsletter of the Mel Fisher Maritime Heritage Society* 13.11-12 (1998).

Marken, M.W., *Pottery from Spanish Shipwrecks 1500-1800* (University Press of Florida, 1994).

Marley, D., *Wars of the Americas: a Chronology of Armed Conflict in the Western Hemisphere, Volume 1* (Santa Barbara, 2008).

Marquez, O. and Ramos Navarro, L., *Compilation of Colonial Spanish Terms and Document Related Phrases* (Midway City, 1998).

Marshall, J., *A New Universal Gazetteer Containing a Description of the Principal Nations, Empires, Kingdoms... of the Known World* (New York, 1832).

Marx, R.F., *Shipwrecks in Florida Waters* (Florida, 1969).

Mathewson, D., *Treasure of the Atocha* (Houston, 1986).

McKinnon, J.F. and Scott-Ireton, D.A., 'Florida's Mystery Wreck', *International Journal of Nautical Archaeology* 35.2 (2006), 187-94.

Moore, D., *Preliminary Site Analysis, Tortugas Site* (Seahawk, 1991, Unpublished).

Murphy, L.E. and Jonsson, R.W., 'Fort Jefferson National Monument Documented Maritime Casualties'. In L.E. Murphy (ed.), *Dry Tortugas National Park. Submerged Cultural Resources Assessment* (National Park Service, 1993), 143-65.

Nater, L., 'The Spanish Empire and Cuban Tobacco during the Seventeenth and Eighteenth Centuries'. In P.A. Coclanis (ed.), *The Atlantic Economy during the Seventeenth and Eighteenth Centuries* (University of South Carolina, 2005), 252-76.

Nater, L., 'Colonial Tobacco: Key Commodity of the Spanish Empire, 1500-1800'. In S. Topik, C. Marichal and Z.L. Frank (eds.), *From Silver to Cocaine. Latin American Commodity Chains and the Building of the World Economy, 1500-2000* (Duke University Press, 2006), 93-117.

Navarrete, M.F. de, *Colección de documentos y manuscriptos compilados por Fernandez de Navarrete* (Liechtenstein, 1971).

Orche, E., 'Exploitation of Pearl Fisheries in the Spanish American Colonies', *De Re Metallica* 13 (2009), 19-33.

Ortega, A.V., *Cartagena de Indias en la Articulacion del Espacio Regional Caribe, 1580-1640: la Produccion Agrarian* (Agrija Ediciones, 2002).

Page, M.E. (ed.), *Colonialism: an International Social, Cultural, and Political Encyclopedia* (Santa Barbara, 2003).

Parry, J.H., *The Age of Reconnaissance. Discovery, Exploration and Settlement 1450-1650* (University of California Press, 1963).

Piñero, E., *The Town of San Felipe and Colonial Cacao Economies* (Transactions of the American Philosophical Society 84.3, Philadelphia, 1994).

Reiss, O., *Blacks in Colonial America* (Jefferson, North Carolina, 1997).

Rodríguez Mendoza, B.M., *Standardization of Spanish Shipbuilding: Ordenanzas para la Fábrica de Navíos de Guerra y Mercante – 1607, 1613, 1618* (MA Thesis, Texas A&M University, 2008).

Rondón, Y., 'La Región Histórica Margariteña y su Influencia en la Conformación de Redes Comerciales en el Caribe', *Revista Digital de Historia y Arqueología desde el Caribe Colombiano* 6.11 (2009), 97-127.

Rouse, I. and Cruxent, J.M., *Venezuelan Archaeology* (Yale University Press, 1963).

Skowronek, R., *Seventeenth Century Spanish Colonial Shipping in the Dry Tortugas: an Archaeological, Geographical, and Historical Overview* (Florida State University, 1982).

Sluiter, E., 'Dutch-Spanish Rivalry in the Caribbean Area, 1594-1609', *The Hispanic American Historical Review* 28.2 (1948), 165-96.

Smith, J., *Fatal Treasure* (Hoboken, New Jersey, 2003).

Smith, R.C., Scott-Ireton, D., McKinnon, J., Beckwith, S., Altmeier, B. and MacLaughlin, L., *Archaeological and Biological Examination of "The Mystery Wreck" (8MO143) off Vaca Key, Monroe County, Florida* (Florida Keys National Marine Sanctuary, 2006).

Stemm, G., Gerth, E., Flow, J., Guerra-Librero, C.L. and Kingsley, S., *The Deep-Sea Tortugas Shipwreck, Florida: A Spanish-Operated Navio of the 1622 Tierra Firme Fleet. Part 2, the Artifacts* (OME Papers 27, Tampa, 2013).

Tarver, H.M. and Frederick, J.C., *The History of Venezuela* (Westport, CT, 2005).

Tedesco, C., 'The Lost Treasures of the *Santa Margarita*', *X-ray Magazine* 34 (2010), 20-1.

Tedesco, C., *The Deep-Sea Tortugas Shipwreck, Florida (1622): the Silver Coins* (OME Papers, Tampa, 2013).

Thompson, J.E.S., *Thomas Gage's Travels in the New World* (University of Oklahoma Press, 1958).

Thomson, J.K.J., 'The Spanish Trade in American Cotton: Atlantic Synergies in the Age of Enlightenment', *Revista de Historia Económica* 26 (2008), 277-313.

Van Ittersum, M.J., 'Mare Liberum in the West Indies? Hugo Grotius and the Case of the *Swimming Lion*, a Dutch Pirate in the Caribbean at the Turn of the Seventeenth Century', *Itinerario* 31 (2007), 59-94.

Von Humboldt, A., Bonpland, A. and Ross, T., *Personal Narrative of Travels to the Equinoctial Regions of America, Vol. 1* (New York, 2009).

Warsh, M.A., *Adorning Empire: A History of the Early Modern Pearl Trade, 1492-1688* (Doctor of Philosophy Thesis, Johns Hopkins University, Baltimore, 2009).

Whitehead, N.L., *Lords of the Tiger Spirit. A History of the Caribs in Colonial Venezuela and Guyana 1498-1820* (Leiden, 1988).

5

The Deep-Sea Tortugas Shipwreck, Florida: the Animal Bones

Philip L. Armitage

Curator, Brixham Heritage Museum, UK

The excavation of the Tortugas shipwreck between 1990-91 at a depth of 405m off the Tortugas islands in the Florida Keys incorporated the pioneering use of a sediment removal and filtration sieving system (SeRF), which was built into the rear of the Remotely-Operated Vehicle Merlin. Coupled with excavation by Remotely-Operated Vehicle, this tool enabled a collection of 165 animal bones to be recovered from this Tierra Firme fleet *navio* lost in 1622 and identified as the Portuguese-built and Spanish-operated 117-ton *Buen Jesús y Nuestra Señora del Rosario*.

The bones were re-examined by the author in 2011, which resulted in the identification of a typical assemblage characterized by the consumption onboard ship of pig, sheep, cattle and chickens. The presence of black rat bones is not unexpected in light of the historically attested 'plague' that ran riot on the 1622 fleet. More rare are the discovery of the ship's cat and the unparalleled identification of a small parrot (cf. blue-headed), possibly a type of high-status cargo formerly known only from historical sources.

© Odyssey Marine Exploration, 2013

1. Introduction

A collection of 165 animal bones was recovered from the deep-sea Tortugas shipwreck in 1990-91 and was submitted for analysis in 2011. Analytical techniques followed standard zooarchaeological procedures. Wherever possible, identifications of taxa and anatomy were made using the author's modern comparative osteological collections and with reference to established works (Boessneck *et al.*, 1964; Gilbert *et al.*, 1981; Kozuch and Fitzgerald, 1989; Schmid, 1972). For specimens of species outside the range of the author's collections, identifications were made with the kind assistance of colleagues working at the Natural History Museum (Tring) and Royal Albert Memorial Museum, Exeter.

Measurements (in mm) were taken on selected specimens using Draper dial calipers (graduated 0.02mm), following the system of von den Driesch (1976) for the mammal and bird bones and Kozuch and Fitzgerald (1989) for the shark vertebrae. Determination of sex in the sheep innominate (TOR-90-00175-BN) was based on the criteria of Armitage (1977: 78-81) and the criteria of West (1982) for the domestic fowl tarsometatarsus (TOR-90-00216-BN). Wear stages recorded in the pig molar teeth followed the classification system of Grant (1982). A summary of the results of the analysis carried out on the recovered faunal assemblage is presented in Tables 1-2.

2. Preservation

Although a few of the Tortugas shipwreck's bones were remarkably well preserved, the majority were assessed as poorly/moderately well preserved with many exhibiting evidence of post-depositional attritional damage from seabed sedimentary disturbance and, in some cases, also corrosion effects from prolonged exposure in sea water.

Whereas the overall condition of the bones and pattern of butchery recorded in the cattle vertebra, pig mandible and bird radius was consistent with that of other 17th-century archaeological food waste examined by the author, the two sawn pieces of pig vertebrae raised some concerns owing to their exceptionally good state of preservation, unstained appearance and evidence of fine-toothed sawing, all of which suggested the distinct possibility that these specimens were intrusive.

The use of saws in butchery practice dates from the latter half of the 18th century at the earliest; before this period, disjointing/cutting up the carcass in preparation for cooking was performed using axes, cleavers and boning knives. It seemed highly improbable, therefore, that the sawn pig vertebrae were contemporary with the other food bones from the shipwreck. This observation is further supported by the fact that these specimens match exactly bones of modern pork chops/'baby back ribs' in the author's comparative osteological collections. In consequence, these specimens have been omitted from the final analysis and interpretation below.

Three other specimens displayed evidence of butchery marks contemporary with the final voyage. The thoracic vertebra of a cattle bone (TOR-90-00182-BN; Fig. 21) had been chopped, as had the mandible of a pig (TOR-90-00192-BN; Fig. 9). The radius of a bird, possibly a turkey (TOR-90-00301-BN; Fig. 15), exhibited knife cuts.

Class	Taxon	Common Name	NISP
Mammalia	*Bos* (domestic)	Cattle	3
	cf. *Bos* (domestic)	cf. cattle	2
	Ovis (domestic)	Sheep	1
	Ovis/Capra (domestic)	Sheep/Goat	3
	Sus (domestic)	Pig	22
	Sus (?) (domestic)	Pig (?)	4
	Felis (domestic)	Domestic cat	2 (MNI = 1)
	Rattus rattus	Black Rat	21 (MNI = 5)
	Family *Delphinidae*	Dolphin	1
	Indeterminate		18
Aves	*Gallus gallus* (domestic)	Chicken	4
	cf. *Pionus menstruus*	cf. blue-headed parrot	2 (MNI = 1)
	Meleagris gallopavo (?)	Turkey (?)	1
	Unidentified		3
Elasmobranchiomorphi	Family *Carcharhinidae*	Requium sharks	6
Osteichthyes	Family *Serranidae*	Grouper spp.	3
	Unidentified	Reef fishes	37
Reptilia	Family *Chelonidae*	Marine turtle	1
	Unidentified	Turtle/tortoise (?)	5
Indeterminate	Bone fragments		26

Table 1. Numbers of animal bones present (NISP) on the Tortugas shipwreck.

3. Interpretation & Discussion

Numerically (even after excluding the two sawn vertebrae), pig bones from the wreck predominated over those of cattle and sheep/goats (Table 1; Figs. 1-12), reflecting the significant contribution this animal made to the diet of Spanish mariners serving on board Indies ships, an observation in keeping with the official ration system for such vessels in the 17th century (Phillips, 1986: 241). Some of the bones on the Tortugas wreck could have derived from live pigs carried on board ship to provide fresh meat for the captain's table during the trans-Atlantic crossing, a common practice testified in historical accounts (cf. Newton, 1928: 374).

However, other historical sources suggest an alternative interpretation should also be considered for the pig extremity foot bones. Among the supplies of foodstuffs carried on board the *Nina* for the voyage to the New World in 1498 were "three pannier baskets of pigs' feet" (Lyon, 1989: 64). Pigs' feet are also mentioned in the official ration lists for sailors serving on Spanish Indies

ships in the 17th century (Phillips, 1986: 168). Based on such records, it is suggested that the seven metapodial bones from the Tortugas wreck may not necessarily have derived from live animals, but could instead represent the remains of preserved (dried/salted) pigs' trotters.

Similarly, it was not possible to establish with any confidence whether the chopped pig jawbone (TOR-90-00192-BN; Fig. 9) from the wreck originated from a live animal that had been slaughtered/butchered on board as a source of fresh meat or was from preserved salt pork that formed part of the ship's store of provisions. In the Tortugas specimen the bone had been chopped/cleaved transversely through the ascending ramus just below the condylar process, a butchery technique similarly noted on four pig jawbones from the wreck of the Spanish Armada wreck *La Trinidad Valencera* of 1588, which were believed to be cured (dry-salted) cheek pieces (including the tongue) – a convenient, easily packed/transported meat ration (Armitage, 1995a: 35-6).

Inv. No.	Class/Taxon/ Common Name	Bone Element/ NISP/Side	Preservation; Corroded/Eroded; Abraded/Attrition; Staining	Notes
CATTLE				
TOR-90- 00165-BN	Mammalia, *Bos* (domestic), cattle	Patella 1	Moderate/good; corroded, pitted, abraded; grayish iron staining	
TOR-90- 00176-BN	Mammalia, *Bos* (domestic), cattle	Radius 1	Good; graying brown staining	Piece of shaft, spiral fractured/broken
TOR-90- 00182-BN	Mammalia, *Bos* (domestic), cattle	Thoracic vertebra; 1	Good; brownish staining	Chopped piece of centrum/ fused epiphysial plate
TOR-90- 00194-BN	Mammalia, cf. cattle	Vertebra 1	Moderate/good; abraded; dark graying staining	Broken piece of unfused/ detached epiphyseal plate
TOR-90- 00195-BN	Mammalia, cf. cattle	Vertebra 1	Moderate; pitted; some abrasion; creamy with iron staining	Broken piece of unfused/ detached epiphyseal plate
SHEEP/GOAT				
TOR-90- 00175-BN	Mammalia, *Ovis* (domestic), sheep	Innominate; 1 Right	Good; some erosion & abrasion; graying brown staining	Female; depth rim of acetabulum 1.54mm, LA 28.1mm, LAR 26.7mm
TOR-90- 00179-BN	Mammalia, *Ovis*/*Capra* (domestic), sheep/goat	Rib 1	Poor; corroded; very abraded; brownish gray staining	2 broken pieces of shaft
TOR-90- 00180-BN	Mammalia, *Ovis*/*Capra* (domestic), sheep/goat	Rib 1	Moderate/good; browning staining	Articular end & shaft
TOR-90- 00309-BN	Mammalia, *Ovis*/*Capra* (domestic), sheep/goat	Rib 1	Moderate/slightly abraded; grayish staining	Shaft
PIG				
TOR-90- 00166-BN	Mammalia, *Sus* (domestic), pig	Femur 1	Moderate/good; corroded & abraded; grayish iron staining	Shaft only survives; from young animal
TOR-90- 00167-BN	Mammalia, *Sus* (domestic), pig	Radius 1	Moderate/good; corroded & abraded; grayish staining	Shaft - prox. & distal epiphyses unfused/ detached; from young animal under 1 year
TOR-90- 00169-BN	Mammalia, *Sus* (domestic), pig	Femur; 1 Right	Good; grayish with iron streaks	Shaft with prox. & distal epiphyses unfused/detached; subadult
TOR-90- 00177-BN	Mammalia, *Sus* (domestic), pig	Humerus; 1 Right	Very poor; heavily corroded & abraded; creamy white	Shaft
TOR-90- 00178-BN	Mammalia, *Sus* (domestic), pig	Metapodial 1	Very poor; heavily corroded & abraded; creamy white	Distal end only; distal epiphysis unfused/detached
TOR-90- 00181-BN	Mammalia, *Sus* (domestic), pig	Metapodial 1	Good; very pale graying staining	Distal epiphysis unfused/detached
TOR-90- 00183-BN	Mammalia, *Sus* (domestic), pig	Metacarpus IV 1	Good; slightly; very slightly; grayish staining	Complete except for unfused/ detached distal epiphysis

Table 2A. Catalogue of diagnostic faunal remains from the Tortugas shipwreck.

Inv. No.	Class/Taxon/ Common Name	Bone Element/ NISP/Side	Preservation; Corroded/Eroded; Abraded/Attrition; Staining	Notes
(PIG)				
TOR-90-00184-BN	Mammalia, *Sus* (domestic), pig	Fibula 1	Poor; very corroded; very eroded; light grayish staining	Piece of shaft only
TOR-90-00185-BN	Mammalia, *Sus* (domestic), pig	Tibia; 1 Right	Good; graying/ tinged iron staining	Unfused/detached distal epiphysis; young animal
TOR-90-00190-BN	Mammalia, cf. pig	Vertebra 1	Very good; creamy white	Unfused/detached epiphyseal plate
TOR-90-00191-BN	Mammalia, cf. pig	Vertebra 1	Very good; creamy White/slight iron staining	Part of an unfused/ detached epiphyseal plate
TOR-90-00192-BN	Mammalia, *Sus* (domestic), pig	Mandible; 1 Left	Good; very slightly abraded; brownish gray staining	Condylar process/piece of ascending ramus; butchered/chopped
TOR-90-00290-BN	Mammalia, *Sus* (domestic), pig	Metapodial 1	Moderate; slightly abraded; grayish staining	Distal epiphysis unfused/detached
TOR-90-00292-BN	Mammalia, *Sus* (domestic), pig	Metapodial 1	Moderate; slightly abraded; grayish staining	Distal epiphysis unfused/detached
TOR-90-00294-BN	Mammalia, *Sus* (domestic), pig	Metapodial 1	Moderate; abraded; grayish staining	Distal end broken off
TOR-90-00295-BN	Mammalia, *Sus* (domestic), pig	Metapodial 1	Good; grayish staining	Distal epiphysis only/ unfused & detached
TOR-90-00302-BN	Mammalia, *Sus* (domestic), pig	Incisor 1	Very good; not stained	
TOR-90-00303-BN	Mammalia, *Sus* (domestic), pig	Premolar tooth 1	Very good; not stained	Lower P2
TOR-90-00304-BN	Mammalia, *Sus* (domestic), pig	dp4 1	Very good; not stained	Deciduous fourth premolar tooth; wear stage d
TOR-90-00305-BN	Mammalia, *Sus* (domestic), pig	Molar tooth 1	Good; some patches brown staining	Some damage (post depositional) to roots, otherwise complete; cf. second lower molar, left; wear stage b
TOR-90-00306-BN	Mammalia, *Sus* (domestic), pig	Molar tooth 1	Good/fragment; not stained	Crown only survives, in pieces
TOR-90-00307-BN	Mammalia, *Sus* (domestic), pig	Molar tooth 1	Good/fragment; not stained	Crown only survives, in pieces
TOR-90-00308-BN	Mammalia, *Sus* (domestic), pig	Molar tooth 1	Good; not stained	Some damage (post depositional) to roots, otherwise complete; bag includes small frag. from another molar tooth (not acc. separately)
CAT				
TOR-90-00193-BN	Mammalia, *Felis catus*, domestic cat	Mandible 2 Right & left	Very good; white	Right & left paired jawbones from adult cat. Measurements (mm): [1] 53.5; [5] 18.4; [7] 6.7; [8] 24.9; diastema 5.9
BLACK RAT				
TOR-90-00196-BN	Mammalia, *Rattus rattus*, black rat	Tibia 1 Right	Good; gray brown staining	Tibia & fibula intact except for unfused/detached prox. Epiphysis (dist. epiphysis is fused)

Table 2B. Catalogue of diagnostic faunal remains from the Tortugas shipwreck.

(BLACK RAT)				
TOR-90-00197-BN	Mammalia, *Rattus rattus*, black rat	Tibia 1 Right	Good; gray brown staining	Lacks fibula, otherwise intact apart from unfused/detached prox. epiphysis
TOR-90-00198-BN	Mammalia, *Rattus rattus*, black rat	Tibia 1 Left	Moderate; gray brown staining	Lacks fibula plus part of proximal end/broken off
TOR-90-00199-BN	Mammalia, *Rattus rattus*, black rat	Tibia 1 Right	Moderate; slightly abraded; gray brown staining	Lacks fibula plus part of proximal end/broken off
TOR-90-00200-BN	Mammalia, *Rattus rattus*, black rat	Tibia 1 Left	Good; slightly abraded; gray brown staining	Lacks fibula plus part of proximal end/broken off
TOR-90-00201-BN	Mammalia, *Rattus rattus*, black rat	Innominate 1 Right	Moderate; slightly abraded; gray brown staining	Acetabulum is fused (adult); owing to broken/incomplete ischium unable to ascertain sex
TOR-90-00202-BN	Mammalia, *Rattus rattus*, black rat	Femur 1 Right	Moderate; gray brown staining	Shaft intact except for damaged distal end; prox. epiphysis unfused/detached, probably same with distal Epiphysis
TOR-90-00203-BN	Mammalia, *Rattus rattus*, black rat	Humerus 1	Poor/moderate; slightly abraded; gray brown staining	Shaft, distal end broken off; prox. epiphysis unfused/detached
TOR-90-00204-BN	Mammalia, *Rattus rattus*, black rat	Humerus 1 Left (?)	Poor; abraded; gray brown staining	Shaft fragment
TOR-90-00205-BN	Mammalia, *Rattus rattus*, black rat	Metapodial 2	Good; gray brown staining	Two complete metapodials (foot bones)
TOR-90-00206-BN	Mammalia, *Rattus rattus*, black rat	Incisor 1	Good	Upper incisor
TOR-90-00207-BN	Mammalia, *Rattus rattus*, black rat	Incisor 1	Good	Upper incisor
TOR-90-00208-BN	Mammalia, *Rattus rattus*, black rat	Incisor 1	Good	Upper incisor
TOR-90-00209-BN	Mammalia, *Rattus rattus*, black rat	Incisor 2	Good	1 upper & 1 lower incisor
TOR-90-00210-BN	Mammalia, *Rattus rattus*, black rat	Incisor 1	Good	1 lower incisor
TOR-90-00211-BN	Mammalia, *Rattus rattus*, black rat	Incisor 1	Good	1 lower incisor
TOR-90-00287-BN	Mammalia, *Rattus rattus*, black rat	Metapodial 1	Fragment; abraded; grayish staining	Dist. part of bone
TOR-90-00289-BN	Mammalia, *Rattus rattus*, black rat	Metapodial 2	Good; gray brown staining	Complete; distal epiphysis fused
DOMESTIC FOWL				
TOR-90-00212-BN	Aves, *Gallus gallus*, domestic fowl	Coracoid; 1 Left	Good; gray brown staining	Small scrawny chicken. Measurements (mm): GL 51.0 est.; Lm 48.5; BF - ; Bb -
TOR-90-00214-BN	Aves, *Gallus gallus*, domestic fowl	Humerus 1	Moderate; gray staining	Shaft; prox. & distal ends damaged (post deposition); SC 6.2; rat gnawing (incisor grooves) marks mid shaft

Table 2C. Catalogue of diagnostic faunal remains from the Tortugas shipwreck.

(DOMESTIC FOWL)				
TOR-90-00216-BN	Aves, *Gallus gallus*, domestic fowl	Tarsometatarsus 1	Moderate/good; very slightly abraded; gray staining	Prox. end missing; unspurred = female; Measurements (mm): SC 5.4
TOR-90-00224-BN	Aves, *Gallus gallus*, domestic fowl	Carpometacarpus 1 Left	Moderate; some abrasion; gray brown staining	Broken/incomplete specimen; small scrawny chicken
PARROT				
TOR-90-00170-BN	Aves, cf. *Pionus menstruus*, blue-headed parrot	Tarsometatarsus 1 Left	Moderate; some damage, whitish	Measurements (mm): GL 17.3; Bp 7.0; Bd 8.8; SC 4.0
TOR-90-00217-BN	Aves, cf. *Pionus menstruus*, blue-headed parrot	Femur 1 Left	Good; very slightly abraded; gray staining	Measurements (mm): GL 38.35; Bp 6.9; Bd 6.4; SC 2.9
MISCELLANEOUS				
TOR-90-00168-BN	Mammalia, unidentified	Fragments 2 --	Poor/moderate; corroded & abraded; grayish staining	
TOR-90-00186-BN	Mammalia, not pig (?)	1	Moderate; abraded/ waterworn; grayish staining	
TOR-90-00213-BN	Aves, indeterminate	Tibiotarsus 1	Moderate; slightly abraded; gray brown staining	Shaft fragment
TOR-90-00215-BN	Aves, indeterminate	Tibiotarsus 1	Moderate; very slightly abraded; gray staining	Shaft only
TOR-90-00296-BN	Aves, indeterminate	Humerus 1	Moderate/good; grayish brown staining	Shaft only; both ends broken
TOR-90-00301-BN	Aves, indeterminate	Radius 1	Moderate; orange staining	Proximal part of radius of an immature bird, cf. size of a turkey; knife cut marks present
TURTLE				
TOR-90-00174-BN	Reptilia, Family *Chelonidae*, turtle	Coracoid 1	Poor; very corroded; very abraded; waterworn; whitish with iron staining	Large marine turtle (cf. size of green turtle)
cf. GROUPER				
TOR-90-00235.1-BN	Osteichthyes, Family *Serranidae*, grouper	1 Left	Very good; pale graying staining	
TOR-90-00235.2-BN	Osteichthyes, Family *Serranidae*, grouper	1	Very good; pale graying staining	
TOR-90-00237-BN	Osteichthyes, Family *Serranidae*, grouper	1 Right	Moderate; slightly abraded; graying staining	

Table 2D. Catalogue of diagnostic faunal remains from the Tortugas shipwreck.

SHARK				
TOR-90-00225-BN	Elasmobranchio-morphi, Family *Carcharhinidae*, Requiem shark	Vertebra 1	Poor; corroded; heavily abraded; chalky white	Post-depositional damage; measurements (mm): MLB 22.5; CCL 12.4; DVH - ; intraformaninal width 4.5; interforaminal width 6.3
TOR-90-00226-BN	Elasmobranchio-morphi, Family *Carcharhinidae*, Requiem shark	Vertebra 1	Poor; corroded; heavily abraded; chalky white	Post-depositional damage; measurements (mm): MLB [23.8]; CCL [14.1]; DVH [22.5]; intraformaninal width 3.4; interforaminal width 4.3
TOR-90-00227-BN	Elasmobranchio-morphi, Family *Carcharhinidae*, Requiem shark	Vertebra 1	Poor; corroded; heavily abraded; chalky white	Post-depositional damage; measurements (mm): too heavily abraded/worn
TOR-90-00228-BN	Elasmobranchio-morphi, Family *Carcharhinidae*, Requiem shark	Vertebra 1	Poor; corroded; heavily abraded; chalky white	Post-depositional damage; measurements (mm): MLB 17.3; CCL 6.6 ; DVH 17.2; intraformaninal width 3.1; interforaminal width 2.9
TOR-90-00229-BN	Elasmobranchio-morphi, Family *Carcharhinidae*, Requiem shark	Vertebra 1	Poor; corroded; heavily abraded; chalky white	Post-depositional damage; measurements (mm): MLB - ; CCL 4.5 ; DVH 13.7; intraformaninal width 2.1; interforaminal width 3.8
TOR-90-00230-BN	Elasmobranchio-morphi, Family *Carcharhinidae*, Requiem shark	Vertebra 1	Poor; corroded; heavily abraded; chalky white	Post-depositional damage; measurements (mm): MLB 14.8; CCL 7.9 ; DVH - ; intraformaninal width 3.6; interforaminal width 4.9

Table 2E. Catalogue of diagnostic faunal remains from the Tortugas shipwreck.

Four domestic fowl *Gallus gallus* bone elements were identified (one coracoid, one carpometacarpus, one humerus, one tarsometatarsus), which were not unexpected because it is well documented that live chickens were commonplace on Spanish ships sailing to and from the Americas in this period (Figs. 13-14). For instance, in the official records of the fleet sailing to New Spain in 1631, 210 hens were noted as having been consumed by sick sailors during the voyage (Hamilton, 1929: 441). An indication of the numbers of chickens carried onboard Spanish vessels is further revealed in records relating to the ill-fated galleon *Nuestra Señora de Los Tres Reyes*. When loading supplies at Portobello in preparation for the homeward voyage in 1634, 87 "live chickens in a cage" taken on board were intended for feeding sick sailors during the trans-Atlantic crossing (Phillips, 1990).

Measurements taken on selected *Gallus gallus* bones revealed that those on board the Tortugas vessel were scrawny, bantam-sized birds compared to modern boiling and laying chickens (Tables 4-5). The Tortugas chickens in this respect matched those from 16th-century Spanish St. Augustine, Florida, whose very small size was "comparable to a Mediterranean class of Brown Leghorn Bantam" (Reitz and Scarry, 1985: 71).

In addition to hens, live sheep were frequently carried on Spanish ships to provide special food for sick sailors, as well as to supplement the diet of the ships' higher-ranking officers/passengers (Phillips, 1986: 178). This practice probably accounts for the presence of the female sheep pelvis bone (TOR-90-00175-BN; Fig. 16) among the faunal assemblage recovered from the wreck.

Apart from a single specimen, little could be inferred from so few specimens of cattle bones other than that they are probably representative of the salt beef and/or fresh beef consumed on board (Figs. 16-21). Specimen TOR-90-00182-BN, a thoracic vertebra (Fig. 21), however, was particularly noteworthy because it exhibited evidence of multiple chopping, a tertiary butchery pattern observed previously by the author in five cattle vertebrae recovered from the wreck of the 1588 Spanish Armada vessel *La Trinidad Valencera* (Armitage, 1995a).

Skeletal Remains	Cattle	Cf. Cattle	Sheep	Sheep/Goat	Pig	Cf. Pig
Mandible					1	
Incisor					1	
Upper/Lower Cheek Teeth					6	
Indet. Vertebral Fragment		2				4
Thoracic Vertebra	1					
Lumbar Vertebra					1	
Rib				3		
Humerus					1	
Radius	1				1	
Metacarpus IV					1	
Innominate			1			
Femur					2	
Tibia					1	
Fibula					1	
Patella	1					
Metapodial					6	
TOTALS	**3**	**2**	**1**	**3**	**22**	**4**

Table 3. Skeletal elements of the main domesticates from the Tortugas shipwreck.

Site	Date		N	Mean	Min.	Max.	Reference
St. Augustine, Florida	16th century	GL	3	52.0	51.0	53.0	Reitz &
		Lm	5	48.0	46.0	50.0	Scarry, 1985
Tortugas shipwreck, Florida, inv. TOR-90-00212-BN	1622	GL*	1			51.0 est.	Armitage, 2012
		Lm	1			48.5	
Earl of Abergavenny shipwreck, Dorset	1805	GL	2		54.5	62.4	Armitage, 2002
		Lm	2		51.7	59.2	
Laying hen, Booth Museum collections (102093)	Modern	GL	1			60.6	Armitage
		Lm	1			57.6	
Black Minorca bantam, English Heritage collections (AML 2787)	Modern	GL	1			52.9	Armitage
		Lm	No data				

* The Tortugas shipwreck specimen's GL value is estimated and
allows for the slight reduction by post-depositional damage.

Table 4. Size of the chicken coracoid from the Tortugas shipwreck
in comparison with archaeological and modern specimens.
Measurements (in mm): GL greatest (diagonal) length; Lm medial length.

Such chopped pieces of vertebrae reveal the extent to which cattle carcasses were cut up in preparation for cooking meals onboard ship and perhaps were the basis of the "dishes of broth" referenced by Italian Priest Gemelli during his Pacific voyage from the Philippines to Mexico in the late 17th century (Macintyre, 1979: 115). Significantly, both the Tortugas wreck and *La Trinidad Valencera* bones derived from very small cattle. Similar small-sized cattle were represented by vertebrae examined from the 16th-century Emanuel Point shipwreck, Pensacola, Florida (Baker, 1995). Comparison may be made with the exceptionally large/robust cattle raised by the Spanish on Hispaniola during the same period – as evidenced by the zooarchaeological evidence from Puerto Real (Reitz and Ruff, 1994: 706) – and said to be much superior in size and appearance to those from Spain (Reitz, 1992: 87).

Site	Date	SC	N	Mean	Min.	Max.	Reference
St. Augustine, Florida	16th century	SC	4	5.1	4.6	6.0	Reitz & Scarry, 1985
Tortugas shipwreck, Florida, inv. TOR-90-00216-BN	1622	SC	1			5.4	Armitage, 2012
Stonewall Spanish shipwreck, Bermuda	Mid-17th century	SC	4	6.3	5.2	7.1	Armitage, 1997
Readers Point British wreck, Jamaica	18th century	SC	1			6.1	Armitage, 1995c
Earl of Abergavenny shipwreck, Dorset	1805	SC	1			6.6	Armitage, 2002
Laying hen, Booth Museum collections (102093)	Modern	SC	1			8.0	Armitage
Boiling hen (author's collections)	Modern	SC	1			7.6	Armitage

Table 5. Size of the chicken tarsometatarsus from the Tortugas shipwreck in comparison with archaeological and modern specimens. Measurement (in mm): SC minumum shaft width. All specimens female (unspurred).

Distinctive rodent tooth gnawing marks were identified on the mid shaft of a chicken humerus from the wreck (TOR-90-00214-BN; Fig. 13) and indicated that this bone had been scavenged by a hungry shipboard rat. Even more tangible evidence for the presence of these rodents on this vessel was provided by 21 bone elements indentified as the remains of at least five black rats, *Rattus rattus* (Figs. 22-27):

• Incisor: 7
• Humerus: 2
• Innominate: 1
• Femur: 1
• Tibia: 5
• Metapodial: 5

The Tortugas rat evidence sheds further light on the known problem of rat infestation on the 1622 fleet. Contemporary accounts reveal that the crews not only suffered hurricanes, but were also threatened by a plague of rats. On one ship, over one thousand were killed while the vessel was in Havana, with several thousand more subsequently discovered when the vessel was at sea (Phillips, 1986: 157). These rats reportedly caused widespread destruction, gnawing through stored food supplies and contaminating the fresh water in barrels, as well as invading the chicken coops to attack and eat the fowl (Stemm *et al.*, 2013: 55).

Despite the often reputed strong swimming abilities of rats, experiments carried out by Spennermann and Rapp (1987) revealed that even in the relatively calm and warm lagoonal waters of the South Pacific black rats experienced difficulties remaining afloat for more than 20 minutes. On the basis of such evidence it is to be presumed that rats trying to swim away from the doomed vessels of the 1622 fleet would very quickly have become exhausted and drowned in the turbulent storm-tossed sea. Others trapped below decks also drowned; their bones found in the wreck serve as testimony to their fate.

Given the commonplace occurrence of rats on European vessels of the period (cf. Macintyre, 1979: 110; Phillips, 1986: 157; Armitage 1989; Armitage, 1995b), it is not surprising that cats were frequently taken on board in order to attempt to control the numbers of such unwelcome vermin. Contemporary eyewitness references were made to ships' cats (see, for example, Pedro Fernandez de Quiros: Markham, 1967: 393). Faunal remains from shipwrecks also bear witness to this practice, including from the Tortugas wreck, which yielded right and left lower jawbones (TOR-90-00193-BN; Figs. 28-29) from an adult cat. Metrical comparison with archaeological and modern data revealed that the Tortugas cat would have been of below average size for the 17th century and a very small individual when judged against the majority of present day domestic cats (Table 6).

Cat bones are also associated with a small number of Spanish and English shipwrecks of differing status. An ulna was recovered from the Spanish armada *Trinidad Valencera*, lost off the coast of Donegal, Ireland, in 1588 (Armitage, 1995a). The English merchant vessel *Sea Venture*, which foundered off Bermuda in 1609, contained a cat's fibula (Armitage, 1987; 1989), while a cat's mandible was present on HMS *Sapphire*, wrecked in Bay Bulls, Newfoundland, in 1696 (Cumbaa, 1979).

Although the majority of the bones of reef fishes in the Tortugas shipwreck faunal assemblage was probably intrusive material, deriving from fish that had lived and died in the vicinity of the wreck, and are thus omitted from this study, the three bones of grouper (dentary, maxilla and premaxilla) (TOR-90-00235.1-BN, TOR-90-00235.2-BN and TOR-90-00237-BN) may perhaps represent waste from food consumed on board. According to Randall (1968: 57), "groupers are [today considered] the most valuable food fishes of the tropical seas" and European mariners in the 17th century were also clearly acquainted with the food value of such fish, as illustrated by William Dampier's declaration that the "grooper [sic] is good sweet meat" (Dampier, 1697; Gray, 1968: 70).

Archaeological evidence for the consumption of grouper on board a mid 17th-century Spanish ship lost off Bermuda was provided by a butchered (chopped) dentary of this species recovered from the Stonewall wreck (Armitage, 1997). Burnt and cut Cravalle Jack *(Caranx hippos)* bone elements from the wreck of the *Nuestra Señora de Atocha* further support the inclusion of fresh caught fish in the Spanish shipboard diet (Chapin, 1990: 40). It must be presumed that the Stonewall and *Atocha* specimens are not isolated instances of Spanish mariners exploiting locally abundant reef fishes as a food source. Historical sources reveal that crews of Spanish Indies treasure ships in this period were encouraged to augment their shipboard rations while at anchor and awaiting departure from New World ports, and for this purpose their ships were routinely equipped with "fish hooks and other fishing paraphernalia" (Hamilton, 1929: 437).

As with the reef fish bones, the Requiem shark vertebrae found on the Tortugas wreck could be intrusive material, but it is notable that while English seamen of the period considered sharks to be "malevolent fish" and "unwholesome as food" (see Unwin, 1961: 113), and would only catch and eat such creatures when faced with starvation (cf. Dampier, 1684: Masefield, 1906: 107), their Spanish counterparts in the New World apparently held no such qualms at eating shark meat. As noted by Reitz and Scarry (1985: 76) and Reitz (1992: 88-9), together with rays and marine bony fishes, sharks were a major vertebrate group exploited by 16th-century Spanish coastal settlements in Florida. However, all the shark vertebrae from the wreck site had every appearance of being intrusive owing to their poor preservation and absence of any evidence of butchery.

The single, positively identified marine turtle bone, a coracoid (TOR-90-00174-BN; Fig. 30) may be considered intrusive to the site in the absence of any butchery marks and the poor preservation (leached/abraded/waterworn condition). The identification of other presumed

Site	Date	N	Min.	Max.	Mean
Tortugas shipwreck, Florida	1622	1		18.4	
Cheapside	*c.* 1600	1		18.2	
Aldgate	First half 17th century	2	18.8	19.9	
London Wall	Mid-17th century	1		17.5	
Fulham Pottery	*c.* 1660-80	3	18.3	19.1	18.8
Modern Cats	Modern	7	18.5	23.6	20.6

Table 6. Size of the cat jawbone from the Tortugas shipwreck in comparison with archaeological examples from London and modern specimens. Measurement (in mm): [5] length of cheektooth row P3 - M1.

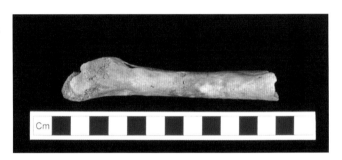

Fig. 1. Femur, Mammalia, Sus *(domestic), pig (TOR-90-00166-BN).*

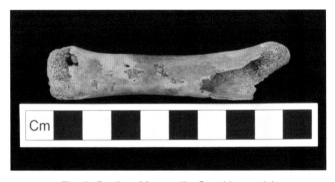

Fig. 2. Radius, Mammalia, Sus *(domestic), pig (TOR-90-00167-BN).*

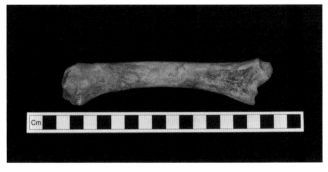

Fig. 3. Femur, Mammalia, Sus *(domestic), pig (TOR-90-00169-BN).*

Specimen	Greatest Length	Proximal Width	Distal Width	Min. Shaft Width
Tortugas shipwreck *	38.55	6.9	6.4	2.9
Comparative Femur				
Pionus menstruus, 1896.6.9.2	37.5	7.1	7.4	2.9
Pionus menstruus, 1925.1.27.1	38.2	7.1	7.1	3.0
Pionus menstruus, 1996.57.1	36.5	7.1	7.4	2.9

* Note that the Tortugas shipwreck specimens' GL, PW, DW are surviving dimensions, which are slightly reduced by damage.

Table 7. Measurements (in mm) taken from the Tortugas shipwreck parrot femur (TOR-90-00217-BN) in comparison with modern specimens of the blue-headed parrot Pionus menstruus *held by the Bird Group, Department of Zoology, Natural History Museum. Data source: Dr. Joanne Cooper, Natural History Museum, Tring, UK.*

reptile bones (turtle/tortoise) among the faunal assemblage proved elusive, despite consultation with several zooarchaeological colleagues. It is suggested, however, that these other specimens probably also represent intrusive remains of marine turtles. A periodic (inner ear bone) of a dolphin (TOR-90-00335-BN) was recovered from the wreck site and is also intrusive. These specimens are not listed in the diagnostic faunal site catalogue.

By far the most remarkable specimens in the Tortugas shipwreck faunal assemblage were two parrot bones: a tarsometatarsus (TOR-90-00170-BN; Fig. 30) and a femur (TOR-90-00217-BN; Fig. 31) believed to derive from a single individual. This unfortunate bird had probably been abandoned below decks and drowned when the vessel sank.

An initial identification of the tarsometatarsus as the remains of a parrot (Family *Psittacidae*) by Armitage was subsequently confirmed by Dr. Joanne Cooper, Curator of Avian Anatomical Collections, Bird Group, Natural History Museum, UK, who also found the morphology of the femur was consistent with parrots. Due to the preservation of the specimens, and the great diversity of smaller parrots in the Caribbean and Central South American region, it was difficult to assign the parrot bones without doubt to a specific taxon. However, the femur was compared to a wide range of small to medium Caribbean, South American and Africa taxa and was found to most closely resemble the genus *Pionus*, a genus of medium-sized, chunky, short-tailed parrots. In terms of size, the bones appear to be most similar to the Blue-headed *Pionus menstruus* (Table 7). According to Dr. Cooper, both bones are highly likely to be from the same bird and their identification as possibly *Pionus* is significant for several reasons (Cooper and Armitage, forthcoming).

Firstly, the seven species of *Pionus* are essentially birds indigenous to Central and northern South America

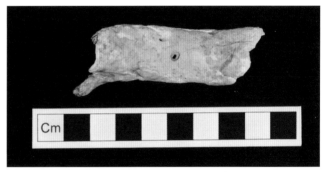

Fig. 4. Humerus, Mammalia, Sus *(domestic), pig (TOR-90-00177-BN).*

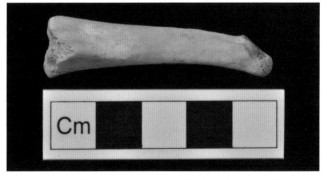

Fig. 5. Metapodial, Mammalia, Sus *(domestic), pig (TOR-90-00181-BN).*

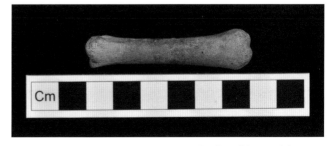

Fig. 6. Metacarpus IV, Mammalia, Sus *(domestic), pig (TOR-90-00183-BN).*

*Fig. 7. Tibia, Mammalia, Sus (domestic),
pig (TOR-90-00185-BN).*

*Fig. 8. Incisor, Mammalia, Sus (domestic),
pig (TOR-90-00302-BN).*

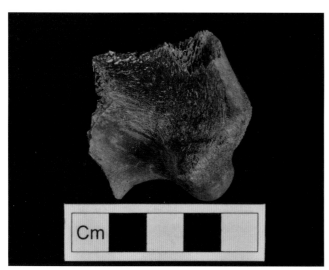

*Fig. 9. Mandible, Mammalia, Sus (domestic),
pig (TOR-90-00192-BN).*

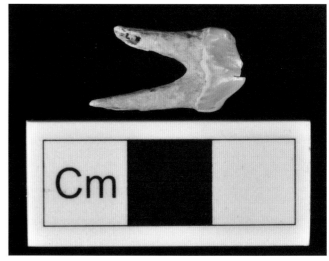

*Fig. 10. Premolar tooth, Mammalia,
Sus (domestic), pig (TOR-90-00303-BN).*

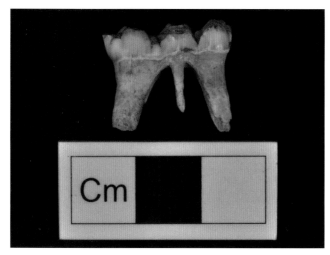

*Fig. 11. Dp4, Mammalia, Sus (domestic),
pig (TOR-90-00304-BN).*

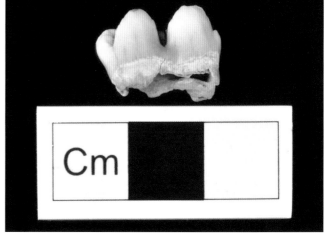

*Fig. 12. Molar tooth, Mammalia, Sus (domestic),
pig (TOR-90-00306-BN).*

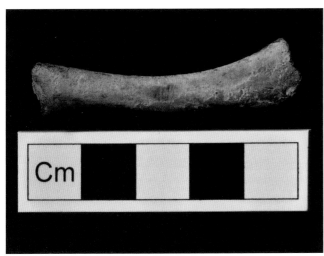

Fig. 13. Humerus, Aves, Gallus gallus, domestic fowl (TOR-90-00214-BN).

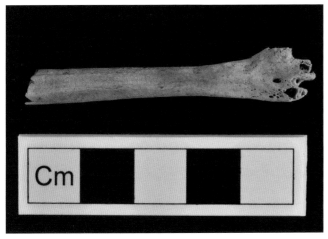

Fig. 14. Tarsometatarsus, Aves, Gallus gallus, domestic fowl (TOR-90-00216-BN).

Fig. 15. Radius, Aves, indeterminate (TOR-90-00301-BN).

(including the Amazon region), and are not birds of the Caribbean Islands, suggesting trade with the mainland rather than the archipelagos. Opportunities for such trade would have been possible when the Spanish Tierra Firme fleet of galleons called at the important ports/way stations of Portobello (Panama) and Cartagena (Columbia) to load gold and silver from the mines of Peru, Ecuador, Venezuela and Columbia before sailing to join the convoy at Havana and the trans-Atlantic crossing to Seville, Spain (Mathewson, 1986: 18-19).

Secondly, evidence of trade in smaller parrot species is scarce, and indeed physical evidence of any parrots almost non-existent. The trade in parrots from the New World became established in the late 15th century, led by Spanish and Portuguese explorers and merchants. As early as 1494, 60 "long-tailed parrots (macaws)" were shipped to Cadiz from Hispaniola (George, 1980: 80). By 1526, New World parrots were so familiar that Gonzalo Fernandez de Oviedo was able to remark in his *General and Natural History of the Indies* that "so many species have been carried to Spain, it is hardly worth while to take time to describe them here" (Boehrer, 2004).

This sentiment was echoed in 1684 when buccaneer John Esquemeling observed that it was well known that parrots in Europe had been transported from the New World (Stallybrass, 1992: 42-3), indicating that mariners had discovered the profitability of bringing back live parrots (as well as other animals, notably monkeys: Armitage, 1983) in order to satisfy the demand for ownership of exotic creatures, especially those destined for royal menageries, such as at Versailles. Some idea of the profit in this trade is indicated by the cost of parrots sold in late 17th-century Amsterdam for "roughly sixty guilders" (Margócsy, 2010: 67).

Exotic and expensive, parrots commonly featured in paintings of the 1500s and 1600s, perhaps as inhabitants of paradise or accompanying images of their owners in portraits as status symbols. A review of the collections of the Museo del Prado, Madrid, reveals that macaws and amazons were most frequently depicted during this time, with smaller parrots rarely shown (Gomez Cano *et al.*, 2010). However, despite their abundance in art and other documentation, physical evidence of parrots in 16th and 17th-century Europe is extremely rare, limited to one other archaeological find amongst 17th-century rubbish excavated in Norwich, England (Albarella *et al.*, 1997: 51-2).

4. Conclusion

Alongside the Tortugas shipwreck, two other shipwreck faunal assemblages associated with the ill-fated 1622 homeward bound Tierra Firme fleet have been studied and

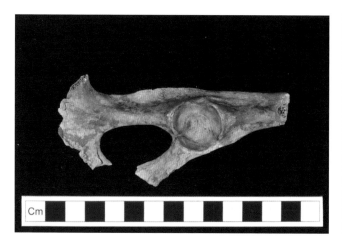

*Fig. 16. Innominate, Mammalia, Ovis (domestic),
sheep (TOR-90-00175-BN).*

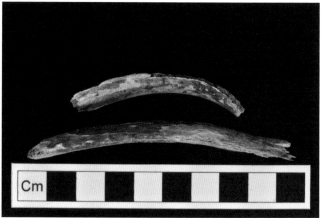

*Fig. 17. Rib, Mammalia, Ovis/Capra (domestic),
sheep/goat (TOR-90-00179-BN).*

*Fig. 18. Rib, Mammalia, Ovis/Capra (domestic),
sheep/goat (TOR-90-00309-BN).*

*Fig. 19. Patella, Mammalia, Bos (domestic),
cattle (TOR-90-00165-BN).*

*Fig. 20. Radius, Mammalia, Bos (domestic),
cattle (TOR-90-00176-BN).*

*Fig. 21. Thoracic vertebra, Mammalia, Bos (domestic),
cattle (TOR-90-00182-BN).*

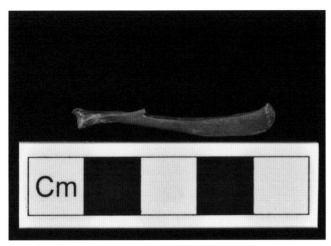

Fig. 22. Tibia, Mammalia, Rattus rattus, *black rat (TOR-90-00197-BN).*

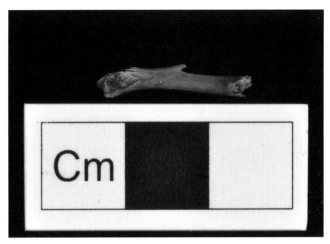

Fig. 23. Tibia, Mammalia, Rattus rattus, *black rat (TOR-90-00199-BN).*

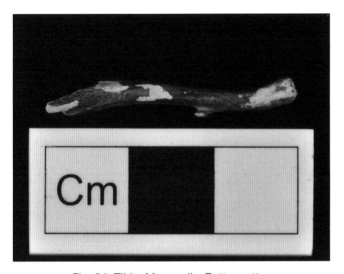

Fig. 24. Tibia, Mammalia, Rattus rattus, *black rat (TOR-90-00200-BN).*

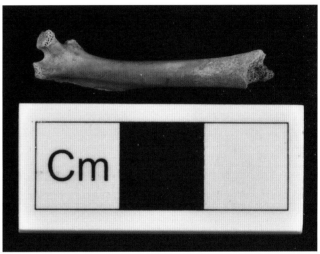

Fig. 25. Femur, Mammalia, Rattus rattus, *black rat (TOR-90-00202-BN).*

Fig. 26. Incisor, Mammalia, Rattus rattus, *black rat (TOR-90-00206-BN).*

Fig. 27. Incisor, Mammalia, Rattus rattus, *black rat (TOR-90-00210-BN).*

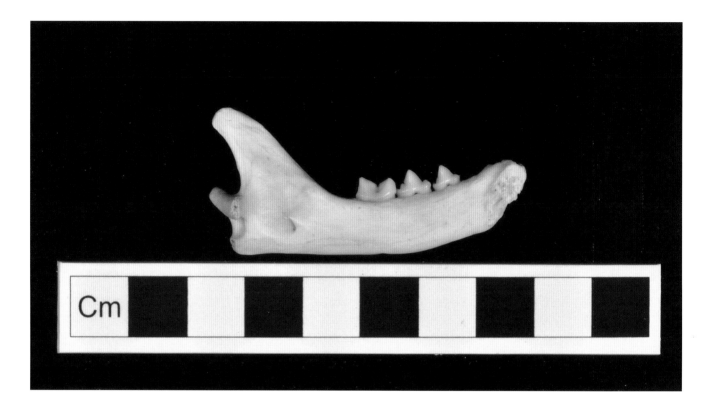

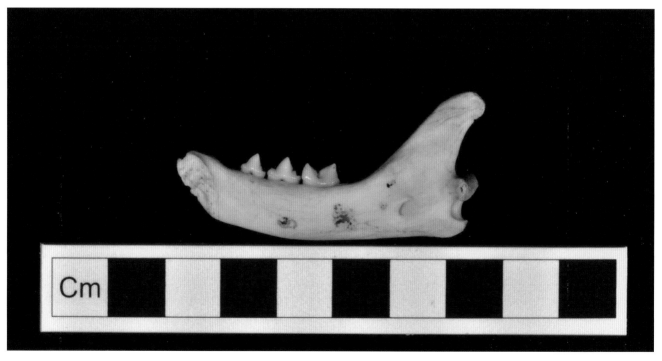

Figs. 28-29. Mandible, Mammalia, Felis catus *domestic cat (TOR-90-00193-BN).*

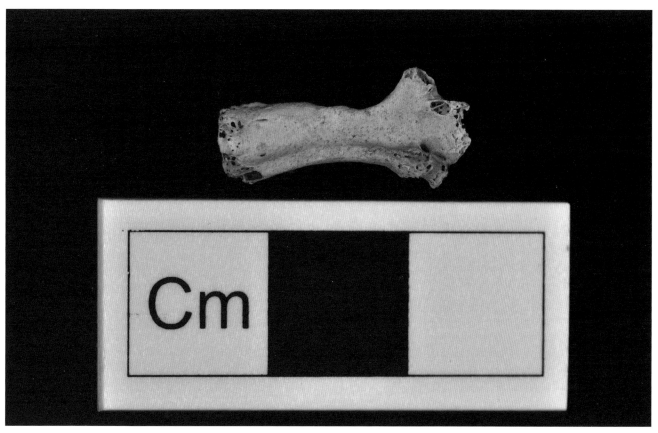

Fig. 30. Tarsometatarsus, Aves, cf. Pionus menstruus, *blue-headed parrot (TOR-90-00170-BN).*

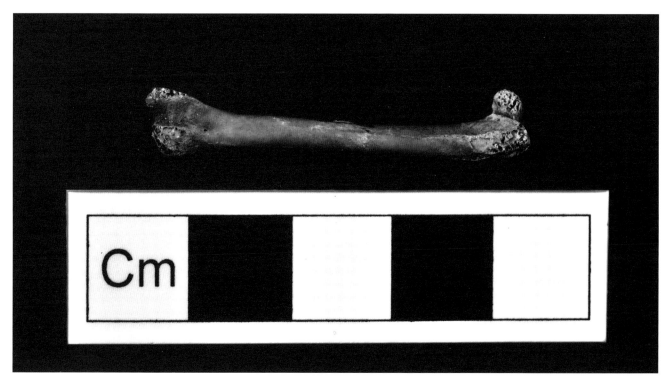

Fig. 31. Femur, Aves, cf. Pionus menstruus, *blue-headed parrot (TOR-90-00217-BN).*

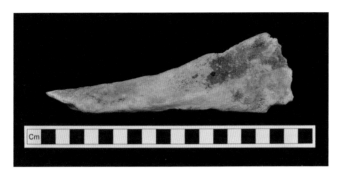

Fig. 32. Coracoid, Reptilia, Family Chelonidae, *turtle (TOR-90-00174-BN).*

documented and derive from the *Atocha* and the *Santa Margarita* (Chapin, 1990). The present analysis of the Tortugas material provides further insights into the preserved and fresh meat provisions of mariners serving on board vessels engaged in transatlantic voyages in the 17th century.

For all three vessels examined there is a concordance that demonstrates a heavy reliance on the customary Old World domesticates (pigs, cattle, sheep/goats and chickens) as principal sources of meat consumption, which was supplemented by lesser contributions from New World exotic animals (notably turtle and marine fish). Unlike the *Atocha* and *Margarita*, however, there is no evidence among the Tortugas wreck faunal remains that the vessel was carrying live horses and donkeys. At 550 tons each, these galleons were significantly larger than the 117-ton *Buen Jesús y Nuestra Señora del Rosario* and, therefore, probably were better suited through capacity to accommodate these animals.

However, the *Buen Jesús* differs from these other companion vessels in carrying at least one live parrot, which was perhaps originally part of a larger caged consignment. This discovery provides an unparalleled archaeological glimpse into the commercial trade of European merchants in exotic New World parrots in the 17th century. The importance of the Tortugas discovery lies in the fact that there are few other archaeological finds indicative of the transportation and trade in exotic New World fauna. Other identified examples include the remains of a South American yellow-footed land tortoise, *Geochelone denticulate*, in the wreck of a Dutch vessel of *c.* 1620-40 off Bermuda (Armitage, 1989) and a jawbone of a South American capuchin monkey, Cebus *nigrivittatus*, dated *c.*1640-80 from the River Thames foreshore (Armitage, 1983).

Acknowledgements

The author wishes to express his gratitude to Dr. Sean Kingsley (Director, Wreck Watch Int.) for his continued encouragement and support throughout the faunal analysis. Special thanks are due to Dr. Joanne Cooper (Curator of Avian Anatomical Collections, Bird Group, Natural History Museum, UK) for all her comprehensive work on the parrot bones and their historical and archaeological significance. Sincere thanks also go to other colleagues for very helpful assistance in this project: Dr. Alison Locker (Andorra) for identifying the grouper bones and Mr. Dave Bolton (Curator of Zoology) for arranging access to the zoological collections at the Royal Albert Memorial Museum, Exeter, UK. The photos in this article were taken by Alan Bosel, Odyssey Marine Exploration.

Bibliography

Albarella, U., Beech, M. and Mulville, J., *The Saxon, Medieval and Post-Medieval Mammal and Bird Bones Excavated 1989-91 from Castle Mall, Norwich, Norfolk* (English Heritage AML Report 72/97, 1997).

Armitage, P.L., *The Mammalian Remains from the Tudor Site of Baynard's Castle, London: A Biometrical and Historical Analysis* (Ph.D. Thesis, Royal Holloway College & the British Museum (Natural History, 1977).

Armitage, P.L., 'Jawbone of a South American Monkey from Brooks Wharf, City of London', *The London Archaeologist* 4.10 (1983), 262-70.

Armitage, P.L., 'Victuals and Vermin: Life on Board the "Sea Venture" in 1609', *Bulletin of the Institute of Maritime History and Archaeology (Bermuda)*, 10 (1987), 8-10.

Armitage, P.L., 'Ship Rats, Salted Meat and Tortoises: Selected Aspects of Maritime Life in the "Great Age of Sail" (1500-1800s)', *Bermuda Journal of Archaeology and Maritime History* 1 (1989), 143-59.

Armitage, P.L., *Report on the Mammalian Bones Excavated from the Spanish Armada Shipwreck 'La Trinidad Valencera'* (1588) (Unpublished Report to Dr. Colin Martin, Scottish Institute of Maritime Studies, University of St. Andrews, 1995a).

Armitage, P.L., 'Black Rats and House Mice'. In R.C. Smith, J. Spirek, J. Bratten & D. Scott-Ireton, *The Emanuel Point Ship: Archaeological Investigations, 1992-1995, Preliminary Report* (Bureau of Archaeological Research, Division of Historical Resources, Florida Department of State, 1995b), 78-81.

Armitage, P.L., *Report on the Mammalian, Bird, Reptile and Fish Bones Excavated from the Shipwreck of a Late Eighteenth-Century British Merchant Vessel, St. Ann's Bay, North Shore of Jamaica* (Unpublished Report to Greg Cook, Director, Reader's Point Shipwreck Project, Greenville, North Carolina, USA, 1995c).

Armitage, P.L. *Mammalian, Bird and Fish Bones from the Stonewall Wreck, Bermuda* (Unpublished Report to Richard Kelly Bumpass, Program in Maritime & Nautical Archaeology, East Carolina University, 1997).

Armitage, P.L., 'Study of the Animal Bones – Section 1'. In E. Cumming (ed.), *The Earl of Abergavenny Historical Record and Wreck Excavation* (CD ROM, MIBEC Enterprises, 2002).

Baker, B.W., *Emanuel Point Shipwreck Faunal Analysis* (Unpublished Report, Texas A&M University, 1995).

Boehrer, B.T., *Parrot Culture: Our 2,500 Year Long Fascination with the World's Most Talkative Bird* (University of Pennsylvania Press, 2004).

Boessneck, J., Müller, H.-H. and Teichert, M., 'Osteologische Unterscheidungmerkmale Zwischen Schaf (*Ovis aries* Linné) und Ziege (*Capra hircus* Linné)', *Kühn-Archiv* Bd. 78 (1964), H.1-2.

Chapin, R.L., *A Faunal Analysis of the 17th Century Galleon Nuestra Senora De Atocha* (MA Thesis, The University of Arizona, 1990).

Cooper, J.H. and Armitage, P.L., 'A Parrot of the Caribbean? A Remarkable Find from a 17th Century Spanish Shipwreck', *Bulletin of the British Ornithologists' Club* (forthcoming).

Cumbaa, S.L., *An Analysis of Animal Bones from the 1696 Wreck of HMS Sapphire, Bay Bulls, Newfoundland* (Unpublished Report, Parks Canada, Ref. 32, 1979).

George, W., 'Sources and Background to Discoveries of New Animals in the Sixteenth and Seventeenth Centuries', *History of Science* 18.2, No. 40 (1980), 79-104.

Gilbert, B.M., Martin, L.D. and Savage, H.G., *Avian Osteology* (Laramie, Wyoming: 1981).

Gómez Cano, J., Orellana Escudero, G. and Varela Simó, J., *Las Aves en el Museo del Prado* (Madrid, 2010).

Grant, A., 'The Use of Tooth Wear as a Guide to the Age of Domestic Ungulates'. In B. Wilson, C. Grigson and S. Payne (eds.), *Ageing and Sexing Animal Bones from Archaeological Sites* (BAR British Series 109, Oxford, 1982), 91-108.

Gray, A., *A New Voyage Round the World by William Dampier* (New York, 1968).

Hamilton, E.J., 'Wages and Subsistence on Spanish Treasure Ships, 1503-1660', *The Journal of Political Economy* 37 (1929), 430-50.

Kozuch, L. and Fitzgerald, C., 'A Guide to Identifying Shark Centra from Southeastern Archaeological Sites', *Southeastern Archaeology* 8.2 (1989), 146-57.

Lyon, E., 'Nina, Ship of Discovery'. In J.T. Milanch and S. Milbrath (eds.), *First Encounters. Spanish Explorations in the Caribbean and the United States, 1492-1570* (University of Florida Press, Gainesville, 1989), 55-65.

Macintyre, D., *The Adventure of Sail 1520-1914* (London, 1979).

Margócsy, D., '"Refer to Folio and Number": Encyclopedias, the Exchange of Curiosities, and Practices of Identification before Linnaeus', *Journal of the History of Ideas* 71.1 (2010), 63-89.

Markham, C., *The Voyages of Pedro Fernandez de Quiros 1595 to 1606. Vols. I & II* (Klaus Reprint Series II, Vols. 14-15, New York, 1967).

Masefield, J. (ed.), *Dampier's Voyages by Captain William Dampier. Vol. I. A New Voyage Round the World* (New York, 1906).

Mathewson III, D.R., *Treasure of the Atocha* (Houston, Texas, 1986).

Newton, A.P. (ed.), *Thomas Gage. The English-American. A New Survey of the West Indies, 1648* (London, 1928).

Phillips, C.R., *Six Galleons for the King of Spain. Imperial Defense in the Early Seventeenth Century* (John Hopkins University Press, Baltimore, 1986).

Phillips, C.R., *The Short Life of an Unlucky Spanish Galleon: Los Tres Reyes 1628-1634* (The University of Minnesota Press, Minneapolis, 1990).

Randall, J.E., *Caribbean Reef Fishes* (London, 1968).

Reitz, E.J., 'The Spanish Colonial Experience and Domestic Animals', *Historical Archaeology* 2.1 (1992), 84- 91.

Reitz, E.J. and Ruff, B., 'Morphometric Data for Cattle from North America and the Caribbean Prior to the 1850s', *Journal of Archaeological Science* 21 (1994), 699-713.

Reitz, E.J. and Scarry, C.M., *Reconstructing Historic Subsistence with an Example from Sixteenth-century Spanish Florida* (Society for Historical Archaeology Special Publication 3, 1985).

Schmid, E., *Atlas of Animal Bones* (Amsterdam, 1972).

Spennermann, D.H.R. and Rapp, G., 'Swimming Capabilities of the Black Rat (Rattus rattus) in Tropical Lagoonal Waters in Tonga', *Alafua Agricultural Bulletin (Western Samoa)* 12.2 (1987), 17-19.

Stallybrass, W.S. (ed.), *The Buccaners of America* (Rio Grande Press, Inc., Glorieta, New Mexico, 1992).

Stemm, G., Gerth, E., Flow, J., Lozano Guerra-Librero, C. and Kingsley, S., *The Deep-Sea Tortugas Shipwreck, Florida: A Spanish-Operated Navio of the 1622 Tierra Firme Fleet. Part 2: The Artifacts* (OME Papers 27, Tampa, 2013).

Unwin, R., *The Defeat of John Hawkins. A Biography of his Third Slaving Voyage* (London, 1961).

Von den Driesch, A., *A Guide to the Measurement of Animal Bones from Archaeological Sites* (Peabody Museum Bulletin 1, 1976).

West, B.A., 'Spur Development: Recognising Caponised Fowl in Archaeological Material'. In B. Wilson, C. Grigson and S. Payne (eds.), *Ageing and Sexing Animal Bones from Archaeological Sites* (BAR British Series 109, Oxford, 1982), 255-61.

6

The Deep-Sea Tortugas Shipwreck, Florida: the Silver Coins

Carol Tedesco

Historic Research and Certification, Inc., Key West, Florida, USA

Between 1990 and 1991 an assemblage of 1,184 silver cob coins was excavated from the 400m-deep Tortugas shipwreck off the Florida Keys, a merchant vessel from the 1622 Spanish Tierra Firme fleet most plausibly identified as the 117-ton *Buen Jesús y Nuestra Señora del Rosario*. A sample of 648 coins retained in the collection of Odyssey Marine Exploration in Tampa, Florida, was re-examined in 2011 to obtain optimum quantitative data about the coins' denominations, mint origins, dates and assayer administrators. Silver *reales* coins were identified from predominantly, and unexpectedly, the mint of Mexico, followed by Potosí and a 'Bogotá/Cartagena or Old World' class.

Although vast quantities of comparable silver coins have been recovered from the shallow-water wrecks of the *Atocha* and *Margarita* from the same homeward-bound 1622 Spanish fleet, this material has not been subjected to formal quantification. The value of the Tortugas collection lies in its association with a small Tierra Firme fleet merchant vessel, and as an important archaeological counterpoint to the more renowned large treasure-laden *flota* warships. The Tortugas wreck thus reflects the smaller scale maritime trade conducted between Colonial Spain and the Americas that is less conspicuous within the archaeological record.

1. Introduction: Wealth, War & Inheritance

The marriage in 1469 of Isabella, heir to the throne of Castile, and Ferdinand, King of Sicily and heir to the throne of Aragon, set the stage for the unification of multiple Iberian Peninsula kingdoms and the birth of the Kingdom of Spain (Elliott, 1963: 23). Their sponsorship of the 1492 voyage of Christopher Columbus, intended to establish a western route to the Orient, but resulting in the 'discovery' of the Americas, was the precursor to the rise of a global empire (Fuson, 1987).

Previous to 1732, when the Mexico City mint began producing circular milled coins using screw press technology (Walton, 1994: 167), all coins in the Americas were made by hand, one at a time. Each tells a unique story. Those produced before the infamous mid-17th century Potosí mint scandal, and its resulting die insignia transition (Menzel, 1995: 15), reflect the birth of coin minting in the Americas, a fascinating, intricate and often mysterious evolution that archival researchers and coin scholars continue to explore, study and debate.

By the time King Philip IV ascended to the throne in 1621, Spain was the most powerful country in the world, controlling much of Europe, as well as the Caribbean, Mexico and the Americas – the New World. However, maintaining this position of supremacy was expensive, and financial problems plagued the nation. Spain was engaged in costly warfare much of the time, and Philip's throne had inherited past generations of debt.

The New World was abundant in desirable riches, in particular the precious metal silver, and in the relatively short timespan between the first voyages of Columbus and the rise of Philip IV to the throne, at age 16, Spain had become profoundly dependent on the Americas. In order to control the vast wealth emerging from the Spanish colonies, mints were established and operated in key areas throughout the New World. Wooden ships were built to transport massive amounts of plundered riches, which sailed in organized fleets, or *flotas*, each with a particular purpose and route.

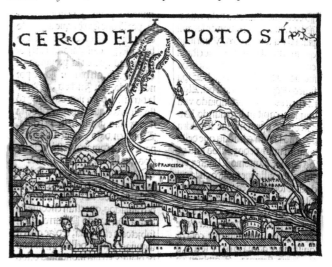

Fig. 1. View of the city of Potosí located in the geographic area of the viceroyalty of Peru, modern Bolivia, at the foot of the mountain for which it was named, renowned for its mineral deposits, especially silver and tin. Engraving: from La Cronica del Peru, *1553.*

Fig. 2. 'Slaves at Work in the Silver Mines of Peru' from R. Johnson, The History of South America *(London, 1789: 166).*
Slaves wield pick-axes to extract ore and crush the ore in a vessel, while a third works the bellows for a European smelter.
Source: www.slaveryimages.org, compiled by Jerome Handler and Michael Tuite, and sponsored by the Virginia
Foundation for the Humanities and the University of Virginia Library.

Each year these ships voyaged from Spain to the Americas along a route know as the Carrera de Indias.

When eight ships of the Tierra Firme fleet met their fate in 1622, New World silver in the form of the Spanish dollar, also called *pesos* or 'pieces of eight' (Walton, 1994: xiii), was the most coveted and widely traded money on Earth. In September of that year the Tierra Firme fleet – whose purpose was to transport Peruvian and South American treasures (Mathewson, 1986: 19; Walton, 1994: 47-9) – departed from Havana, Cuba, en route for Spain. The 28 vessels that formed the fleet (Lyon, 1989: Appendix B, *Communication from Marquis of Cadereita to the Crown, Havana, January 10, 1623,* AGI *Santo Domingo* 132) strained under cargos of vast imperial, private and commercial wealth: tons of Peruvian silver, fortunes in New World gold, Cuban copper, indigo and mercury. With officers, crew and passengers came personal belongings, such as medical tools, navigational utensils, tableware, precious gems and jewelry, and artistic and cultural souvenirs.

Spain and her creditors awaited the return of the fleet anxiously since its arrival was anticipated to refresh the royal coffers, repay loans and ease financial pressures (Lyon, 1989: 41-3). But two days subsequent to departing from the island of Cuba, eight of the ships were destroyed, as a contemporary account reported, victims of a "storme

and fearfull tempest" *(A True Relation of that Which Lately Hapned to the Great Spanish Fleet, and Galleons of Terra Firma in America,* London, 1623: 4). More than 500 lives were lost in the fleet disaster of 1622 (Lyon, 1989: Appendix B). Also lost was a king's ransom in 'treasure', a serious setback for Spain, whose supremacy in the world was upheld by the wealth of the Indies.

In 1980 and 1985 respectively, the Mel Fisher company, Treasure Salvors, Inc., discovered in the Florida Straits sections of two of the Tierra Firme fleet's richest vessels, the *Santa Margarita* and the *Nuestra Señora de Atocha.* Between 1990 and 1991, Seahawk Deep Ocean Technology excavated a shipwreck discovered off the nearby Dry Tortugas Islands from the same 1622 fleet, most plausibly identified as the Portuguese-built and Spanish-operated 117-ton *Buen Jesús y Nuestra Señora del Rosario* homeward-bound from Nueva Cordoba, Cumana on the north coast of Venezuela (Kingsley, 2013).

2. Making Money

Because no ship's manifest seems to survive for the *Buen Jesús y Nuestra Señora del Rosario,* it is impossible to propose how many silver coins it may have originally carried. The *Atocha* transported approximately 250,000 registered silver coins (Lyon, 1989: 58) and the *Margarita's* manifest listed

Fig. 3. A 16th-century woodcut depicting the workings of a New World mint, with blanks being cut from sheets of silver, struck into coins, weighed and registered.

component of the coin's design. Sometimes die punches were used to repair or update a directly engraved die; alternatively, both die punches and additional direct engraving would be employed (Armstrong, 1997: 9-13). Appropriately sized dies were made for each denomination of coin.

3. The Spanish Dollar

The value of money was determined by the purity and weight of the metal. Silver coin denominations were counted in *reales*. With the exception of a seemingly single Mexico City mint ½ *reale* coin documented on the Tortugas site (Flow, 1999: 88), four denominations of silver coins prevail on the wrecks from the 1622 Tierra Firme fleet: 8 *reales*, 4 *reales*, 2 *reales* and 1 *reale*, with 8 *reales* being by far the most abundant.

Purity was mandated to be .93 fine (Craig, 1989: 2). The 8 *reales* of silver equaled the one-ounce Spanish silver dollar of 27.47 grams (Craig, 1989: 2), which is less than the troy ounce standard today. The 4 *reales* coins weighed

more than 140,000 registered silver issues (pers. comm. Eugene Lyon to Mel Fisher, 27 May 1980). No gold coins were listed on the manifests of either the *Atocha* or the *Margarita* (Mathewson, 1986: 131). To date, however, the *Margarita* shipwreck has produced 77 gold coins and the *Atocha* 128 examples. With the exception of a small sample of gold coins struck with an 'SF' mintmark representing the recently opened (*c.* 1622) Santa Fe de Bogotá mint – the first mint authorized to produce gold coins in the Americas (Menzel, 2004: 383) – gold coins on 1622 fleet shipwrecks were the European struck private funds of individuals and therefore exceedingly rare.

Although mechanically produced coins had been introduced to some areas of Europe by the mid-16th century,[1] until the year 1732 coins in the Americas were all struck individually by hand. First, blanks were hand-cut from strips of silver. Next, the blank, or planchet, was heated, sandwiched between double dies and struck with a hammer (Fig. 3). Any silver in excess of the requisite weight was trimmed from the outer coin's edges until the weight was correct. This resulted in irregularly shaped coins whose insignia were frequently off center (Menzel, 2004: 7-8). The dies themselves were made of steel, with insignia impressed into them by direct engraving or by the sinking (stamping) of multiple die punches, each punch being a

Figs. 4-5. Loose silver coins in situ *just beyond the sternpost on the Tortugas shipwreck (and close-up detail).*

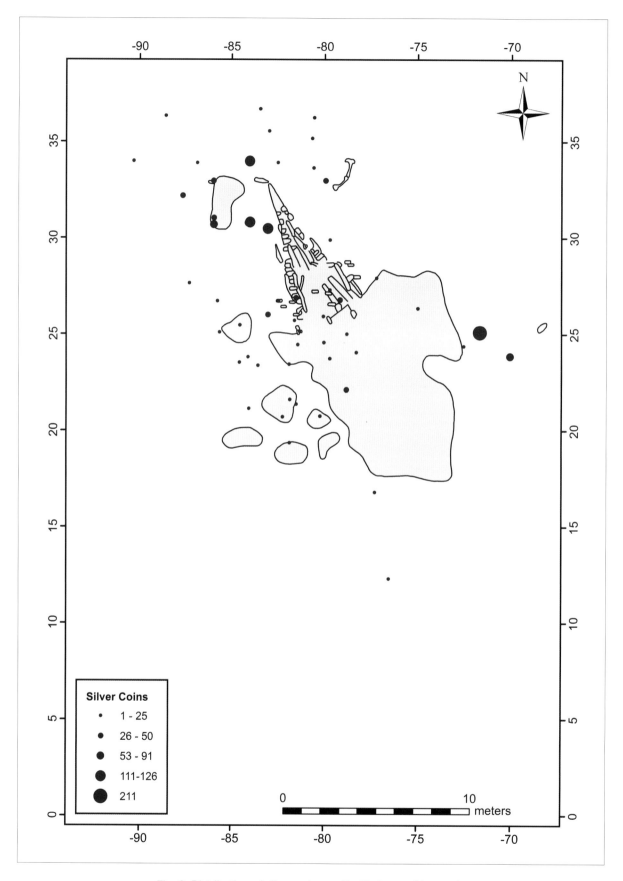

Fig. 6. Distribution of silver coins on the Tortugas shipwreck.

½ ounce each, 2 *reales* coins one-quarter of an ounce and the 1 *reale* one-eighth of an ounce.

As stated, an initial study of the Tortugas shipwreck's silver coins lists a single ½ *reale* coin from the Mexico mint (Flow, 1999: 88), but the report contains no corroborating photograph. Although ½ and ¼ *reale* denominations were produced intermittently throughout the Spanish Colonial period, there is no record of either having been recovered from the *Nuestra Señora de Atocha* or the *Santa Margarita*. If the attribution is not erroneous (bearing in mind the potential for substantial metallic erosion within the marine environment), and a single ½ *reale* coin was indeed recovered from the Tortugas shipwreck, like most of the gold coins on these shipwrecks it would have functioned as the pocket money of an individual and would be one of the most rare coins in the 1622 collections.

4. Tortugas Coin Die Insignia

The silver coins from the Tortugas shipwreck bear unified iconography (Figs. 7-8). Thus, at random, on a Potosi mint coin dated to 1620, the crowned shield occurs on the obverse and the lions of Léon and the castles of Castile, quartered by a Greek cross and surrounded by a curving Moorish design called a tressure, or quatrefoil, characterizes the reverse. On either side the symbols are encircled within dots and a legend.

Fig. 7. The Habsburg shield, the arms of King Philip III of Spain, and with some variations, of the other Habsburg Kings: Philip II, Philip IV and Charles II. The symbols that compose the shield represent the various individual arms of lands under Spanish rule.

Fig. 8. Potosi mint silver coin die design. Obverse, to left, the crowned Habsburg shield with 'P' mintmark and assayer initial 'T' (Juan Ximénez de Tapia, 1618 intermittently through 1648). Reverse, to right, the lions of Léon and castles of Castile, quartered by a Greek cross and surrounded by a curving Moorish quatrefoil. On either side the symbols are encircled within dots and a legend.

The shield depicted is the Habsburg Shield, the arms of King Philip III of Spain, and, with some variations, of the other Habsburg kings: Philip II, Philip IV and Charles II (r. 1556-1700). The symbols comprising the shield represent the various individual arms of lands under Spanish rule at the time (Sedwick and Sedwick, 2007: 23-4). Therefore, the obverse symbolizes and advertises the power of the Kingdom of Spain. When the power base changed, the shield changed as well.

To the left of the shield, typically, are two initials, one set above the other, although placement of elements can vary. The upper initial on a Potosi mint coin is a 'P' representing Potosi or Peru. Below the letter 'P' the chief assayer of the mint (responsible for guaranteeing coins of legal weight and purity) was required to place his own initial. Therefore, this letter changes (Craig, 1989: 5).

To the right of the shield on the obverse is a numeral expressing the coin's value. This value can appear in the form of a traditional Roman numeral, or in Arabic form, or in a manner reflecting the handwritten style of the times, which often includes an 'o' above the value. The custom of the 'o' derives from handwritten traditions, which often included placing the final letter of a word above the first letter – the 'o' above 'M' mintmark representing the Mexico mint, for instance. In the case of coin values, however, the 'o' would represent the final letter in quatro *reales*, or ocho *reales* (Sedwick and Sedwick, 2007: 28).

Potosi coins minted during the reign of Philip II did not carry a date and do not display an ordinal number, so the legend (using 'V' for 'U' in the Latin style) reads "PHILIPVS D.G. HISPANIARVM ET INDIARVM REX", meaning "Philip By the Grace of God D.G. [Dei Gratia] Spain and the Indies King." When Philip III took the throne the ordinal 'III' was added to the legend, thus "PHILIPVS III D.G. HISPANIARVM ET INDIARVM REX". The Potosi mint did not introduce dates into its coin legends until 1617. Therefore, beginning in 1617 the legend reads "PHILIPVS III D.G. HISPANIARVM ET INDIARVM REX ANO (abbreviation for Ano Domeni) 16--".

Coin die insignia varied from mint to mint. Sometimes the differences are obvious, and sometimes quite subtle, as in the case of issues produced around the reign of Philip II from the Potosi and Lima mints. Early Philip II period coins (*c.* 1574-81) from the Potosi mint are so similar in appearance to Philip II shield style coins of the Lima, Peru, mint that for some years the coins of early assayers bearing the initials 'R', 'M', 'B' and 'L' were mistakenly attributed to Lima.

Prior to the discovery of 37 intact chests of silver coins on the *Atocha* site in 1985, a prominent numismatist, E.A. Sellschopp, attributed the coins of early assayers 'R' (Alonso de Rincón), 'M', 'B' and 'L' to the Lima mint (and assayer 'C' to a mint at La Plata) (Sellschopp, 1971). Sellschopp's attributions were based on the artistic similarities between the coins carrying these assayers' initials with those of the confirmed Lima mint assayer Diego de la Torre. Comparing the workmanship, stylistic features and artistic rendering of these early Potosi coins with Diego de la Torre's Lima mint coins, it is easy to understand how their appearance led Sellschopp to arrive at this presumption. Other numismatic authors perpetuated his attributions.

However, research conducted by Cunietti-Ferrando (1989) and Dym (1989) provided documentary evidence that placed the assayers 'R' (beginning in 1574) and 'B' (beginning *c.* 1577) at the Potosi mint. Direct observation of assayer initial erasures and overstrikes definitively connect assayers 'L' and 'C' to assayer 'B', and hence to the Potosi mint. Assayer initials 'M' struck over 'R', and 'L' struck over 'M' specimens, are documented, as well as coins bearing 'M' to right of shield and 'L' to left of shield (Sedwick and Sedwick, 2007: 93), indicating a period of joint assayership. Therefore, 'M' must also be attributed to Potosi.

Currently, documentary evidence has yet to be uncovered that places assayers 'M', 'B' or 'L' at the Lima mint (although Sellschopp's earlier theories were reiterated in the 1992 revision of his book). However, Sellschopp did correctly place assayer/engraver Alonso de Rincón in Lima. Rincón opened both the Lima and the Potosi mints, and a third that operated briefly in La Plata. However, his Lima mint issues all date to *c.* 1568-70, struck in the Lima mint's original 'pillars' format, a style that was discontinued and replaced with the crowned shield before the opening of the Potosi (1574) and La Plata (1573) mints (Cunietti-Ferrando, 1989: 62-4).

As a result of a Royal edict issued in 1570 (Dargent Chamot, 1989: 48), by 1572 both the Mexico City and the Lima, Peru, mints had transitioned from a previous 'pillars' design to the Habsburg shield. At the directive of the Viceroy of Peru, in 1573 Alonso de Rincón left the city of Lima to establish a new mint in La Plata (now Sucre, Bolivia), taking Lima mint tools and, by then, shield type dies with him to begin the work (Cunietti-Ferrando, 1989: 53-4). La Plata's very brief and sparse production of coins occurred in late 1573. The endeavor quickly proved to be ill advised and Rincón was subsequently dispatched to Potosi with the directive of re-establishing operations there. Again Rincón began his work with tools and dies originally from Lima.

The timely transition from 'pillar' style dies to the crowned shield style serves as a key chronological marker that allows Rincón's Lima issues and his La Plata/Potosi issues to be differentiated.

5. The Condition, Grading & Identity of the Tortugas Coins

Coins are graded by quality and, in the case of shipwreck coins, quality is largely determined by degree of exposure to the elements and erosion. The coins from the Tortugas shipwreck were found scattered individually under light sediment cover, usually less than 5-10cm deep, but exhibit a degree of wear and erosion typical of unprotected coins on high energy sites (Figs. 4-6). This suggests that the coins were exposed to the water column and seabed surface before being gradually buried. Such a state of preservation is also true of many silver coins discovered on the shallow-water *Margarita* shipwreck.

By contrast, the *Atocha* site has to date produced 52 'chests' of coins. Each *Atocha* rosewood chest contained between 1,192 and 4,533 coins, for an average of 1,982 coins per chest. The lids and bases measured on average 57.2cm long and 22.3cm wide and were built with 2-3cm thick planks (Malcom, 2001). These plain, rectangular wooden boxes largely decayed and disintegrated over time. Because of a chemical reaction between the metal and the saltwater, silver sulfide both blackened the coins and fused them together, thus retaining the shape of their chests. Coins from the interior of such conglomerations, having been protected from the elements, tend to be in mint or near mint condition, those on the outer perimeter less so. No evidence for comparable chests was encountered on the Tortugas shipwreck, where the coins were not being transported as cargo but seemingly as part payment, alongside the gold bars, for the outward-bound consignments (cf. Kingsley 2013: 10-12).

The Tortugas collection was graded for this study following a widely accepted set of guidelines whereby, based on surface condition, each coin is assigned a grade category of one to five, with special features noted separately. For instance, a coin may be noteworthy because it exhibits a full or partial date or because of a rare assayer initial, but while increasing its interest these features do not influence its grade. Because the coins under consideration are not uniform or machine made, no two are identical. The grading process involves both measurable criteria and individual subjectivity.

- Grade One coins display little or no visible ocean wear, show little or no roughness or pitting, and, therefore, look much as they did when new. Both sides are in Very Good to Excellent condition and the obverse and reverse features resulting from the original strike are defined and easily identifiable.
- Grade Two coins were partly exposed to the elements. The coin may not be completely intact or it may look

Fig. 9. A rare 1543-72 pillars and waves style Mexico City mint coin recovered from the Tortugas shipwreck. The single dot between the pillars represents the 1 reale *denomination value. Unless otherwise stated, Figs. 9-42 © Odyssey Marine Exploration.*

more 'sand-blasted' than a Grade One, but the quality is still Good and most of the features resulting from the original strike are easily identifiable.
- Grade Three coins are in Fair overall condition, but ocean wear is very apparent. Many Grade Three coins were typically located on the outer layer of a shipping chest and, therefore, the side of the coin that faced into the chest will be of Grade One or Grade Two quality. The opposite side, exposed to the elements following the wooden chest's deterioration, is completely worn away. Other Grade Three coins might incorporate ocean wear distributed across both sides of the coin. On Grade Three coins, obverse and/or reverse sides will still offer easily identifiable characteristics that have definition.
- Grade Four coins are still identifiable as Spanish Colonial coins, but they have been subject to much wear and tear and the markings are faint and have little or no definition.
- Grade Five coins are just above a fragment in quality, but can still be identified as a coin taking into consideration factors such as shape and provenience.
- A Fragment is a piece of silver recovered among concentrations of coins, but with no markings to identify it as a coin.

Grading assessments need to take into consideration additional external criteria affecting form and preservation. For instance, almost all handmade coins display areas of smooth 'soft strike' on which the markings appear to have been erased. Often this feature is actually due to the blanks of silver used to make the coins not being uniformly flat, as well as coin dies that wore down unevenly with use over time. The feature can also be the result of tongs used to hold the coins during production. Soft strike still represents the 'mint' condition of a coin and should not be confused with ocean wear, which can make a coin look rough, pitted or sand-blasted.

Denomination	Mexico	Potosi	Bogotá/ Cartagena or Old World	Unknown
8 *reales*	199	34	3	107
4 *reales*	28	9	2	20
2 *reales*	5	3	1	12
1 *reale*	23	2	0	4
Unknown	60	4	1	130
Total	315 (48.6%)	52 (8.0%)	7 (1.1%)	274 (42.3%)

Table 1. Tortugas shipwreck silver coins by quantity, denomination and mint (2011 analysis of 648 coins).

In August 2011, the author re-analyzed 648 silver coins from the Tortugas shipwreck in the collection of Odyssey Marine Exploration in Tampa, Florida (Figs. 12-42). Crucial criteria for distinguishing between mints are the fact that Mexico City coins are easily identified because each of the cross's four flared extensions end in an orb. (A mint at Santo Domingo, Dominican Republic, also produced shield-type coins with orbed crosses in 1578: Sedwick and Sedwick, 2007: 75. However, few are known to exist, and these may be identified by the location of the assayer initial on the coin reverse, a trait not seen on other American minted coins.) Potosi mint coins, by contrast, bear an unadorned Greek cross, as do coins from the Lima, Panama, Santa Fe de Bogotá/Cartagena and Spanish Peninsular mints.

The Lima mint closed in 1588 and, except for an additional brief production in 1592 (Sedwick and Sedwick, 2007: 52), did not reopen until after the 1622 fleet disaster near the Florida Keys, making coins from this mint fairly old and significantly rare on shipwrecks of this period. The Nuevo Reino de Granada (New Kingdom of Granada) mints of Santa Fe de Bogotá and Cartagena, authorized in 1620, did not begin production until at least mid-1621 (AGI *Santa Fe* 192) and are also exceedingly rare in 1622

Denomination	Unknown + Assume Potosi
8 *reales*	66
4 *reales*	17
2 *reales*	11
1 *reale*	4
Unknown	32
Total	130

Table 2. Tortugas shipwreck silver coins for the 'Unknown + Assume Potosi' class by quantity and denomination.

fleet coin assemblages. Lastly, Spanish Peninsular minted coins discovered on shipwrecks departing from the Americas were twice-traveled wealth, having originated in Europe, crossed the ocean to the New World, entered into circulation and in September 1622 were en route back to Europe. Spanish Peninsular coins, therefore, are also exceedingly rare on 1622 shipwrecks in the Americas.

Due to its location and date of sinking, one might assume that most coins from the Tortugas shipwreck bearing the Greek cross would be Potosi issues. Because this proved not to be the case (Table 1), for the purpose of this study a coin was attributed to a specific mint only if indicators were visibly identifiable. Where no visible indicators existed, the coin was designated an 'Unknown' classification. If a coin was labeled 'Unknown', but displayed a Greek cross, had the overall appearance of a Potosi mint coin and no other markings to suggest otherwise, it was given an additional label of 'Unknown + Assume Potosi' (Table 2).

In the case of the 1622 shipwrecks the *Atocha* and *Margarita*, 8 *reales* denomination coins are most numerous, followed by 4 *reales*, with 2 *reales* denominations relatively rare and 1 *reale* denominations scarce. For example, of the silver coins recovered in 1985 from the *Atocha* site, 0.001% (110) were 1 *reale* denominations, 15.0% (17,088) were 2 *reales* denominations, 21.8% (24,853) were 4 *reales* denominations, and 63.1% (71,808) were 8 *reales* denominations (Malcom, 2001).

This makes sense since small denominations may have been most desirable for local trade, but shipping cargos long-distance in large denomination form was most efficient. Because the Tortugas shipwreck coin collection included a fairly high percentage of 'unknown' denomination coins, a decision was made with Odyssey artifact data specialist Eric Tate to distinguish between higher denomination coins of 8 or 4 *reales* and lower denomination issues. This study demonstrated that nearly twice as many 'unknown' coins were higher denominations varieties:

- Total 'Unknown': 130
- Unknown (either 4 or 8 *reales*): 28
- Unknown (either 1 or 2 *reales*): 15
- Unknown (unidentifiable): 87

As stated previously, the Tortugas shipwreck coins were discovered loose and scattered under light sediment cover in deep waters (not in coin chests or conglomerations; Fig. 6), and exhibit a degree of erosion typical of exposed coins associated elsewhere with high-energy marine environments. The predominance of 207 Grade Four (31.9%) and 334 Grade Five (51.5%) coins amongst the Tortugas collection must be attributable to their unprotected state

over a long period. Only a single coin (0.1% of the assemblage) was attributed to Grade One and Two:

- Grade One: 0
- Grade Two: 1
- Grade Three: 57
- Grade Four: 207
- Grade Five: 334
- Fragment: 49

The Tortugas coin collection is surprising for a vessel of the 1622 Tierra Firme fleet for two reasons (Table 1). Firstly, this study has demonstrated that the majority of coins were manufactured at the Mexico City mint (48.6% of the total sample; Figs. 12-21). The primary purpose of the Tierra Firme fleet was to transport Peruvian and South

Fig. 10. Five better-preserved (Grades 2 and 3) Tortugas shipwreck silver coins. Top left: Habsburg shield with letters 'o' above 'M' to left of shield signifying the Mexico City mint, above assayer initial 'D'; denomination unconfirmed. 'D' assayer coins appear c. 1598/1599, 1618-34, and possibly at intervals before 1618. Identification of the 'D' assayers is at present unconfirmed. Top right: coin reverse displaying lions of Léon and castles of Castile in inverted positions, quartered by a Greek cross and surrounded by a curving quatrefoil; mint and denomination unconfirmed. Center: Habsburg shield with 'oM' signifying the Mexico City mint, with assayer initial 'D' (as above); denomination unconfirmed. Bottom left: coin reverse displaying the lions of Léon and castles of Castile, quartered by a Greek cross and surrounded by a curving quatrefoil; letters 'DIA' preserved on the right outer edge, part of 'INDIARVM' meaning 'Indies'; mint and denomination unconfirmed. Bottom right: a 8 reales coin obverse, the initial 'P' to left of shield signifying the Potosi mint, and 'o' over 'viii' to right signifying the 8 reales denomination.

Denomination	Mexico	Potosi	Bogotá/ Cartagena or Old World	Unknown
8 *reales*	335	212	6	9
4 *reales*	157	67	4	4
2 *reales*	66	45	2	6
1 *reale*	104	31	1	1
½ *reale*	1	--	--	--
Unknown	--	--	--	133
Total	663 (56.0%)	355 (29.9%)	13 (1.1%)	153 (13.0%)

Table 3. Tortugas shipwreck silver coins by quantity, denomination and mint (1999 analysis of 1,184 coins).

American 'treasure' (Mathewson, 1986: 19; Walton, 1994: 47-49). Thus, the majority of coin cargo would be expected to have originated in Potosi (Figs. 1-2), then a territory of the Viceroyalty of Peru (and today of Bolivia). Coins minted in Mexico City, by contrast, would have been transported overland to Veracruz on the east coast of Mexico for consignment to New Spain fleet ships (Mathewson, 1986: C2-C3).

Even when the 52 Potosi (8.0%) and the 130 'Assume Potosi' (20.1%) issues in the 2011 Tortugas wreck collection are combined (Table 2; Figs. 22-34), Mexico mint issues still outnumber those from Potosi (315 Mexico coins compared to 182 Potosi/Assume Potosi: 48.6% compared to 28.1%). Even adding the 52 Potosi coins to all of the 274 'Unknown' origin coins (thereby assuming for the sake of this exercise that all 'Unknowns' were minted in Potosi), the number of Potosi to Mexico coins is still only slightly higher (48.6% Mexico compared to 50.3%). Thus, the Tortugas ship was transporting an unusually high percentage of Mexico City mint coins. Notably the *Atocha* and the *Margarita* wrecks also produced a large representation of Mexico City mint coins for Tierra Firme fleet shipwrecks, but unlike the Tortugas assemblage Potosi mint coins proved to be by far the majority, with 85-90% of *Atocha* coins originating there (pers. comm. Corey Malcom, 12 September 2012).

The second curiosity amongst the Tortugas assemblage examined in 2011 is the comparatively high percentage of 1 *reale* denomination coins, also from the Mexico mint (Table 1; Figs. 12-14), although these may simply represent a personal or merchant shipment belonging to an individual/s with business interests in New Spain. In total the collection contains 343 8 *reales* issues, 59 4 *reales*, 21 2 *reales* and 29 1 *reale*. Of these, the 1 *reale* issues account for 7.3% of the Mexico coins, compared to 3.8% for the wreck's Potosi coins (see Table 3 for the figure of 1 *reale*

coins accounting for a far higher 15.7% of Mexico issues from the 1999 data set).

One explanation for the interpretation of these Mexico City mint coins, other than as 'pocket money', may be proposed. The Tierra Firme and New Spain fleets shared one port-of-call in common, Havana, Cuba. Havana was the final meeting point for all ships before undertaking the return voyage to Spain (Mathewson, 1986: C2-C3; Walton, 1994: 53). According to Dr. Eugene Lyon, the foremost authority on the history of the 1622 shipwrecks, having converged that year in Portobello with a guard fleet under the command of the Marquis de Cadereita, the Tierra Firme fleet was traveling far behind schedule. The New Spain fleet reached Havana in advance of the combined Tierra Firme and Guard fleets. With hurricane season and its dangers upon them, the commander of the New Spain fleet chose not to wait any longer before disembarking.

The New Spain fleet thus departed for Spain, unfortunately leaving its valuables behind in Havana for the well armed, but ill timed combined Tierra Firme and Guard ships to transport. According to Dr. Lyon, coins, ingots and agricultural products from New Spain fleet ships were loaded onto the *Atocha* and *Margarita* in Havana, a scenario which is to account for most of the Mexico mint coins in the assemblage (pers. comm. Eugene Lyon, April 2010).

Comparing the original sample of 1,184 silver coins recovered from the Tortugas wreck (Table 3), from which 1,051 issues were examined prior to 1999 (Flow, 1999: 88), with the 2011 reanalysis presents a remarkably similar overall quantitative picture (Fig. 11). From the larger 1999 data set the Mexico mint is again dominant amongst the assemblage (56.0% of the total compared to 48.6% for 2011), while Potosi is represented by 29.9% of the coins compared to 28.1% (filtering the 'Unknown + Assume Potosi' coins into the equation), while the Bogotá/Cartagena or Old World source issues are identical at 1.1%, and

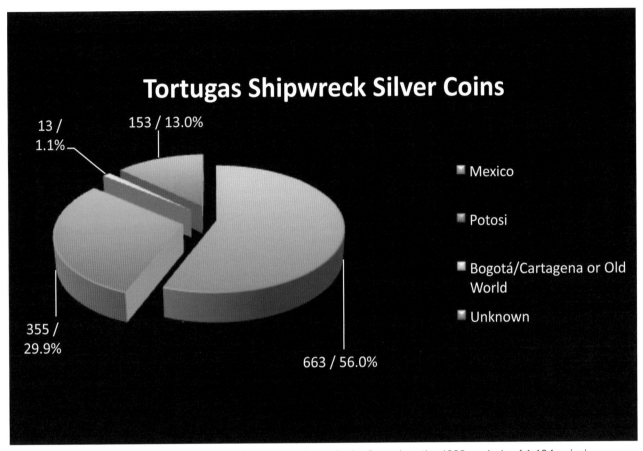

Fig. 11. Tortugas shipwreck silver coins by quantity and mint (based on the 1999 analysis of 1,184 coins).

a lower 13.0% are unknown (compared to 22.2% from the 2011 analysis).

In total, the 1999 collection contains 562 8 *reales*, 232 4 *reales*, 119 2 *reales* and 137 1 *reales*, plus one apparent ½ *reale*. Of these, the 1 *reale* issues account for 15.7% of the Mexico coins, compared to 8.7% for the wreck's Potosi coins. It is suggested that the numerically superior 1999 sample is utilized for official site statistics. Thus, from the Tortugas coin assemblage 53.5% of coins are 8 *reales* issues, 22.1% 4 *reales*, 11.3% 2 *reales*, 13.0% 1 *reale* and 0.1% ½ *reale*.

6. Tortugas Mints, Assayers & Dates

Only three of the 648 coins from the current study of the Tortugas shipwreck exhibit a date and all are incomplete: TOR-90-00517-CN and TOR-90-00784-CN both read '162-' (Figs. 38, 41), while TOR-90-00894-CN has a partial date of '16--' (Fig. 19). A fourth coin examined in 1999 is dated '--21' for the year 1621 (Fig. 35). Dated

coins on early 17th-century shipwrecks in the Americas are rare in general. Prior to 1607 in Mexico City, and to 1617 in Potosi, coins did not carry a date. When the year of issue was eventually added to the coin dies, it was located at about the 11 o'clock position on the outer perimeter of the coin's obverse (Mexico) and reverse (Potosi and Santa Fe de Bogotá/Cartagena). Because the coins were hand struck and hand cut, most of the wording in the legends and most of the dates were sacrificed in the process of obtaining the desired weight by edge clipping.

Of the 648 Tortugas coins examined in 2011, all that are identifiable fall into three categories: Mexico City, Potosi and Santa Fe de Bogotá/Cartagena or possibly Old World. All are of the crowned shield variety.

The Mexico City mint was the first to issue coins in the Americas, beginning in 1536 (Utberg, 1963: 8) during the monarchy of Johanna and Charles I (r. 1516-56). Mexico coins produced prior to *c.* 1572 displayed a 'pillars' design, rather than a crowned shield (Dargent Chamot, 1989: 48). Two coins illustrated in the earlier analysis (Flow, 1999: 87) are of the *c.* pre-1572 pillar design (Fig. 9). Both appear to be from the Mexico City mint, although the Lima, Peru, mint also produced pillar style coins prior to *c.* 1572. One appears to be an extremely rare early Mexico coin assayed by 'L,' Luis Rodríguez (*c.* 1547?-53? and *c.* 1554?-1569: Sedwick and Sedwick, 2007:63-64) (*c.* 1548-67: Menzel, 2004: 69). Since no 'pillar' issues were represented amongst the 2011 study of 315 Mexico City examples in the Tortugas assemblage, it is clear that other than these rare anomalies the vast majority of the ship's coins were minted after *c.* 1572, beginning in the second half of the reign of Philip II (1556-98).

Assayer tenures often span more than one monarch's reign. For example, the previously mentioned Mexico City assayer Luis Rodríguez took his post late in the reign of Charles and Johanna (r. 1515-56) and held it for more than ten years into the reign of Philip II. Potosí's assayer 'B', Juan de Ballesteros Narváez, performed this office intermittently during the years *c.* 1577-1615 under both Philip II and Philip III (Dym, 1989: 84; Menzel, 2004: 243). An undated coin that bears a king's ordinal number in the legend may narrow down its possible date range. While the Mexico City mint included the ordinal 'II' in coin legends, Potosi, which began operations in 1574 (Dym, 1989: 80), did not. Both the Mexico and the Potosi mints included the ordinal's 'III' and 'IIII'. It is to be expected that the majority of the Tortugas coins would have been minted during the reign of Philip III, and two were identified as bearing a visible ordinal 'III' in their legend; none possessed a visible ordinal 'II' or a visible ordinal 'IIII'. Nine Tortugas coins were identifiable as Philip II period issues: five Potosi, two Mexico, one seemingly early Potosi or Lima, and one an 'Unknown/Assume Potosi' with Philippus spelled with double 'PP' (TOR-90-00949-CN; Fig. 25), a typical Philip II era coin characteristic.

Coins may display certain features that help place undated examples within broad dates of production. A chief assayer's initial is the most valuable such feature. While some assayers' years of operations are confirmed, others such as those struck before dates were included in the coin legend, and particularly those minted during the reign of Philip II, are in many cases chronological estimates based on historical information derived from archives and incomplete records. Evolving artistic styles of coin die emblems, and assayer initial overstrikes and combinations, also help pinpoint date ranges.

Of the 315 Mexico City mint coins examined (Figs. 12-21), 30 incorporate a visible assayer's initial:

- One coin 'A': Antonio de Morales, *c.* 1608-10 (TOR-90-00999-CN; Fig. 17).

- 27 coins 'D': an assayer using the initial 'D' is confirmed to have worked at the Mexico City mint from 1618 into the 1630s (TOR-90-00382-CN; Fig. 16), and also possibly intermittently prior to 1618. An assayer 'D' is confirmed *c.* 1598/1599 working jointly with assayer 'F' on coins known bearing both assayers initials, one to the left of the shield and the other to the right, with some examples bearing the ordinal 'II' and some the ordinal 'III' (Sedwick and Sedwick, 2007: 66-7). The 'D' assayer initial does not necessarily represent the same individual for the above date ranges.

- Two coins 'O': Bernardo de Oñate *c.* 1571?-1578? and Luis de Oñate *c.* 1578-1589 (Sedwick and Sedwick, 2007: 65-6) (TOR-90-00780-CN, TOR-90-00920-CN).

Of the 52 Potosi mint coins examined (Figs. 22-34), 30 have a visible assayer's initial:

- Two coins 'B': for Juan de Ballesteros Narváez, intermittently *c.* 1577-1615; also Hernando Ballesteros substituting for Juan de Ballesteros (Dym, 1989: 84), similarly also using the letter 'B'. One of the two 'B' coins (TOR-90-00402-CN; Fig. 30) is of the Philip II period style; the other is undetermined (TOR-90-00462-CN).

- One coin 'M': Juan Muñoz, 1616-17 (TOR-90-00422-CN; Fig. 33).

- 13 coins 'Q': Agustín de la Quadra, 1613-16 (see TOR-90-00762-CN, TOR-90-01041-CN; Figs. 23, 32).

- Seven coins 'R': TOR-90-01003-CN is a Philip II period type 'R' (Fig. 22), either representing Alonso de Rincón (*c.* 1574-76) or Baltasar Ramos Leceta, who served as assayer intermittently between *c.* 1590-98 (and also during the reign of Philip III). I suspect that the coin in question was issued under Ramos Leceta, *c.* 1590-98. With the exception of coins TOR-90-00737-CN and TOR-90-00377-CN, which are of unconfirmed reign, the remaining 'R' coins were all issued under Baltasar Ramos Leceta and are Philip III types (TOR-90-00481-CN, TOR-90-00379-CN, TOR-90-00777-CN, TOR-90-01009-CN; Figs. 27, 31).

- Seven coins 'T': Juan Ximénez de Tapia, 1618 into the late 1640s (TOR-90-00398-CN, TOR-90-00435-CN, TOR-90-00478-CN, TOR-90-00640-CN, TOR-90-00798-CN, TOR-90-01054-CN, TOR-90-00506-CN; Figs. 24, 29, 34).

Seven of the coins examined in 2011 originated from the Nuevo Reino de Granada (New Kingdom of Granada) mints of Santa Fe de Bogotá or Cartagena, located in northern South America, or alternatively derived from a Spanish Peninsular mint (Fig. 35). In any case, they are exceedingly rare. In 1620, King Philip III authorized military engineer Don Alonso Turrillo de Yebra to establish two mints in Nuevo Reino de Granada (Lasser, 1989: 132). The first to be approved was Santa Fe de Bogotá. Cartagena was then approved as an ancillary mint (AGI *Santa Fe* 536, book 11, folio 228 vº). It is known that the first dies, intended for Bogotá, were crafted in Madrid, and in a document dated 25 May 1620 (AGI *Santa Fe* 536, book 11, folio 226 vº) King Philip III ordered their delivery to Turrillo.

Turrillo first set up establishment in Cartagena in 1621, but its city officials created impediments that caused him to transfer his employees and coin-making tools to Bogotá, from where he wrote that with the approval of Audiencia officials he had struck coins of both gold and silver, "with much more perfection than that which is styled in some of the other mints…" and that these coins had entered the stream of commerce. From Bogotá, Turrillo continued to petition the king for intervention regarding the minting house in Cartagena, to enable him to commence operations there. It is certain that Turrillo produced authorized coins of silver at Cartagena in 1621 and coins of both silver and gold at Bogotá in 1622, and that some of these were "lost on one of the (1622) galleons which were flooded" (AGI *Santa Fe* 192).

Turillo's earliest Nuevo Reino de Granada coins bore mintmarks of 'S' above the letter 'F' (for Sante Fé); 'S' without a visible letter 'F' below the 'S'; and 'R' above 'N' for Nuevo Reino. All bear the assayer initial 'A'. While a comprehensive study of his coins is beyond the scope of this report, there are two features that in the absence of an assayer's initial can make a 'Turrillo coin' difficult to distinguish from an Old World minted one. The first is the 'S' mintmark, which appears on some of Turrillo's coins, but problematically also on all coins issued by the Seville mint in Spain. The second feature is the presence of the arms of Portugal within the crowned upper third center shield. This feature is found on seven Tortugas shipwreck coins examined in 2011, six of which do not have visible mintmarks, one of which has a visible 'S' mintmark and none of which exhibit a visible assayer's initial (TOR-90-00410-CN visible 'S' mintmark, TOR-90-00517-CN, TOR-90-00567-CN, TOR-90-00784-CN, TOR-90-00813-CN, TOR-90-00911-CN, TOR-90-01014-CN).

An eighth Nuevo Reino de Granada coin from the Tortugas shipwreck bears the partial date of '--21' and assayer initial 'A' (TOR 000628.0058; Fig. 35), definitively linking it to Alonso Turrillo de Yebra and his Nuevo Reino de Granada mints. This example is one of only four known Nuevo Reino de Granada coins struck with the date 1621, the first year of issue for Turrillo's mints. The three others were recovered from the *Atocha* shipwreck.

In 1580 Philip II expanded his empire territorially with the annexation of the Portuguese throne, after which the Portuguese arms were incorporated into the shield of coins produced in Spanish Peninsular mints. The Nuevo Reino de Granada mints of Bogotá and Cartagena were the only New World mints to include this feature on their coin dies. Examples of Turrillo's Nuevo Reino de Granada silver coins have been discovered on the *Atocha*, the *Margarita* and now the Tortugas wreck sites (Flow, 1999: 84; Fig. 35).

7. Gold Coins

Two gold coins were seemingly recovered from the Tortugas shipwreck, both of Spanish peninsular origin (Flow, 1999: 82; Stemm *et al.*, 2013: 21, fig. 33). This scarcity of gold coins is not surprising. As stated above, Don Alonso Turrillo de Yebra possessed the first imperial authorization to mint gold coins in the Americas, a grant issued in the year 1620. With the exception of Turrillo's documented sample of gold coins "lost on one of the [1622] galleons which were flooded" – the first known to depart from the Americas on a vessel bound for the Old World – gold coins on 1622 ships in the Americas were the European struck private funds of individuals and, therefore, were exceedingly rare. Their value also ensured their rarity: counted in *escudos* (and with 8 *escudos* coins required to be of .92 fineness and equaling the silver 8 *reales* coin in weight: Craig, 1989: 2), the gold to silver value ratio in 1622 was 16:1 (Walton, 1994: 20). Of the two documented gold coins, only L01051.0078 is illustrated in an earlier unpublished report (Flow, 1999: 82). The lack of the arms of Portugal confirms that it is of pre-1580 Spanish peninsular origin.

8. What Would a Spanish Dollar Buy?

While it has been widely quoted that a common worker would need to labor a month to earn one or two Spanish dollars (also called *pesos* and 'pieces of eight'), each consisting of 8 *reales* of silver, just like today the value of money fluctuated as a result of inflation, recession and geography. As a general indication of income, Walton (1994: xiii) has suggested that in the era of Columbus the richest aristocrat in Spain earned over 80,000 *pesos* a year from his estates, while a typical laborer made about 25 *pesos* annually. In 1622, the year of the Tortugas shipwreck sinking, and in 1623, a master carpenter could make 238 *maravedís* a day (34 *maravedís* = 1 *reale*), a master mason 272 *maravedís*, a laborer 136 *maravedís*, a gardener 25 *maravedís* and a female cook 11 *maravedís* a day.

In the period covering 1600-49, building craftsmen in Madrid earned 20.1 grams of silver per day, by far the

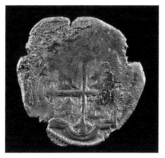

Fig. 12. Mexico City mint; 1 reale denomination (TOR-90-00763-CN). Obverse: the small framed pomegranate symbolizing New Granada, upper-center, clearly depicted. Reverse: a cross whose four extensions each end in an orb, indicative of the Mexico City mint, quarters the lions of Léon and castles of Castile. Diam. 2.0cm, Grade 3.

Fig. 13. Mexico City mint; 1 reale denomination (TOR-90-00770-CN). Obverse: Habsburg shield; the letters 'o' above 'M' to left of shield signifying the Mexico City mint. Reverse: the lions of Léon and castles of Castile quartered by an orbed cross, surrounded by a curving quatrefoil. Diam. 2.0cm, Grade 3.

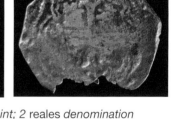

Fig. 14. Mexico City mint; 1 reale denomination (TOR-90-01005-CN). Obverse: crowned Habsburg shield. Reverse: an orbed cross quarters the lions of Léon and castles of Castile, surrounded by a curving quatrefoil. The legend displays preserved letters 'IARUM ET IN,' representing a section of 'HISPANIARUM ET INDIARUM', with colon punctuation indicating striking during the reign of Philip II. Diam. 2.3cm, Grade 3.

Fig. 15. Mexico City mint; 2 reales denomination (TOR-90-00901-CN). Obverse: mintmark 'oM' to left of crowned Habsburg shield; Roman numeral 'II' denomination value to right of shield. Reverse: eroded lions of Léon and castles of Castile quartered by an orbed cross, surrounded by a curving quatrefoil. Diam. 2.6cm, Grade 3.

Fig. 16. Mexico City mint; 4 reales denomination (TOR-90-00382-CN). Obverse: mintmark 'oM' to left of shield, above assayer initial 'D.' Kings' ordinal 'III' clearly visible at the 6:00 position. Reverse: lions of Léon and castles of Castile, quartered by an orbed cross and surrounded by a curving quatrefoil. Diam. 3.1cm, Grade 3.

Fig. 17. Mexico City mint; 4 reales denomination (TOR-90-00999-CN). Obverse: 'oM' to left of Habsburg shield above assayer initial 'A,' representing Antonio de Morales (c. 1608-10). Reverse: lions of Léon and castles of Castile, quartered by an orbed cross and surrounded by a curving quatrefoil. Diam. 2.5cm. Grade 3.

Fig. 18. Mexico City mint; 4 reales denomination (TOR-90-01025-CN). Obverse: Arabic numeral '4' to right of shield represents denomination value. Reverse: lions of Léon and castles of Castile, quartered by an orbed cross and surrounded by a curving quatrefoil. Diam. 3.0cm, Grade 3.

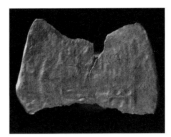 

Fig. 19. Mexico City mint; denomination unknown (TOR-90-00894-CN). Obverse: mintmark 'oM' to left of shield; partial date '16--' on outer perimeter, 10:00-11:00 position, confirms that this coin was struck during the reign of Philip III or Philip IV. Reverse: features entirely eroded. Note that the Mexico City mint is the only New World mint whose year of strike appears on the die obverse. The coin diameter indicates this is most probably an upper denomination 4 or 8 reales. Diam. 3.6cm, Grade 5.

 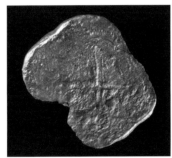

Fig. 20. Mexico City mint; 8 reales denomination (TOR-90-00365-CN). Obverse: Arabic numeral '8' to right of shield representing denomination value. Reverse: lions of Léon and castles of Castile, quartered by an orbed cross and surrounded by a curving quatrefoil. Diam. 3.3cm, Grade 3.

 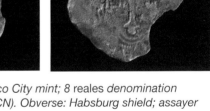

Fig. 21. Mexico City mint; 8 reales denomination (TOR-90-01000-CN). Obverse: Habsburg shield; assayer unknown. Reverse: eroded lions of Léon and castles of Castile, quartered by an orbed cross and surrounded by a curving quatrefoil. Diam. 3.8cm, Grade 3.

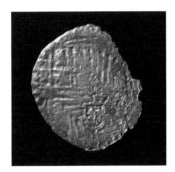 

Fig. 22. Potosi mint; 1 reale denomination (TOR-90-01003-CN). Obverse: mintmark 'P' to left of shield above assayer initial 'R' representing either Alonso de Rincón (c. 1574-76) or Baltasar Ramos Leceta (Philip II period, c. 1590 to 1598). Reverse: lions of Léon and castles of Castile quartered by a Greek cross and surrounded by a curving quatrefoil. Diam. 2.2cm, Grade 3.

Fig. 23. Potosi mint; 2 reales denomination (TOR-90-00762-CN). Obverse: crowned Habsburg shield; mintmark 'P' above 'Q' for assayer Agustín de la Quadra (1613-16). Reverse: lions of Léon and castles of Castile, quartered by a Greek cross and surrounded by a curving quatrefoil. Diam. 2.4cm, Grade 3.

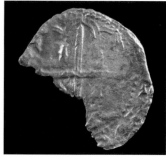

*Fig. 24. Potosi mint; 2 reales denomination
(TOR-90-00798-CN). Obverse: mintmark 'P' above
assayer initial 'T' signifying Juan Ximénez de Tapia
(1618 intermittently through 1648). Reverse: lions of Léon
and castles of Castile, quartered by a Greek cross and
surrounded by a curving quatrefoil. Diam. 2.1cm, Grade 4.*

*Fig. 25. Potosi mint; 2 reales denomination
(TOR-90-00949-CN). Obverse: 'Philippus' spelled double
'P', a typical feature during the reign of Philip II; 'dot' punctuation in the legend represents a die type that began during
an era commonly described as the 'third period' of assayer
'B,' approximated to have commenced c. 1581; lasting until
1586. Assayer 'A,' Juan Alvarez Reinaltes continued the style
during his tenure, 1586-89. Reverse: partial lions of Léon and
castles of Castile quartered by a Greek cross, surrounded by
a curving quatrefoil. The notably tiny castles also point to
this period of assayers 'B' and 'A.' Diam. 2.4cm, Grade 3.*

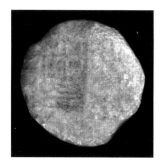

*Fig. 26. Potosi mint; 8 reales denomination (TOR-90-00506-
CN). Obverse: faint Habsburg shield with the initial 'T' to
left for assayer Juan Ximénez de Tapia (1618 intermittently
through 1648). Reverse: the lions of Léon and castles of
Castile in inverted positions, quartered by a Greek cross and
surrounded by a curving quatrefoil. Diam. 3.4cm, Grade 3.*

*Fig. 27. Potosi mint; 4 reales denomination (TOR-90-00777-
CN). Obverse: mintmark 'P' to left of shield above assayer
initial 'R' Baltasar Ramos Leceta (Philip III period, 1598-1612;
possibly 'R' over 'B' overstrike/monogram, which would
have concluded c. 1610). Reverse: lions of Léon and castles
of Castile, quartered by a Greek cross and surrounded
by a curving quatrefoil. Diam. 3.0cm, Grade 3.*

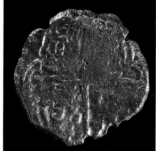

*Fig. 28. Potosi mint; 4 reales denomination (TOR-90-00800-
CN). Obverse: eroded Habsburg shield. Reverse: lions of
Léon and castles of Castile, quartered by a Greek cross and
surrounded by a curving quatrefoil. Castles feature a multi-
window design reflecting that the die was carved c. 1589-
1616 under one of three assayers, 'B,' 'R' or 'Q,' as by the
time 'Q' left office in 1616 the multi-window design had been
replaced with 'Sevilla' style castles. Diam. 2.6cm, Grade 4.*

*Fig. 29. Potosi mint; 4 reales denomination
(TOR-90-01054-CN). Obverse: Habsburg shield with
mintmark 'P' above the initial 'T' for assayer Juan Ximénez de
Tapia (1618 intermittently through 1648). Reverse: the lions of
Léon and castles of Castile, quartered by a Greek cross and
surrounded by a curving quatrefoil. Diam. 2.3cm, Grade 4.*

Fig. 30. Potosi mint; 8 reales denomination (TOR-90-00402-CN). Obverse: crowned Habsburg shield with mintmark 'P' to left, above the initial 'B' signifying assayer Juan de Ballesteros Narváez. Reverse: the lions of Léon and castles of Castile, quartered by a Greek cross and surrounded by a curving quatrefoil. A Philip II era issue that would have been struck c. 1577-98. Diam. 3.8cm, Grade 3.

Fig. 31. Potosi mint; 8 reales denomination (TOR-90-01009-CN). Obverse: Habsburg shield with mintmark 'P' above the initial 'R' signifying assayer Baltasar Ramos Leceta during the reign of Philip III (1598-1612). Reverse: the lions of Léon and castles of Castile, quartered by a Greek cross and surrounded by a curving quatrefoil. Diam. 3.5cm, Grade 4.

Fig. 32. Potosi mint; 8 reales denomination (TOR-90-01041-CN). Obverse: mintmark 'P' to left of shield above assayer initial 'Q' for Agustín de la Quadra (1613-16) during the reign of Philip III. Reverse: an eroded Greek cross. Diam. 3.3cm, Grade 3.

 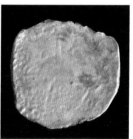

Fig. 33. Potosi mint; 8 reales denomination (TOR-90-00422-CN). Obverse: mintmark to left of shield above assayer initial 'M' representing assayer Juan Muñoz (1616-17). The king's ordinal 'III' is visible in the legend, 5:00 position. Reverse: the lions of Léon and castles of Castile, quartered by a Greek cross and surrounded by a curving quatrefoil. Diam. 3.8cm, Grade 4.

Fig. 34. Potosi mint; 8 reales denomination (TOR-90-00398-CN). Obverse: partially crowned Habsburg shield; mintmark 'P' above assayer initial 'T' signifying Juan Ximénez de Tapia (1618 intermittently through 1648) during the reigns of Philip III and IV. Reverse: the lions of Léon and castles of Castile, quartered by a Greek cross and surrounded by a curving quatrefoil. Diam. 3.3cm, Grade 3.

Fig. 35. Nuevo Reino de Granada/Cartagena; 8 reales denomination (Tortugas 000628.0058). Obverse: crowned Habsburg shield displaying arms of Portugal; assayer initial 'A' to right of shield. Reverse: the lions of Léon and castles of Castile, quartered by a Greek cross surrounded by a curving quatrefoil; partial date of '--21' at 11:00 to 12:00 position. This coin is highly important: it is the sole example from the Tortugas wreck bearing both the Portuguese arms and the assayer initial 'A', thus definitively linking it to Alonso Turrillo de Yebra and his Nuevo Reino de Granada mints; it is also one of only four known existing Nuevo Reino de Granada coins struck with the date 1621, the first year of issue for Turrillo's mints. The other three known Turrillo coins struck 1621 were recovered from the Atocha shipwreck. Diam. 4.2cm, Grade 2. Photo: courtesy of Dr. Susan Pearson and Bill Pearson.

   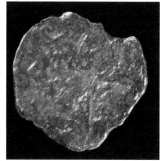

Fig. 36. Unidentified mint; 2 reales denomination (TOR-90-00567-CN). Obverse: upper section of Portuguese arms within the Habsburg shield, indicative of either a Spanish peninsular mint origin or one of Turrillo's Nuevo Reino de Granada mints; 'PH' for 'PHILIPVS' visible in the legend. Reverse: an eroded Greek cross which originally quartered the lions of Léon and castles of Castile. Diam. 2.0cm, Grade 3.

Fig. 37. Unidentified mint; 4 reales denomination (TOR-90-00911-CN). Obverse: faint Habsburg shield with visible Portuguese arms, indicative of either a Spanish peninsular mint origin or one of Turrillo's Nuevo Reino de Granada mints. Denomination value 'IIII' located vertically to right of shield. Reverse: an eroded Greek cross originally quartered the lions of Léon and the castles of Castile. Diam. 2.5cm, Grade 4.

Fig. 38. Unidentified mint; 4 reales denomination (TOR-90-00784-CN). Obverse: details eroded. Reverse: the lions of Léon and the castles of Castile, quartered by a Greek cross surrounded by a curving quatrefoil; partial date of '162-' on the outer left edge, 11:00 position. The style of the lions and castles is indicative of either a Spanish peninsular mint or one of Turrillo's Nuevo Reino de Granada mints. Diam. 2.7cm, Grade 3.

Fig. 39. Unidentified mint; 4 or 8 reales denomination (TOR-90-00813-CN). Obverse: details entirely eroded. Reverse: the lions of Léon and castles of Castile, quartered by a Greek cross. Elaborate open-mouthed lions suggest either a Spanish peninsular mint origin or one of Turrillo's Nuevo Reino de Granada mints. Diam. 2.4cm, Grade 4.

Fig. 40. Unidentified mint; 8 reales denomination (TOR-90-01014-CN). Obverse: partially crowned Habsburg shield bearing Portuguese arms. The Portuguese arms suggest either a Spanish peninsular mint origin or one of Turrillo's Nuevo Reino de Granada mints. Reverse: a partial Greek cross surrounded by a curving quatrefoil. Diam. 3.0cm, Grade 4.

Fig. 41. Unidentified mint; 8 reales denomination (TOR-90-00517-CN). Obverse: eroded. Reverse: lions of Léon and castles of Castile quartered by a Greek cross surrounded by a curving quatrefoil; partial date of '162-' at 11:00 position. The elaborate open-mouthed lions and rendering of the castles suggest either a Spanish peninsular origin or production in one of Turrillo's Nuevo Reino de Granada mints. Diam. 3.5cm, Grade 3.

Fig. 42. Unidentified mint; 8 reales denomination (TOR-90-00410-CN). Obverse: crowned Habsburg shield bearing Portuguese arms; the initial 'S' indicative of either the Seville or Bogota mints. Reverse: lions of Léon and 0the castles of Castile quartered by a Greek cross. Diam. 3.0cm, Grade 4.

highest wage across Europe (compared to 12.6 ounces of silver in Antwerp in the same date range, the second largest wage bracket). Building laborers, meanwhile, made 8.0 grams of silver per day in Madrid (Allen, 2001: 416). In these years the annual 'subsistence basket' has been estimated at costing 439 grams of silver in Madrid, 391 grams of silver in Mexico, 201 grams in London and 152 grams in Amsterdam (Allen *et al.*, 2011: 44).

The Archivo General de Indias Lima reveals that in 1591 20,200 *pesos* purchased the valuable and prestigious office of Potosi mint assayer for one Juan de Ballesteros Narváez (Dym, 1989: 83), while at the same mint in 1598 the annual salaries for key mint officials in *pesos* were 3,500 for a treasurer, 1,800 for an assayer, 1,400 for a weight master and 150 for a master smelter (Menzel, 2004: 7). Finally, an example depictive of the Americas in the later part of the 17th century, embedded in some pirate's Articles of agreement listed in John Esquemeling's *The Buccaneers of America* (1967: 59), states that "Lastly, they stipulate in writing what recompense or reward each one ought to have, that is either wounded or maimed in his body, suffering the loss of any limb, by that voyage. Thus they order for the loss of a right arm six hundred pieces of eight, or six slaves; for the loss of a left arm five hundred pieces of eight, or five slaves; for a right leg five hundred pieces of eight, or five slaves..."

9. Conclusion

There are no mints, timeframes or assayers represented in the Tortugas shipwreck coin assemblage that have not been documented amongst the *Nuestra Señora de Atocha* and *Santa Margarita* shipwreck collections. The coins examined in 2011 are consistent with those found on the *Atocha* and *Margarita*. Thus, assayer 'D' is the final assayer to represent the Mexico City mint, assayer 'T' is the final assayer from the Potosi mint and assayer 'A' is the only operative to represent the mints of Nuevo Reino de Granada. Each of

these officers held their posts immediately previous to and beyond the years when the 1622 fleet vessels sank. Because Philip IV had only been king for the short period of 17 months before the fleet disaster of 6 September, it is to be expected that the majority of the coins lost on these ships would date from the reign of King Philip III.

The latest date to appear on a Tortugas shipwreck coin is (16)21, appearing on the single example to display both the arms of Portugal and the assayer initial 'A' (Fig. 35). The *Atocha* and *Margarita* collections have both produced coins featuring the ordinal 'IIII' and coins dated '1622', mostly from Spanish American mints, but even a few coins minted in Seville. While exceedingly scarce relative to the *Atocha/Margarita* collections as a whole, amongst Old World coins in general those from Seville have the greatest representation, which is not surprising as the port of Seville was the hub of all maritime commerce to and from the 'Indies'.[2]

Acknowledgements

For providing me with the opportunity to further my studies of shipwreck coins and for its commitment to consistently excellent professionalism and teamwork, I extend my gratitude to Odyssey Marine Exploration, in particular to CEO and Director, Greg Stemm; President and COO, Mark Gordon; Director of Archaeology, Research and Conservation, John Oppermann; Archaeological Curator, Ellen Gerth; Director of Business Development, John Longley; Artifact Data Specialist Eric Tate; as well as to Kathy Salvant and Adam Tate for their ongoing support. Dr. Sean Kingsley, Wreck Watch Int., London, is to be thanked for his valuable archaeological and scientific input as well as for his editing expertise.

The coins' photography in this report was conducted by Alan Bosel and the image captions were formulated by Eric Tate (both of Odyssey Marine Exploration, Tampa, Florida), who also carried out the preliminary division of the collection by denomination, date and grade. AGI *Santa Fe 192* was translated by linguist Christine O'Connor. Obverse and reverse photographs of the Tortugas assayer 'A' Nuevo Reino de Granada coin dated (16)21 (inv. 000628.0058) are courtesy of Dr. Susan Pearson and Bill Pearson.

Thanks are also due to Dr. Patrick C.A. Gossweiler for his assistance translating and interpreting documents (originally translated from the old Spanish by John Friede and Luis Ospina Vasquez) on the foundation of the mint at Santa Fe de Bogotá (1614-35) kept in the Archivo General de Indias, Seville and published at http://www.banrep-cultural.org.

Notes

1. See: http://www.segoviamint.org/english/history.htm.
2. For further research related to coins from the 1622 Tierra Firme and other coins of the period, see: Tedesco, C., *Treasure Coins of the Nuestra Señora de Atocha and Santa Margarita* (SeaStory Press, 2010); Tedesco, C., *Pieces of Eight - Treasure Coins of the 1622 Shipwrecks Nuestra Senora de Atocha, Santa Margarita, and the Portuguese Carrack São José* (SeaStory Press, forthcoming); and Tedesco, C., 'The Treasures Within the Treasure', *X-Ray International Dive Lifestyle Magazine* (April 2010).

Bibliography

Allen, R.C., 'The Great Divergence in European Wages and Prices from the Middle Ages to the First World War', *Explorations in Economic History* 38 (2001), 411-47.

Allen, R.C., Murphy, T.E. and Schneider, E.B., *The Colonial Origins of the Divergence in the Americas: A Labour Market Approach* (Economics Series Working Papers 559, University of Oxford, 2011).

A True Relation of that Which Lately Hapned to the Great Spanish Fleet, and Galleons of Terra Firma in America (London, 1623; reprinted by En Rada Publications, West Palm Beach, Florida).

Armstrong, D.R., 'Steel and Die Making for New World Hand-Hammered Coins', *Treasure Quest Magazine* (November-December 1997), 9-13.

Craig, F., 'Coinage of the Viceroyalty of El Peru – an Overview'. In W.L. Bischoff (eds.), *The Coinage of El Peru. Coinage of the Americas Conference at the American Numismatic Society, New York, October 29-30, 1988* (New York, 1989), 2-5.

Cunietti-Ferrando, A.J., 'Documentary Evidence Regarding the La Plata Mint and the First Issues of Potosí'. In W.L. Bischoff (eds.), *The Coinage of El Peru. Coinage of the Americas Conference at the American Numismatic Society, New York, October 29-30, 1988* (New York, 1989), 53-54, 62-64, 62-66.

Dargent Chamot, E.D., 'The Early Lima Mint'. In W.L. Bischoff (eds.), *The Coinage of El Peru. Coinage of the Americas Conference at the American Numismatic Society, New York, October 29-30, 1988* (New York, 1989), 48.

Dym, K., 'The First Assayers at Potosí'. In W.L. Bischoff (eds.), *The Coinage of El Peru. Coinage of the Americas Conference at the American Numismatic Society, New York, October 29-30, 1988* (New York, 1989), 80, 83,84.

Elliott, J.H., *Imperial Spain 1469-1716* (London, 1963).

Esquemeling, J., *The Buccaneers of America* (New York, 1967).

Flow, J., *Tortugas Deep Water Shipwreck. Interim Report* (Tampa, 1999, Unpublished).

Fuson, R.H. (tr.), *The Log of Christopher Columbus* (Southampton, 1987).

Kingsley, S., *The Identity and Maritime History of the Deep-Sea Tortugas Shipwreck* (OME Papers 28, Tampa, 2013).

Lasser, J.R., 'Silver Cobs of Columbia, 1622-1748'. In W.L. Bischoff (eds.), *The Coinage of El Peru. Coinage of the Americas Conference at the American Numismatic Society, New York, October 29-30, 1988* (New York, 1989), 132.

Lyon, E., *Search for the Atocha* (Florida Classics Library, 1989).

Malcom, C., 'The Cargo of Coins Aboard Nuestra Señora de Atocha, or "The Treasure Chest Defined"', *The Navigator: Newsletter of the Mel Fisher Maritime Heritage Society* 16.5 (2001).

Mathewson, R.D., *Treasure of the Atocha* (London, 1986).

Menzel, S.H., *The Potosi Mint Scandal and Great Transition of 1652* (Florida, 1995).

Menzel, S.H., *Cobs, Pieces of Eight and Treasure Coins. The Early Spanish-American Mints and their Coinages, 1536-1773* (New York, 2004).

Sedwick, D. and Sedwick, F., *The Practical Book of Cobs* (Florida, 2007).

Sellschopp, E.A., *Las Acuñaciones de las Cecas de Lima, La Plata y Potosí 1568-1651* (Barcelona, 1971).

Stemm, G., Gerth, E., Flow, J., Lozano Guerra-Librero, C. and Kingsley, S., *The Deep-Sea Tortugas Shipwreck, Florida: A Spanish-Operated Navio of the 1622 Tierra Firme Fleet. Part 2: The Artifacts* (OME Papers 27, Tampa, 2013).

Utberg, N.S., *The Coins of Mexico 1536-1963* (self-published, Texas, 1963).

Walton, T.B., *The Spanish Treasure Fleets* (Sarasota, 1994).